Fodor's

SEATTLE

P9-DZP-112

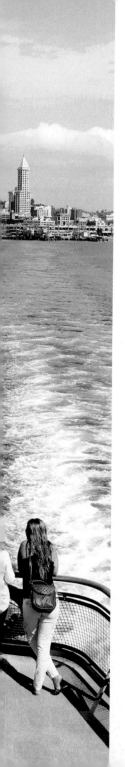

WELCOME TO SEATTLE

Seattle is a city of many personalities: eclectic, urban, outdoorsy, artsy, gritty, down-to-earth, or posh—it's all here, from the quirky character of the eccentric "Republic of Fremont," to hipsters walking baby carriages past aging mansions on Capitol Hill. There's something for just about everyone within this vibrant Emerald City. Taking a stroll, browsing a bookstore, or enjoying a cup of coffee can feel different in every one of Seattle's neighborhoods. It's the adventure of exploring that will really introduce you to the character of Seattle.

TOP REASONS TO GO

★ **Fresh Seafood:** Shop for local produce and seafood at the Pike Place Market, and then eat at Seattle's renowned restaurants.

★ **Craft Beer:** Seattle is so obsessed with the stuff that its annual Beer Week actually lasts for two.

★ **Art and Architecture:** Chihuly Garden and Glass is located at the base of the Space Needle.

★ **Coffee Culture:** Seattle may be the birthplace of Starbucks, but you'll find cool local coffee shops on every corner.

★ **Gardens and Parks:** Visit Alki Beach or make time for a stroll through the Olympic Sculpture Park.

Fodor's SEATTLE

Design: Tina Malaney, *Associate Art Director*

Photography: Jennifer Arnow, *Senior Photo Editor*

Maps: Rebecca Baer, *Senior Map Editor*; David Lindroth and Mark Stroud (Moon Street Cartography), *Cartographers*

Production: Angela L. McLean, *Senior Production Manager*; Jennifer DePrima, *Editorial Production Manager*

Sales: Jacqueline Lebow, *Sales Director*

Business & Operations: Chuck Hoover, *Chief Marketing Officer*; Joy Lai, *Vice President and General Manager*; Stephen Horowitz, *Head of Business Development and Partnerships*

Writers: Lauren Kelley, Kade Krichko, Conor Risch, AnnaMaria Stephens, Naomi Tomky

Editor: Teddy Minford

Production Editor: Jennifer DePrima

6th Edition

ISBN 978-0-14-754682-1

ISSN 1531–3417

SPECIAL SALES

This book is available at special discounts for bulk purchases for sales promotions or premiums. For more information, e-mail specialmarkets@penguinrandomhouse.com.

PRINTED IN THE UNITED STATES OF AMERICA

10 9 8 7 6 5 4 3 2 1

CONTENTS

Fodor's Features

CONTENTS

MAPS

ABOUT THIS GUIDE

Fodor's Recommendations

Everything in this guide is worth doing—we don't cover what isn't—but exceptional sights, hotels, and restaurants are recognized with additional accolades. Fodor'sChoice★ indicates our top recommendations. Care to nominate a new place? Visit Fodors.com/contact-us.

Trip Costs

We list prices wherever possible to help you budget well. Hotel and restaurant price categories from **$** to **$$$$** are noted alongside each recommendation. For hotels, we include the lowest cost of a standard double room in high season. For restaurants, we cite the average price of a main course at dinner or, if dinner isn't served, at lunch. For attractions, we always list adult admission fees; discounts are usually available for children, students, and senior citizens.

Hotels

Our local writers vet every hotel to recommend the best overnights in each price category, from budget to expensive. Unless otherwise specified, you can expect private bath, phone, and TV in your room. For expanded hotel reviews, facilities, and deals visit Fodors.com.

Top Picks

★ Fodor'sChoice

Listings

✉ Address
✉ Branch address
☎ Telephone
📠 Fax
🌐 Website
📧 E-mail
🎟 Admission fee
🕒 Open/closed times
[M] Subway
✥ Directions or Map coordinates

Hotels & Restaurants

🏨 Hotel
🛏 Number of rooms
🍴 Meal plans
🍷 Restaurant
✍ Reservations
👔 Dress code
💳 No credit cards
[$] Price

Other

⇨ See also
☞ Take note
🏌 Golf facilities

Restaurants

Unless we state otherwise, restaurants are open for lunch and dinner daily. We mention dress code only when there's a specific requirement and reservations only when they're essential or not accepted. To make restaurant reservations, visit Fodors.com.

Credit Cards

The hotels and restaurants in this guide typically accept credit cards. If not, we'll say so.

EUGENE FODOR

Hungarian-born Eugene Fodor (1905–91) began his travel career as an interpreter on a French cruise ship. The experience inspired him to write *On the Continent* (1936), the first guidebook to receive annual updates and discuss a country's way of life as well as its sights. Fodor later joined the U.S. Army and worked for the OSS in World War II. After the war, he kept up his intelligence work while expanding his guidebook series. During the Cold War, many guides were written by fellow agents who understood the value of insider information. Today's guides continue Fodor's legacy by providing travelers with timely coverage, insider tips, and cultural context.

EXPERIENCE SEATTLE

WHAT'S WHERE

1 Downtown. This part of town is easy to pick out—it's the only part of Seattle with skyscrapers. Seattle's governmental buildings are here, along with most of the city's hotels and many popular tourist spots, including the evolving waterfront, recently expanded Pike Place Market, and Seattle Art Museum. Just north of Downtown, Belltown is home to the Olympic Sculpture Park, as well as boutiques and nightlife.

2 Seattle Center, South Lake Union, and Queen Anne. Queen Anne, north of Belltown, rises up from Denny Way to the Lake Washington Ship Canal. At the bottom are the Space Needle, the Seattle Center, and the Experience Music Project museum. South Lake Union—home to Amazon's massive HQ and a neighborhood in major transition—has the REI superstore, lakefront, and some eateries and hotels.

3 Pioneer Square. Seattle's oldest neighborhood has historic redbrick and sandstone buildings, plus galleries, niche shops, and a small cluster of innovative eateries. A few sketchy elements clash with the carefully maintained facades.

4 International District. Once called Chinatown, the I.D. is a fun place to shop and eat. The stunning Wing Luke Museum of the Asian Pacific American Experience and Uwajimaya shopping center anchor the neighborhood.

5 First Hill and the Central District. Nicknamed "Pill Hill" for its abundance of hospitals, the First Hill neighborhood has only one must-see: the Frye Art Museum. Farther east is the Central District, which is way off the tourist track, but has some beautiful churches and street art.

6 Capitol Hill. The Hill has two faces: On one side, it's young and edgy, full of artists, musicians, and students. On the other side, it's elegant and upscale, with tree-lined streets, 19th-century mansions, and John Charles Olmsted's Volunteer Park. It has some of the city's best restaurants and nightlife.

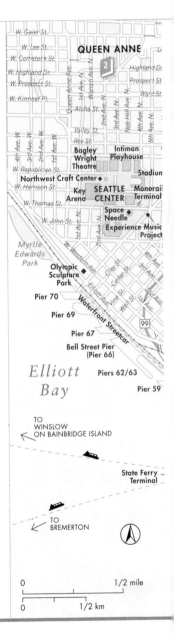

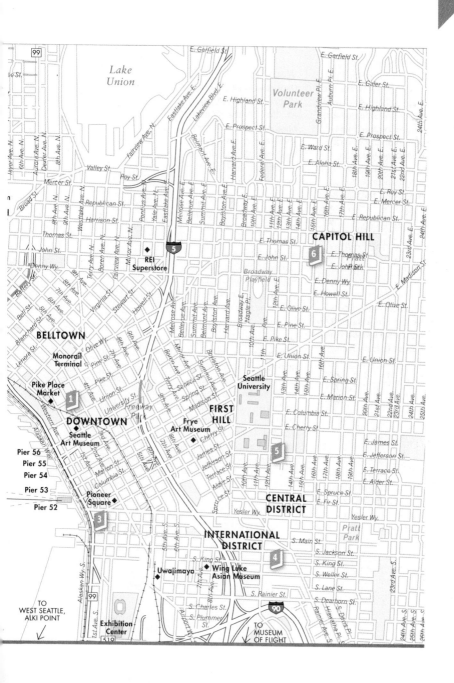

WHAT'S WHERE

7 Fremont. This 'hood on the northern side of the Lake Washington Ship Canal used to be *the* neighborhood for artists and hippies; it's now an interesting mix of pricey boutiques and restaurants obsessed over by foodies. Up the hill, residential Phinney Ridge includes the Woodland Park Zoo.

8 Ballard. Skirting the mouth of Shilshole Bay, Ballard's main tourist attraction is the Hiram M. Chittenden Locks. This historically Scandinavian neighborhood is now booming with new builds, and is worth a visit for the dining, shopping, and year-round farmers' market.

9 Wallingford. A large residential neighborhood that keeps a low profile, Wallingford starts at the ship canal with the wonderful waterfront Gas Works Park. Its booming commercial strip along North 45th Street has a few excellent restaurants. Directly north of Wallingford is Green Lake, whose park has a 3-mile paved path that circles the lake.

10 The "U District." The University of Washington's vast campus is truly lovely, and the surrounding neighborhood can be both gritty and inviting. Loads of ethnic restaurants and a large student population keep things lively.

11 West Seattle. On a peninsula west of the city proper, West Seattle's California Avenue has some appealing shops and restaurants. Gorgeous Alki Beach offers views of the Seattle skyline. Lincoln Park is an ideal place to hike or relax on the beach.

12 Eastside. East of Lake Washington, the Eastside suburbs are home to Microsoft. Bellevue is the most citylike, with its own skyline, an art museum, and high-end shops and restaurants. You can also visit Redmond, Woodinville wineries, Marymoor Park, or head into the mountains.

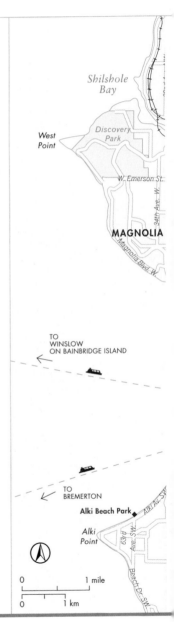

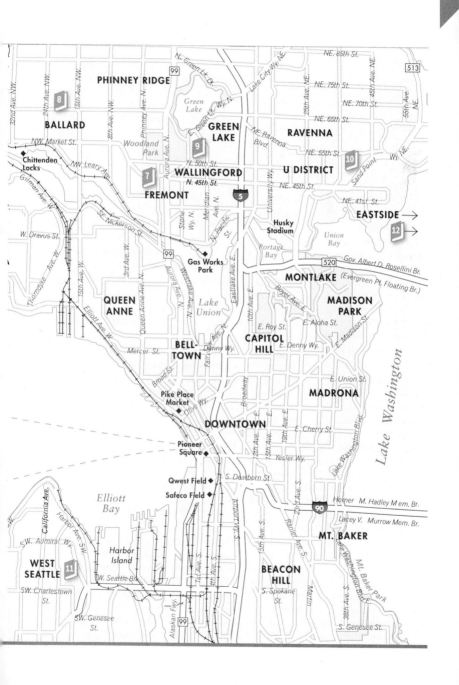

SEATTLE PLANNER

Getting Here and Around

GETTING HERE

The major gateway is Seattle–Tacoma International Airport (SEA), known locally as Sea-Tac. The airport is south of the city and reasonably close to it—non-rush-hours trips to Downtown sometimes take less than a half hour. Sea-Tac is a midsize, modern airport that is usually pleasant to navigate. You can take Sound Transit's **Link light-rail** (⊕ *www.soundtransit.org*), which will take you right to Downtown or beyond in 35 minutes for just $3.

GETTING AROUND

Biking is a popular but somewhat tricky endeavor, thanks to a shortage of safe bike routes and some daunting hills. Walking is fun, though distances and rain can sometimes get in the way. Several neighborhoods—from Pioneer Square to Downtown, or from Belltown to Queen Anne, for example—are close enough to each other that even hills and moisture can't stop walkers.

The bus system will get you anywhere you need to go, although some routes require a time commitment and several transfers. Within the Downtown core, however, the bus is efficient and affordable. Another option for public transport is the bright red streetcars that connects Downtown to South Lake Union and Pioneer Square to Capitol Hill.

Access to a car is *almost* a necessity if you want to explore the residential neighborhoods beyond their commercial centers, but parking can cost upwards of $50 per night in the urban center. Alternatives like Car2Go, Lyft, or Uber are great options, and many high-end hotels offer complimentary town-car service around Downtown and the immediate areas.

Ferries are a major part of Seattle's transportation network, and they're the only way to reach Vashon Island and the San Juans. You'll get outstanding views of the skyline and the elusive Mt. Rainier from the ferry to Bainbridge.

Helpful Websites and Apps

⊕ *www.ridethecity.com/seattle* helps cyclists find the best route.

⊕ *www.wsdot.com/traffic/seattle* has bridge and road closures and live traffic updates.

⊕ *www.wsdot.com/ferries* has live cams and wait times for ferries.

⊕ *www.tripplanner.kingcounty.gov* makes finding bus route easy.

⊕ *www.accessmap.io* helps users navigate Seattle's hills, curb cuts, and construction. It's designed for the handicapped but has useful information for others as well.

Visitor Information

Contact the **Seattle Visitors Bureau and Convention Center** (⊕ *www.visitseattle.org* ☎ 206/461–5800) for help with everything from sightseeing to booking spa services. You can also follow their Twitter feed (⊕ *twitter.com/seattlemaven*). The main visitor information center is Downtown, at the Washington State Convention and Trade Center on 8th Avenue and Pike Street; it has a full-service concierge desk open daily 9 to 5 (in summer; weekdays only in winter). There's also an info booth at Pike Place Market.

When to Go

Unless you're planning an all-indoor museum trip, Seattle is most enjoyable May through October. June can be surprisingly rainy, but July through September is almost always dry, with warm days that range from the mid-70s and 80s with the occasional serious scorcher; nights are cooler, though it doesn't get dark until 9 or 10 pm. Although the weather can be dodgy, spring (particularly April) and fall are also excellent times to visit, as lodging and tour costs are usually much lower (and the crowds much smaller). In winter, the days are short, dark, and wet, but temperatures rarely dip below the low 40s, and winter events—especially around the holidays—are plentiful. You might even luck into a sunny winter day with crisp air and clear views of snowy mountains.

Festivals

The Seattle Convention and Visitors Bureau has a full calendar of events at ⊕ *www.visitseattle.org/cultural.* Foodies will want to hit up **Taste of Washington** (spring ⊕ *www.tastewashington.org*) for the best of food and wine, as well as **Bite of Seattle** (July ⊕ *www.biteofseattle.com*), the Northwest Chocolate Festival (September ⊕ *www.nwchocolate.com*) and Seattle International Beer Fest (July ⊕ *www.seattlebeerfest.com*). The **Seattle International Film Festival** presents more than 200 features (May and June ⊕ *www.siff.net*).

Music lovers have three major events to keep them happy: **Bumbershoot** (September ⊕ *www.bumbershoot.com*) is Seattle's premier music festival, packed with major acts, as well as dance and theater, while Northwest Folklife Festival (May ⊕ *www.nwfolklife.org*) is a free, family-friendly event featuring folk music and dance from around the globe. Hipsters will want to check out Capitol Hill Block Party (July ⊕ *www.capitolhillblockparty.com*) for the best indie pop, rock, hip-hop, and alt-country.

The **Seattle Pride Festival** (June ⊕ *www.seattlepride.org*) has the Northwest's biggest gay, lesbian, and transgender pride parade. A local favorite, the quirky **Fremont Fair Summer Solstice Parade** (June ⊕ *www.fremontfair.org*) provides a glimpse into the true character of the city. **Seafair** (July and August ⊕ *www.seafair.com*) is the biggest summer festival; hydroplane races are just one major event.

SEATTLE TODAY

Seattle is a city that doesn't stand on convention. From its well-earned reputation for quirky music and art, to its laid-back population of obsessive foodies, this is a place that defies easy categorization. You're as likely to see millionaires riding the bus as PhDs behind the counter at a coffee shop. Grizzled fishermen mingle at Ballard bars alongside mustachioed hipsters, techies in performance clothing, and tattooed moms. It's an international city, with a strong Asian influence and a history of innovation. This is a place that successfully rallied for the statewide legalization of marijuana, yet people still refuse to jaywalk, even during protests.

Today's Seattle

... is influenced by its environment. The Seattleite way of life is shaped by the mountains, water, and massive evergreen trees that hang like verdant shrouds over Craftsman homes. You can see it in Seattleite fashion—for many, waterproof gear and sensible shoes take precedence over trends. You can see it in the hobbies—with the most sailors per capita, nearly everyone has a boat or knows someone who does. REI started here for a reason: this outdoorsy, active population is constantly on a hike, bike, or paddle adventure. With such a connection to nature, Seattleites are rabid recyclers and composters and the city recently enacted a plastic bag ban. The rain makes the population maudlin, introspective, and dark—which they channel into wildly imaginative writing, art, and music.

... is highly educated. This is a city of nerds. Go ahead, make that obscure reference to Hessian fighters or binary code—you'll find an appreciative audience. Seattle is the most educated city in the country, and constantly vies for most literate with Minneapolis. It has always attracted educated, creative people, from the first influx of Boeing engineers and University of Washington students to today's high-tech innovators.

... is liberal, progressive, and alternative. One of the most liberal cities in the country, Seattle can be counted on to vote at least 80% Democrat in any given election. This progressive hotbed is also host to one of the largest LGBT populations, the highest mixed-race population nationwide, and a hugely influential alternative press—including *The Stranger, Seattle Weekly,* and the many active neighborhood blogs. Which is not to say they're always tolerant—conservatives are shunned in the city limits and people aren't quick to advertise their church attendance.

... is growing. Fast. With a near-constant influx of newcomers arriving, the population is growing ahead of the national average. Newbies now outweigh natives—a fact many old-timers lament. Hemmed by the geographical limits of mountains and water, the city has had no choice but to expand skyward. Density is growing, as are light-rail and other forms of mass transit. And not a moment too soon—Seattle now boasts the fifth-worst traffic in the country. Luckily, the city is walkable and bike-able, and most neighborhoods are well equipped with all the necessities within walking distance. With all this expansion, housing costs are sky-high and Seattle is fast becoming one of the most expensive cities. Understandably, you won't see a lot of kids—only San Francisco boasts fewer families with children. Dogs, however, are another story. The canine-to-kid ratio is decidedly in Fido's favor.

FREE AND ALMOST FREE

Free Art

The Olympic Sculpture Park has installations from sculptors like Alexander Calder set against the backdrop of the sparkling waters of the Sound.

Pioneer Square has the largest concentration of art galleries in the city, all of which are free. Elsewhere in the city, Belltown and Capitol Hill also have free galleries.

Beloved sculptures like the *Fremont Troll*, the statue of Lenin, and *Waiting for the Interurban* are free to visit, too.

Free Music

Unless it's a major ticketed venue, cover charges at small music venues tend to be cheap ($5–$8) or free.

Throughout the year, City Hall hosts free lunchtime concerts, mostly jazz and world music.

Local indie music station KEXP, which has an international audience, and Seattle Center host the Concerts at the Mural series at the Mural Amphitheatre lawn in late July and August (⊕ *www.kexp.org/ events*; KEXP also offers free tours of its new HQ near the Space Needle).

All shows at the four-day (Memorial Day weekend) **Northwest Folklife Festival** (⊕ *www.nwfolklife.org*) are free, but donations are appreciated.

Free Words

Only residents can check out materials, but the gorgeous main branch of the Rem Koolhaas– and Joshua Ramus–designed Seattle Public Library is open to everyone—check email, take a tour, listen to a CD from the music library, or catch up on reading in one of the many lounges. Many of their evening lectures are also free.

Elliott Bay Book Company (⊕ *www.elliott-baybook.com*), Third Place Books (⊕ *www. thirdplacebooks.com*), and **Open Books**

(⊕ *www.openpoetrybooks.com*) often have free author readings.

Town Hall, the city's premier venue for lectures, sometimes has free series—and tickets to most lectures are only $5 (⊕ *www.townhallseattle.org*).

Free Theater

Free (and cheap) theater can be found in Seattle year-round, but the best time to score that live theater fix is October, during Arts Crush (⊕ *www.artscrush.org*). For the entire month, the city teems with live theater (along with music, literature, film, and dance) events, many of which are free. If you're visiting in July or August, you can enjoy a free Shakespeare in the Park production from Wooden O Theater (⊕ *www.seattleshakespeare.org*) or Green Stage (⊕ *www.greenstage.org*). Head to Volunteer Park for free children's theater from Theater Schmeater (⊕ *www.schmeater.org*).

Free Museums and Attractions
Always Free

The Center for Wooden Boats

Coast Guard Museum on Pier 36

Frye Art Museum

Hiram M. Chittenden "Ballard" Locks

Klondike Gold Rush Museum

Kubota Garden

Pike Place Market

Seattle Art Museum Sculpture Park

Uwajimaya

Volunteer Park Conservatory

Woodland Park Zoo's Rose Garden

QUINTESSENTIAL SEATTLE

Coffee

If Seattle had a soundtrack it would surely include the whir, hiss, and hum of espressos being pulled by baristas. It may be a cliché, but coffee fuels a huge part of Seattle's cultural identity. Starbucks has local fans, but to understand the coffee culture—and to get a great cup of joe—visit one of the numerous independent shops and local minichains, many of which roast their own beans on-site. With what appears to be half the city telecommuting at any given time, coffeehouses are the de facto workplace for many Seattleites. Spend an hour or two in a shop and you'll notice business meetings and small armies of freelancers tapping away on their laptops. Some shops, particularly in the north end, host play groups and story times, and an increasing number offer beer and wine as well as evening trivia or music events. Occasionally, shops feature hard-to-get coffees at special "cupping" events, which take on the feel of wine tastings.

Music

Let's get this out of the way: the city that brought the world grunge has never stopped evolving. While you still might catch a glimpse of grunge royalty, our current crop of local bands is proof we've moved on. Today you're more likely to catch alt-country bands, underground hip-hop, or eclectic folk-pop like the Fleet Foxes in the city's many little clubs, theaters, and music festivals. Seattle's love of music is demonstrated more outside its clubs than in them. You can see it in the independent record shops, where staff members handwrite poetic recommendations; in the continued success of local label Sub Pop Records; in the fanatical support for local radio station KEXP; in the health of midsize venues that can draw national acts; and the tendency of coffeehouse baristas to treat their shifts like DJ sessions.

If you want to savor the Emerald City like a local, start by familiarizing yourself with some of its passions. Seattle's culture is best experienced in its coffee shops, music clubs, restaurants, and the surrounding mountains and waterways.

Pacific Northwest Cuisine

Fresh, local, organic, and wild—this is a city that takes these buzzwords seriously, and it shows. Over the last decade, Seattle has emerged as a foodie mecca, with a distinctive farm- (and sea-) to-table style and a heavy Pacific Rim influence. Many restaurants get their ingredients from farmers' markets, Pike Place Market, and in some cases from their own organic farms and rooftop gardens. We'd be remiss if we didn't push you to try seafood throughout the city—from sustainable sushi to the season's best offerings at midlevel and high-end eateries. Your exploration shouldn't be limited to the fanciest eateries—be sure to hit hole-in-the-wall pho joints, tiny diners, fish-and-chips shops, bakeries, and food trucks—many of which feature high-quality, local ingredients and a devoted following. ⊕ *www.seattlefoodtruck.com*

The Great Outdoors

Yes, it rains a lot … in winter. But summers are gorgeous (as are most falls and springs), and with a major mountain range on each side and Mt. Rainier rising to the south, it's no wonder that Seattleites are obsessed with the outdoors. The best adventures—heading east to hike in the Cascade range; south to Mt. Rainier or Mt. St. Helens national parks; west to camp, hike, and spot wildlife in Olympic National Park; or across the Sound to explore one of many nearby islands on foot or by canoe or kayak—involve leaving the city, but even within Seattle proper, there's plenty to do. Rent a bike or kayak or take a walk around Discovery Park, Washington Park Arboretum, and Seward Park. Enjoying an outdoor adventure is easy and memorable here.

IF YOU LIKE

Arts and Culture

The Great Outdoors gets so much attention it's easy to overlook Seattle's Great Indoors—the myriad galleries, museums, music clubs, independent bookstores, theaters, and cinemas. The city teems with visual artists and sculptors; several excellent film festivals attest to the number of resident cinephiles. Nearly every local coffee shop (and many restaurants, bars, and stores) serves as an impromptu art gallery; some even hold official openings with food, drinks, and music when exhibits change.

A great way to get an overview of Seattle's art scene—and mingle with locals in the process—is to participate in one of the city's **art walks**, which include stops at galleries, coffeehouses, restaurants, shops, and public works of art in all their quirky glory. The First Thursday Art Walk in Pioneer Square (first Thursday of every month from noon to 8 pm ⊕ *www.firstthursdayseattle.com*) starts at Main Street and Occidental and takes you through the city's gallery district, as well as to some Downtown spots. There are also smaller walks in every neighborhood in Seattle (⊕ *www.seattle.gov.arts.experience.artwalks*). Some of our favorites are Capitol Hill (second Thursdays from 5 pm to 8 pm ⊕ *www.capitolhillartwalk.com*), Fremont (first Fridays from 6 pm to 9 pm ⊕ *www.fremontfirstfriday.blogspot.com*), and Ballard (second Saturdays from 6 pm to 9 pm ⊕ *www.ballardchamber.com*).

Check out what local writers are up to at readings at the **Hugo House, Open Books, the Elliott Bay Book Company,** and at other local bookstores and venues citywide (⊕ *www.thestranger.com/seattle/books* for weekly listings).

The grande dame of the art scene, the **Seattle Art Museum** has rotating exhibitions and a broad permanent collection. SAM's outdoor branch, **Olympic Sculpture Park,** is where striking sculptures compete with views of the Puget Sound. Other favorite museums include the **Wing Luke Museum of the Asian Pacific American Experience** and the **Frye Art Museum,** along with the Chihuly Garden and Glass museum.

A nonprofit that aids Seattle's budding filmmakers, the **Northwest Film Forum** (⊕ *www.nwfilmforum.org*) has the scoop on independent film in the Northwest. At NWFF's hip screening room, film geeks can catch hard-to-find documentaries and feature films or revisit classic films from masters like Jean Renoir and Akira Kurosawa.

Water

Bound and sliced by impressive stretches of water, even longtime residents can be found gawking at the mountain-backed Puget Sound and its bays.

A must-see on any itinerary, the **Seattle Aquarium** shows you what's going on underneath the surface, with special exhibits concerning the ecosystems of the Pacific Northwest. Get an up-close look at all sorts of craft, from research boats to posh yachts, as they navigate the Lake Washington Ship Canal and the **Hiram M. Chittenden (aka "Ballard") Locks.**

If you're not content with views alone, **rent a canoe or kayak** from Agua Verde Paddle Club and tool around the ship canal or head into Lake Union to see Seattle's famous houseboats. Experienced sailors might want to consider renting a sailboat from the Center for Wooden Boats; lessons are available for landlubbers.

On hot days, the swimming rafts in **Lake Washington** beckon. Several beaches along the western shore of this massive lake have lifeguards and other amenities. The eastern shore of **Green Lake** also has a beach and swimming raft and offers a more subdued dip—a good way to cool off after you join Seattleites in a jog around the lake's nearly 3-mile pedestrian path.

To experience a little taste of California in Seattle, with beach volleyball and a general SoCal beachy feel, take the **West Seattle water taxi** (⊕ *www.kingcounty. gov*) across Elliott Bay. Stroll or bike along Alki Beach, dip a toe or a kayak in the water, and enjoy a panorama of city skyline, mountains, and sea. Riding a **Washington State ferry**—perhaps a trip from Downtown Seattle to Bainbridge Island—is pure exhilarating joy, with the views, the waves, the seagulls, the spray of water, and the seals frolicking.

Lazy Days

Despite all the activities they enjoy, Seattleites appreciate the beauty of slowing the pace and spending a few quiet hours away from distractions.

Grab a few books, **find a coffee shop**, and spend a couple of hours reading and writing postcards.

Instead of jostling with joggers around Green Lake or power walking in Discovery Park, head to **Gas Works Park** and stake out a piece of green. From the park's hill you can watch the boats in Lake Union.

Take the ferry to nearby islands of **Vashon** or **Bainbridge**. Rent a bike and tool around past parkland, farmland, and orchards; then pop into charming galleries and crafts shops if you feel so inclined. Or just find a piece of beach and relax for a few hours.

Wining and Dining

It's no secret that Seattle has excellent restaurants as well as an obsession with wine. Many restaurants showcase the best of Northwest wine alongside international selections, and the city's most upscale dining options often offer sommelier services. Oenophiles should also plan to visit the Woodinville wine country. Just 30 minutes outside Seattle, the region features numerous wineries and tasting rooms.

Craft beer is a big deal in Seattle. An annual spring beer fest celebrates the best of the city and beyond, while low-key brewpubs continue to crop up in every neighborhood. Ballard features a growing concentration of microbreweries, many of which are kid-friendly and include ample seating. Other locally produced tipples are trending as well, including craft cider and spirits.

Out of all of the city's current favorite restaurants, **Canlis, Cascina Spinasse, Sitka & Spruce, the Walrus and the Carpenter, Tilth, How to Cook a Wolf, Poppy, Anchovies & Olives, Matt's in the Market,** and **Lark** are just a few that get a special nod for excellent food and wine choices that never disappoint. **Café Juanita** and **the Herbfarm**, in the city's eastern suburbs, take special-occasion dining to a whole new level with multiple courses and wine pairings.

To indulge during daylight hours, **create the perfect picnic** with food from **Salumi Cured Meats** in Pioneer Square, **Paseo** in Fremont, or **DeLaurenti**'s at Pike Place Market (be sure to grab a few choice bottles from the **Pike & Western Wine Shop** nearby).

SEATTLE
TOP ATTRACTIONS

The World of SAM

(A) Downtown's Seattle Art Museum (SAM) is known for its collection of modern and Native American art. A sleek addition to the original building—complete with a stylish café and gift shop—is the proper modern aesthetics for Picasso and Warhol. SAM'S Olympic Sculpture Park, in Belltown, overlooks Puget Sound and the Olympic Mountains and showcases works by Calder and Serra amidst lovely green spaces. On Capitol Hill explore Volunteer Park.

Seattle Aquarium

(B) Seattle's homage to its marine habitats and inhabitants sits, fittingly, on one of its piers. This small but delightful aquarium has a well-rounded selection of Northwest-focused exhibits, from river otters to a salmon ladder. Watch divers feed fish in a replica of Neah Bay, then pay a visit to a giant Pacific octopus.

Discovery Park

(C) Well off the radar, on a peninsula in a residential neighborhood called Magnolia, this park always feels like a serendipitous discovery. Though the city has many other impressive green spaces, none of them has such variety: densely forested trails spill out onto beaches with jaw-dropping vistas of Puget Sound.

Seattle Center, the Space Needle, MoPOP, Chihuly Garden and Glass, and more

(D) Almost every trip, especially an inaugural one, includes a stop at Seattle Center, which was built for the 1962 World's Fair and is home to the Space Needle, museums, and performance halls. Most of the city's major events are held here, but even on quiet weekends there's something for everyone: Pacific Science Center and Children's Museum, Experience Music Project/Science Fiction Museum, a skatepark, the SIFF Film Center, and the

brand-new Chihuly Garden and Glass exhibit. You can catch opera or ballet at McCaw Hall and theater performances at Intiman Theatre.

Local Farmers' Markets

(E) A tour of the Northwest's seasonal bounty should start at glorious Pike Place Market. Then visit smaller neighborhood markets in the University District, West Seattle, Columbia City, and along historic Ballard Avenue, and Broadway on Capitol Hill.

The Burke-Gilman Trail

(F) This major cycling corridor stretches from Ballard all the way around the northern tip of Lake Washington into the Eastside suburbs. Along the way it skirts the canal and Lake Union, goes through the UW campus, passes lakeside Magnuson Park, and spends its last leg along the shore of Lake Washington.

Washington Park Arboretum

(G) From autumn's effulgent colors to the tiny pink petals of spring, the Washington Park Arboretum is a 230-acre reminder that Seattle is a city with seasons. Easy-to-navigate paths include the Shoreline Trail. One of the many highlights is the beautiful Japanese Garden.

Hiram M. Chittenden Locks

Also called the Ballard Locks, this attraction is an important passage within the Lake Washington Ship canal, connecting Puget Sound to Lake Washington.

GREAT ITINERARIES

Seattle Highlights

Though Seattle's not always the easiest city to navigate, it's small enough that you can see a great deal of it in a week. If you've only got a long weekend here, you can easily mix and match any of the days in this itinerary. Before you explore, you'll need three things: comfortable walking shoes, layered clothing, and a flexible mind-set: it's easy and advisable to meander off track.

Day 1: Pike Place Market and Downtown's Major Sights

Spend the first day seeing some of the major sights around Downtown. Get up early and stroll to Pike Place Market. Grab a latte or have a hearty breakfast at a café, then spend the morning wandering through the fish, fruit, flower, and crafts stalls. When you've had your fill, head a bit south to the Seattle Art Museum or take the steps down to the docks and visit the Seattle Aquarium. Other options include taking a stroll to Belltown to take in the views at the Olympic Sculpture Park or getting a roving view of the landscape from atop the new Seattle Great Wheel. Stop for a simple lunch at Storyville Coffee or Macrina Bakery. If you're not too tired, head to 1st Avenue in Belltown or to Downtown's Nordstrom and thereabouts for some late-afternoon shopping. Have dinner and drinks in either Belltown or Downtown—both have terrific restaurants that will give you a first taste of that famous Pacific Northwest cuisine.

Day 2: Seattle Center or Pioneer Square

Take the two-minute monorail ride from Downtown's Westlake Center to the Seattle Center. Travel up the Space Needle for 360-degree city views. Then take in one of Seattle Center's many ground-level attractions: the Pacific Science Center, the Children's Museum, the Chihuly Garden and Glass exhibit, or the Experience Music Project/Science Fiction Museum. If you didn't visit it the day before, walk southwest down Broad Street to the Olympic Sculpture Park. From there, take a cab or the bus to the International District. Visit the Uwajimaya superstore, stroll the streets, and have dinner in one of the neighborhood's many restaurants.

Option: If you don't need to start out with the Space Needle, skip Seattle Center and start your day in Pioneer Square. Tour a few galleries (most of which open late morning), peek into some shops, and then head to nearby International District for more exploring—don't miss the Wing Luke Museum of the Asian Pacific American Experience. If you still want to see the Space Needle, you can go after dinner; the observation deck is open until 9:30 pm most nights.

Day 3: Side Trips from the City

Now that you've seen some of the city, it's time to get out of town and get closer to nature. Hikers have almost too many options, but Mt. Rainier National Park never disappoints. Alternatively, Crystal Mountain, a popular ski resort (from Highway 410, the left-hand turnoff to Crystal Mountain Blvd. is just before the entrance to the national park), offers gondola rides to the summit, where you can take in unparalleled views of Mt. Rainier and the Cascade Range (to get back to the base, hop back on the gondola or hike down). Plan a whole day for any hiking excursion—between hiking time and driving time, you'll probably need it. When you return to the city, tired and probably ravenous, grab a hearty, casual meal and maybe an art flick—Capitol Hill is a great neighborhood for both, as is Wallingford and the University District.

If you'd rather take to the water, get on a ferry and visit either Bainbridge or Vashon islands. Bainbridge is more developed, but it's pretty and has large swaths of protected land with trails. The Bloedel Reserve is a major attraction, with trails passing through a bird refuge, forest, and themed gardens (a Japanese garden and a moss garden are just two). It's always serene, thanks to a limit on the number of daily visitors (make reservations). Vashon is more agricultural and low-key. The most popular way to explore either island is by bicycle, though note that Bainbridge has some hills. Both islands have beach strolls, too. Bainbridge also has many shops and good restaurants, so it's easy to grab a bite before heading back into the city. You'll need less time to explore the islands than you'll need to do a hiking excursion, so you can probably see one or two sights Downtown before going to the pier. If you haven't made it to the aquarium yet, its proximity to the ferry makes it a great option.

Day 4: Stepping Off the Tourist Trail
Since you covered Downtown on Days 1 and 2, today you can sleep in a bit and explore some of the different residential neighborhoods. Check out Capitol Hill for great shopping, strolling, café culture, and people-watching. Or head north of the Lake Washington Ship Canal to Fremont and Ballard. Wherever you end up, you can start your day by having a leisurely breakfast or getting a coffee fix at an independent coffee shop. To stretch your legs, make the rounds at Volunteer Park in Capitol Hill or follow the Burke-Gilman Trail from Fremont Center to Gasworks Park. Both the Woodland Park

> **TIPS**
>
> ■ Pike Place Market and waterfront attractions are open daily all year.
>
> ■ The ride to the top of the Needle is not worth the charge if the day is overcast or rainy.
>
> ■ Remember that Pioneer Square's galleries may not be open on Monday. They do, however, have late hours on the first Thursday of every month.
>
> ■ When leaving the city for an all-day hiking trip, try to time things so that you're not hitting I-5 during evening rush hour. Unless you get a very early start—or don't leave until 9:30 am or 10 am—you probably won't be able to avoid sitting in aggravating morning rush-hour traffic.

Zoo (slightly north of Fremont) and the Hiram M. Chittenden Locks ("Ballard" Locks) are captivating. In Capitol Hill or in the northern neighborhoods, you'll have no problem rounding out the day by ducking into shops and grabbing a great meal. If you're looking for late-night entertainment, you'll find plenty of nightlife options in both areas, too.

Day 5: Last Rays of Sun and Loose Ends
Spend at least half of your last day in Seattle outdoors, exploring Discovery Park or renting kayaks in the University District, from Agua Verde Café and Paddle Club, for a trip around Portage Bay or into Lake Washington. Linger in your favorite neighborhood (you'll have one by now). Note that you can combine a park visit with kayaking if you head to the Washington Park Arboretum and Japanese Garden first. From there, it's a quick trip to the U-District.

SEATTLE THEN AND NOW

The Early Days

"There is plenty of room for one thousand settlers. Come at once." Upon receiving his brother's note, Arthur Denny set out from Portland on the schooner *Exact* with two dozen settlers. It landed at Alki Point on November 13, 1851.

The Denny party wasn't the first to arrive at the wild land that would become the Emerald City, though: the Duwamish tribe had been living there for millennia and British explorers surveyed the same spot in 1792. But Arthur Denny was the first of Seattle's many mad visionaries. He dreamed of creating a future endpoint for the transcontinental railroad, one to rival the already steadily developing Portland. The party moved to Elliot Bay's eastern shore in 1852; in 1853, the first boundaries of the city were marked on present-day Pioneer Square and Belltown, and Seattle—named after Chief Seattle (Si'ahl) of the Duwamish and Suquamish tribes—was born.

The Gold Rush

Amid all the growth came a series of disasters. In 1889, the Great Fire burned 64 acres. Then the "Panic of 1893" stock-market crash crippled the local economy. Seattle seemed down on its luck until, in 1897, a boat docked carrying gold from the Klondike, heralding the last Gold Rush.

The city quickly repositioned itself as the "Gateway to Alaska" (Alaska being the preferred point of entry into the Klondike). The assay office that journalist Erastus Brainerd convinced the federal government to open was just part of the city's Gold Rush revenue—Canada's Northwest Mounted Police required that each prospector show up with a year's worth of supplies, and Seattle merchants profited heavily from the edict.

Floatplanes and Postwar Prosperity

William E. Boeing launched his first floatplane from Lake Union in 1916. This marked the start of an industry that would define the city and long outlast timber. World War I bolstered aircraft manufacturing enough that Boeing moved south to a former shipyard.

Seattle was devastated by the Great Depression, with its only growth the result of New Deal programs that built parks, housing, and roads, including the floating bridge that links Seattle and Mercer Island. But entry into World War II again buoyed shipbuilding and aircraft industries. Boeing produced the B-29 bomber, the aircraft used to drop atomic bombs on Hiroshima and Nagasaki.

Seattle's renewed prosperity, which prompted it to host the 1962 World's Fair, remained tethered to Boeing, and the early '70s "Boeing Bust," when loss of federal funding caused Boeing to lay off tens of thousands of employees, sunk the city back into recession. After that, although Boeing would remain an influential employer, new industries would start to take its place. In 1963, Seattle had spent $100 million to upgrade its port in a successful bid to lure cargo traffic from Asia away from Portland and San Francisco. In 1970, six Japanese shipping lines started calling at Seattle.

The Tech Boom and Today's Seattle

The tech boom may have defined the '90s, but it planted its roots in Seattle in the '70s. In 1978, Microsoft moved from Albuquerque to the Eastside suburb of Bellevue, bringing the first influx of tech money—even today "Microsoft money" is shorthand for wealthy techies (Microsoft moved to its current Redmond campus in 1986). In 1994, Amazon.com became incorporated in the State of Washington; it is now one of Seattle's largest employers and has such a significant presence in South Lake Union that many locals refer to it as Amazonia. Although the dot-com bust temporarily took the wind out of Seattle's entrepreneurial sails, the city has continued to define itself as a major tech player, with companies such as Facebook, Google, and Zynga having local offices. And an increasing number of other companies are basing themselves here, including BuddyTV.com, Expedia.com, Zillow.com, AllRecipes.com, Drugstore.com, and Redfin.com. Today, the metro area of more than 3.5 million holds a diverse portfolio: one part of the port is dominated by container ships while the other side welcomes Alaska-bound ships to Smith Cove Cruise Terminal. The food and beverages industries are a major part of the economy, with coffee giant Starbucks and Redhook Ale Brewery standing alongside such major seafood companies as Trident Seafoods. Like tech, the gaming industry is huge here, with Big Fish Games, PopCap, Nintendo of America, and Wizards of the Coast based in the metro area. T-Mobile's national headquarters is here, too, as is a long list of hardware companies. The University of Washington is a national leader in medical research, and a biotech hub is rising in the city center. Retail giants Nordstrom, Tommy Bahama, REI, Costco, and, of course, Amazon, keep money flowing into the area.

Important Dates

1851 Denny party arrives in Seattle.

1861 University of Washington is established.

1889 Seattle's Great Fire destroys the commercial core.

1889 Washington becomes the 42nd state.

1903 John C. Olmsted arrives; his master plan creates most of the city's parks.

1910 Washington women get the vote, 10 years before the rest of the nation.

1941 After Pearl Harbor is attacked, 8,000 Japanese immigrants are sent to internment camps.

1962 The World's Fair (and Space Needle) opens and runs for six months.

1982 Visitors Bureau starts using nickname "Emerald City." Seattle has also been called Queen City, Jet City, Rat City, and, of course, Rain City.

2001 Sesquicentennial coincides with a 6.8 earthquake that causes more than $1 billion in damage.

2004 The Central Library opens, the crown jewel in the city's massive "Libraries for All" project.

2015 *The New Yorker* publishes Pulitzer-winning "The Really Big One," which predicts a devastating PNW earthquake.

2016 The city celebrates a newly expanded light-rail system and passes a $54 billion transit bill to keep the improvements coming.

2017 Pike Place Market debuts a new expansion, and Seattle continues to develop a new, tourist-friendly waterfront.

WITH KIDS

Seattle is great for kids. After all, a place where floatplanes take off a few feet from houseboats, and where harbor seals might be spotted on a routine ferry ride, doesn't have to try too hard to feel like a wonderland. And if the rain falls, there are plenty of great museums to keep the kids occupied. A lot of child-centric sights are easily reached via public transportation, and the piers and the Aquarium can be explored on foot from most Downtown hotels. A few spots (Woodland Park Zoo, the Ballard Locks, and the Discovery and Gas Works parks) are easier to visit by car.

Museums

Several museums cater specifically to kids, and many are conveniently clustered at the Seattle Center. The Center's winning trio is the **Pacific Science Center,** which has interactive exhibits and IMAX theaters; the **Children's Museum,** which has exhibits on Washington State and foreign cultures plus plenty of interactive art spaces catering to kids ages 10 months to 10 years; and, of course, the **Space Needle.** For older, hipper siblings there's a skatepark; the Vera Project, a teen music and art space; and the Experience Music Project/Science Fiction Museum.

Downtown there are miles of waterfront to explore along the piers. The **Seattle Aquarium** is here and has touch pools and adorable otters—what more could a kid want?

Parks and Outdoor Attractions

Discovery Park has an interpretive center, a Native American cultural center, easy forest trails, and accessible beaches. **Alki Beach** in West Seattle is lively and fun; a wide paved path is the perfect surface for wheels of all kinds—you can rent bikes and scooters, or take to the water on rented paddleboats and kayaks. **Gas Works Park** has great views of the skyline, floatplanes over Lake Union, and the evocative rusty remnants of the old machinery. **Volunteer Park** and Green Lake have wide lawns and shallow pools made for splashing toddlers.

The **Woodland Park Zoo** has 300 different species of animals, from jaguars to mountain goats, cheap paid parking, and an adjacent playground; stroller rentals are available. Watching an astonishing variety of boats navigate the ship canal at the **Ballard Locks** will entertain visitors of any age. The **Northwest Puppet Center** has a museum and weekend marionette plays.

Hotels

Downtown, the **Hotel Monaco** offers a happy medium between sophisticated and family-friendly. The colorful, eccentric decor will appeal to kids but remind adults that they're in a boutique property. Fun amenities abound, like optional goldfish in the rooms, and toys in the lobby. Surprisingly, one of the city's most high-end historic properties, the **Fairmont Olympic,** is also quite kid-friendly. The grand staircases in the lobby will awe most little ones, and there's a great indoor pool area. In addition, the hotel offers babysitting, a kids' room-service menu, as well as toys and board games.

Several properties offer kitchenette suites that help families save some money on food costs. The **Silver Cloud Inn,** in Lake Union, has suites with kitchens. It's north of Downtown on Lake Union, but the South Lake Union streetcar is across the street and gets you into Downtown and to bus connections quickly.

TOURS WORTH NOTING

Bike Tours

Bike rentals are becoming increasingly common in the city, and many hotels and hostels offer daily and hourly rates to tour the city on wheels. If you'd rather go with a guide, there are a number of bicycle touring companies in Seattle for nearly every type of traveler. ■TIP➔ Seattle is a city built on hills, so bike tours are recommended for riders with moderate to advanced skills only.

Seattle Cycling Tours. Tours explore Pioneer Square, the Waterfront, and Seattle Center, West Seattle, Ballard, or Bainbridge Island. ✉ *714 Pike St., Downtown* ☎ *206/356–5803* ⊕ *www.seattle-cycling-tours.com.*

Terrene Tours. Terrene Tours offers upscale bike tours to the San Juan Islands, the Cascade Mountains, and Washington wine country—food and drinks are provided, and a van is on hand if you get tired. ✉ *3810 E Galer St., Madison Park* ☎ *206/325–5569* ⊕ *www.terrenetours.com.*

Orientation Tours

Show Me Seattle. Show Me Seattle takes up to 14 people in vans on three-hour tours of the major sights. This is an extremely touristy program that makes stops at places like the flagship Nordstrom store, the first Starbucks, and the *Sleepless in Seattle* floating home, but it also stops by a few sites many tourists miss, like the Fremont Troll and the north-end neighborhoods. ✉ *8110 7th Ave. S* ☎ *206/633–2489* ⊕ *www.showmeseattle.com* ✉ *$58.*

Or, you could always take a free, self-guided tour of five historic Seattle neighborhoods by downloading HistoryLink. org's walking tours at ⊕ *www.seattle.gov/ tour/historicdistricts.*

Self-Guided Tours

Seattle CityPASS. CityPASS provides admission to many of the top attractions at a steeply discounted rate. The booklet of tickets comes with a map, coupons, and a guide to the Space Needle, Seattle Aquarium, Argosy Cruises Harbor Tour, either the Chihuly Garden of Glass or the Pacific Science Center, and either the Museum of Pop Culture (MoPOP, formerly EMP) or the Woodland Park Zoo. Your pass is good for nine days and allows you to skip most ticket lines. Note that tickets must be removed from the booklet by attraction staff to be valid. ☎ *888/330–5008* ⊕ *www.citypass.com/seattle* ✉ *$74.*

Walking Tours

Chinatown Discovery Tours. Tours are offered Tuesday through Saturday at 2 pm and include admission to the Wing Luke Asian Museum. ☎ *206/623–5124* ⊕ *www.seattlechinatowntour.com* ✉ *$19.95.*

Market Ghost Tours. These weekend tours weave in local ghost stories, eerie history, and fun facts about haunted places. ✉ *1410 Post Alley, Downtown* ☎ *206/805–0195* ⊕ *www.seattleghost.com.*

Savor Seattle Food Tours. Options include a Chocolate Indulgence tour, a Gourmet Seattle tour, and a Pike Place Market tour. ✉ *1st Ave. and Pike St., Downtown* ☎ *888/987–2867* ⊕ *www.savorseattletours.com.*

Seattle Free Walking Tours. Follow the tour guide with a flag around Pike Place Market or through Pioneer Square down to the Waterfront district. Reservations are required and, while there's no charge, tips are definitely appreciated. ✉ *Seattle* ☎ *425/770–6928* ⊕ *www.seattlefreewalkingtours.org.*

SEATTLE'S BEST PARKS

Mountain ranges, ocean waters, and islands may surround the city, but Seattleites are often content to stay put on sunny weekends. Why? Because the incredible park system makes for fantastic outdoor adventures, offering everything from throwing beach rocks into the ocean against the backdrop of the Olympics to hiking under canopies of old growth, and from eating ice cream next to gurgling fountains in the center of town to wandering pathways of traditional Japanese gardens.

Luckily for today's residents, more than a century ago, the city's Board of Commissioners had the wisdom to hire the Olmsted Brothers (who had inherited the firm from Frederick Law Olmsted, designer of New York's Central Park) of Brookline, Massachusetts, to conduct a survey of the potential for a park system. J.C. Olmsted's visionary plan not only placed a park, playground, or playing field within walking distance of most homes in Seattle, it also created a 20-mile greenway connecting many of the urban parks, starting at Seward Park on Lake Washington and traveling across the city to Woodland Park and Discovery Park. Later the architect created plans for the campus of the University of Washington and the Washington Park Arboretum.

What follows are our top picks for best parks in the city. *(See also the Neighborhoods listings for more in-depth reviews of top parks.)*

Best for Families and Picnics

Cal Anderson Park. An urban park in every sense, this Capitol Hill expanse has a lovely water sculpture, a playing field, and green space. Grab an ice cream at nearby **Molly Moon's** (*917 E. Pine St.*) and enjoy. *1635 11th Ave., Capitol Hill.*

Gas Works Park. Reachable by the Burke-Gilman Trail, this Wallingford park gets its name from the remains of an old gasification plant. Twenty acres of rolling green space look out over Lake Union and the city skyline. *North end of Lake Union at N. Northlake Way and Meridian Ave. N, Wallingford.*

Volunteer Park. Capitol Hill's best green spot houses a plant conservatory, a water tower, paths, and an Isamu Noguchi sculpture (along with a great view). *14th Ave. E at Prospect St., Capitol Hill.*

(See also Carkeek Park, Marymoor Park, Olympic Sculpture Park, and Warren G. Magnuson Park.)

Best for Seasonal Blooms

Kubota Garden. It may be far south, but Kubota Garden is striking, with 20 acres of landscaped gardens blending Japanese and native plants and techniques. *817 55th Ave. S, South Seattle.*

Washington Park Arboretum. The park system's crown jewel may well be this 230-acre expanse, with flowering fruit trees in early spring; vibrant rhododendrons and azaleas in late spring and early summer; and brightly hued trees and shrubs in fall. *2300 Arboretum Dr. E, Washington Park.*

(See also Bellevue Botanical Gardens.)

Best Views

Alki Point. West Seattle comes to life in summer, and there's no better way to enjoy it than walking along this beachfront path to enjoy the sparkling views of Puget Sound, the Seattle skyline, and the Olympics. *1702 Alki Ave. SW, West Seattle.*

Carkeek Park. North of Ballard, Carkeek has awe-inspiring views of Puget Sound and the Olympics. Its Pipers Creek, playgrounds, picnic areas, and forest trails make this a fun family spot. *950 N.W. Carkeek Park Rd., Broadview.*

Discovery Park. Seattle's largest park, in Magnolia, is all about variety, with shaded forest, open meadows, pebbled beach stretches, and even sand dunes. A lighthouse, plus sweeping views of Puget Sound and the mountains make this an extremely picturesque spot. *3801 W. Government Way, Magnolia.*

Golden Gardens. This Ballard park, perched on Puget Sound, is the best place for beachcombers. Loads of facilities and a pretty pathway make this spot even more special. *8498 Seaview Pl. NW, Ballard.*

Myrtle Edwards. Adjacent to the Olympic Sculpture Park, Myrtle Edwards has a short bike-and-pedestrian path along Elliott Bay, with vistas of the Sound and the mountains. *3130 Alaskan Way W, Downtown.*

Olympic Sculpture Park. The Seattle Art Museum's 9-acre outdoor playground, located in Belltown, has fabulous views of Elliot Bay and the Olympics, complemented by huge works of art by the likes of Alexander Calder. *Western Ave. at Broad St., Belltown.*

(See also Gas Works Park.)

Best Walking Trails

Green Lake. The almost 3-mile loop around the lake is a favorite spot for joggers, bikers, kids, and dog walkers alike. You can rent a paddleboat and explore the waters. *E. Green Lake Dr. N and W. Green Lake Dr. N, Green Lake.*

Seward Park. Old-growth forest, views of the mountains and Lake Washington, and a very fun walking loop make this a beloved spot at the southwest side of

Lake Washington. *5902 Lake Washington Blvd.*

Warren G. Magnuson Park. Northeast of University District, this large green space has great playgrounds, walkable trails, and one of the largest off-leash dog parks in the city. *Sand Point Way NE at 65th St., Sand Point.*

(See also Discovery Park.)

Best Ocean-side Parks

Lincoln Park. With old-growth forest and rocky beaches, as well as facilities like a pool and tennis courts, this is a West Seattle favorite. *5551 S.W. Admiral Way, West Seattle.*

(See also Alki Point, Discovery Park, Golden Gardens Park, Lincoln Park, and Myrtle Edwards Park.)

Best Parks on the Eastside

Bellevue Botanical Gardens. Perennial borders, colorful rhododendron, rock gardens, and the lovely Lost Meadow Trail fill the 36 acres of this spot in Bellevue. *510 Bellevue Way NE, Bellevue, Eastside.*

Marymoor Park. Six hundred and forty acres of fun can be found at this huge Redmond green space, including a climbing rock, tennis courts, game fields, an off-leash dog area, and a path along the Sammamish River. *6046 W. Lake Sammamish Pkwy. NE, Redmond, Eastside.*

SEATTLE'S SIPPING CULTURE
ARTISAN COFFEES, CRAFT MICROBREWS, AND BOUTIQUE WINES

by Carissa Bluestone

Seattle's beverage obsession only *begins* with coffee. Whether you're into hoppy microbrews, premium wines, or expertly crafted cappuccinos, prepare to devote much of your visit to sipping the best Seattle and Washington State have to offer.

Seattle may forever be known as the birthplace of Starbucks, but nowadays foodies are just as likely to talk about Washington state's wine industry as the city's coffeehouses. Not to pronounce coffee dead, however. After a few years of inertia, the coffee scene is growing again with more independent roasters and shops than ever.

In fact, in the past few years the city's seen a profusion of potables: New microbreweries and wineries are opening, and hip new bars, taprooms, and tasting rooms are thriving more than ever. Like its sister city, Portland, Seattle is a hotspot for entrepreneurial spirit—it's this energy, mixed with a passion for local and organic ingredients, that has raised the bar on everything artisan.

COFFEE

Although Seattle owes much of its coffee legacy to Starbucks, the city's independent coffee shops rule the roast here. Their ardent commitment to creating premium artisanal blends from small batches of beans is what truly defines the scene. The moment you take your first sip of an expertly executed cappuccino at a coffeehouse such as **Caffé Vita** or **Espresso Vivace** you realize that the drink is never an afterthought here. Perfectly roasted beans ground to specification and pulled into espresso shots using dual-boiler machines and velvety steamed milk are de rigueur. In most restaurants, your coffee is likely to be a personal French press filled with a brew roasted just a few blocks away.

The "rosetta," a common latte design.

LATTE ART

Latte art is a given in Seattle. Designs vary by barista, but the most common flourish is the rosetta, which resembles a delicate fern. Here's how it's done:

1. THE BASE. A latte consists of a shot (or two) of espresso and hot, frothy milk.

2. THE POUR. First the shot is poured. The milk pitcher gets a few gentle swirls and taps (to burst the largest bubbles), then the milk is poured at a steady pace into the center of the tilted cup.

3. THE SHAKE. When the cup's about three-quarters full, the milk is streamed with tiny side-to-side strokes up and down the cup's center line. The "leaves" will start to fan out.

4. THE TOP. When the cup's almost full, the milk is drawn towards the bottom. With the last stroke the "stem" is drawn through the center of the leaves.

BEST COFFEEHOUSES

Many Seattle roasters obtain their beans through Direct Trade, sourcing directly from growers rather than brokers. They travel across the globe to meet with farmers, often paying them well above Fair Trade prices to ensure the highest-quality beans. Local roasters are also intensely community-minded: Caffé Vita, for example, recently partnered with the much-loved local chocolate factory Theo to produce sublime espresso-flavored chocolate bars.

Stumptown

CAFFÉ VITA. Though now a mini-chain (with locations in Fremont, Queen Anne, Pioneer Square, and Seward Park), Vita's roasting operations (and heart and soul) are in Capitol Hill. ⊠ *1005 E. Pike St., Capitol Hill* ☎ *206/709–4440* ⊕ *www.caffevita.com*

Caffé Vita

ESPRESSO VIVACE. A top roaster, Vivace has two tidy coffee shops (the other's by REI in South Lake Union), and a sidewalk espresso stand at Broadway and Harrison. ⊠ *532 Broadway Ave E, Capitol Hill* ☎ *206/860–2722* ⊕ *www.espressovivace.com*

FREMONT COFFEE COMPANY. Known for its awesome wraparound porch and exceptional brews, this friendly shop is the city's latest small-batch roaster. ⊠ *459 N. 36th St., Fremont* ☎ *206/632–3633* ⊕ *www.fremontcoffee.net*

HERKIMER. This cheerful small-batch roaster is a northern neighborhoods

favorite. ⊠ *7320 Greenwood Ave. N, Phinney Ridge* ☎ *206/784–0202* ⊕ *www.herkimercoffee.com*

STUMPTOWN. This hip Portland powerhouse has two branches (the other is on Pine and Boylston). The 12th Ave. branch has the roasting facility. ⊠ *1115 12th Ave., Capitol Hill* ☎ *206/323–1544* ⊕ *www.stumptowncoffee.com*

VICTROLA COFFEE. The original branch on 15th Avenue is a favorite standby, but the newer branch at 310 E. Pike St. in the Pike-Pine Corridor has a great view of the roasting room from its cafe tables. ⊠ *310 E. Pike St., Capitol Hill* ☎ *206/624–1725* ⊕ *www.victrolacoffee.com*

Victrola Coffee

BEER

Craft brews have fewer ingredients than you might think.

Next time you drink a beer, thank the state of Washington. More than 70% of the nation's hops is grown in the Yakima Valley, and Washington is the fourth-largest producer of malting barley. The state's 80-plus breweries combine top-notch ingredients with crystal-clear snowpack waters to make high-quality craft beers. Seattle has at least a dozen breweries within its city limits, plus many fine gastropubs with standout locals on tap.

GREAT BREWERIES

ELLIOTT BAY BREWING. A dozen of Elliott Bay's beers are certified organic. The pub is a neighborhood favorite for its good, locally sourced food. ✉ *4720 California Ave NW, West Seattle* ☎ *206/932–8695* ⊕ *www.elliottbay-brewing.com*

PIKE PUB. The most touristy of the local breweries, Pike Pub also has a small microbrewery museum. The pale ale and the Kilt Lifter Scottish ale have been local favorites for two decades.

There's a full pub menu. ✉ *1415 1st Ave, Downtown* ☎ *206/622–6044* ⊕ *www.pikebrewing.com*

ELYSIAN BREWING COMPANY. Known for its Immortal IPA and good seasonal brews and pub grub, Elysian has three branches, in Capitol Hill, Green Lake, and across from Qwest Field. ✉ *1221 E. Pike St., Capitol Hill* ☎ *206/860–1920* ⊕ *www.elysianbrewing.com*

FREMONT BREWING. This newcomer (2008) makes small-batch pale ales using organic hops. The Urban Beer

Elysian Brewing Company

Hale's beer

Garden is open Thurs.–Sat. 4–8:30. ✉ *3409 Woodland Park Avenue N, Fremont* ☎ *206/420-2407* ⊕ *www.fremontbrewing.com*

GEORGETOWN BREWING CO. This brewery offers a very small list, including Manny's Pale Ale and a special namesake porter for neighborhood bar the Nine Pound Hammer. Visit the store to pick up souvenirs or a growler of beer. Open weekdays 10–6 and Sat. 9–noon. ✉ *5200 Denver Ave. S., Georgetown* ☎ *206/766–8055* ⊕ *www.georgetownbeer.com*

HALE'S ALES. One of the city's oldest craft breweries (1983), Hale's does cask-conditioned ales and nitrogen-conditioned cream ales. The Mongoose IPA is also popular. The pub serves a full menu and has a great view of the fermenting room. ✉ *4301 Leary Way NW, Fremont* ☎ *206/706–1544* ⊕ *www.halesbrewery.com*

REDHOOK. This brewery specializes in amber ales—their ESB is an award-winner. The Forecaster's Pub has a full menu. It's open Mon.–Thurs. 11–10, Fri. and Sat. 11–midnight, and Sun. 11–9. ✉ *14300 NE 145th St, Woodinville* ☎ *425/483–3232* ⊕ *www.redhook.com.*

TWO BEERS BREWING CO. A small list of ales and IPAs, and interesting seasonal experiments—such as a summer ale with coriander and sweet orange peel. Tasting room open Thurs. and Fri. 3–7. No food. ✉ *4700 Ohio Ave. S., SoDo* ☎ *206/414–2224* ⊕ *www.twobeersbrewery.com*

BEER FESTIVALS

Washington Brewers Festival (⊕ www.washingtonbeer.com/festival_cask.htm; June/Father's Day weekend).

Fremont Oktoberfest (⊕ www.fremontoktoberfest.com; September).

Tacoma Craft Beer Festival (⊕ www.tacomacraftbeerfest.com; October).

Washington Cask Beer Festival (⊕ www.washingtonbeer.com/cbf.htm; end of March).

Pike Pub

Fremont Oktoberfest

WASHINGTON STATE WINE REGIONS

Second only to California in U.S. wine production, Washington has more than 500 wineries and 11 official American Viticultural Areas. The state is increasingly becoming known for its fine cabernet sauvignons after decades-strong on its crisp chardonnays and complex merlots. Here's a sampling of some of the state's best grape varieties.

Orchards and vineyard near Wishram, WA

WHITE WINES

CHARDONNAY. The French grape widely planted in eastern Washington, where the wines range from light to big and complex.

GEWÜRTZTRAMINER. A German-Alsatian grape in the Columbia Gorge and the Yakima Valley that produces a spicy, aromatic wine.

RIESLING. A German grape that makes a delicate, floral wine.

Château Ste. Michelle

SAUVIGNON BLANC. Herbal, dry wine from this Bordeaux grape, fermented in oak, is sold as fumé blanc.

VIOGNIER. A Rhône Valley grape that in eastern Washington makes fragrant wine with a good acid content.

WINERY SAMPLING

Amavi Cellars
(🌐 www.amavicellars.com)

Chateau Ste. Michelle
(🌐 www.ste-michelle.com)

Columbia Crest
(🌐 www.columbiacrest.com)

Cote Bonneville
(🌐 www.cotebonneville.com)

DeLille (🌐 www.delillecellars.com)

Gramercy Cellars
(🌐 www.gramercycellars.com)

L'Ecole no. 41 (🌐 www.lecole.com)

Long Shadows
(🌐 www.longshadows.com)

Mark Ryan (🌐 www.markryanwinery.com)

Maryhill (🌐 www.maryhillwinery.com)

àMaurice (🌐 www.amaurice.com)

RED WINES
CABERNET FRANC.
A Bordeaux grape
that produces well-
balanced wine in
the Walla Walla and
Yakima Valleys and
Columbia Gorge.
**CABERNET SAUVI-
GNON.** The famed
Bordeaux grape
grows well in the
Columbia Valley and
makes deeply tannic
wines in Walla Walla
and Yakima.
MERLOT. A black
grape yielding a
softer, more supple
wine than cabernet
sauvignon, merlot
has recently experi-
enced a boom, es-
pecially in the Walla
Walla Valley.

Columbia Crest

SYRAH. A Rhône
grape that produces
complex, big-bodied
wines; increas-
ingly planted in the
Yakima and Walla
Walla Valleys.
ZINFANDEL. A hot-
climate grape that
in the Yakima Valley
and the Columbia
Gorge makes big,
powerful wines.

BEST TASTING ROOMS AND WINE BARS

Almost every wine list in Seattle includes at least some regional choices, even when the cuisine has origins far from the Pacific Northwest.

BRICCO DELLA REGINA ANNA. Less comprehensive on the Northwest selec- tions than some of its peers, Bricco com- pensates with a good list of Italian wines. ✉ *1525 Queen Anne Ave N, Queen Anne* ☎ *206/285–4900* 🌐 *www.briccoseattle.com*

PIKE & WESTERN. This well-respected wine shop holds weekly tastings—limited- production bottles are sampled Wed. 4–6 PM ($5); new arrivals are tested Fri. 3–6 PM. ✉ *1934 Pike Pl., Downtown* 🌐 *www.pike- andwestern.com*

POCO WINE ROOM. Feels like both a date spot and a friendly neighborhood hangout. Reasonably priced Pacific Northwest wines are the focus. ✉ *1408 E. Pine St., Capitol Hill* ☎ *206/322–9463* 🌐 *www.pocowineroom.com*

PORTALIS. A cozy wine bar and well- stocked shop, Portalis has happy hours, prix-fixe dinners, and regular thematic tastings. ✉ *5205 Ballard Ave NW, Ballard* 🌐 *www.portaliswines.com*

PURPLE CAFE AND WINE BAR. Rumor has it that the imposing tower at this lofty wine bar contains more than 5,000 bottles. It should be no surprise, then, that this sprawl- ing downtown spot has one of the largest local wine selections in the city, with more than 50 choices from Washington state alone and hundreds from around the globe. Try the wines on their own or with snacks like Gorgonzola-stuffed dates, beef tartare, or meat and cheese plates. ✉ *1225 4th Ave., Downtown* ☎ *206/829-2280* 🌐 *www.purplecafe.com*

THE TASTING ROOM. Wine shop and tasting bar with hard-to-find boutique Washington wines. *Tast- ings range from $2 to $6.* ✉ *1924 Post Alley, Downtown* 🌐 *www. tastingroomseattle.com*

Cabernet Sauvignon,
Chateau Ste. Michelle

SEATTLE NEIGHBORHOODS

Updated by
AnnaMaria
Stephens

Seattle is a city of many neighborhoods: eclectic, urban, outdoorsy, artsy, gritty, down-to-earth, or posh—it's all here, from the quirky character of the Seattle Waterfront and the eccentric "Republic of Fremont," to hipsters walking baby carriages past aging mansions on Capitol Hill. There's something for just about everyone within this vibrant Emerald City.

Indeed, part of Seattle's diversity lies in the topography: the city is a feat of environmental engineering. Once Seattle started to grow, its residents literally changed the landscape. Massive Denny Hill once occupied the Belltown neighborhood, but it simply had to go. The multistage "regrade" started in 1899 and was completed 32 years later. The Denny Hill Regrade was just one of dozens of projects; another equally ambitious earth-moving mission was the construction of the canal that links Lake Washington to Puget Sound. Today, the city is once again moving a lot of earth around with the construction of a light-rail line across the city; it's changing the look, feel, and energy of neighborhoods as a result.

It's hard to think of Seattle as anything but natural, though. After all, the city owes much of its appeal to its natural features—the myriad hills that did survive settlement offer views of mountain ranges and water, water, water. Outside Downtown and other smaller commercial cores, Seattle's neighborhoods fan out in tangles of tree-lined streets. Massive parks like Discovery, Magnuson, and Washington Park Arboretum make Seattle one of the greenest and most livable cities in the nation. From the peaks of the Olympics or Cascades to an artistically landscaped garden in front of a classic Northwest bungalow, nature is in full effect every time you turn your head.

Taking a stroll, browsing a bookstore, or enjoying a cup of coffee can feel different in every one of Seattle's neighborhoods. It's the adventure of exploring that will really introduce you to the character of Seattle.

DOWNTOWN AND BELLTOWN

Sightseeing
★★★★★
Dining
★★★★
Lodging
★★★★★
Shopping
★★★★★
Nightlife
★★★★

Downtown is easy to recognize—it's the only part of Seattle with skyscrapers. Nearby Belltown is a hot spot for restaurants and nightlife, but is perhaps best known for its Olympic Sculpture Park. Nestled near both neighborhoods is Pike Place Market, with the Waterfront District a short walk away.

DOWNTOWN

Except for the busy areas around the Market and the piers, and the always-frenetic shopping district, a lot of Downtown can often seem deserted, especially at night. Still, while it may not be the soul of the city, it's definitely the heart, and there's plenty to do—nearly all of it easily reachable by foot. There's the city's premier art museum, the eye-popping Rem Koolhaas–designed Central Library, lively Pike Place Market, and a major shopping corridor along 5th Avenue and down Pine Street. And, of course, there's the water: Elliott Bay beckons from every crested hill.

Within the core of Downtown—which is bounded on the west by Elliott Bay and on the east by I–5, stretching from Virginia Street to Yesler Way—are several different experiences. The waterfront and much of 1st Avenue are lively and at times quite touristy, thanks to Pike Place Market, the Seattle Art Museum (SAM), and the piers, which have several kid-friendly sights as well as ferries to Bremerton and to Bainbridge Island. As you head east from Pike Place Market, you soon hit Downtown's shopping and entertainment district. The flagship Nordstrom department store is here, and the Westlake Center and Pacific Place shopping centers offer plenty of opportunities to part with your money. In addition to the shopping at Pacific Place, there are multiplex movie theaters, a multistory arcade, and a few popular chain restaurants.

MARIJUANA LEGALIZATION

In 2012, Washington voted to legalize recreational marijuana, one of the first two states in the United States to blaze the trail. Since 2014, when the first handful of legal locations opened in Washington, pot shops have cropped up in every Seattle neighborhood. Just two years after the initial roll out, state residents and visitors had consumed more than $1 billion in marijuana products, which generated roughly $250 million for the state through a 37% excise tax at the point of purchase. Steep taxes mean legal weed doesn't come as cheap as black-market goods, but as demand has grown, average prices have dropped significantly, from $25 per gram in 2014 to $10 per gram in 2016. That's good news for tourists who'd like to try it!

If you're inclined to explore the legal scene, it's a good idea to do a bit of research first. Shopping options range from hole-in-the-wall storefronts to upscale boutiques that stock impressive selections of marijuana along with various accessories. Check sites like ⊕ leafly.com or ⊕ weedmaps.com to locate stores and check on what strains they carry. You must be 21 or up with a valid ID to purchase marijuana in Washington. You can buy or possess an ounce of weed at a time, or up to 6 ounces of solid marijuana-infused edibles. When it comes to consumption, treat it like booze. Don't partake in public, and don't get high and drive. If you'd like a guided introduction to Emerald City's green offerings, check out Kush Tourism (⊕ www.kushtourism.com).

Heading south of Pike Street, the Central Business District holds mostly office and municipal buildings. There are a few sights scattered about, including the remarkable Central Library, a handful of art galleries, and a sampling of higher-end shops. There are a few major cultural sights, too, including the Seattle Symphony's elegant concert venue, Benaroya Hall.

TOP ATTRACTIONS

FAMILY

Fodor's Choice

★

Pike Place Market. One of the nation's largest and oldest public markets dates from 1907, when the city issued permits allowing farmers to sell produce from parked wagons. At one time the market was a madhouse of vendors hawking their produce and haggling with customers over prices; now you might find fishmongers engaging in frenzied banter and hilarious antics, but chances are you won't get them to waver on prices. There are many restaurants, bakeries, coffee shops (including the flagship Starbucks), lunch counters, and ethnic eateries. Go to Pike Place hungry and you won't be disappointed. The flower market is also a must-see—gigantic fresh arrangements can be found for around $10. It's well worth wading through dense crowds to enjoy the market's many corridors, where you'll find specialty-food items, quirky gift shops, tea, honey, jams, comic books, beads, eclectic crafts, and cookware. In spring 2017, Pike Place Market debuted a significant expansion, fulfilling a decades-long vision for Seattle's Market Historic District. The market's new digs feature artisanal-food purveyors, an on-site brewery, four public art installations, and a 30,000-square-foot open public

The stunning Seattle Central Library

space with a plaza and a viewing deck overlooking Elliott Bay. ☒ *Pike Pl. at Pike St., west of 1st Ave., Downtown* ☏ *206/682–7453* ⊕ *www.pikeplacemarket.org.*

FAMILY
Fodor's Choice
★

Seattle Aquarium. Located right at the water's edge, the Seattle Aquarium is one of the nation's premier aquariums. Among its most engaging residents are the sea otters—kids, especially, seem able to spend hours watching the delightful antics of these creatures and their river cousins. In the Puget Sound Great Hall, "Window on Washington Waters," a slice of Neah Bay life, is presented in a 20-foot-tall tank holding 120,000 gallons of water. The aquarium's darkened rooms and large, lighted tanks brilliantly display Pacific Northwest marine life. The "Life on the Edge" tide pools re-create Washington's rocky coast and sandy beaches—kids can touch the starfish, sea urchins, and sponges. Huge glass windows provide underwater views of the harbor seal exhibit; go up top to watch them play in their pools. If you're visiting in fall or winter, dress warmly—the Marine Mammal area is outside on the waterfront and catches all of those chilly Puget Sound breezes. The café serves Ivar's chowder and kid-friendly food like burgers and chicken fingers; the balcony has views of Elliott Bay. ☒ *1483 Alaskan Way, Pier 59, Downtown* ☏ *206/386–4300* ⊕ *www.seattleaquarium.org* ☒ *$24.95.*

A GOOD COMBO

If you plan to spend the morning exploring Pike Place Market or the Seattle Art Museum, but still have energy for a walk, head north into the Belltown neighborhood, grab lunch to go at Macrina Bakery, and stroll down to the Olympic Sculpture Park: views, works of art, and chairs aplenty await.

Getting Oriented

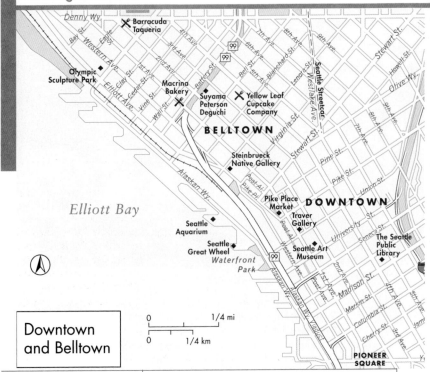

Denny Wy.

Barracuda Taqueria

Bay St.
Eagle St.
Western Ave.
Elliott Ave.
Clay St.
Vine St.
Cedar St.
Wall St.
Battery St.
1st Ave.
2nd Ave.
3rd Ave.
4th Ave.
5th Ave.
6th Ave.
7th Ave.
8th Ave.
9th Ave.

99
99

Olympic Sculpture Park

Macrina Bakery

Suyama Peterson Deguchi

Yellow Leaf Cupcake Company

Bell St.
Blanchard St.
Lenora St.

Seattle Streetcar
Westlake Ave.
Stewart St.
Howell St.
Olive Wy.

BELLTOWN

Steinbrueck Native Gallery

Virginia St.
Stewart St.
Pine St.
Pike St.

Post Alley
Pike Pl.
Alaskan Wy.

Pike Place Market

DOWNTOWN

Traver Gallery

Union St.

Elliott Bay

Seattle Aquarium

Seattle Great Wheel

Waterfront Park

Post Alley
University St.
Seneca St.

Seattle Art Museum

The Seattle Public Library

99

1st Ave.
2nd Ave.
3rd Ave.
4th Ave.
5th Ave.

Madison St.
Marion St.
Columbia St.
Cherry St.

Alaskan Wy. Viaduct

PIONEER SQUARE

Downtown and Belltown

0   1/4 mi

0   1/4 km

GETTING AROUND

Both Downtown and Belltown are very easy to explore on foot—walking from one neighborhood to the other is easy, too—but if you head down to the waterfront, be prepared for some major hills on the way back up toward your hotel or the main shopping area. Buses are $2.75 (peak, one-zone or $2.50 off-peak, all zones; two-hour transfer included), a small price to pay when you're hoofing it in a hilly area.

PLANNING YOUR TIME

A Downtown day can have a variety of combinations. All itineraries should include a stop at Pike Place Market. Two other can't-miss sights are the Olympic Sculpture Park in Belltown and the Seattle Art Museum Downtown. If you have children in tow, consider the aquarium, a ride on the Seattle Great Wheel, and the sights along the waterfront.

Try to arrive at Pike Place Market in the morning when it's a bit calmer (before cruise ships have docked). The aquarium gets crowded midday, but it's a happy kind of chaos and likely preferable to getting stuck negotiating the midday Market crowds.

Even though the shops in both neighborhoods are concentrated in small areas, doing a comprehensive shopping tour will take all day and you shouldn't try to schedule much sightseeing—just plan to hit Belltown when you start to get tired, as there are good cafés along 1st and 2nd Avenues.

QUICK BITES

Cherry Street Coffee House. A variety of yummy breakfast, lunch, and vegan items are on the menu, including smoothies and breakfast bagels. ⊠ *5th and Denny, Belltown* ☎ *206/812–1298* ⊕ *cherryst.com/locations/denny* ▭ *No credit cards.*

Macrina. Macrina, close to the Olympic Sculpture Park, is famous for its delicious breads, sandwiches, cookies, and coffee cakes. ⊠ *2408 1st Ave., Belltown* ☎ *206/448–4032* ⊕ *macrinabakery.com* ▭ *No credit cards.*

Pike Place Market. The best place for a quick snack is Pike Place Market. You can get anything from chowder and pierogi to gourmet tea and decadent desserts. ⊠ *85 Pike St.* ☎ *206/682-7453* ⊕ *www.pikeplacemarket.org* ▭ *No credit cards.*

Storyville Coffee. In addition to perfectly pulled espresso drinks, Storyville offers fresh pastries, light lunch items, and beer and wine. ⊠ *94 Pike St. #34* ☎ *206/780-5777* ⊕ *www.storyville.com.*

TOP REASONS TO GO

Find your perfect souvenir—along with yummy breakfast or lunch—at **Pike Place Market.**

Visit the **Seattle Art Museum**—consider doing it on a First Thursday or during a Remix event.

Hit the **shopping areas**: On Pike and Pine between 4th and 6th Avenues are favorite chains, department stores, and high-end labels. Belltown has boutiques, design stores, and a big branch of Patagonia. Western Avenue on the waterside of the market has upscale furniture stores that are fun to browse.

Make time for a stroll in the **Olympic Sculpture Park,** or, if you're traveling with kids, make a beeline for the **Seattle Aquarium** to watch sea otters frolic.

Attend a concert at **Benaroya Hall.** The home of the Seattle Symphony is renowned for its near-perfect acoustics. The hall is stunning, and tours are available.

SEATTLE ART MUSEUM

✉ *1300 1st Ave., Downtown*
☎ *206/654–3100* ⊕ *www.seattleartmuseum.org*
📷 *Suggested donation $20; fee for special exhibitions; free first Thurs. of the month.*

TIPS

■ SAM's free floors have the best attractions for kids. Select second Saturdays are Family Fun days, with kid-focused tours, performances, and workshops from 10 am to noon.

■ SAM hosts special exhibitions throughout the year. Blockbuster shows can attract record-setting crowds, so consider purchasing tickets in advance if there's something you really want to see.

■ You can download SAM Audio—podcasts about the museum's collection—to your iPod or smartphone.

■ TASTE (*www.tastesam. com*), the museum's stylish restaurant, has good weekday happy-hour deals and a solid wine and beer list. It's a pleasant spot for a sit-down meal, too, but if you want more variety, remember, Pike Place Market is only a block away.

Sculptor Jonathan Borofsky's several-stories-high "Hammering Man" greets visitors to SAM, as locals call this pride of the city's art scene. The genre-spanning museum features plenty of free public space. The first floor includes the SAM's fantastic gift shop, a café that focuses on local ingredients, and spaces for drop-in workshops where the whole family can get creative.

HIGHLIGHTS

SAM's permanent collection surveys American, Asian, Native American, African, Oceanic, and pre-Columbian art. Collections of African dance masks and Native American carvings are particularly strong. Kanye Quaye's *Mercedes Benz Coffin* installation and the Italian Room, a reproduction of typical Lombard Renaissance–era room, are also favorites.

The grand staircase in the original South Building, with its imposing Chinese funerary statues, has always been fun to climb.

Arty film series take place monthly in the Plestcheeff Auditorium. Select Third Thursdays and Third Sundays of the month, visitors can experience a tea ceremony in the superbly crafted teahouse on the third floor. Second Thursdays feature evening jazz ensembles. The real party, however, is SAM Remix, which happens on select Fridays (8–midnight). The exhibits are open and complemented by live music and DJ sets, talks, and provocative performance art.

A steel sculpture by Richard Serra at the Olympic Sculpture Park

FAMILY **Seattle Great Wheel.** Want to hitch a ride to a soaring Seattle vantage point? At the end of Pier 57, just steps from Pike Place Market and the Seattle Aquarium, the Seattle Great Wheel is a 175-foot (about 17 stories tall) Ferris wheel. As you round the top, enjoy views of the city skyline, the Puget Sound, and the Olympic and Cascade mountain ranges (on a clear day, of course). Rides are slow and smooth, lasting 15 to 20 minutes, with three revolutions total. Each gondola can hold six people (up to eight if some are children) and, generally speaking, parties get to stick together. The Seattle Great Wheel also lights up the waterfront after dark with dazzling colors, making it a romantic option for date night. Advance tickets are recommended—you'll still have to wait in line, but the line is a lot shorter. ■TIP→ If you're afraid of heights, you should definitely skip this attraction. ✉ *1301 Alaskan Way (Pier 56), Downtown* ☎ *206/623–8600* ⊕ *www.seattlegreatwheel.com* ✆ *$13; $50 for VIP Gondola.*

Fodor'sChoice **The Seattle Public Library.** The hub of Seattle's 27-branch library system
★ is a stunning jewel of a building that stands out against the concrete jungle of downtown. Designed by renowned Dutch architect Rem Koolhaas and Joshua Ramus, this 11-story structure houses more than 1 million books, a language center, terrific areas for kids and teens—plus hundreds of computers with Internet access, an auditorium, a "mixing chamber" floor of information desks, and a café. The building's floor plan is anything but simple; stand outside the beveled glass-and-metal facade of the building and you can see the library's floors zigzagging upward. Tours are self-guided via a laminated sheet you can pick up at the information desk; there's also a number you

can call on your cell phone for an audio tour. The reading room on the 10th floor has unbeatable views of the city and the water, and the building has Wi-Fi throughout. Readings and free film screenings happen on a regular basis; check the website for more information. ✉ *1000 4th Ave., Downtown* ☎ *206/386–4636* ⊕ *www.spl.org/ locations/central-library.*

WORTH NOTING

Traver Gallery. One block north of the Seattle Art Museum, Traver Gallery is like a little slice of SoHo in Seattle, with large picture windows and uneven wood floors. The focus is on contemporary studio glass, paintings, sculpture, and installation art from local and international artists. Pieces are exquisite—never whimsical or gaudy—and the staff is extremely courteous. After you're done tiptoeing around the gallery, head back downstairs and around the corner to **Vetri** (*1404 1st Ave.*), which sells smaller-scale glass art and home objects from emerging artists at reasonable prices. ✉ *110 Union St., Suite 200, Downtown* ☎ *206/587–6501* ⊕ *www.travergallery.com* 🎟 *Free.*

ARCHITECT'S TOUR

Within a few blocks on 4th Avenue (between University and Madison), you'll find two very different iconic buildings: the historic Fairmont Olympic Hotel (go inside for a look at the grand staircase or to have afternoon tea) and the ultramodern, Rem Koolhaas–designed Central Library.

BELLTOWN

Belltown is Downtown's younger sibling, just north of Virginia Street (up to Denny Way) and stretching from Elliott Bay to 6th Avenue. Not so long ago, Belltown was home to some of the most unwanted real estate in the city. Today, Belltown is increasingly hip, with luxury condos, trendy restaurants, swanky bars, and a number of boutiques. (Most of the action happens between 1st and 4th Avenues and between Bell and Virginia Streets.) You can still find plenty of evidence of its edgy past—including a gallery exhibiting urban street art, a punk-rock vinyl shop, and a major indie rock music venue that was a cornerstone of the grunge scene—but today Belltown is almost unrecognizable to long-term residents. Except for the stunning Olympic Sculpture Park—which, especially on a gorgeous day, is not to be missed— the area doesn't have much in terms of traditional sights, but it's an interesting extension of Downtown. Though the number of homeless people in the neighborhood can be off-putting, Belltown is generally safe during the day and is very pleasant to explore.

TOP ATTRACTIONS

Fodor's Choice **Olympic Sculpture Park.** An outdoor branch of the Seattle Art Museum ★ is a favorite destination for picnics, strolls, and quiet contemplation. Nestled at the edge of Belltown with views of Elliott Bay, the gently sloping green space features native plants and walking paths that wind past bigger-than-life public artwork. On sunny days, the park frames an astounding panorama of the Olympic Mountains, but even the grayest afternoon casts a favorable light on the site's sculptures.

The grounds are home to works by such artists as Richard Serra, Louise Bourgeois, and Alexander Calder, whose bright-red steel "Eagle" sculpture is a local favorite (and a nod to the bald eagles that sometimes soar above). "Echo," a 46-foot-tall elongated girl's face by Spanish artist Jaume Plensa, is a beautiful and bold presence on the waterfront. The park's PAC-CAR Pavilion has a gift shop, café, and information about the artworks. ⊠ *2901 Western Ave., between Broad and Bay Sts., Belltown* ☎ *206/654–3100* ⊕ *www.seattleartmuseum.org/visit* 🎟 *Free.*

WORTH NOTING

Steinbrueck Native Gallery. Prints, masks, drums, sculptures, baskets, and jewelry by local Native artists fill the space of this elegant Belltown gallery near Pike Place Market. Alaskan and Arctic art is also on display, including beautiful sculptural pieces carved from ivory, wood, and soapstone. ⊠ *2030 Western Ave., Belltown* ☎ *206/441–3821* ⊕ *www.steinbruecknativegallery.com* 🎟 *Free.*

Suyama Peterson Deguchi. The brainchild of art advocate and noted local architect George Suyama, this nonprofit gallery located within the architecture firm of Suyama Peterson Deguchi exhibits large-scale, site-specific contemporary installations three times a year. Unlike many of Seattle's galleries, this is not a commercial venue—its programming is made possible through grants and donations—which is just another reason to stroll through the lofty space. To visit, ring the bell at 2324 2nd Avenue for entry. ⊠ *2324 2nd Ave., Belltown* ☎ *206/256–0809* ⊕ *www.suyamaspace.org* 🎟 *Free.*

DOG-FRIENDLY SEATTLE

Seattle routinely ranks as one of the top dog cities in the country, with more canines living here than children. Pooches are pampered with 14 off-leash areas within city boundaries, including 9-acre Magnuson Park, which provides access to a stretch of beach on Lake Washington and a special area for small dogs. More than 70 hotels allow furry friends to stay for free or a fee, and some go out of their way to make pets feel as welcome as their human pals (Hotel Vintage, for example, puts out a special bed and bowls for canine companions and offers pet-sitting services and a list of Fido-friendly attractions).

SEATTLE CENTER, SOUTH LAKE UNION, AND QUEEN ANNE

Sightseeing
★★★★
Dining
★★★
Lodging
★★
Shopping
★★
Nightlife
★

Almost all visitors make their way to Seattle Center at some point, to visit the Space Needle or other key Seattle sites like the MoPOP building, the Pacific Science Center, or the stunning new Chihuly Garden and Glass. The neighborhoods that bookend Seattle Center couldn't be more different: Queen Anne is all residential elegance (especially on top of the hill), while South Lake Union, once completely industrial, is quickly becoming Seattle's next hot neighborhood.

SEATTLE CENTER

Seattle Center is the home to Seattle's version of the Eiffel Tower—the Space Needle—and is anchored by Frank Gehry's wild MoPOP building, the acclaimed Pacific Science Center, and the dazzling new Chihuly Garden and Glass. This area is a key destination for the museums or to catch a show at one of the many performing arts venues.

Seattle Center's 74-acre complex was built for the 1962 World's Fair. A rolling green campus with multiple venues is organized around the massive International Fountain. Among the arts groups based here are the Seattle Repertory Theatre, Intiman Theatre, the Seattle Opera, and the Pacific Northwest Ballet. It's also the site of three of summer's largest festivals—Northwest Folklife Festival, Bite of Seattle, and Bumbershoot. The Pacific Science Center, Seattle Children's Museum, and the Bill & Melinda Gates Visitor Center offer engaging activities for visitors of all ages.

TOP ATTRACTIONS

FAMILY **Bill & Melinda Gates Foundation Visitor Center.** The Bill & Melinda Gates Foundation has some lofty goals, and it's here, across the street from Seattle Center, where you get to witness their plans in action. Exhibits are thought provoking and interactive, inviting you to offer up your own solutions to complex global problems like poverty and climate change. The "Innovation & Inspiration" gallery is the most fun, providing dozens of creative activities for visitors of all ages. ⊠ *440 5th Ave N, South Lake Union* ☎ *206/709–3100* ⊕ *www.gatesfoundation.org/Visitor-Center* ⊡ *Free.*

Fodor's Choice **Chihuly Garden and Glass.** Just steps
★ from the base of the Space Needle, fans of Dale Chihuly's glass works will be delighted to trace the artist's early influences—neon art, Native American Northwest Coast trade baskets, and Pendleton blankets, to name a few—to the vibrant chandelier towers and architectural glass installations he is most known for today. There are eight galleries total, plus a 40-foot-tall "Glasshouse," and an outdoor garden that serves as a backdrop for colorful installations that integrate with a dynamic Northwest landscape, including native plants and a 500-year-old western cedar that washed up on the shores of Neah Bay. Chihuly, who was born and raised in Tacoma, was actively involved in the design of the exhibition as well as the whimsical Collections Cafe, where you'll find Chihuly's quirky personal collections on display—everything from tin toys to vintage cameras to antique shaving brushes. Indeed, so many of his personal touches are part of the exhibition space, you can almost feel his presence in every room (look for the guy with the unruly hair and the black eye patch). Chihuly is kid-friendly for all but the littlest ones. ⊠ *305 Harrison St., under Space Needle, Central District* ☎ *206/753–4940* ⊕ *www.chihulygardenandglass.com* ⊡ *$22.*

FAMILY **The Children's Museum, Seattle.** If you're traveling with kids, you already know that a good children's museum is like gold at the end of a rainbow. This colorful, spacious museum, located on the lower level of The Armory in the heart of Seattle Center, provides hours of exploration and fun. Enter through a Northwest wilderness setting, with winding trails, hollow logs, and a waterfall. From there, you can explore the Global Village where rooms with kid-friendly props show everyday life in Ghana, the Philippines, and Japan. Cog City is a giant game of pipes, pulleys, and balls; kids can also test their talent in a mock recording studio. There's a small play area for toddlers and plenty of crafts to keep everyone engaged. ⊠ *305 Harrison St., Central District* ☎ *206/441–1768* ⊕ *www.thechildrensmuseum.org* ⊡ *$10.50.*

CHIEF SEATTLE

At the southeast side of Seattle Center (on the corner of 5th Avenue and Denny Way) stands a statue of Chief Seattle (originally Si'ahl), of the Duwamish tribe. The chief was among the first Native Americans to have contact with the white explorers who came to the region. His fellow tribesmen considered him to be a great leader and peacemaker. The sculpture was created by local artist James Wehn in 1912 and dedicated by the chief's great-great-granddaughter, Myrtle Loughery.

2

Getting Oriented

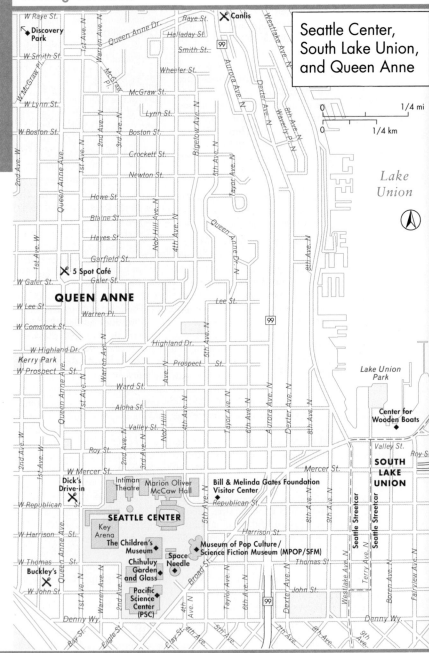

Seattle Center,
South Lake Union,
and Queen Anne

GETTING HERE AND AROUND

The monorail runs from Westlake Center (5th Avenue and Pine Street) and makes getting here easy from Downtown. It runs daily from 9 am to 11 pm (with slightly shorter hours in winter), with departures every 10 minutes. Traffic and parking around the Center can be nightmarish during special events and festivals, so try to walk or take public transportation. Walking to Seattle Center from the Olympic Sculpture Park is a ½-mile (about 15-minute) stroll northeast on Broad Street.

From Downtown, multiple bus lines run up 3rd and 1st Avenues to Seattle Center. Buses also climb Queen Anne Avenue, making the commercial districts easy to reach from Downtown or Seattle Center; the rest of that neighborhood will require a car to tour.

From Downtown, South Lake Union is served by the Seattle Streetcar (⊕ *www.seattlestreetcar.org*). The #30 bus connects Lake Union to Seattle Center.

TOP REASONS TO GO

Visit (or gaze up at) the **Space Needle** and rock out at **MoPOP**; leave a couple of hours to visit **Chihuly Garden and Glass,** the **Children's Museum** (best for kids ages 10 months to 10 years), or the nearby **Bill & Melinda Gates Visitor Center.**

Kerry Park has outstanding views of the skyline and Elliott Bay. It's an all-time favorite spot for snapshots and public displays of affection.

Seattle Center houses the city's opera and ballet, and the headquarters of **SIFF Cinema**. Don't miss **On the Boards** (⊕ *www.ontheboards.org*), a small but important performing-arts space.

Rent a small boat at the **Center for Wooden Boats** to tour Lake Union and go back in time with a visit to the **Museum of History and Industry.**

PLANNING YOUR TIME

Depending on your endurance, you can combine a visit to the Space Needle with one museum visit before exhaustion sets in. Schedule more time for the Pacific Science Center and MoPOP than other sights—both have a lot of interactive exhibits. The Space Needle is open late.

QUICK BITES

Citizen. A rustic coffee shop in a converted warehouse, this ultrachic spot serves up crepes, breakfast tacos, salads, and wine. ⊠ *706 Taylor Ave. N, Queen Anne* ☎ *206/284–1015* ⊕ *www.citizencoffee.com.*

Dick's Drive In Restaurant. You won't find a quicker or more affordable snack than a few burgers and a milk shake here. ⊠ *500 Queen Anne Ave. N, Lower Queen Anne* ☎ *206/285–5155* ⊕ *www.ddir.com.*

The 5 Spot. Popular with families, you'll find breakfast, lunch, and dinner, with American and Cuban food on the menu. ⊠ *1502 Queen Anne Ave. N, Queen Anne* ☎ *206/285–7768* ⊕ *www.chowfoods.com/5-spot.*

Pho Viet Anh. This popular Vietnamese spot draws a lively local crowd with the best banh mi in town. ⊠ *372 Roy St., Lower Queen Anne* ☎ *206/352–1881* ⊕ *www.phovietanh.com.*

MUSEUM OF POP CULTURE (MOPOP)

✉ *325 5th Ave. N, between Broad and Thomas Sts., Central District* ☎ *206/770–2700* ⊕ *www.mopop.org* 🎟 *$25.*

TIPS

■ MoPOP is a great place for teenagers. It regularly holds teen-artist workshops in songwriting, rock band, and sci-fi writing; check the education calendar for details. IPod audio guides offer an enhanced experience, with music playlists and commentary about the exhibits.

■ As with most Seattle museums, MoPOP is least crowded early in the morning (before 11 am) and after 6 pm.

■ There's a café on-site, Pop Kitchen + Bar, serving fresh entrées and seasonal microbrews.

Formerly EMP, Seattle's most controversial architectural statement is the 140,000-square-foot complex designed by architect Frank Gehry, who drew inspiration from electric guitars to achieve the building's curvy metallic design. It's a fitting backdrop for rock memorabilia from the likes of Bob Dylan and the grunge-scene heavies.

HIGHLIGHTS

Complementing the amazing "Roots and Branches" installation, a 35-foot tower made of guitars, this beautiful collection, starting with a model from the 1770s and leading up to the Gibsons, Fenders, and Les Pauls of today, traces the history of guitar amplification.

Two permanent exhibits provide a primer on the evolution of Seattle's music scene. "Nirvana: Taking Punk to the Masses" features rare and unseen artifacts and photography from the band, their crews, and families. "Jimi Hendrix: An Evolution of Sound" illustrates Hendrix's rise from his early days in Seattle, including sound effects and mixing interactives, showing Hendrix as an innovator and forefather of modern recording technology.

The interactive space has 12 ministudio rooms where you can jam with friends on real or MIDI-compatible instruments. You can also channel your inner rock star in front of a virtual audience in the "On Stage" exhibit, complete with smoke, hot lights, and screaming fans.

In the Science Fiction Museum and Hall of Fame—now a permanent exhibit—you'll find iconic artifacts from sci-fi literature, film, television, and art, including an Imperial Dalek from *Doctor Who,* the command chair from the classic television series *Star Trek,* and Neo's coat from *The Matrix Reloaded.*

2

FAMILY **Pacific Science Center.** If you have kids, this nonprofit science center in
Fodor's Choice the heart of Seattle is a must-visit, home to more than 200 indoor
★ and outdoor hands-on exhibits, two IMAX theaters, a Laser Dome,
a butterfly house, and a state-of-the-art Planetarium. The dinosaur
exhibit—complete with moving robotic reproductions—is a favorite,
and tots can experiment with water at the ever-popular stream table.
Machines analyze human physiology in the *Body Works* exhibit.
When you need to warm up, the Tropical Butterfly House is 80°F
and home to colorful butterflies from South and Central America,
Africa, and Asia; other creatures live in the Insect Village and saltwater tide-pool areas. IMAX movies, Planetarium shows, Live Science
Shows, and Laser Dome rock shows run daily. Look for the giant
white arches near the Space Needle and make a day of the surrounding sights. ■TIP→ Pacific Science Center offers a number of lectures,
forums, and "Science Cafes" for adults, plus a variety of educational
programs for kids, including camp-ins, monthly parents' night outs,
workshops, and more. See website for schedule information. ⌂ *200
2nd Ave. N, Central District* ☎ *206/443–2001* ⊕ *www.pacsci.org*
⌨ *Center $19.75, IMAX $10–15.50, laser shows $7–$10.50, combined museum/IMAX $31.25.*

FAMILY **Space Needle.** More than 50 years old, Seattle's most iconic building
is as quirky and beloved as ever. The distinctive, towering, 605-foot-
high structure is visible throughout much of Seattle—but the view
from the inside out is even better. A less-than-one-minute ride up to
the observation deck yields 360-degree vistas of Downtown Seattle,
the Olympic Mountains, Elliott Bay, Queen Anne Hill, Lake Union,
and the Cascade Range. Built for the 1962 World's Fair, the Needle
has educational kiosks, interactive trivia game stations for kids, and
the glass-enclosed SpaceBase store and Pavilion spiraling around the
base of the tower. The top-floor SkyCity restaurant is "revolutionary"
(literally—watch the skyline evolve as you dine) and the elevator trip
and observation deck are complimentary with your reservation. If the
forecast says you may have a sunny day during your visit, schedule
the Needle for that day! If you can't decide whether you want the
daytime or nighttime view, for an extra 10 bucks you can buy a ticket
that allows you to visit twice in one day. (Also look for package deals
with Chihuly Garden and Glass.) ⌂ *400 Broad St., Central District*
☎ *206/905–2100* ⊕ *www.spaceneedle.com* ⌨ *$22.*

QUEEN ANNE

Just west of the Seattle Center is the intersection of Queen Anne
Avenue North and Denny Way. This marks the start of the Queen
Anne neighborhood, which stretches all the way up formidable Queen
Anne Hill to the ship canal on the other side. The neighborhood is split
into Upper and Lower Queen Anne, and the two are quite different:
Lower Queen Anne is a mixed-income neighborhood that has a small,
interesting mix of independent record shops and bookstores, laid-back
pubs, and a few upmarket restaurants and bars. Past Aloha Street, the
neighborhood starts to look more upscale, with the snazzy Galer Street

commercial strip marking the heart of Upper Queen Anne. Queen Anne doesn't have many sights, but the residential streets west of Queen Anne Avenue in Upper Queen Anne are fun to stroll, and sunny days offer gorgeous views. This ribbon of residential turf extends to the Magnolia neighborhood. There's only one sight to see in off-the-beaten-path Magnolia, but it's a terrific one: Discovery Park.

TOP ATTRACTIONS

FAMILY **Discovery Park.** You won't find more spectacular views of Puget Sound, Fodor's Choice the Cascades, and the Olympics. Located on Magnolia Bluff, northwest ★ of Downtown, Seattle's largest park covers 534 acres and has an amazing variety of terrain: shaded, secluded forest trails lead to meadows, saltwater beaches, sand dunes, a lighthouse, and 2 miles of protected beaches. The North Beach Trail, which takes you along the shore to the lighthouse, is a must-see. Head to the South Bluff Trail to get a view of Mt. Rainier. The park has several entrances—if you want to stop at the visitor center to pick up a trail map before exploring, use the main entrance at Government Way. The North Parking Lot is much closer to the North Beach Trail and to Ballard and Fremont, if you're coming from that direction. First-come, first-served beach parking passes for the disabled, elderly, and families with small children are available at the Learning Center. Note that the park is easily reached from Ballard and Fremont. It's easier to combine a park day with an exploration of those neighborhoods than with a busy Downtown itinerary. ✉ 3801 *W. Government Way, Magnolia* ✥ *From Downtown, take Elliot Ave. W (which turns into 15th Ave. W), and get off at Emerson St. exit and turn left onto W. Emerson. Make a right onto Gilman Ave. W (which eventually becomes W. Government Way). As you enter park, road becomes Washington Ave.; turn left on Utah Ave.* ☎ *206/386–4236* ⊕ *seattle.gov/parks/environment/discovery.htm* ◪ *Free.*

FAMILY **Kerry Park.** While in Seattle, if the mood strikes you to "pop the question" Fodor's Choice (any question will do, really), you'll find the answer at Kerry Park. ★ Famous for engagements, sweeping views of the city skyline and, on clear days, Mt. Rainier, camera buffs and romantic types can't help but linger at this 1¼-acre sliver of a city park, which is a short but steep walk up from the shops and restaurants of Lower Queen Anne. The sculpture "Changing Form" by Doris Chase was added in 1971. There's a terrific little park and play area for kiddos at Bayview-Kinnear Park, just below the viewpoint of Kerry Park. ✉ *211 W. Highland Dr., Queen Anne* ☎ *206/684–4075* ⊕ *www.seattle.gov/parks.*

SOUTH LAKE UNION

South Lake Union, on the east side of Seattle Center, is a destination in itself. Though it's still in transition (construction is underway in many areas), Amazon's new headquarters here has brought more amenities, such as boutiques and upscale restaurants, including several Tom Douglas eateries. The biggest attractions are Lake Union itself as well as the incredible REI megastore.

TOP ATTRACTIONS

FAMILY **Museum of History & Industry.** Located in the Lake Union Park's converted Naval Reserve Building, the 20,000-square-foot MOHAI offers visitors an in-depth slice of regional history with a permanent collection featuring more than 100,000 objects ranging from vintage souvenirs to everyday household items. Permanent exhibitions include the Center for Innovation, which showcases Seattle's role as a place where innovation and entrepreneurship flourish; the exhibit is supported by a $10 million gift from Jeff Bezos, founder and CEO of Seattle-based Amazon.com (which has its corporate headquarters a few blocks away). Special temporary exhibitions examine everything from chocolate to stories of Jewish merchants in Washington State. ✉ *860 Terry Ave. N, at Lake Union Park, South Lake Union* ☎ *206/324–1126* ⊕ *www.mohai.org* 💲 *$19.95, free 1st Thurs. of month (excluding special exhibitions).*

WORTH NOTING

Center for Wooden Boats. Though it used be considered an off-the-beaten-path gem, the Center for Wooden Boats is now a major feature of Lake Union Park. The center gives free boat rides on the lake every Sunday; they sail on the hour from 1 to 3 pm, but the first-come, first-served slots tend to go fast, so you should queue up at the Center as soon as it opens. You may also rent a variety of small craft—pedal boats, canoes, rowboats, and small sailboats—to explore the lake on your own (lessons are available if you don't have much experience). Rates are $25–$50 per hour. Check out the events calendar for weekend workshops or to schedule one-on-one sailing lessons. ✉ *1010 Valley St., South Lake Union* ☎ *206/382–2628* ⊕ *www.cwb.org* 💲 *Free.*

Lake Union Park. Before this scenic park at the foot of Lake Union was completed, most people traveled up to Wallingford's Gas Works Park to enjoy Lake Union from a green space. Now the southern shore is more accessible and vibrant than ever—this 12-acre park includes a model boat pond, a boardwalk, a beach where you can launch small craft like kayaks and rowboats to paddle past the houseboats, a spray area for little kids, plus the Museum of History & Industry and the Center for Wooden Boats. Several cruise options also depart from the park. A 45-minute narrated Ice Cream Cruise on the Seattle mini ferry is a family favorite on Sundays (on the hour from 11 to 3, $12). ✉ *860 Terry Ave. N, South Lake Union* ☎ *206/684–4075* ⊕ *www.atlakeunionpark.org* 💲 *Free.*

PIONEER SQUARE

Sightseeing
★★★
Dining
★
Lodging
★
Shopping
★★★
Nightlife
★★★

The Pioneer Square district, directly south of Downtown, is Seattle's oldest neighborhood. It attracts visitors for elegantly renovated (or in some cases replica) turn-of-the-20th-century redbrick buildings and art galleries. It's the center of Seattle's arts scene and the galleries in this small neighborhood make up the majority of its sights.

Today's Yesler Way was the original "Skid Road," where, in the 1880s, timber was sent to the sawmill on a skid of small logs laid crossways and greased so that the cut trees would slide down to the mill. The area later grew into Seattle's first center of commerce. Many of the buildings you see today are replicas of the wood-frame structures destroyed by fire in 1889.

Nowadays, the role Pioneer Square plays in the city today is harder to define. Despite the concentration of galleries, the neighborhood is no longer a center for artists per se, as rents have risen considerably; only established gallery owners can rent loftlike spaces in heavily trafficked areas.

By day, you'll see a mix of Downtown workers and tourists strolling the area. Sadly, the local parks are mainly inhabited by homeless people. Pioneer Square has a well-known nightlife scene, but these days it's a much-derided one, thanks to the meat-market vibe of many of the clubs. If you want classier venues, you'll be smart to head north up First Avenue to Belltown or to select spots on Capitol Hill.

When Seattleites speak of Pioneer Square, they usually speak of the love they have for certain neighborhood spots—the original Grand Central Bakery in the historic Grand Central Arcade, Zeitgeist coffeehouse, a beloved art gallery, a friend's loft apartment, a great store—than the love they have for the neighborhood as a whole. Pioneer Square is always worth a visit, but reactions do vary. Anyone seriously interested in doing the gallery circuit will be impressed and foodies will find a few

Getting Oriented

DOWNTOWN

Bill Speidel's
Underground Tour

James St.

Smith Tower

Yesler Wy.

Yesler Wy.

99

Delicatus

Tat's

PIONEER
SQUARE

Gallery 110

G. Gibson
Gallery

S Washington St.

Occidental
Park

Grand Central Bakery

Waterfall
Garden

Greg Kucera
Gallery

Foster/White
Gallery

Kobe
Terrace
Park

S Main St.

AXIS Pioneer Square

Davidson
Galleries

Last Resort
Fire Dept.
Museum

Salumi

James Harris Gallery

Flury & Co

S Jackson St.

Klondike Gold Rush
National Historical Park

Stonington Gallery

Zeitgeist
Coffee

INTERNATIONAL
DISTRICT

1st Ave. S

Occidental Ave. S

2nd Ave. S

S King St.

2nd Ave. Ext. S

3rd Ave. S

4th Ave. S

5th Ave. S

6th Ave. S

S Weller St.

0   1/8 mi

0   1/8 km

S Lane St.

Alaskan Wy. S

S Dearborn St.

S Dearborn St.

Airport Wy. S

Century
Link
Field

99

90

1st Ave. S

Occidental Ave. S

S Royal Brougham Wy.

519

Pyramid
Ale House

Safeco
Field

Pioneer Square

GETTING HERE AND AROUND

Pioneer Square is directly south of Downtown, which means you can easily walk here. However, the stretch between the two neighborhoods is not the most scenic trip, so you can also hop on a bus heading south on 1st Avenue.

Pioneer Square is pretty small; you'll easily be able to walk to all the galleries. If you've driven in from a more distant neighborhood, most of the pay parking lots and garages are on South Jackson Street.

Most people combine Pioneer Square with a trip to the International District, which together would make a full day of sightseeing. Pioneer Square is also the closest neighborhood to CenturyLink Field and Safeco Field, so it also makes sense to end a touring day here before heading to a game.

TOP REASONS TO GO

Leave the Space Needle to the masses and check out the observation deck at 38-story **Smith Tower** at 506 2nd Avenue and Yesler Way.

Gallery hop on First Thursday art walks—perhaps the best time to see Pioneer Square, when animated crowds walk from gallery to gallery, viewing the new exhibitions. Or tour on your own: Greg Kucera, G. Gibson, James Harris, and the Tashiro-Kaplan Building are must-sees, as is the lobby of the Arctic Hotel Seattle, which features a gold-rush-era vibe.

Soak up some weird and wonderful historic Seattle tidbits on the zany **Bill Speidel's Underground Tour.**

Explore totally unique taxidermy, jewelry, art, and other oddities at **The Belfry** (309 A 3rd Avenue).

Catch your reflection in the hood of an antique fire truck at **Last Resort Fire Department Museum.**

Cheer for one of the home teams at CenturyLink or Safeco Field. (See Sports and Activities listing).

TOURS

At a kiosk on Occidental between Main and Jackson Streets, you can pick up a booklet that outlines three walking tours around the historic buildings of Pioneer Square.

The Underground Tour shows you the remnants of passageways and buildings buried when the city regraded the streets in the 1880s. The tour is fun and full of Seattle-history tidbits, though younger kids might be bored as there's not much to see.

QUICK BITES

Grand Central Bakery. This bakery serves hearth-baked breads, artisanal pastries, paninis, soups, and salads. ⊠ 214 1st Ave. S, Pioneer Square ☎ 206/622–3644 ⊕ www.grandcentralbakery.com.

Il Corvo Pasta. This tiny lunch-only spot serves only a couple of delicious handmade pasta choices each day. ⊠ 217 James St., Pioneer Square ☎ 206/538–0999.

Salumi Artisan Cured Meats. Salumi serves artisanal cured meats in heavenly sandwiches. ⊠ 309 3rd Ave. S, Pioneer Square ☎ 206/621–8772 ⊕ www.salumicuredmeats.com.

Zeitgeist. The best-loved coffee shop in the neighborhood. ⊠ 171 S. Jackson St., Pioneer Square ☎ 206/583–0497 ⊕ zeitgeist-coffee.com.

Foster/White Gallery's massive exhibition space

buzzworthy options. And the recently renovated Smith Tower, once the tallest building on the West Coast, beckons with an observation deck and a speakeasy on the 35th floor. That said, those looking for a vibrant, picture-perfect historic district that invites hours of contented strolling will be underwhelmed.

Pioneer Square is a gateway of sorts to the stadium district, which segues into SoDo (South of Downtown). First comes CenturyLink Field, where the Seahawks and the Sounders play. Directly south of that is Safeco Field, where the Mariners play. There's not much to see in this industrial area, but if you're a sports fan you can easily make a run from Pioneer Square to one of the stadiums' pro shops. There are also a few good brewpubs close to the stadiums.

TOP ATTRACTIONS

AXIS Pioneer Square. Soaring 18-foot ceilings, classic brick arches, and antique wood floors make a dramatic backdrop for monthly rotating exhibits with a contemporary bent. Part of a multitasking, 6,000-square-foot studio space, the gallery features a roster of local, national, and international artists and photographers. AXIS hosts new shows with entertainment during First Thursday Art Walk. ⊠ *308 1st Ave. S, Pioneer Square* ☎ *206/681–9316* ⊕ *www.axispioneersquare. com* 🔳 *Free.*

Bill Speidel's Underground Tour. Present-day Pioneer Square is actually one story higher than it used to be. After the Great Seattle Fire of 1889, Seattle's planners regraded the neighborhood's streets, which had been built on filled-in tide lands and regularly flooded. The result? There is now an intricate and expansive array of subterranean passageways and basements beneath Pioneer Square, and Bill Speidel's Underground Tour is the only way to explore them. Speidel was an irreverent historian, PR man, and former *Seattle Times* reporter who took it upon himself to preserve historic Seattle, and this tour is packed with his sardonic wit and playful humor. It's

> ## GALLERY WALKS
>
> It's fun to simply walk around Pioneer Square and pop into galleries. South Jackson Street to Yesler between Western and 4th Avenue South is a good area. The first Thursday of every month, galleries stay open late for First Thursday Art Walk, a neighborhood highlight. Visit ⊕ *www. firstthursdayseattle.com.*

very informative, too—if you're interested in the general history of the city or salty anecdotes about Seattle's early denizens, you'll appreciate it that much more. Younger kids will probably be bored, as there's not much to see at the specific sites, which are more used as launching points for the stories. Comfortable shoes, a love for quirky historical yarns, and an appreciation of bad puns are musts. Several tours are offered daily, and schedules change month to month: call or visit the website for a full list of tour times. ⊠ *608 1st Ave., Pioneer Square* ☎ *206/682–4646* ⊕ *www.undergroundtour.com* 🖾 *$20.*

OFF THE BEATEN PATH

CenturyLink Field. Located directly south of Pioneer Square, CenturyLink Field hosts two professional teams, the Seattle Seahawks (football) and the Seattle Sounders FC (soccer). The open-air stadium has 67,000 seats; sightlines are excellent, thanks to a cantilevered design and the close placement of lower sections. Tours start at the pro shop (be sure to arrive at least 30 minutes prior to purchase tickets), and last an hour and a half. You'll get a personal look at behind-the-scenes areas as well as the famous 12th Man Flag Pole, and have a chance to sink your feet into the same playing surface as your favorite Seahawks and Sounders stars. ⊠ *800 Occidental Ave. S, SoDo* ☎ *206/381–7582* ⊕ *www. centurylinkfield.com* 🖾 *$14.*

Foster/White Gallery. One of the Seattle art scene's heaviest hitters has digs as impressive as the works it shows: a century-old building with high ceilings and 7,000 square feet of exhibition space. Works by internationally acclaimed Northwest masters Kenneth Callahan, Mark Tobey, Alden Mason, and George Tsutakawa are on permanent display. ⊠ *220 3rd Ave. S, Pioneer Square* ☎ *206/622–2833* ⊕ *www. fosterwhite.com* 🖾 *Free.*

Fodor's Choice ★ **G. Gibson Gallery.** Vintage and contemporary photography is on exhibit in this elegant corner space, including work by the likes of Michael Kenna, Walker Evans, Jule Blackman, Lori Nix, and JoAnn Verburg. The gallery also shows contemporary paintings, sculpture, and mixed-media pieces. The gallery's taste is always impeccable and shows rotate every six weeks. ⊠ *300 S. Washington St., Pioneer Square* ☎ *206/587–4033* ⊕ *www.ggibsongallery.com* 🖾 *Free.*

Fodor's Choice ★ **Greg Kucera Gallery.** One of the most important destinations on the First Thursday gallery walk, this gorgeous space is a top venue for national and regional artists. Be sure to check out the outdoor sculpture deck on the second level. If you have time for only one gallery visit, this is the place to go. You'll see big names that you might recognize—along with newer artists—and the thematic group shows are always thoughtful and well presented. ⊠ *212 3rd Ave. S, Pioneer Square* ☎ *206/624–0770* ⊕ *www.gregkucera.com* 💰 *Free.*

OFF THE BEATEN PATH **Safeco Field.** This 47,000-seat, open-air baseball stadium with a state-of-the-art retractable roof is the home of the Seattle Mariners. If you want to see the stadium in all its glory, take the one-hour tour, which brings you onto the field, into the dugouts, back to the press and locker rooms, and up to the posh box seats. Tours depart from the Team Store on 1st Avenue, and you purchase your tickets there, too (at least 15 minutes prior to the scheduled tour). Afterward, head across the street to the Pyramid Alehouse for a local brew. ⊠ *1250 1st Ave. S, SoDo* ☎ *206/622–4487* ⊕ *seattle.mariners.mlb.com/sea/ballpark/safeco_field_tours.jsp* 💰 *$12.*

Smith Tower. When this iconic landmark opened in 1914, it was the tallest office building outside New York City and the fourth-tallest building in the world. (It remained the tallest building west of the Mississippi for nearly 50 years.) The Smith Tower Observation Deck on the 35th floor is an open-air wraparound deck providing panoramic views of the surrounding historic neighborhood, ball fields, the city skyline, and the mountains on clear days. It's also a superb spot to take in a sunset. The top floor also includes the speakeasy-themed Temperance café and bar. Once home to the Chinese Room, the new space features striking original architectural details and a cocktail and nibbles menu that pays homage to the Prohibition era. Smith Tower's ground-floor Provisions General Store, where you'll find a nostalgic soda fountain and locally inspired gifts, is also worth a visit. ⊠ *506 2nd Ave. S, Pioneer Square* ☎ *206/622–4004* ⊕ *www.smithtower.com* 💰 *$12.*

Stonington Gallery. You'll see plenty of cheesy tribal art knockoffs in tourist-trap shops, but this elegant gallery will give you a real look at the best contemporary work of Northwest Coast and Alaska tribal members (and artists from these regions working in the Native style). Three floors exhibit wood carvings, paintings, sculpture, and mixed-media pieces from the likes of Robert Davidson, Joe David, Preston Singeltary, Susan Point, and Rick Barto. ⊠ *119 S. Jackson St., Pioneer Square* ☎ *206/405–4040* ⊕ *www.stoningtongallery.com* 💰 *Free.*

WORTH NOTING

Davidson Galleries. Davidson has several different departments in one building: the Contemporary Print & Drawing Center, which holds the portfolios of 50 print artists; the Antique Print Department; and the Painting and Sculpture Department. Though the Antique Print Department is more of a specialized interest, the contemporary-print exhibits are always interesting and worth a look. ⊠ *313 Occidental Ave. S,*

Fallen Firefighters Memorial at Pioneer Square

Pioneer Square ☎ *206/624–7684 contemporary prints, 206/624–6700 antique prints, 206/624–7684 painting and sculpture* ⊕ *www.davidsongalleries.com* ✉ *Free.*

Flury & Co. One of the largest collections of vintage photographs by Edward Curtis, along with Native American antiques, traditional carvings, baskets, masks, jewelry, and tools are showcased in a historic space that's as interesting as the store's wares. ⊠ *322 1st Ave. S, Pioneer Square* ☎ *206/587–0260* ⊕ *www.fluryco.com.*

Gallery 110. Gallery 110 works with a collective of 30 contemporary artists (primarily Northwest-based) showing pieces in its small space that are energetic, challenging, and fresh. On-site exhibitions change monthly, and once a year the gallery hosts a juried exhibition. ⊠ *110 3rd Ave. S, Pioneer Square* ☎ *206/624–9336* ⊕ *www.gallery110.com* ✉ *Free.*

James Harris Gallery. One of Seattle's oldest and most respected galleries, James Harris Gallery is known for creating small shows that selectively and impeccably survey both local and international work. Three exhibition rooms provide intimacy and connectivity to tightly curated shows, including work from artists like Steve Davis, Squeak Carnwath, Claire Cowie, Karin Davie, Richard Rezac, and Akio Takamori. ⊠ *312 2nd Ave. S, Pioneer Square* ☎ *206/903–6220* ⊕ *www.jamesharrisgallery.com* ✉ *Free.*

Klondike Gold Rush National Historical Park. A tiny yet delightful museum illustrating Seattle's role in the 1897–98 Gold Rush in the Klondike region, this gem is located inside a historic redbrick building with wooden floors and soaring ceilings. Walls are lined with photos of gold miners, explorers, and the hopeful families who followed them. Film presentations, gold-panning demonstrations (daily in summer, at 10 and 3), and rotating exhibits are scheduled throughout the year. Other sectors of this park are in southeast Alaska. ⊠ *319 2nd Ave. S, Pioneer Square* ☎ *206/220–4240* ⊕ *nps.gov/klse/index.htm* 🎟 *Free.*

Last Resort Fire Department Museum. Occupying the bottom floor of the Seattle Fire Department's headquarters, the museum includes eight historic rigs from Seattle dating from the 19th and early 20th centuries, as well as artifacts (vintage helmets and uniforms, hose nozzles, and other equipment) and photos, logs, and newspaper clippings recording historic fires. ⊠ *301 2nd Ave. S, Pioneer Square* ☎ *206/783–4474* ⊕ *www.lastresortfd.org* 🎟 *Free.*

Occidental Park. This shady, picturesque cobblestone park is the geographical heart of the historic neighborhood—on first Thursdays it's home to a variety of local artisans setting up makeshift booths. Grab a sandwich or pastry at the Grand Central Bakery (arguably the city's finest artisanal bakery) and get in some good people-watching at the outdoor patio. Note that this square is a spot where homeless people congregate; you're likely to encounter more than a few oddballs. The square is best avoided at night. ⊠ *Occidental Ave. S and S. Main St., Pioneer Square.*

Punch Gallery. This small artist-run gallery is a local favorite for its eclectic shows, which combine the many mediums of its founding members—painting, digital media, sculpture, and collage. Punch is one of several artist collectives in the Tashiro Kaplan Building at 3rd Avenue South and Washington Street. SOIL and Platform are also worth checking out in this complex; there are also open studios (be sure to make the rounds on First Thursdays) and a great coffeehouse. ⊠ *119 Prefontaine Pl. S, Pioneer Square* ☎ *206/621–1945* ⊕ *www. punchgallery.org* 🎟 *Free.*

Waterfall Garden. A tranquil spot to take a break, this small garden surrounds a 22-foot (artificial) waterfall that cascades over large granite stones. There are a few café tables; it's a great place to rest for a few minutes and seek out your next destination in the guidebook. ⊠ *219 2nd Ave. South, Pioneer Square* ☎ *206/624–6096.*

2

INTERNATIONAL DISTRICT

Sightseeing
★★
Dining
★★★★
Lodging
★
Shopping
★★★
Nightlife
★

Bright welcome banners, 12-foot fiberglass dragons cling-ing to lampposts, and a traditional Chinese gate confirm you're in the International District. The I.D., as it's locally known, is synonymous with delectable dining—it has many inexpensive Chinese restaurants (this is the neigh-borhood for barbecued duck and all manner of dump-lings), but the best eateries reflect its Pan-Asian spirit: Vietnamese, Japanese, Malay, Filipino, Cambodian. With the endlessly fun Uwajimaya shopping center, the gorgeously redesigned Wing Luke Museum, and several walking tours to choose from, you now have something to do in between bites.

The I.D. used to be called Chinatown; it began as a haven for Chinese workers who came to the United States to work on the transcontinen-tal railroad. It was later a hub for Seattle's growing Japanese popula-tion, and now one of the biggest presences is Vietnamese, both in the center of the I.D. and in "Little Saigon," directly east of the neigh-borhood. Though the neighborhood has weathered the anti-Chinese riots and the forced eviction of Chinese residents during the 1880s and the internment of Japanese-Americans during World War II, it's become increasingly less vital to its communities. Many of the people who actually live in the neighborhood are older—the northern and southern suburbs of the city are where the newer generations are being raised (though young people still often make the I.D. an obligatory snack stop before heading home after a night out in Seattle).

Getting Oriented

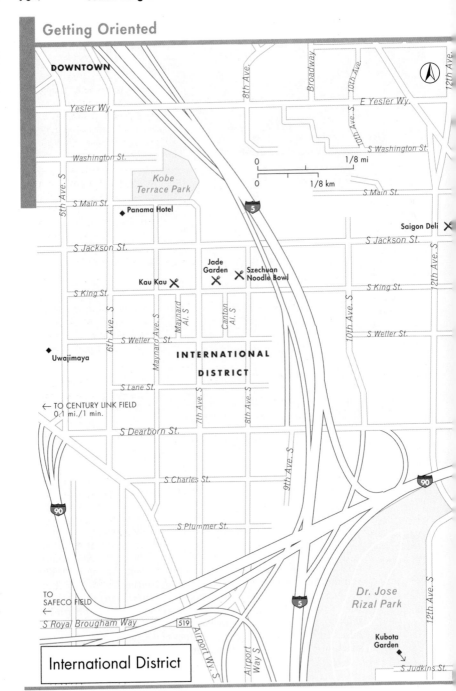

DOWNTOWN

Yesler Wy.

E Yesler Wy.

8th Ave.

Broadway

10th Ave.

12th Ave.

Washington St.

S Washington St.

10th Ave. S

0   1/8 mi

0   1/8 km

Kobe Terrace Park

S Main St.

5th Ave. S

S Main St.

◆ Panama Hotel

Saigon Deli ✕

S Jackson St.

S Jackson St.

12th Ave. S

Jade Garden ✕

Szechuan Noodle Bowl ✕

Kau Kau ✕

S King St.

S King St.

6th Ave. S

Maynard Ave. S

Maynard Al. S

Canton Al. S

10th Ave. S

S Weller St.

S Weller St.

◆ Uwajimaya

INTERNATIONAL

DISTRICT

S Lane St.

7th Ave. S

8th Ave. S

← TO CENTURY LINK FIELD
0.1 mi./1 min.

S Dearborn St.

S Charles St.

9th Ave. S

90

S Plummer St.

90

TO
SAFECO FIELD
←

Dr. Jose Rizal Park

12th Ave. S

S Royal Brougham Way   519

5

Airport Wy. S

Airport Way S

Kubota Garden ◆

S Judkins St.

International District

GETTING AROUND

The I.D. is southeast of Pioneer Square, and the neighborhoods are often combined in one visit—you may find yourself wandering into the I.D. anyway, along South Jackson Street, which is the main thoroughfare connecting the two neighborhoods.

From the center of Downtown, walking to the I.D. takes about 20 minutes. However, it's not a scenic route, so unless you need the leg stretch, take a bus or hail a cab or Uber. Buses 7, 14, and 36 pick up on Pine (at 3rd or 4th Avenues). Bus 99 picks up by each of the major piers and travels along Alaskan Way.

TOP REASONS TO GO

Browse for unique gifts, souvenirs, and trinkets at **Uwajimaya** and **Kobo at Higo.** Uwajimaya has an amazing selection of Asian foods, plus a great bookstore and home section. Kobo, a gallery for local artists, is the spot for classy mementos.

Get a history lesson with your tea at the **Panama Hotel.** Although not one of our top choices for lodging, this hotel is a must-see for its lovely ground-floor teahouse and window into the lives of Japanese Americans shipped to internment camps during World War II.

Tour the neighborhood with docents from the **Wing Luke Museum of the Asian Pacific American Experience.** The museum casts a no-nonsense eye on the story of Asian and Pacific Islander communities, and guided tours point out the living history in the neighborhood.

Sample something from **every major Asian cuisine.**

PLANNING YOUR TIME

The I.D. is a very popular lunchtime spot with Downtown office workers and a popular dinner spot with many Seattleites. You should definitely make a meal here part of your visit. You'll need at least an hour at the Wing Luke Museum. A stop at Uwajimaya is essential. Don't plan on spending a full day here—a morning or an afternoon will suffice. And be forewarned that, as in adjacent Pioneer Square, Seattle's homelessness problem is quite visible here.

QUICK BITES

Jade Garden. The go-to place for dim sum. ⊠ *424 7th Ave. S, International District* ☎ *206/622–8181* ⊕ *www.jadegardenseattle. com.*

KauKau BBQ Restaurant. This simple spot serves the best Chinese barbecue in the I.D. ⊠ *656 S. King St., International District* ☎ *206/682–4006* ⊕ *www.kaukaubbq.com* ⊟ *No credit cards.*

Saigon Deli. The best banh mi in the neighborhood. ⊠ *1237 S. Jackson St., International District* ☎ *206/322–3700* ⊟ *No credit cards.*

Thai Curry Simple. Thai Curry Simple makes its own fresh curry pastes with local ingredients and herbs from Thailand. ⊠ *406 5th Ave. S, International District* ☎ *206/327–4838* ⊕ *www.thai-currysimple.com.*

The I.D. stretches from 4th Avenue to 12th Avenue and between Yesler Way and S. Dearborn Street. The main business anchor is the Uwajimaya superstore, and there are other small businesses scattered among the restaurants, including herbalists, acupuncturists, antiques shops, and private clubs. Note that the area is more diffuse than similar communities in larger cities like San Francisco and New York. You won't find the densely packed streets chockablock with tiny storefronts and markets that spill out onto the sidewalk—scenes that have become synonymous with the word "Chinatown."

When the Wing Luke Museum of the Asian Pacific American Experience moved from its tiny cluttered home to a refurbished historic building on one of the main drags here, it refocused the city's attention on the I.D. as more than a collection of restaurants. There are indeed signs of further improvement, which the neighborhood sorely needs. (As with Pioneer Square, the I.D. is interesting and fun, but can be rough around the edges: it's in these two adjacent neighborhoods that Seattle's horrible homeless problem is most visible.) The I.D. does have more energy these days: students crowd bubble-tea parlors, and the community has been holding more special events like parades and periodic night markets and movie nights in Hing Hay Park.

TOP ATTRACTIONS

Kubota Garden. A serene 20 acres of streams, waterfalls, ponds, and rock outcroppings were created by Fujitaro Kubota, a 1907 emigrant from Japan. The gardens on the Seattle University campus and the Japanese Garden at the Bloedel Reserve on Bainbridge Island are other examples of his work. The garden, a designated historical landmark of the city of Seattle, is free to visitors and tours are self-guided, though you can go on a docent-led tour on the fourth Saturday of every month, April through October, at 10 am. ✉ *9817 55th Ave. S, Mt. Baker* ✛ *From I–5, take Exit 158 and turn left toward Martin Luther King Jr. Way; continue up hill on Ryan Way. Turn left on 51st Ave. S, then right on Renton Ave. S and right on 55th Ave. S to parking lot* ☎ *206/684–4584* ⊕ *www.seattle.gov/parks/find/parks/kubota-garden* ⊿ *Free.*

A GOOD COMBO

For a great day of walking and exploring, start your day with breakfast at Pike Place Market, then bus, cab, or stroll down 1st Avenue to Pioneer Square (you'll pass SAM en route—another option!). After visiting some art galleries (which generally open between 10:30 and noon) and stopping at any of the neighborhood's coffee shops (such as Zeitgeist or Grand Central Bakery), walk southeast to the International District for some retail therapy at Uwajimaya and a visit to the Wing Luke Museum. Then cab it back to your hotel.

FAMILY
Fodor'sChoice
★

Uwajimaya. This huge, fascinating Japanese supermarket is a feast for the senses. A 30-foot-long red Chinese dragon stretches above colorful mounds of fresh produce and aisles of delicious packaged goods—colorful sweets and unique savory treats from countries throughout Asia. A busy food court serves sushi, Japanese bento-box meals, Chinese stir-fry

Historic Chinatown Gate in the International District

combos, Korean barbecue, Hawaiian dishes, Vietnamese spring rolls, and an assortment of teas and tapioca drinks. You'll also find authentic housewares, cosmetics (Japanese-edition Shiseido), toys (Hello Kitty) and more. There's also a fantastic branch of the famous Kinokuniya bookstore chain, selling many Asian-language books. The large parking lot is free for one hour with a minimum $7.50 purchase or two hours with a minimum $15 purchase—don't forget to have your ticket validated by the cashiers. ⊠ *600 5th Ave. S, International District* ☎ *206/624–6248* ⊕ *www.uwajimaya.com.*

WORTH NOTING

Kobe Terrace Park. Follow pathways adorned by Mt. Fuji trees at this lovely hillside pocket park. The trees and a 200-year-old stone lantern were donated by Seattle's sister city of Kobe, Japan. Despite being so close to I–5, the terrace is a peaceful place to stroll and enjoy views of the city, the water, and, if you're lucky, Mt. Rainier; a few benches line the gravel paths. The herb gardens you see are part of the Danny Woo Community Gardens, tended to by the neighborhood's residents. Across the street from the park is the historic Panama Hotel, featured in the novel *Hotel on the Corner of Bitter and Sweet* by Jamie Ford. Artifacts from the days of Japanese internment are on display, including a window on the floor showing a basement storage space that still contains a time capsule of unclaimed belongings. ⊠ *Main St. between 6th Ave. S and 7th Ave. S, International District* ☎ *206/684–4075* ▨ *Free.*

WING LUKE MUSEUM OF THE ASIAN PACIFIC

✉ *719 S. King St., International District* ☎ *206/623–5124* ⊕ *www.wingluke.org* 🎟 *$14.95, free 1st Thurs. and 3rd Sat. of month.*

TIPS

■ The museum is a great place to start your tour of the I.D., as it will provide a context to the neighborhood and the communities living here that you won't get by simply wandering around.

■ Parts of the historic building can only be visited on the Museum Experience tour.

■ Note that in addition to participating in First Thursdays, the museum is also free on the third Saturday of each month. The museum is open until 8 pm both days.

■ Be sure to check out what's going on in the Tateuchi Story Theater. The museum has long supported Asian-American playwrights, musicians, and artists, and its cultural offerings keep getting better. Shows range from concerts of traditional instruments to avant-garde theater to documentary film screenings. Third Saturdays are Family Days, offering free events and children's crafts 1–3 pm.

AMERICAN EXPERIENCE

The only museum in the United States devoted to the Asian Pacific American experience provides a sophisticated and often somber look at how immigrants and their descendants have transformed (and been transformed by) American culture. The evolution of the museum has been driven by community participation—the museum's library has an oral history lab, and many of the rotating exhibits are focused around stories from longtime residents and their descendants. Museum admission includes a guided walk-and-talk tour through the East Kong Yick building, where scores of immigrant workers from China, Japan, and the Philippines first found refuge in Seattle.

HIGHLIGHTS

The museum includes re-creations of typical early-20th-century one-room apartments, a communal kitchen, and the Yick Fung Company store.

The George Tsutakawa Art Gallery presents group shows of established and up-and-coming Asian-Pacific-American artists.

The museum offers three tours. The "Museum Experience" includes the current exhibits and the 1910 Historic Hotel and Yick Fung Company buildings. The second, "Touch of Chinatown," is a 90-minute guided stroll around the I.D. The "Hotel on the Corner of Bitter and Sweet Tour" (based on the bestselling book by Jamie Ford) includes walks in the area and lasts 90 minutes, every Saturday at 1. Tickets are $19.95 and include admission to the museum.

FIRST HILL AND THE CENTRAL DISTRICT

Sightseeing
★★
Dining
★★
Lodging
★
Shopping
★
Nightlife
★

The little-visited neighborhoods of First Hill and the Central District are nonetheless important pieces of the city's fabric. First Hill is an eastern extension of Downtown, and one tree-lined street has something truly spectacular: the Frye Art Museum. The Central District, mostly residential and off the beaten path, is the historic hub of Seattle's African American community, though to the dismay of many, the neighborhood is rapidly gentrifying.

FIRST HILL

Smack between Downtown and Capitol Hill, First Hill is an odd mix of sterile-looking medical facility buildings (earning it the nickname "Pill Hill"), old brick buildings that look like they belong on a college campus, and newer residential towers. There are a few businesses along Boren Avenue, but they're mostly unremarkable. The main draws of the neighborhood are the Frye Art Museum, which is well worth a detour, and the fantastic historic Sorrento Hotel.

THE CENTRAL DISTRICT

The predominantly residential Central District, or the "C.D.," lies south of Capitol Hill and northeast of the International District. Its boundaries are roughly 12th Avenue on the west, Martin Luther King Jr. Boulevard on the east, East Madison to the north, and South Jackson Street to the south. As Downtown Seattle rapidly develops, the C.D. is facing a transitional period. Community groups are working hard to ensure that the "revitalization" of the area doesn't come at the expense of stripping the city's oldest residential neighborhood of its history or breaking up and pricing out the community that's hung in there during years of economic blight. It has a few monuments honoring the city's

Getting Oriented

First Hill and the
Central District

Broadcast Coffee. Grab Stumptown coffee, pastries from Macrina Bakery, bagels, and salads here. ⊠ *1918 E. Yesler Way, Central District* ☎ *206/322-0807* ⊕ *www.broadcastcoffee.com.*

Ezell's. This Seattle institution, does one thing to perfection: crispy, juicy fried chicken with all the fixings. ⊠ *501 23rd Ave., Central District* ☎ *206/324-4141* ⊕ *www.ezellschicken.com.*

Katy's Corner Café. A tiny, unpretentious neighborhood spot with homemade pastries, quiches, and sandwiches. ⊠ *2000 E. Union St., Central District* ☎ *206/329-0121.*

Med Mix. The original purveyor of the "Original Seattle Cream Cheese Dog" mostly offers well-priced, hearty Mediterranean favorites like falafel, gyros, and Greek salad. ⊠ *1400 23rd Ave., Central District* ☎ *206/257-4397.*

GETTING AROUND

Because the sights are so spread out here, having a car is essential. This is especially true if you want to tool around the Central District to see the landmark buildings and houses, or if you want to visit the Northwest African American Museum, which is far south of everything else, in the Rainier Valley area. If you're busing it to the Northwest African American Museum from Downtown, take Bus 7 to Rainier Avenue South and South State Street. From Capitol Hill take Bus 48 from 23rd Avenue and East Madison Street to 23rd Avenue and South Massachusetts Street, which is right in front of the museum. If you're just visiting the Frye and the Sorrento Hotel, you can walk from either Downtown or Capitol Hill. By bus, take the 2, 10, 11, or 14 from Downtown.

TOP REASONS TO GO

Spend a quiet, art-filled afternoon at the **Frye Art Museum,** the only real attraction in First Hill, and one of Seattle's best museums. The Frye mixes representational art with rotating exhibits of folk and pop art, so there's something for everyone.

Settle into an overstuffed chair for a drink at the Sorrento Hotel's delightfully fussy **Fireside Room.** This is an especially pleasant stop on a chilly, rainy day—a few leather easy chairs are parked in front of a crackling fireplace.

Redefine dinner theater at **Central Cinema.** This off-the-beaten-path movie house serves beer, wine, burgers, pizzas, and salads. Screenings are a mix of classics (*The Shining, Animal House*) and small independent films.

PLANNING YOUR TIME

Both of these neighborhoods are best as detours from other itineraries. First Hill is adjacent to Downtown, and the C.D. is close to the International District. The Northwest African American Museum requires at least an hour. A visit to the small but captivating Frye Art Museum could take anywhere from one to three hours.

FRYE ART MUSEUM

✉ *704 Terry Ave., First Hill*
☎ *206/622–9250* ⊕ *www. fryemuseum.org* ✉ *Free.*

TIPS

■ The museum is small enough that you can move through it in an hour, but you could easily spend more time here, too.

■ The café, which serves made-from-scratch soups and sandwiches, Macrina Bakery pastries, and loose-leaf teas, is a local favorite. It also has free Wi-Fi access.

■ The Frye is best midweek. Because of its size, weekend crowds can overwhelm the space and detract from its charm.

■ Public and private tours are available, including "Tea and Tours" every Tuesday at 2 pm during the first four weeks of a new show, in which visitors can discuss what they've seen over tea in the café with Frye curators.

■ Download podcasts on exhibits past and present at www.fryemusem.org/podcasts.

In addition to its beloved permanent collection—predominately 19th- and 20th-century pastoral paintings—the Frye hosts eclectic and often avant-garde exhibits, putting this elegant museum on par with the Henry in the U-District. No matter what's going on in the stark, brightly lighted back galleries, it always seems to blend well with the permanent collection, which is rotated regularly. Thanks to the legacy of Charles and Emma Frye, the museum is always free, and parking is free as well.

HIGHLIGHTS

Charles and Emma Frye amassed a huge collection of late-19th- and early-20th-century European, particularly German, paintings. Their core collection is particularly strong on the Munich Secession artists and includes *Sin* by Franz von Stuck.

In addition, the Frye's permanent collection features paintings by American artists, including Albert Bierstadt, William Merritt Chase, and John H. Twachtman.

Perhaps because of the challenges of integrating such a conservative collection with avant-garde contemporary works, the Frye excels at providing context for its shows. Supplemental materials are clear and accessible, and public programs, lecture series, and classes are often on offer.

African American community, as well as some good restaurants and a few landmarks that provide a fairly good survey of architectural trends throughout the decades. ■TIP➔ Several pop-culture icons hail from the C.D., including Jimi Hendrix, Quincy Jones, Bruce Lee, and Sir Mix-a-Lot.

WORTH NOTING

Crespinel Martin Luther King Jr. Mural. Heading west on Cherry Street in the Central District, you'll see a 17-foot-tall mural of Dr. Martin Luther King Jr. Pacific Northwest artist James Crespinel painted the mural in the summer of 1995 on the eastern face of the building and touched up his work in 2016 while the community gathered to watch. ⊠ *Corner of Martin Luther King Jr. Way and Cherry St., Central District.*

CENTRAL DISTRICT LANDMARKS

■ Immaculate Conception Church (1904) at 820 18th Ave.

■ Old Firehouse #23 (1909) at 722 18th Ave.

■ Victorian House (1900) at 1414 S. Washington St.

■ Langston Hughes Cultural Arts Center (built in 1912 as the Bikur Cholim Synagogue) at 104 17th Ave.

■ James Washington Jr. Home and Studio (1918) at 1816 26th Ave.

■ First African Methodist Episcopal Church (1912) at 14th Ave. and Pine St.

Douglass-Truth Neighborhood Library. A city landmark that offers a little something for history buffs, architecture fans, and public-art lovers alike, this 1914 library was the first to be funded entirely by Seattle. After a lauded remodel and expansion a decade ago that followed strict historic preservation guidelines, Douglass-Truth remains a cherished community gathering spot. It also houses one of the largest collections of African American literature and history on the West Coast. Local artists Marita Dingus and Vivian Linder created sculptures and three-dimensional relief panels for the branch, which can be seen in the spacious corridor connecting the two buildings. Paintings of former slaves and abolitionists Frederick Douglass and Sojourner Truth by artist Eddie Ray Walker are also on display. Don't miss the Soul Pole, a totem pole depicting African American history, located outside on the grassy area on the corner of 23rd Avenue and E. Yesler Way. ⊠ *2300 E. Yesler Way, Central District* ☎ *206/684–4704* ⊕ *www.spl.org/locations/douglass-truth-branch.*

First African Methodist Episcopal Church. Founded in 1886, the state's oldest African American church and the community's nexus has operated out of this historic building since 1912. Their gospel choirs are among the city's best, and discussions with and among intellectuals, authors, artists, and the community are regularly scheduled. Rapidly growing church attendance (now around 1,700 members) has led to an extra service out of a satellite site in Kent. ⊠ *1522 14th Ave., Central District* ☎ *206/324–3664* ⊕ *www.fameseattle.org.*

Martin-Zambito Fine Art. David Martin and Dominic Zambito are well-known in Seattle's art scene for expanding the study of regional Northwest art by uncovering little-known, unknown, or long-forgotten artists, many of them women and minorities. The gallery, located in the historic Henry H. Dearborn House, focuses primarily on 19th- and 20th-century American art, especially WPA-era and figurative works. ✉ *1117 Minor Ave., First Hill* ☎ *206/726–9509* ⊕ *www. martin-zambito.com* ✉ *Free.*

Mount Zion Baptist Church. Gospel-music fans are drawn to the home of the state's largest African American congregation. The church's first gatherings began in 1889; back then its prayer meetings were held in homes and in a store. The church was incorporated in 1903, and after a number of moves, settled in its current simple but sturdy brick building. Eighteen stained-glass windows, each with an original design that honors a key African American figure, glow within the sanctuary. Beneath the bell tower, James Washington's sculpture *The Oracle of Truth,* a gray boulder carved with the image of a lamb, is dedicated to children struggling to find truth. ✉ *1634 19th Ave., Central District* ☎ *206/322–6500* ⊕ *www.mountzion.net.*

JAZZY SCHOOL

Garfield High School (400 23rd Avenue) is one of the Central District's historic landmarks. Alumni include Quincy Jones and Jimi Hendrix; today the school enjoys national attention for its jazz program. The 30-piece ensemble often performs at local festivals, including Earshot Jazz Festival in October and Folk Life in May. ⊕ *www.garfieldjazz.org*

OFF THE BEATEN PATH

Northwest African American Museum. Focusing on the history of African Americans in the Northwest, this museum tells stories through a diverse collection of well-curated and insightful photos, artifacts, and compelling narratives. Past exhibits have included "Xenobia Bailey: The Aesthetics of Funk," and "The Test: The Tuskegee Project," focusing on the first African American aviation units in the U.S. military to serve in combat. One gallery is dedicated to the work of local artists. Adjacent to the museum, which is housed in an old school building, the Jimi Hendrix Park is in its second phase of construction, part of a six-year project. Eventually, the 2½-acre park will feature a colorful structure that will serve as a gathering space and an amphitheater. ✉ *2300 S. Massachusetts St., Leschi* ☎ *206/518–6000* ⊕ *www.naamnw.org* ✉ *$6.*

OFF THE BEATEN PATH

Seward Park. Seward Park, about 10 minutes southeast of Downtown, is a relatively undiscovered gem on the shores of Lake Washington. The 300-acre park includes trails through old-growth forest, mountain views, eagles' nests, a 2½-mile biking and walking path, a native plant garden, art studio, and a small swimming beach. Free walking tours are offered by Friends of Seward Park at 11 am on most first Saturdays (check the website to confirm), departing from the Seward Park Environmental and Audubon Center. ■ TIP→ **Turn your park visit into a bike tour on select summer Sundays for Bicycle Sunday, when Lake Washington Boulevard (south of Mount Baker Beach to the entrance of Seward Park) is closed to motorized traffic, 10 am–6 pm. Check www. seattle.gov/parks/bicyclesunday.** ✉ *5895 Lake Washington Blvd. S, Columbia City–Seward Park, Mt. Baker* ⊕ *www.sewardpark.org, www. seattle.gov/parks/bicyclesunday.*

2

CAPITOL HILL

Sightseeing
★★★
Dining
★★★★★
Lodging
★★★
Shopping
★★★★
Nightlife
★★★★★

The Hill has two faces: on one side, it's young and edgy, full of artists, musicians, and students. Tattoo parlors and coffeehouses abound, as well as thumping music venues and bars. On the other side, it's elegant and upscale, with tree-lined streets, 19th-century mansions, and John Charles Olmsted's Volunteer Park. Converted warehouses, modern high-rises, colorfully painted two-story homes, and brick mansions all occupy the same neighborhood. There are parks aplenty and cute, quirky shops to browse, including one of the best bookstores in the city.

The Pike–Pine Corridor (Pike and Pine Streets running from Melrose Avenue to 15th Avenue) is the heart of the Hill. Pine Street is a slightly more pleasant walk, but Pike Street has more stores—and unless you're here in the evening (when the area's restaurants come to life), it's the stores and coffee shops that will be the main draw. The architecture along both streets is a mix of older buildings with small storefronts, a few taller buildings that have lofts and office spaces, and garages and warehouses (some converted, some not). Pine skirts Cal Anderson Park—a small, pleasant park with an unusual conic fountain and reflecting pool—a lovely place to take a break after walking and shopping. Depending on weather, the park can be either very quiet or filled with all kinds of activities from softball games to impromptu concerts.

The Hill's other main drag is Broadway East (a north–south avenue that crosses both Pike and Pine). Seattle's youth culture, old money, gay scene, and everything in between all converge on Broadway's lively if somewhat seedy stretch between East Denny Way and East Roy Street. Broadway is undergoing a renaissance, thanks to a few new high-profile

Getting Oriented

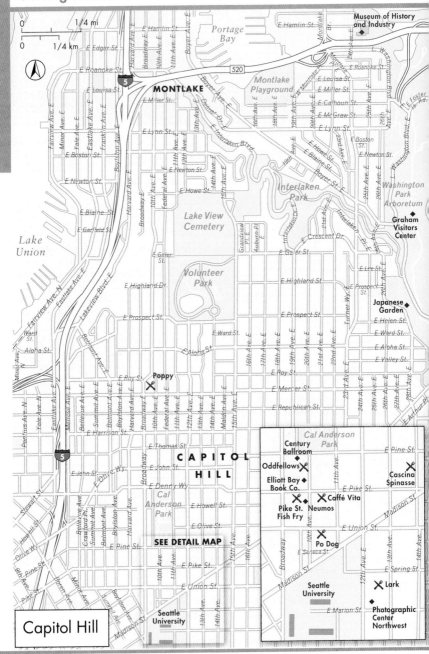

Capitol Hill

TOP REASONS TO GO

Browse the stacks at **Elliott Bay Book Company**, Seattle's biggest independent bookstore. Then find a sunny reading spot in **Cal Anderson Park**, a block away.

After you've stocked up on books, visit the surrounding shops, ice-cream shops, coffeehouses, and restaurants that make the **Pike–Pine Corridor** so hip and happening.

Rock out at **Neumos,** to anything from indie music to national touring acts.

Sample fantastic restaurants and coffeehouses, including **Poppy, Sitka & Spruce, Anchovies & Olives,** and **Cascina Spinasse** (for food); and **Stumptown, Espresso Vivace,** and **Caffé Vita** (for caffeine).

See the season's colors at nearby **Washington Park Arboretum.**

QUICK BITES

Baguette Box. Baguette Box serves gourmet sandwiches, salads, and sides. ✉ *1203 Pine St., Capitol Hill* ☎ *206/332–0220* ⊕ *www.baguetteboxseattle.com* ⊟ *No credit cards.*

Oddfellows Cafe + Bar. Scones, fluffy eggs, and Stumptown coffee in the morning, rustic sandwiches and salads midday, and pan-seared salmon and tasty quinoa cakes in the evening—the ever-hip Oddfellows is a Capitol Hill hot spot. ✉ *1525 10th Ave., Capitol Hill* ☎ *206/325–0807* ⊕ *www.oddfellowscafe.com* ⊟ *No credit cards.*

Pike Street Fish Fry. Pike Street Fish Fry has perfectly fried cod, halibut, salmon, calamari, and seasonal smelt, served with chips or a fresh Macrina roll. ✉ *1122 E. Pike St., 10th and Pike (next to Neumos), Capitol Hill* ☎ *206/329–7453* ⊟ *No credit cards.*

GETTING HERE AND AROUND

You can walk from Downtown, taking Pine or Pike Street across I–5 to Melrose Avenue, but keep in mind that touring the neighborhood itself will require a lot of walking, and it's uphill from Downtown.

Light-rail runs from Westlake Center to Capitol Hill. Buses 10, 11, and 49 all pick up on Pike Street Downtown and travel up Pine Street after crossing I–5. This is the easiest crosstown route to Capitol Hill's Pike–Pine Corridor. The 10 and the 49 continue up toward Volunteer Park. The 8 connects Seattle Center to Capitol Hill via Denny Way. The 11 and the 43 (the latter also picks up on Pike Street Downtown) will get you the closest to the Washington Park Arboretum, which is technically several neighborhoods out of Capitol Hill (most people usually drive or bike there).

Street parking here is difficult. Keep an eye out for pay lots, which are numerous.

PLANNING YOUR TIME

Not much gets going on the Hill until late morning, so spend the morning at Volunteer Park and Washington Park Arboretum. Stop for coffee first—there are many great coffeehouses to choose from. If you visit in the afternoon, stroll and shop, grab a coffee, then stick around for dinner and barhopping—the Hill's real attractions.

The water tower at Volunteer Park.

condo buildings and a light-rail station. Although it's got a few spots of note (Jerry Traunfeld's excellent restaurant, Poppy, for one), it's still mostly a cluttered stretch of cheap restaurants, even cheaper clothing stores, and a few bars. Many people still find the area compelling because of its human parade. If you really want to see Seattle in all its quirky glory, head to Dick's Drive-In around midnight on a weekend night.

The neighborhood's reputation as one of the city's hippest and most vibrant is bringing some good developments, too—Seattle's beloved Elliott Bay Book Company relocated here in the hopes that the constant street traffic and focus on the arts would revitalize its business. It's within walking distance of several great pizzerias, ice-cream shops, and coffeehouses.

TOP ATTRACTIONS

Volunteer Park. Nestled among the grand homes of North Capitol Hill sits this 45-acre grassy expanse that's perfect for picnicking, sunbathing (or stomping in rain puddles), and strolling. You can tell this is one of the city's older parks by the size of the trees and the rhododendrons, many of which were planted more than a hundred years ago. The Olmsted Brothers, the premier landscape architects of the day, helped with the final design in 1904; the park has changed surprisingly little since then. In the center of the park is the **Seattle Asian Art Museum (SAAM, a branch of the Seattle Art Museum)**, housed in a 1933 art moderne–style edifice; note the museum is closed for renovations until 2019.

LAKESIDE BEACHES NEARBY

Madison Park. In the late 19th century, Madison Park was the most popular beach in the city, with a promenade, floating bandstands, gambling halls, and ship piers. Now it's a lakefront park with sloping lawns, a swimming area, playgrounds, and tennis courts. The whole area is usually bustling with activity—there are a number of upscale coffee shops, restaurants, and boutiques nearby. It may not be obvious at first, but this is where the city's old money runs deep. The beach has picnic tables, restrooms, and showers, and lifeguards on duty in summer, and the recently renovated children's playground is among the city's best. From Downtown, go east on Madison Street; it'll take you straight down to the lake. ⊠ *Madison St. and 43rd Ave., Madison Park.*

Madrona Park. Several beach parks and green spaces front the lake along Lake Washington Boulevard; Madrona Park is one of the largest. Lifeguards are on duty in the summer and young swimmers have their own roped-in area, while teens and adults can swim out to a floating raft with a diving board. The mile-long trail along the shore is a great jogging spot. Grassy areas encourage picnicking; there are grills, picnic tables, phones, restrooms, and showers. From Downtown, go east on Yesler Way about 2 miles to 32nd Avenue. Turn left onto Lake Dell Avenue and then right; go to Lake Washington Boulevard and take a left. ⊠ *853 Lake Washington Blvd., Madrona.*

A focal point of the park, at the western edge of the hill in front of the Asian Art Museum, is Isamu Noguchi's sculpture, *Black Sun*, a natural frame from which to view the Space Needle, the Puget Sound, and the Olympic Mountains. ⊠ *Park entrance, 1400 E. Prospect St., Capitol Hill* ☎ *206/654–3100 museum.*

OFF THE
BEATEN
PATH
Washington Park Arboretum. As far as Seattle's green spaces go, this 230-acre arboretum is arguably the most beautiful. On calm weekdays, the place feels really secluded. The seasons are always on full display: in warm winters, flowering cherries and plums bloom in its protected valleys as early as late February, while the flowering shrubs in Rhododendron Glen and Azalea Way bloom March through June. In autumn, trees and shrubs glow in hues of crimson, pumpkin, and lemon; in winter, plantings chosen specially for their stark and colorful branches dominate the landscape. In 2016, as part of a 20-year master plan, the arboretum broke ground on a 1¼ mile trail that connects to an existing path to create a 2½-mile loop, giving guests access to areas that were previously hard to reach. March through October, visit the peaceful **Japanese Garden,** a compressed world of mountains, forests, rivers, lakes, and tablelands. The pond, lined with blooming water irises in spring, has turtles and brightly colored koi. An authentic Japanese teahouse is reserved for tea ceremonies and instruction on the art of serving tea (visitors who would like to enjoy a bowl of tea and sweets can purchase a $10 "Chado" tea ticket at the Garden ticket booth). The Graham Visitors Center at the park's north end

has descriptions of the arboretum's flora and fauna (which include 130 endangered plants), as well as brochures, a garden gift shop, and walking-tour maps. Free tours are offered most of the year; see website for schedule. ⊠ *2300 Arboretum Dr. E., Capitol Hill* ☎ *206/543–8800 arboretum, 206/684–4725 Japanese garden* ⊕ *www.depts.washington. edu/uwbg* ⊠ *Free, Japanese garden $6.*

WORTH NOTING

Lakeview Cemetery. One of the area's most beautiful cemeteries, dating back to 1872, looks east toward Lake Washington from its elevated hillside directly north of Volunteer Park. Several of Seattle's founding families are interred here (names you will likely recognize from street names and public places) and Bruce Lee's grave and that of his son Brandon are the most visited sites. Maps are available at the cemetery office. ⊠ *1554 15th Ave. E, Capitol Hill* ☎ *206/322–1582* ⊕ *www. lakeviewcemeteryassociation.com* ⊠ *Free.*

Photographic Center Northwest. A small, starkly attractive gallery space occupies the front of this photo education center. Curated shows often feature well-respected photographers, ranging from journalistic to fantastical, and "crash course" workshops are open to the public. The gallery is convenient to the Pike–Pine Corridor—it's a few blocks south of Pike. ⊠ *900 12th Ave., Capitol Hill* ☎ *206/720–7222* ⊕ *www.pcnw. org* ⊠ *Free.*

FREMONT AND PHINNEY RIDGE

Sightseeing
★★
Dining
★★★★
Lodging
★
Shopping
★★★★★
Nightlife
★★★

The pretty neighborhoods of Fremont and Phinney Ridge are great side trips when you've done with your major Seattle sightseeing and are in the mood for shopping, strolling along the canal, or sampling artisanal goodies.

FREMONT

For many years, Fremont enjoyed its reputation as Seattle's weirdest neighborhood, home to hippies, artists, bikers, and rat-race dropouts. But Fremont has lost most of its artist cachet as the stores along its main strip turned more upscale, luxury condos and town houses appeared above the neighborhood's warren of small houses, and rising rents sent many longtime residents reluctantly packing (many to nearby Ballard). On weekend nights, the Downtown strip sometimes looks like one big party, as a bunch of bars draw in a young crowd from Downtown, the University District, and the city's suburbs.

The mixed bag of "quintessential sights" in this neighborhood reflects the intersection of past and present. Most of them, like Seattle's favorite photo stop, the Fremont Troll, are works of public art created in the 1980s and '90s. Others, like Theo Chocolate and Fremont Brewing, celebrate the independent spirit of the neighborhood but suggest a much different lifestyle than the founders of the "republic of Fremont" espoused. Still others are neutral and timeless, like a particularly lovely section of the Burke Gilman Trail along the Lake Washington Ship Canal.

WORTH NOTING

FAMILY **Theo Chocolate factory tour.** If it weren't for a small sign on the sidewalk pointing the way, you'd never know that Fremont has its own chocolate factory. Theo has helped to boost the Northwest's growing artisanal chocolate scene and has taken the city by storm, thanks to

Getting Oriented

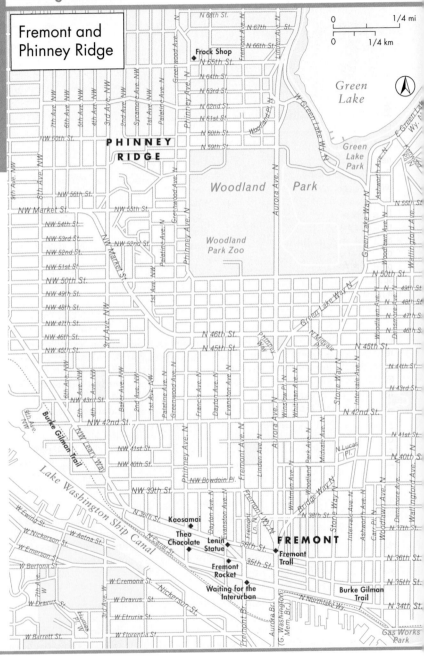

Fremont and
Phinney Ridge

0   1/4 mi

0   1/4 km

Green
Lake

Frock Shop

PHINNEY
RIDGE

Woodland   Park

Green
Lake
Park

Woodland
Park Zoo

NW Market St.

Burke Gilman Trail

Lake Washington Ship Canal

Kaosamai
Theo
Chocolate
Lenin
Statue
FREMONT
Fremont
Troll
Fremont
Rocket
Waiting for the
Interurban
Burke Gilman
Trail
Gas Works
Park

FREMONT SOLSTICE PARADE

If you want to know where all of Fremont's legendary weirdness has retreated, look no further than the Fremont Arts Council's warehouse on Fremont Avenue North. For months leading up to the Fremont Solstice Parade (held on the summer solstice weekend in June), half-finished parade floats spill out of the workshop. The parade is Seattle's most notorious summer event—some of the floats and costumes are political and/or wacky, and the "highlight" is a stream of naked bicyclists, only some of whom don elaborate body paint. And the professionally built floats and puppets are truly spectacular: past participants have included giant robots and a papier-mâché Flying Spaghetti Monster.

QUICK BITES

Flying Apron. "I can't believe this is vegan!" is a common reaction to the delicious pastries, cookies, and muffins made by the Flying Apron. All items are also gluten- and wheat-free. ✉ 3510 Fremont Ave. N, Fremont ☎ 206/442–1115 ⊕ www. flyingapron.com ▭ No credit cards.

PCC Natural Markets. PCC Natural Markets, an upscale food co-op, has all the fixings you need for a picnic along the canal, including sandwiches and salads. ✉ 600 N. 34th St., Fremont ☎ 206/632–6811 ⊕ www.pccnaturalmarkets.com ▭ No credit cards.

Red Mill. People line up out the door at Red Mill for juicy burgers and milk shakes in yummy flavors like mandarin-chocolate and butterscotch. ✉ 312 N. 67th St., Greenwood ☎ 206/783–6362 ⊕ www.redmillburgers.com ▭ No credit cards.

Royal Grinders. Royal Grinders serves hearty hot subs on soft crusty rolls. The Crown and the Italian are the best. ✉ 3526 Fremont Pl. N, behind Lenin statue, Fremont ☎ 206/545–7560 ⊕ www.royalgrinders.com ▭ No credit cards.

GETTING HERE AND AROUND

Buses 26, 28, and 5 will drop you in Fremont center. Driving, take either Aurora Avenue North (Route 99) and exit right after you cross the bridge, or take Westlake Avenue North and cross the Fremont Bridge into the neighborhood's core. Phinney is at the top of a big hill. If you want to walk it, the best strategy is to thread your way up through the charming residential streets. If not, take Bus 5 bus up Fremont Avenue.

TOP REASONS TO GO

Follow the **Burke-Gilman Trail** along the Fremont section of the Lake Washington Ship Canal.

Bring your credit card for some retail therapy at the area's **boutiques.** Mandatory stops on the shopping tour include Les Amis and Burnt Sugar in Fremont and the Frock boutique in Phinney Ridge.

Sip some brews at a **neighborhood tap house.**

Take a spin on a historic wooden carousel, then hang out with Sumatran tigers, snow leopards, and grizzly bears at the nearby **Woodland Park Zoo.**

Tour an artisanal-chocolate factory: **Theo Chocolate's** inventive, rich confections are best sampled after seeing the cocoa roasters and chocolate makers at work.

Fremont Like a Local

WACKY PUBLIC ART

Kick-start your tour under the north end of the Aurora Bridge at N. 36th Street, where you'll find the **Fremont Troll**, a two-ton, 18-foot-tall concrete troll clutching a real Volkswagen beetle in his massive hand. The troll appeared in 1991, commissioned by the Fremont Arts Council. Pose for a shot atop his head or pretending to pull his beard.

Next, head west down the hill to the statue of **Lenin** (✉ N. 36th St. at Fremont Place and Evanston Ave. N). Constructed by Bulgarian sculptor Emil Venkov for the Soviets in 1988, the 16-foot, 7-ton statue was removed shortly after the Velvet Revolution and eventually made its way to Seattle. Visitors here during Gay Pride Week might catch a glimpse of him in drag. The annual Lenin lighting, part of the Fremont Festivus in early December, is also a popular tradition.

A few blocks away you'll find the **Fremont Rocket** (✉ N. 35th St. and Evanston Ave. N), a 53-foot Cold War–era rocket nonchalantly strapped to the side of a retail store—which just may mark the official "center of the universe." This Seattle landmark was rescued from a surplus store in 1991 and successfully erected on its current locale in '94, when neon lights were added, along with the crest "De Libertas Quirkas," meaning "Freedom to Be Peculiar."

Walk along the water toward the Fremont Bridge, past the offices of Adobe, Getty Images, and Google (among others) to visit the cast-aluminum sculpture **Waiting for the Interurban** (✉ N. 34th St. and Fremont Ave. N). Artist Richard Beyer created this depiction of six people and a dog waiting for a trolley in 1979. Observe that the dog's face is actually that of a man—story goes this is the face of recycling pioneer (and onetime honorary mayor of Fremont) Armen Stepanian, who made disparaging remarks about the statue. It's been a long local tradition to "vandalize" the sculpture with anything from brightly colored umbrellas to signs congratulating newlyweds.

THAI FOOD AND CHOCOLATES AND T-SHIRTS, OH MY!

If the comrades are hungry, opt for Thai food. On sunny days, choose **Kaosamai** (⊕ www.kaosamai.com), a crowd-pleasing eatery with a large deck. On rainy days, you might prefer cozy **Kwanjai Thai** (✉ 469 N. 36th St. ☎ 206/632–3656), where you can dive into home-style Thai curries.

After you've had your fill of spicy food, peruse nearby **Destee-Nation** (⊕ www.desteenation.com), a cool little shop that sells vintage-looking T-shirts from independent restaurants and establishments across Seattle.

Next stop is **Theo Chocolate Factory** (⊕ www.theochocolate.com), an organic and fair-trade chocolate factory offering tours. You'll learn all about the chocolate-making process and get to sample some of Theo's favorites. Be sure to try the coconut-curry bar!

Check out the neighborhood's website (⊕ www.fremontuniverse.com) for more information.

high-quality chocolate creations. Theo uses only organic, fair-trade cocoa beans, usually in high percentages—yielding darker, less sweet, and more complex flavors than some of their competitors. You'll see Theo chocolate bars for sale in many local businesses, from coffee shops to grocery stores. Stop by the factory to buy exquisite "confection" truffles—made daily in small batches—with unusual flavors like basil-ganache, lemon, fig-fennel, and burnt sugar. The super-friendly staff is known to be generous with samples. You can go behind the scenes as well: informative, hour-long tours are offered daily; reservations aren't always necessary, but it's a good idea to reserve ahead, particularly on weekends. ⊠ *3400 Phinney Ave. N, Fremont* ☎ *206/632–5100* ⊕ *www.theochocolate.com* ☞ *Tour $10.*

PHINNEY RIDGE

Phinney Ridge, above Fremont, is almost entirely residential, though it shares the booming commercial street of Greenwood Avenue North with its neighbor to the north, Greenwood. Although not as strollable as similar districts in Fremont or Ballard, Greenwood Avenue has a lot of boutiques, coffee shops, and restaurants that range from go-to diner food to pricey Pacific Northwest.

WORTH NOTING

FAMILY **Woodland Park Zoo.** Ninety-two acres are divided into bioclimatic zones here, allowing many animals to roam freely in habitat areas. A jaguar exhibit is the center of the Tropical Rain Forest area, where rare cats, frogs, and birds evoke South American jungles. The Humboldt penguin exhibit is environmentally sound—it uses geothermal heating and cooling to mimic the climes of the penguins' native home, the coastal areas of Peru. With authentic thatch-roof buildings, the African Village has a replica schoolroom overlooking animals roaming the savanna; the Trail of Vines takes you through tropical Asia; and the Northern Trail winds past rocky habitats where brown bears, wolves, mountain goats, and otters scramble and play. The Reserve Zoomazium is a nature-themed indoor play space for toddlers and young kids, and the Woodland Park Rose Garden (free; located near the zoo's south entrance) is always a hit. ⊠ *5500 Phinney Ave. N, Phinney Ridge* ☎ *206/548–2000* ⊕ *www.zoo.org* ☞ *Oct.–Apr. $13.75, May–Sept. $19.75.*

BALLARD

Sightseeing
★★

Dining
★★★★★

Lodging
★

Shopping
★★★★★

Nightlife
★★★★

Ballard is Seattle's sweetheart. This historically Scandinavian neighborhood doesn't have many sights outside the Hiram M. Chittenden Locks; you'll spend more time strolling, shopping, and hanging out than crossing attractions off your list. It's got a great little nightlife, shopping, and restaurant scene on Ballard Avenue, and an outstanding farmers' market every Sunday.

Ballard used to be almost exclusively Scandinavian and working-class; it was the logical home for the Swedish and Norwegian immigrants who worked in the area's fishing, shipbuilding, and lumber industries. Reminders of its origins still exist—most literally in the Nordic Heritage Museum—but the neighborhood is undergoing inevitable changes as the number of artists, hipsters, and young professionals (many of whom have been priced out of Fremont and Capitol Hill) increases. Trendy restaurants, upscale furniture stores, and quirky boutiques abound along NW Market Street and Ballard Avenue, the neighborhood's main commercial strips. But no matter how tidy it gets, Ballard doesn't feel as gentrified as Fremont or as taken with its own coolness as Capitol Hill—Ballard still stands apart from the rest of the city.

Ballard used to be its own city: it wasn't a part of Seattle until 1907, when Ballard residents voted to be "annexed" by the city. The citizens of Ballard were responding to a water crisis—which would be solved by becoming part of Seattle—as well as to myriad promises of new and better public services made by Seattle's mayor. Today Ballard residents old and new adopt the "Free Ballard" slogan for many reasons. Although a few people would like to see Ballard revert to being its own city, many simply see it as a way to express neighborhood pride—a way to remind themselves and the rest of Seattle that Ballard's unique heritage and way of life must be preserved despite being one of the city's hippest neighborhoods.

TOP ATTRACTIONS

FAMILY

Fodor's Choice

★

Hiram M. Chittenden Locks. There's no doubt—there's something intriguing and eerie about seeing two bodies of water, right next to each, at different levels. The Hiram M. Chittenden Locks (also known as "Ballard Locks") are an important passage in the 8-mile Lake Washington Ship Canal that connects Puget Sound to freshwater Lake Washington and Lake Union. In addition to boat traffic, the Locks see an estimated half-million salmon and trout make the journey from saltwater to fresh each summer, with the help of a fish ladder.

Families picnic beneath oak trees in the adjacent 7-acre Carl S. English Botanical Gardens; various musical performances (from jazz bands to chamber music) serenade visitors on summer weekends; and steel-tinted salmon awe spectators as they climb a 21-step fish ladder en route to their freshwater spawning grounds—a heroic journey from the Pacific to the base of the Cascade Mountains.

In the 1850s, when Seattle was founded, Lake Washington and Lake Union were inaccessible from the tantalizingly close Puget Sound. The city's founding fathers—most notably, Thomas Mercer in 1854—began dreaming of a canal that would connect the freshwater lakes and the Sound. The lure of freshwater moorage and easier transport of timber and coal proved powerful, but it wasn't until 1917 that General Hiram M. Chittenden and the Army Corps of Engineers completed the Lake Washington Ship Canal and the locks that officially bear his name. More than 90 years later, the Locks are still going strong. Tens of thousands of boaters pass through the Locks each year, carrying more than a million tons of commercial products—including seafood, fuel, and building materials.

Guided tours of the Locks are available departing from the visitor center; however, plaques by the locks will give you plenty of information if you don't have time for a tour. ✉ 3015 N.W. 54th St., Ballard ✢ From Fremont, head north on Leary Way NW, west on N.W. Market St., and south on 54th St. ☎ 206/783–7059 ⊕ www.seattle.gov/tour/locks.htm ☑ Free.

WORTH NOTING

Golden Gardens Park. The waters of Puget Sound may be bone-chillingly cold, but that doesn't stop folks from jumping in to cool off. Besides brave swimmers, who congregate on the small strip of sand between the parking lot and the canteen, this Ballard-area park is packed with sunbathers and walkers in summer. In other seasons, beachcombers explore during low tide, and groups gather around bonfires to socialize and watch the glorious Seattle sunsets. The park has drinking water, grills, picnic tables, phones, and restrooms. It also has two wetlands, a short loop trail, and unbelievable views of the Olympic Mountains. From Downtown, take Elliott Avenue North, which becomes 15th Avenue West, and cross the Ballard Bridge. Turn left to head west on Market Street and follow signs to the Ballard Locks; continue about another mile via Seaview Avenue NW to the park.

Getting Oriented

Golden
Gardens
Park

Puget
Sound

Seaview Ave. NW

NW 83rd St.

24th Ave. NW
20th Ave. NW
15th Ave. NW

Loyal Way NW

NW 80th St.
NW 80th St.

33rd Ave. NW
32nd Ave. NW
31st Ave. NW
30th Ave. NW
29th Ave. NW
28th Ave. NW

NW 77th St.
NW 77th St.

NW 75th St.
NW 75th St.

NW 74th St.
NW 73rd St.
NW 73rd St.
NW 73rd St.
NW 72nd St.
NW 71st St.
NW 70th St.

24th Ave. NW
Jones Ave. NW
23rd Ave. NW
22nd Ave. NW

NW 69th St.

NW 68th St.
♦ Nordic Heritage
Museum
NW 67th St.
NW 67th St.

18th Ave. NW
17th Ave. NW
15th Ave. NW

35th Ave.
34th Ave. NW
33rd Ave. NW

NW 66th St.

NW 65th St.
NW 65th St.
NW 64th St.

Earl Ave. NW
25th Ave. NW
26th Ave. NW

NW 64th St.
NW 63rd St.
NW 63rd St.

BALLARD

32nd Ave. NW

NW 62nd St.
NW 61st St.
NW 61st St.

36th Ave.

NW 60th St.
Café
Besalu ✗
NW 60th St.

21st Ave. NW
20th Ave. NW
19th Ave. NW

NW 59th St.
NW 59th St.

28th Ave. NW

NW 58th St.
NW 58th St.

27th Ave. NW

NW 57th St.
NW 57th St.

NW 56th St.
NW 56th St.

Than
Brothers

NW 54th St.
NW 53rd St.

NW Market St.
NW Market St.
La Carta de Oaxaca
Miro Tea
Other Coast Café

Ballard Ave. NW
Leary Ave. NW
Russell Ave. NW
Tallman Ave.

NW 52nd St.
NW 51st St.
NW 50th St.
NW 49th St.

Hiram M.
Chittendon Locks
("Ballard Locks")
♦

Ballard
Farmers'
Market ♦

Shilshole Ave. NW

NW Park Pl.

NW Leary
NW Ballard
NW 46th

W Commodore Way

W Lawton St.

Salmon
Bay

15th Ave. NW

36th Ave. W

W Fort St. Way
W Government W

Gilman Ave. W

27th Ave. W

W Commodore Wy.

✦

0   1/4 mi
0   1/4 km

Ballard

TOP REASONS TO GO

The **Ballard Farmers' Market**, on Ballard Avenue every Sunday from 10 to 3 (rain or shine, year-round), is one of the city's finest farmers' markets.

See a show at the **Sunset Tavern**. Ballard has its own music scene, with several small clubs on Ballard Avenue; The Tractor Tavern is a small venue with a big reputation.

Explore Ballard's **booming beer scene** at one or a few of the kid- and dog-friendly breweries in the area. Among the best: Reuben's, Stoup, and PopLuxe.

Get some **retail therapy**, Ballard-style: the area's artsy galleries and many boutiques, and shoe and clothing stores offer tempting reasons to drop some dough.

Dip your toes in the water at **Golden Gardens Park**.

GETTING HERE AND AROUND

Ballard's main drags are N.W. Market Street and Ballard Avenue. If you're driving from Downtown, the easiest way to reach Ballard's center is to take Western Avenue and follow it as it turns into Elliott Avenue West and then 15th Avenue NW. Cross the bridge and make a left onto N.W. Market Street.

By bus, the 15, 17, and 18 will get you from Downtown to N.W. Market Street. Ballard is well connected to Phinney Ridge, Wallingford, and the U-District—the 44 and 46 buses pick up on N.W. Market Street and make their way to the other northern neighborhoods. Bus 28 connects Fremont's center to N.W. Market Street.

Note that the neighborhood is more spread out than it appears on a map. For example, walking west from the heart of Market Street to the Locks and back is long. Golden Gardens Park may not be worth the effort if you don't have a car.

2

PLANNING YOUR TIME

Set aside an hour or two to visit the Hiram M. Chittenden Locks. After that, you can spend your afternoon one of three ways before having dinner in the neighborhood: stroll and shop on Ballard Avenue; relax on the sand at Golden Gardens Park; or visit the Nordic Heritage Museum and area art galleries.

QUICK BITES

Ballard Pizza Company. Order a fat slice or a whole pie at this popular NYC-style pizza spot. ⊠ *5107 Ballard Ave NW, Ballard* ☎ *206/946–9960* ⊕ *www.ballardpizzacompany.com.*

Cafe Besalu. Cafe Besalu is one of best French bakeries in the city, with long morning lines for chocolate croissants (visit in the afternoon). ⊠ *5909 24th Ave. NW, Ballard* ☎ *206/789–1463* ⊕ *www.cafebesalu.com* ▭ *No credit cards.*

La Carta de Oaxaca. Outstanding margaritas and traditional Mexican favorites are served in this lively space on Ballard Avenue. ⊠ *5431 Ballard Ave. NW, Ballard* ☎ *206/782–8722* ⊕ *www.lacartadeoaxaca.com* ▭ *No credit cards.*

Miro Tea. Modern, hip Miro Tea is the place to go for exotic teas and amazing pastries. ⊠ *5405 Ballard Ave. NW, Ballard* ☎ *206/782–6832* ⊕ *www.mirotea.com* ▭ *No credit cards.*

DID YOU KNOW?

Hiram M. Chittenden Locks (aka Ballard Locks) allow more than just water and boats to pass from Puget Sound to Lake Washington and Lake Union. Every year about a half million salmon and trout climb a 21-step fish ladder en route to their fresh-water spawning grounds.

Note that even though the park has two dedicated parking lots, these quickly fill up on weekends. ⊠ *8498 Seaview Pl. NW, near N.W. 85th St., Ballard* ☎ *206/684-4075* 🎟 *Free.*

FAMILY **Nordic Heritage Museum.** Celebrating the five Nordic cultures of Sweden, Finland, Norway, Iceland, and Denmark (of which there are many descendants in Ballard), this museum in a massive 1900s schoolhouse traces Scandinavian art, artifacts, and heritage all the way from Viking times. Behind the redbrick walls, nine permanent galleries on three floors give an in-depth look at how immigrants came to America and settled in the Pacific Northwest. Among the finds are textiles, china, books, tools, and photographs. Delve into Nordic history in the library; learn a few phrases at the on-site Scandinavian Language Institute; or join in a class or children's program on Nordic arts and crafts. The galleries display paintings, sculpture, and photography by contemporary artists. In 2016, the museum broke ground on a new 58,000-square-foot location about a mile from the original. Featuring a grand central atrium, the $45 million building is expected to open by the end of 2017. ⊠ *3014 N.W. 67th St., Ballard* ☎ *206/789-5707* ⊕ *www.nordicmuseum.org* 🎟 *$8; 1st Thurs. free.*

WALLINGFORD AND GREEN LAKE

Sightseeing
★★
Dining
★★★★
Lodging
★
Shopping
★★
Nightlife
★★★

Wallingford and Green Lake are low-profile neighborhoods without much in the way of sights to see, but these are great spots for strolling, especially around the eponymous lake.

WALLINGFORD

The laid-back neighborhood of Wallingford is directly east of Fremont—the boundaries actually blur quite a bit. There are several lovely parks and residential streets are brimming with colorful Craftsman houses. The main drag, 45th Street NW, has an eclectic group of shops, from a gourmet beer store to an erotic bakery to a Hawaiian merchant, along with a few great coffeehouses, and several notable restaurants.

In the 1920s, Wallingford was one of the city's most important neighborhoods. It went from forest and cow pasture (one of which, incidentally, hosted Seattle's first golf course for a very short time) to a densely populated neighborhood of 50,000 in less than two decades. The game changer was a trolley line from the University District to Fremont—once the tracks were laid, the bungalow-building frenzy started. Although the initial hoopla died down after a major commercial district on Stone Way never materialized, the neighborhood grew steadily, if quietly. In the past 10 years, however, it's been on everyone's radar again, as some of Seattle's most celebrated chefs—Maria Hines of Tilth and Rachel Yang of Revel and Joule, in particular—have chosen the neighborhood for their distinctive and highly praised restaurants. Other eateries and shops have filled in around 45th's other big draw, a popular two-screen movie theater. By the time the fabulous restaurant Cantinetta opened far off the main drag, it came as no surprise to anyone that Wallingford could be a place where you wait two hours for a table.

TOP ATTRACTIONS

FAMILY

Fodor'sChoice

★

Gas Works Park. Far from being an eyesore, the hulking remains of an old 1907 gas plant actually lends quirky character to the otherwise open, hilly, 20-acre park. Get a great view of Downtown Seattle while seaplanes rise up from the south shore of Lake Union; the best vantage point is from the zodiac sculpture at the top of a very steep hill, so be sure to wear appropriate walking shoes. This is a great spot for couples and families alike; the sand-bottom playground has monkey bars, wooden platforms, and a spinning metal merry-go-round. Crowds throng to picnic and enjoy outdoor summer concerts, movies, and the July 4th fireworks display over Lake Union. ■TIP➜ Gas Works can easily be reached on foot from Fremont Center, via the waterfront Burke-Gilman Trail. ✉ *2101 N. Northlake Way, at Meridian Ave. N (the north end of Lake Union), Wallingford.*

GREEN LAKE

The neighborhood of Green Lake surrounds the eponymous lake, which is 50,000 years old. It was formed by the Vashon Glacial Ice Sheet, which also gave Seattle, among other things, Puget Sound. Green Lake (the neighborhood) is a pleasant stroll. It has a few shops and eateries along the lake, and one standout B&B, if you're looking to be far from Downtown's busy streets.

A GOOD
COMBO

A trip to Woodland Park Zoo (on the border of Phinney Ridge and Green Lake), a stroll around (or boat ride on) adjacent Green Lake, and then exploring Wallingford's main drag (45th Avenue NW) is a great way to spend a sunny day. Or, instead of Wallingford, you could drive to Ballard and peruse its many shops and restaurants.

TOP ATTRACTIONS

FAMILY

Green Lake Park. This beautiful 342-acre park is a favorite of Seattleites, who jog, bike, and walk their dogs along the 2½-mile paved path that surrounds the lake. Beaches on both the east and west sides (around 72nd Street) have lifeguards and swimming rafts. Canoes, kayaks, and paddleboats can be rented (seasonally) at Green Lake Boat Rental on the eastern side of the lake. There are also basketball and tennis courts and baseball and soccer fields. A first-rate play area includes a giant sandbox, swings, slides, and all the climbing equipment a child could ever dream of—and the wading pool is a perfect spot for tots to cool off (in summer, when the temp is above 70 degrees.) The park is generally packed, especially on weekends. And you'd better love dogs: the canine-to-human ratio here is just about even. Surrounding the park are lovely homes, plus a compact commercial district where you can grab snacks or dinner after your walk. ✉ *7201 E. Green Lake Dr. N, Green Lake* ☏ *206/684–4075 general info, 206/527–0171 Greenlake Boat Rental* ⊕ *www.seattle.gov/parks/find/parks/green-lake-park.*

Getting Oriented

Wallingford and
Green Lake

GETTING HERE AND AROUND

Bus 16 connects Downtown to North 45th Street in Wallingford (the neighborhood's main drag) and continues north to the east (and main) entrance of Green Lake Park (get out at 71st and East Green Lake Way). From Downtown it takes about a half hour to reach the lake; the trip between the lake and North 45th Street takes about 10 minutes.

To reach Green Lake by car, take either Aurora Avenue North (Route 99) to West Green Lake Way or I–5 to 50th Street (go west back over the highway at that exit). There are parking lots at both Green Lake Park and Woodland Park; lots at the latter are generally less full. Wallingford is a five-minute drive from Green Lake—if there's no traffic.

QUICK BITES

Fainting Goat Gelato. Sample gelato in seasonal flavors like honey-lavender and fig-vanilla. ✉ *1903 N. 45th St., Wallingford* ☎ *206/327–9459* ⊕ *www.faintinggoatseattle.com* ▭ *No credit cards.*

Hiroki. Hiroki makes wonderful Japanese desserts along with some standards like tiramisu. ✉ *2224 N. 56th St.* ☎ *206/547–4128* ▭ *No credit cards.*

Molly Moon's Homemade Ice Cream. Molly Moon's makes rich, delicious ice creams with local ingredients in flavors like balsamic strawberry and salted caramel. ✉ *1622 N. 45th St., Wallingford* ☎ *206/547–5105* ⊕ *www.mollymoon.com* ▭ *No credit cards.*

Rancho Bravo Tacos. Pork tacos are the favorite at this humble taco truck. ✉ *211 N.E. 45th St., between N. Thackeray Pl. and N. 2nd Ave.* ☎ *206/466–1693* ⊕ *www.ranchobravo-tacos.com* ▭ *No credit cards.*

Tutta Bella Neapolitan Pizzeria. Family-friendly Tutta Bella makes delicious pizza and salads. ✉ *4411 Stone Way N, Wallingford* ☎ *206/633–3800* ⊕ *www.tuttabella.com* ▭ *No credit cards.*

PLANNING YOUR TIME

Green Lake is adjacent to Woodland Park Zoo. In summer, you could spend an entire day outdoors, touring the zoo, then strolling around the lake—or floating in a rented rowboat or paddleboat. The Tangletown area of Green Lake can be reached on foot (follow North 55th Street east to the "K" streets of Kenwood, Keystone, Kirkwood, and Kensington) and has a few great casual eateries. Some of the city's best chefs have put down roots in Wallingford, making the neighborhood a good place to end the day.

TOP REASONS TO GO

Enjoy the definitive north-shore view of Lake Union from **Gas Works Park**, which incorporates the rusting remnants of the historic gas works plant.

Go souvenir hunting at **Archie McPhee**, a shrine to irreverence. You'll find great Seattle-themed items here, like Tofu Mints and librarian and barista action figures, amid tons of assorted weirdness and fun *(See the Shopping listing).*

Visit the "poem emporium"— **Open Books** is one of two poetry-only bookstores in the country.

Stroll or jog around **Green Lake's** loop. If your running shoes are a little ragged, stop at Super Jock 'n' Jill (✉ *7210 E. Green Lake Drive N* ☎ *206/522–7711*) for a new pair.

UNIVERSITY DISTRICT

Sightseeing
★★
Dining
★★★
Lodging
★★★
Shopping
★
Nightlife
★★

The U-District, as everyone calls it, is the neighborhood surrounding the University of Washington (UW or "U-Dub" to locals). The campus is extraordinarily beautiful (especially in springtime, when the cherry blossoms are flowering), and the Henry Art Gallery, on its western edge, is one of the city's best small museums. Beyond that, the appeal of the neighborhood lies in its variety of cheap, delicious ethnic eateries, its proximity to the waters of Portage and Union Bays and Lake Washington, and its youthful energy.

The U-District isn't everyone's cup of chai. Almost all businesses are geared toward students, and the area has its own transient population. The U-District often feels like it's separate from the city—and that's no accident. The university was founded in 1861 and was constructed on newly clear-cut land long before there were any convenient ways to get to the city that was growing Downtown. More so than any other northern neighborhood, the U-District had to be self-sufficient, even though the light-rail now links the neighborhood with Capitol Hill and Downtown. Residents don't even have to travel to Downtown to get their shopping done: they have their own upscale megamall, University Village ("U Village"), an elegant outdoor shopping center with an Apple store, chain stores (including H&M, Gap, Eddie Bauer, Crate & Barrel, Room & Board, and Banana Republic), as well as restaurants, boutiques, and two large grocery stores. The Burke-Gilman Trail, Magnuson Park, and the UW Botanic Gardens Center for Urban Horticulture offer scenic detours.

Fascinating exhibits fill the Burke Museum of Natural History and Culture.

TOP ATTRACTIONS

FAMILY **Burke Museum of Natural History and Culture.** Founded in 1899, the Burke is the state's oldest museum, featuring exhibits that survey the natural history of the Pacific Northwest. Highlights include artifacts from Washington's 35 Native American tribes, dinosaur skeletons, and dioramas depicting the traditions of Pacific Rim cultures. An adjacent ethnobotanical garden is planted with species that were important to the region's Native American communities. Check out the schedule for family events and adult classes. ⊠ *University of Washington campus, 17th Ave. NE and N.E. 45th St., University District* ☎ *206/543–5590* ⊕ *www.burkemuseum.org* ✉ *$10, free 1st Thurs. of month.*

Center for Urban Horticulture. Nestled between a residential lakefront neighborhood to the east and the University of Washington campus to the west are the 16-acre landscaped gardens of the Center for Urban Horticulture and the 74-acre Union Bay Natural Area, part of the University of Washington Botanic Gardens. Inside the Center is the Elisabeth C. Miller Library, open to the public and home to 15,000 books and 500 periodicals on gardening techniques. The Union Bay Natural Area serves as an outdoor laboratory for UW research with some of the best bird-watching in the city. With a ¾-mile loop gravel trail, it's also a terrific place for a walk or a jog, and on a nice day, the views of Mt. Rainier and the surrounding waterfront are simply divine. From the U-District, head east on N.E. 45th Street and take a right onto Mary Gates Drive. ⊠ *3501 N.E. 41st St., University District* ☎ *206/543–8616* ⊕ *depts.washington.edu/uwbg/visit/cuh.php.*

Getting Oriented

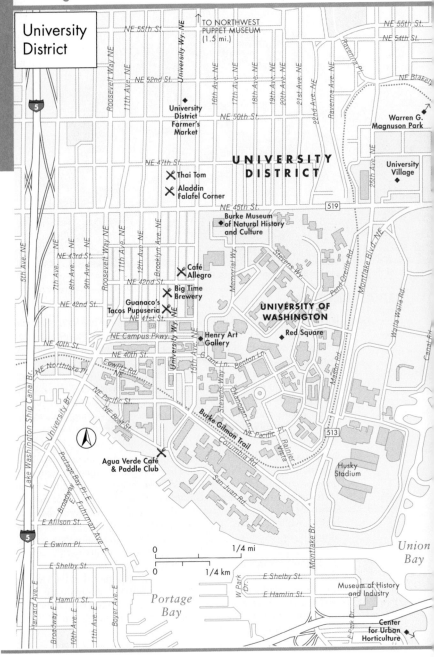

University
District

TO NORTHWEST
PUPPET MUSEUM
(1.5 mi.)

NE 55th St.

NE 54th St.

NE 55th St.

NE Blakely

Warren G.
Magnuson Park

University
District
Farmer's
Market

NE 50th St.

University
Village

NE 47th St.

**UNIVERSITY
DISTRICT**

Thai Tom

Aladdin
Falafel Corner

NE 45th St.

Burke Museum
of Natural History
and Culture

Café
Allegro

Big Time
Brewery

Guanaco's
Tacos Pupuseria

Henry Art
Gallery

**UNIVERSITY OF
WASHINGTON**

Red Square

NE Campus Pkwy.

NE 40th St.

NE Northlake Pl.

NE Pacific St.

Burke-Gilman Trail

Agua Verde Café
& Paddle Club

Husky
Stadium

*Union
Bay*

E Allison St.

E Gwinn Pl.

E Shelby St.

0   1/4 mi

0   1/4 km

E Hamlin St.

*Portage
Bay*

E Shelby St.

E Hamlin St.

Museum of History
and Industry

Center
for Urban
Horticulture

GETTING HERE AND AROUND

A quick light-rail ride takes you from Downtown or Capitol Hill to the Link light-rail underground station next to Husky Stadium. From there it's a 25-minute walk to the heart of the area, or a quick ride on the 73 bus. Driving is the easiest solution; unless you hit traffic, taking I–5 north to 45th Street takes only 10 minutes from Downtown.

Bus 43, which you can catch Downtown along Pike Street, takes a pleasant route through Capitol Hill, over the Montlake Bridge, and stops on the western side of the campus in front of the Henry Art Gallery.

Getting around the U-District is fairly easy. The major action happens on "The Ave" (University Way NE), between 42nd and 50th Streets. Getting to the other northern neighborhoods of Wallingford, Fremont, and Ballard is easy, too. The only thing not convenient is the University Village shopping center, which is a long walk.

TOP REASONS TO GO

See the **Red Square,** UW's main plaza, named for its brick paving. Stop here for views of college life and, on sunny days, Mt. Rainier (it's also one of the best places to spot spring's fleeting cherry-blossom bloom). Then check out the well-curated exhibits at the **Henry Art Gallery.**

Paddle around **Portage Bay** from Agua Verde Café & Paddle Club. They can set you up with a kayak—and a margarita and Mexican grub when you return.

Make a detour to the **Center for Urban Horticulture,** which is across the street from outdoor shopping center **University Village,** on the shores of Lake Washington, for a relaxing stroll, bird-watching, or an evening picnic.

Big Time Brewery & Alehouse. Sidle up to the antique bar at this hot spot for students and faculty from nearby UW, for a good selection of suds and pizza. ⊠ 4133 University Way NE, University District ☎ 206/545–4509 ⊕ www.bigtimebrewery.com.

QUICK BITES

Aladdin Falafel Corner. Lamb gyros, falafel sandwiches, and hummus platters are all excellent here. ⊠ 4541 University Way NE, University District ☎ 206/548–9539.

Café Allegro. This rustic, brick-walled cafe is Seattle's oldest espresso bar. ⊠ 4214 University Way NE, University District ☎ 206/633–3030 ⊕ www.seattleallegro.com.

Guanaco's Tacos Pupusería. Try the fried plantains and *pupusas* (corn pancakes stuffed with meats, veggies, or beans). ⊠ 4106 Brooklyn Ave. NE, Suite 102, University District ☎ 206/547–2369 ⊕ guanacostacos.weebly.com.

Portage Bay Cafe. Portage Bay Cafe serves organic and sustainable breakfast, brunch, and lunch. ⊠ 4130 Roosevelt Way NE, University District ☎ 206/547–8230 ⊕ www.portagebaycafe.com.

PLANNING YOUR TIME

The few sights the neighborhood has are helpfully grouped close together. The Henry Art Gallery and the Burke Museum are on the lovely UW campus. You can combine a museum stop with a campus stroll and then hit The Ave (the area's main drag) for lunch.

The Henry Art Gallery is well worth the trip. Stroll around the UW campus in the morning, especially if you happen to visit during the spring when the school's many cherry blossom trees are blooming. Then pay a visit to the Henry when it opens at 11 am, followed by spicy Vietnamese pho or Thai curry for lunch on The Ave—the U-District's main drag. If you still have energy, stroll from there to the Montlake Bridge; part of your walk can be along the Burke Gilman Trail. The bridge is a fun place to watch passing boats and kayakers in summer.

Fodor's Choice
★

Henry Art Gallery. This large gallery is perhaps the best reason to take a side trip to the U-District and consistently presents sophisticated and thought-provoking contemporary work. Exhibits pull from many different genres and include mixed media, photography, and paintings. Richard C. Elliott used more than 21,500 bicycle and truck reflectors of different colors and sizes in his paintings that fit into the sculpture alcoves on the exterior walls of the museum; in another permanent installation, *Light Reign,* a "Skyspace" from artist James Turrell, an elliptical chamber allows visitors to view the sky. More than a few people have used this as a meditation spot; at night the chamber is illuminated by thousands of LED lights. ⊠ *University of Washington campus, 15th Ave. NE and N.E. 41st St., University District* ☎ *206/543–2280* ⊕ *www.henryart.org* ⊠ *$10.*

University District Farmer's Market. Seattle's largest "farmers only" market (no crafts, imports, or flea-market finds) operates year-round on Saturday from 9 am to 2 pm in the heart of the U-District, rain or shine. With more than 50 Washington State farmers participating, you'll find a great selection of produce, baked goods, preserves, flowers, cheese, soups, pies, wines, pasta, and handmade chocolates. ⊠ *Corner of University Way NE and N.E. 50th St., University District* ⊕ *seattle-farmersmarkets.org/markets/u-district.*

Warren G. Magnuson Park. Also called Sand Point–Magnuson Park and most often simply Magnuson Park, this 350-acre park northeast of the University District was once an active naval air base. Evidence of the park's roots are on full (if somewhat decrepit) display, with barracks and hangars in various stages of use and upkeep. Keep your focus on the areas toward the lake, as the paved trails are wonderful for cycling, jogging, or pushing a stroller. Leashed dogs are welcome on the trails; a gigantic off-leash area includes one of the few public beaches where pooches can swim. Farther south, on the mile-long shore, there's a swimming beach, a seasonal wading pool, and a boat launch. Innovative art is threaded through the grounds, including *Fin Art* (made from submarine fins, on Kite Hill) and "Straight Shot," allowing visitors to experience what a surveyor does. A fabulous playground engages little ones near the north end. To get here from the U-District, you can follow 45th Street northeast past the University Village shopping center until it turns into Sand Point Way, and then follow Sand Point until you reach the park. If you're coming from Downtown, take I–5 to the 65th Street exit and head east on 65th until you reach the park. Note that

The outdoor space of the Henry Art Gallery

traffic around University Village is usually pretty slow, especially on weekends. ⊠ *Park entrance, 6500 Sand Point Way NE, Sand Point* ☎ *206/684–4946* ⊕ *www.seattle.gov/parks/magnuson.*

WORTH NOTING

OFF THE
BEATEN
PATH

Northwest Puppet Center. In a renovated church in the Maple Leaf neighborhood, the only puppet center in the Northwest highlights the renowned marionettes of the Carter family, professional puppeteers trained by masters from Italy, Romania, and China. For their talents they have received a Fulbright Award and a UNIMA/USA Citation of Excellence, the highest award in American puppet theater. New museum exhibits are curated about every six months and may focus on a particular tradition, technique, or historic period. Past exhibits have included "Puppetry from Around the World" and "Cheering up the Great Depression: Puppetry & the WPA." Performances are open to the public on weekends. Recent shows include *Rapunzel, Puss in Boots,* and *Aladdin and the Wonderful Lamp.* The museum is open before and after shows, or by appointment. ⊠ *9123 15th Ave. NE, University District* ✛ *Take I–5 north, Exit 171 to Lake City Way, turn left on 15th Ave. NE and continue to 92nd St.* ☎ *206/523–2579* ⊕ *www.nwpuppet.org* ✉ *Museum is free, performance ticket prices vary; call ahead to reserve.*

WEST SEATTLE

Sightseeing
★★
Dining
★★★
Lodging
★
Shopping
★★
Nightlife
★

Cross the bridge to West Seattle and it's another world altogether. Jutting out into Elliott Bay and Puget Sound, separated from the city by the Duwamish waterway, this out-of-the-way neighborhood covers most of the city's western peninsula—and, indeed, it has an identity of its own. In summer, throngs of people hang out at Alki Beach—Seattle's taste of California—while others head for the trails and playgrounds of Lincoln Park to the west.

The first white settlers parked their boat at Alki Point in 1851, planning to build a major city here until they discovered a deeper logging port at today's Pioneer Square. This makes West Seattle technically the city's oldest neighborhood. West Seattle is huge, and within it are more than a dozen neighborhoods. The two most visitors will see are Alki and West Seattle Junction—the former includes the shoreline and Alki Point; the Alki Point Lighthouse sits on the peninsula's northwest tip, a place for classic sunset views. The main shopping and dining areas line Alki Avenue, next to the beach, and California and Fauntleroy Avenues on the way to the ferry docks. The latter neighborhood, named for a spot where old streetcar lines crisscrossed, is the fastest-growing part of West Seattle and has its own thriving dining scene. It also has most of the area's good shopping and ArtsWest, a community theater and gallery.

The Admiral neighborhood, on the northern bluff, is less vital, but it does have an important old movie house that is one of the venues for the Seattle International Film Festival. Fauntleroy has two main attractions: the lovely Lincoln Park and a ferry terminal with service to Vashon Island and Southworth on the Kitsap Peninsula.

PARKS CLOSE TO ALKI

Lincoln Park. Along the neighborhood's southwest edge, near the Fauntleroy ferry terminal, Lincoln Park sets acres of old forests, rocky beaches, waterfront trails, picnic tables, and a historic saltwater pool against views of Puget Sound. ■TIP→ Colman Pool is a Seattle landmark you won't want to miss in summer. It's located on the water toward the north end of the park. Public swims often sell out on nice days, so get there early. ⊠ *8011 Fauntleroy Way SW, West Seattle* ☎ *206/684–4075*

park, 206/684–7494 Colman pool ⊕ *www.seattle.gov/parks/park_detail. asp?id=460 (park), www.seattle.gov/ parks/aquatics/colman.htm (pool)* ☜ *Park is free; pool, $5.25.*

Schmitz Preserve Park. Marvel at the lustrous 53 acres of rugged forest at Schmitz Preserve, about 15 blocks east of Alki Point. The Preserve was donated to the city in pieces between 1908 and 1912, and features one of the remaining stands of old-growth forest in Seattle. ⊠ *5551 S.W. Admiral Way, West Seattle* ⊕ *www.seattle. gov/parks/park_detail.asp?id=465.*

TOP ATTRACTIONS

FAMILY

Fodor'sChoice

★

Alki Point and Beach. In summer, this is as close to California as Seattle gets—and some hardy residents even swim in the cold, salty waters of Puget Sound here (water temperature ranges from 46 to 56°F). This 2½-mile stretch of sand has views of the Seattle skyline and the Olympic Mountains, and the beachfront promenade is especially popular with skaters, joggers, strollers, and cyclists. Year-round, Seattleites come to build sand castles, beachcomb, and fly kites; in winter, storm-watchers come to see the crashing waves. Facilities include drinking water, grills, picnic tables, phones, and restrooms; restaurants line the street across from the beach. To get here from Downtown, take either I–5 south or Highway 99 south to the West Seattle Bridge (keep an eye out, as this exit is easy to miss) and exit onto Harbor Avenue SW, turning right at the stoplight. Alki Point is the place where David Denny, John Low, and Lee Terry arrived in September 1851, ready to found a city. The Alki Point Lighthouse dates from 1913. One of 195 Lady Liberty replicas found around the country lives near the 2700 block of Alki Avenue SW. Miss Liberty (or Little Liberty) is a popular meeting point for beachfront picnics and dates. ⊠ *1702 Alki Ave. SW, West Seattle.*

OFF THE BEATEN PATH

The Museum of Flight. Boeing, the world's largest builder of aircraft, was founded in Seattle in 1916. This facility at Boeing Field, close to Sea-Tac airport, houses one of the city's best museums, and it's especially fun for kids, who can climb in many of the aircraft and pretend to fly, make flight-related crafts, or attend special programs. The Red Barn, Boeing's original airplane factory, houses an exhibit on the history of flight. The Great Gallery, a dramatic structure designed by Ibsen Nelson, contains more than three dozen vintage airplanes. The Personal Courage Wing showcases World War I and World War II fighter planes, and the Charles Simonyi Space Gallery is home to the NASA Full Fuselage Space Shuttle Trainer. ⊠ *9404 E. Marginal Way S, Tukwila* ⊹ *Take I–5 south to Exit 158, turn right on Marginal Way S* ☎ *206/764–5720* ⊕ *www.museumofflight.org* ☜ *$21.*

Getting Oriented

West Seattle

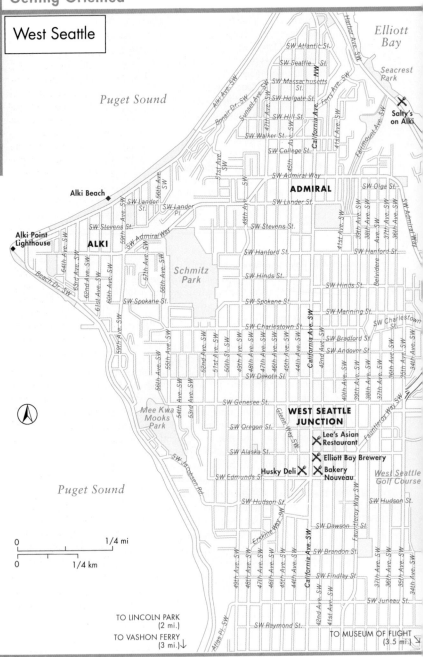

Puget Sound

Elliott Bay

Seacrest Park

Salty's on Alki

ADMIRAL

Alki Beach

Alki Point Lighthouse

ALKI

Schmitz Park

Mee Kwa Mooks Park

Puget Sound

WEST SEATTLE JUNCTION

Lee's Asian Restaurant

Elliott Bay Brewery

Husky Deli

Bakery Nouveau

West Seattle Golf Course

0   1/4 mi

0   1/4 km

TO LINCOLN PARK (2 mi.)
TO VASHON FERRY (3 mi.)↓

TO MUSEUM OF FLIGHT (3.5 mi.)→

GETTING HERE AND AROUND

Driving south on I-5, take the West Seattle Bridge exit (which is easy to miss). The Harbor Avenue SW exit will take you to Alki Beach; S.W. Admiral Way will get you to California Avenue. By bus, take Bus 22, 56, or 57 from Downtown; all travel along 1st Avenue, cross the West Seattle Bridge, and stop at California Avenue. Buses 56 and 57 continue on to the western edge of Alki Beach.

West Seattle is huge and easiest to traverse by car. However, if you arrived by West Seattle Water Taxi (a passenger- and bicycle-only ferry that travels from Pier 50, along the waterfront Downtown, to Seacrest Park at the peninsula's eastern shore), you have several other transit options: You can rent a bicycle at Seacrest, which will get you around the beach areas and up to the restaurants on California Avenue. Or you can take Bus 54 to California Avenue, or hop on Bus 37, which travels around the peninsula almost as far as Lincoln Park.

QUICK BITES

Bakery Nouveau. Bakery Nouveau has an exquisite selection of pastries, sandwiches, croissants, and baguettes. ⊠ *4737 California Ave. SW, West Seattle* ☎ *206/923–0534* ⊕ *www.bakerynouveau.com* ▭ *No credit cards.*

Elliott Bay Brewing Company. Elliott Bay Brewing Company serves craft beers and sandwiches and salads. ⊠ *4720 California Ave. SW* ☎ *206/932–8695* ⊕ *www. elliottbaybrewing.com* ▭ *No credit cards.*

Husky Deli. Grab a handcrafted ice-cream cone at Husky Deli, a Seattle icon. ⊠ *4721 California Ave. SW, West Seattle* ☎ *206/937–2810* ⊕ *www.huskydeli.com* ▭ *No credit cards.*

Salty's on Alki. Salty's is an iconic, family-friendly seafood restaurant with unbeatable views. ⊠ *1936 Harbor Ave. SW, West Seattle* ☎ *206/937–1600* ⊕ *www.saltys.com* ▭ *No credit cards.*

PLANNING YOUR TIME

Head to Alki Beach and follow a path around the peninsula, enjoying the shoreline, Alki Point Lighthouse, and Lincoln Park. This is easiest to do by car. If you arrived by water taxi from Downtown, however, you can rent a bicycle by the terminal and bike the same route; the trip by bike takes roughly 35 minutes. California Avenue, which is in the center of the peninsula, can be your last stop, for sustenance.

TOP REASONS TO GO

See where it all started at **Alki Point.** Any trip to West Seattle should include some beach time on Alki Beach. But be sure to make it around the western edge of the peninsula to see the lighthouse and the spot where the first settlers landed.

Dine on **California Avenue SW.** The stretch between S.W. Genesee and S.W. Edmonds streets has most of West Seattle's notable eateries, from hip coffee shops to delicious restaurants.

Cool off after a beach stroll in the saltwater swimming pool at **Lincoln Park.**

Catch the ferry to **Vashon Island.** The Fauntleroy terminal is the launching point for ferries to Vashon, where you can visit orchards, farms, and wineries.

Climb **Schurman Rock,** an outdoor climbing gym next to the West Seattle Golf Course.

Historic aircraft at the Great Gallery, Museum of Flight

WORTH NOTING

West Seattle Junction Murals. Walk through West Seattle's business district amid the small restaurants, shops, and businesses, and you'll come across murals depicting scenes from local history on various buildings. There are 11 murals total; the project won a national Neighborhood of the Year Award from Neighborhoods, USA, in 1992. A few play tricks with perspective, reminiscent of the paintings Wile E. Coyote used in his attempts to trick the Roadrunner. *The Junction* is a perfect example: if not for the row of neatly trimmed laurel bushes just beneath the wall upon which it's painted, you might be tempted to walk right into the picture's 1918 street scene, painted from the perspective of a streetcar. Another mural is taken from a postcard of 1920s Alki. The most colorful, however, is the *The Hi-Yu Parade*, with its rendition of a *Wizard of Oz*–theme float reminding locals of a 1973 summer celebration. ⊠ *Along California Ave. SW and Fauntleroy Way SW, between 44th and 47th Aves., West Seattle.*

THE EASTSIDE

Sightseeing
★★
Dining
★★★
Lodging
★★★
Shopping
★★★★
Nightlife
★★★

The suburbs east of Lake Washington can easily supplement any Seattle itinerary. The center of East King County is Bellevue, a fast-growing city with its own downtown core, high-end shopping, and a notable dining scene. Kirkland, north of Bellevue, has a few shops and restaurants (including fabulous Café Juanita) plus lakefront promenades. Redmond and Issaquah, to the northeast and southeast respectively, are gateways to greenery. Woodinville, north of Redmond, is the ambassador for Washington State's wine industry, with many wineries and tasting rooms, as well as a growing number of breweries and distilleries. Redmond itself is home to Microsoft's gigantic campus. Drivers now have to pay a toll to cross the 520 Bridge to the Eastside.

Three-quarters of a century ago, Bellevue was a pleasant little town in the country, with rows of shops along Main Street serving the local strawberry farmers. Today it's fast becoming a destination in itself, with snazzy shopping malls, restaurants, and a strong art museum.

Kirkland's business district, along the Lake Street waterfront, is lined with shops, restaurants, pubs, and parks. At the height of summer, it's often warm enough to swim in the sheltered waters of Lake Washington; Juanita Beach Park is a popular spot with an enclosed swimming area.

A string of pretty parks makes Redmond an inviting place to experience the outdoors, and the 13-mile Sammamish River Trail is an attraction for locals and tourists alike. The rapidly expanding city is today one of the country's most powerful business capitals, thanks to the presence of such companies as Microsoft, Nintendo, and Eddie Bauer. Although there are several good malls and a lot of generic strip-mall stores, this isn't a place to shop—locals come here either to work or to play outdoors.

Issaquah is experiencing rapid (and not terribly attractive) development, but it's what lies beyond the subdivisions that counts. The surrounding Cougar, Tiger, and Squak mountain foothills—dubbed the Issaquah Alps—are older than the Cascade Range and pocketed with caves, parks, and trails. This area has some of the most accessible hiking and mountain biking in the Seattle area; Seattleites often use these trails to train on in early spring before the more arduous trails in the Cascades and Olympics open for hiking season.

Woodinville is perhaps the Eastside's most popular day trip. It's the home of Chateau Ste. Michelle and dozens of other wineries plus destination restaurant The Herbfarm. Additionally, luxurious Willows Lodge is walking distance from the main attractions, making Woodinville an ideal place for a romantic getaway.

TOP ATTRACTIONS

Bellevue Arts Museum. A real feather in Bellevue's cap, this museum presents sophisticated exhibits on craft and design, with a focus on regional artists. Past exhibitions have included *High Fiber Diet*—focusing on underexposed media in contemporary art—and *Modern Twist: Contemporary Japanese Bamboo Art*. The dramatic puzzle-piece-looking building, which really stands out in Bellevue's somewhat uninspired downtown core, is worth the trip alone. Tours happen daily at 1 pm and workshops for kids, teens, and adults are offered regularly. In late July, the museum hosts the BAM ARTSfair, a prestigious, high-end street festival held at Bellevue Square and Bellevue Arts Museum. ✉ *510 Bellevue Way NE, Bellevue* ☎ *425/519–0770* ⊕ *www.bellevuearts.org* ⊠ *$12.*

Bellevue Botanical Gardens. This beautiful 53-acre public area next to Wilburton Hill Park and just a short drive from downtown Bellevue is encircled by spectacular perennial borders, brilliant rhododendron displays, and patches of alpine and rock gardens. A new area, the Ravine Experience, encompasses a 5-acre area in the heavily forested southwest corner of the gardens with a 1/3-mile nature trail. A 150-foot suspension bridge crosses a deep ravine in one of the most pristine spaces, allowing visitors to observe unique topography and soaring conifers without disturbing the forest floor. Docents lead tours of the gardens Saturdays and Sundays (April through October), beginning at the visitor center at 2 pm. The Yao Japanese garden is especially beautiful in fall. One of the most interesting features of the park is the Waterwise Garden, which was planted with greenery that needs little water in summer. During the holiday season (late November–late December), the gardens are lit up nightly from 5 to 10 pm for Garden d'Lights, one of the area's most popular seasonal attractions. From downtown Bellevue, head south on 116th to S.E. 1st Street and take a right on Main Street. ✉ *12001 Main St., Bellevue* ☎ *425/452–2750* ⊕ *www.bellevuebotanical.org* ⊠ *Free; winter Garden d'Lights festival, $5.*

Getting Oriented

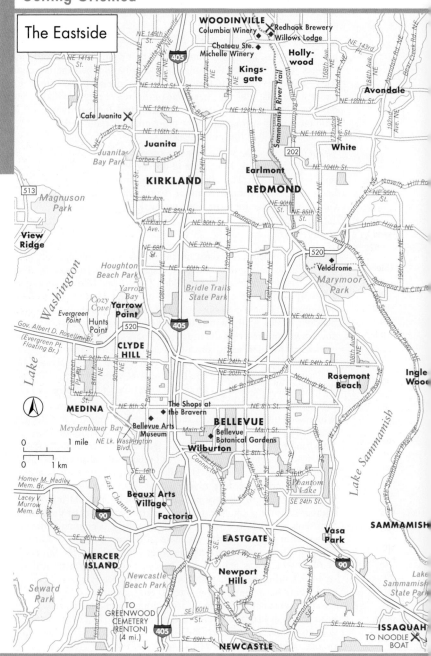

The Eastside

WOODINVILLE
Columbia Winery
Redhook Brewery
Willows Lodge
Chateau Ste.
Michelle Winery
Holly-wood
Kings-gate
Avondale
Cafe Juanita
Juanita
White
Juanita Bay Park
Forbes Creek Dr.
Earlmont
KIRKLAND
REDMOND
Magnuson Park
View Ridge
Velodrome
Houghton Beach Park
Marymoor Park
Bridle Trails State Park
Yarrow Bay
Cozy Cove
Yarrow Point
Evergreen Point
Hunts Point
Gov. Albert D. Rosellini Br.
(Evergreen Pt. Floating Br.)
CLYDE HILL
Lake Washington
Rosemont Beach
Ingle Wood
MEDINA
The Shops at the Bravern
Meydenbauer Bay
Bellevue Arts Museum
BELLEVUE
Bellevue Botanical Gardens
Wilburton
Lake Sammamish
0   1 mile
0   1 km
Homer M. Hadley Mem. Br.
Lacey V. Murrow Mem. Br.
Beaux Arts Village
Phantom Lake
Factoria
East Channel
SAMMAMISH
MERCER ISLAND
Vasa Park
EASTGATE
Seward Park
Newcastle Beach Park
Newport Hills
Lake Sammamish State Park
TO GREENWOOD CEMETERY (RENTON) (4 mi.)
ISSAQUAH
TO NOODLE BOAT
NEWCASTLE

PLANNING YOUR TIME

There are quite a few hotels on the Eastside, mainly in Bellevue, Kirkland, and Woodinville, but unless you're planning an overnight at Willows Lodge after touring Woodinville's wineries, it's not worth staying here. You won't save any money—Bellevue's hotels are just as pricey as and far less interesting than Seattle's—and no local would recommend a daily commute to or from Seattle, especially with the 520 bridge toll.

Instead, plan targeted day trips to the Eastside: a shopping or museum excursion to Bellevue followed by a meal at one of the city's hot restaurants; a winery or brewery crawl in Woodinville; or a day of hiking, biking, or horseback riding that ends in time to return to Seattle for a shower and a nap before a night out.

TOP REASONS TO GO

Explore **Tiger Mountain,** the most popular hiking (and biking) spot a hop, skip, and jump from Seattle, with a large trail system and something for everyone, from grandparents to trail runners.

Feel the wind on your face in the **Velodrome:** Marymoor Park's bicycle racing track is open to the public, and although track bikes are given right-of-way, you can take a spin on any road bike. If you'd rather be a spectator, races are held weekly in summer.

Visit the **Bellevue Botanical Gardens,** a 36-acre park with colorful gardens and trails.

Splurge at the **Shops at the Bravern** in Bellevue. The city has many malls, but the Bravern is the ritziest—one-stop shopping for major international labels like Jimmy Choo, Ferragamo, and Hermès.

Sample Northwest wines in **Woodinville.** The town has more than 140 wineries, wine bars, and tasting rooms, most within easy reach of each other.

2

GETTING HERE AND AROUND

Buses run to the Eastside, but it's easier to get here by car, though you'll pay a toll crossing the 520 floating bridge, and rush-hour traffic is a nightmare. The other route to the Eastside is I–5 South to I–90 East. Bellevue is the most accessible town by public transportation (⊕ www.soundtransit.org). It has a bus hub that's within walking distance of the art museum. The most direct bus route to central Bellevue is the Bus 550.

QUICK BITES

Lunchbox Laboratory. This popular spot serves unique burgers and boozy milk shakes. ⊠ 989 112th Ave. NE #105, Bellevue ☎ 425/505–2676 ⊕ www.lunchboxlaboratory.com.

Noodle Boat. If you're craving Thai food, try delicious Noodle Boat. ⊠ 700 N.W. Gilman Blvd., Issaquah ☎ 425/391–8096 ⊕ www.noodleboat.com ⊜ No credit cards.

Redhook Brewery. The Redhook Brewery serves quality bar food; tours of the brewery are offered daily. ⊠ 14300 N.E. 145th St., Woodinville ☎ 425/483–3232 ⊕ www.redhook.com ⊜ No credit cards.

Twisted Cuban Cafe. This Cuban eatery serves tasty sandwiches and entrées, as well as mojitos. ⊠ 12631 N.E. Woodinville Dr., Woodinville ☎ 425/806–7203 ⊕ www.twistedcubancafe.com.

Chateau Ste. Michelle Winery. One of the state's oldest wineries lies 15 miles northeast of Seattle. Once part of the estate of lumber baron Fred Stimson, these 107 acres include the original trout ponds, a carriage house, a caretaker's cottage, formal gardens, and the 1912 family manor house (which is on the National Register of Historic Places). Complimentary wine tastings and cellar tours run throughout the day. Specialty tours and tastings (vintage reserve tastings and theme tastings) are $10–$20. You're also invited to picnic and explore the grounds on your own; the wine shop sells delicatessen items. In summer Chateau Ste. Michelle hosts nationally known performers and arts events in its amphitheater. ⊠ *14111 N.E. 145th St., Woodinville ✛ From Downtown Seattle take I–90 east to north I–405; take Exit 23 east (Hwy. 522) to Woodinville exit* ☎ *425/488–1133* ⊕ *www.ste-michelle.com* ◪ *Free.*

FAMILY **Marymoor Park.** It's not just famous for its Marymoor Velodrome, the Pacific Northwest's sole cycling arena. This 640-acre park also has a 45-foot-high climbing rock, game fields, tennis courts, a model airplane launching area, a huge off-leash dog park, and the Pea Patch community garden. You can row on Lake Sammamish, rent a free bike via the Blue Bike program or head straight to the picnic grounds or to the Willowmoor Farm, an estate inside the park.

Marymoor has some of the best bird-watching in this largely urban area. It's possible to spot some 24 resident species, including great blue herons, belted kingfishers, buffleheads, short-eared and barn owls, and red-tailed hawks. Occasionally, bald eagles soar past the lakefront. The Sammamish River, which flows through the western section of the park, is an important salmon spawning stream.

Ambitious bikers can follow the Burke-Gilman Sammamish River Trail to access the park; Marymoor is just over 20 miles from Seattle and it's a flat ride most of the way. ⊠ *6046 W. Lake Sammamish Pkwy. NE, Redmond ✛ Take Rte. 520 east to W. Lake Sammamish Pkwy. exit. Turn right (southbound) on W. Lake Sammamish Pkwy. NE. Turn left at traffic light* ☎ *206/296–8687* ⊕ *www.kingcounty.gov/recreation/parks/inventory/marymoor.aspx.*

WORTH NOTING

FAMILY **Burke-Gilman/Sammamish River Trail.** Approximately 27 miles long, the paved, flat, tree-lined Burke-Gilman Trail runs from Seattle's Gas Works Park, on Lake Union, east along an old railroad right-of-way along the ship canal, and then north along Lake Washington's eastern shore. At Blyth Park in Bothell, the trail becomes the Sammamish River Trail and continues for 10 miles to Marymoor Park in Redmond. Except for a stretch of the Sammamish River Trail between Woodinville and Marymoor Park, where horses are permitted on a parallel trail, the path is limited to walkers, runners, and bicyclists. ■TIP➔ **There are a handful of bike rental shops on Sand Point Way, just north of the University of Washington, an easy access point for the trail. For additional access points, view the map online at www.seattle.gov/transportation/burke-gilmantrailmaps.htm.** ⊠ *Seattle* ⊕ *www.ci.seattle.wa.us/parks/burkegilman/bgtrail.htm.*

2

Columbia Winery. A group of UW professors cofounded this winery in 1962, making it the state's oldest. Using only European vinifera-style grapes grown in eastern Washington, the founders' aim was to take advantage of the fact that the vineyards share the same latitude as the best wine-producing areas of France. Wine tastings are held daily; stop in for a glass of Riesling and flatbread pizza Wednesday–Sunday. ⊠ *14030 N.E. 145th St., Woodinville* ✛ *From Downtown Seattle take I–90 east to north I–405; take Exit 23 east (Hwy. 522) to Woodinville exit, go right. Go right again on 175th St., and left on Hwy. 202* ☎ *425/482–7490, 800/488–2347* ⊕ *www.columbiawinery.com* ⊠ *Winery visit free; wine tastings $10–$25.*

Houghton Beach Park. On hot days, sun worshippers, swimmers, and the beach-volleyball crowd flock to this beach south of downtown Kirkland on the Lake Washington waterfront. The rest of the year, the playground attracts families, and the fishing pier stays busy with anglers. Facilities include drinking water, picnic tables, a beach volleyball court, phones, and restrooms. Park the car and slip on some good walking shoes; it's a lovely walk along the waterfront to the shops and restaurants of either Carillon Point or downtown Kirkland. ⊠ *5811 Lake Washington Blvd., Kirkland* ☎ *425/587–3000* ⊕ *www. kirklandwa.gov/depart/parks.*

OFF THE
BEATEN
PATH

Jimi Hendrix Grave Site. Since his death in 1970, the famed guitarist has rested in Greenwood Cemetery. The site includes a memorial with a domed roof and granite columns. ⊠ *350 Monroe Ave. NE, Renton* ✛ *Take I–5 south to I–405 north and WA–169 south (S.E. Maple Valley Hwy.) exit, keeping left at fork in ramp. Merge onto S.E. Maple Valley Hwy./WA–169 north. Take right on Sunset Blvd. N, then right at N.E. 3rd St. Continue 1 mile, as N.E. 3rd St. becomes N.E. 4th St. Turn right at 3rd light* ⊕ *www.jimihendrixmemorial.com.*

FAMILY **Juanita Bay Park.** A 110-acre urban wildlife habitat, this marshy wetland is the perfect spot to don your binoculars to spot songbirds, shorebirds, turtles, beavers, and other small mammals. Interpretive signs are located throughout the park for self-guided tours along paved trails and boardwalks; or take one of the guided tours conducted by volunteer park rangers from the Eastside Audubon Society. ■**TIP**➜ Just to the north of Juanita Bay Park is Juanita Beach Park, a great spot for picnicking, sunbathing, and swimming. On Friday night, May through October, there's a farmers' market. The first Friday of each month is Kid's Day, with crafts, bouncy houses, goats, and puppet shows. ⊠ *2201 Market St., Kirkland* ☎ *425/576–8805 Eastside Audubon Society* ⊕ *www.kirklandwa.gov/depart/parks.*

FAMILY **Lake Sammamish State Park.** Due to Washington State budget cuts, a Discover Pass is now required at all state parks ($10 for the day or $30 for the year), which has made for a more subdued experience at this 512-acre day-use park just off I–90. Though lifeguards are no longer on duty, there are two sandy beaches, plenty of picnic tables (it's best to bring your own basket rather than test the concessions), a playground, and seasonal kayak and paddleboard rentals via Issaquah Paddle Sports (*206/527–1825*). There are a few shady walking trails, and if you head east, you can connect to the Samammish River Trail and walk or bike all the way to Marymoor Park. ⊠ *2000 N.W. Sammamish Rd., Issaquah* ✛ *From I–90, drive east to Exit 15 and follow signs* ☎ *425/455–7010* ⊕ *www.parks.wa.gov/ parks/?selectedpark=lake%20sammamish* ⌲ *Discover Pass required ($10/day or $30/yr).*

Newcastle Beach Park. The most popular beach park in the Bellevue park system, this large park has a big swimming beach, seasonal lifeguards, a fishing dock, nature trails, restrooms, and a large grassy area with picnic tables. The playground is a favorite, thanks to a train that tots can sit in and older kids can climb on and hop from car to car. ⊠ *4400 Lake Washington Blvd. SE, off 112th SE exit from I–405, Bellevue* ☎ *425/452–6885* ⊕ *www.ci.bellevue.wa.us/ newcastle_beach_park.htm.*

WHERE TO EAT

SEATTLE'S BEST FARMERS' MARKETS

If you've been to Pike Place Market in the summer and walked its colorful, aromatic stalls of fresh flowers, berries, and peaches, and if you've had a great meal at a top-rated restaurant, then you know how obsessive Seattle is about its produce and ingredients.

(Above) The University District Farmers' Market (Opposite page top) Wild mushrooms (Opposite page bottom) Local raspberries and blackberries

The many neighborhood farmers' markets throughout the city shape and define how Seattleites eat—from Ballard's year-round colorful and quirky bonanza on Ballard Avenue and Capitol Hill's miniature gem just off Broadway, to West Seattle's weekly bounty and Columbia City's midweek fresh fest. Spend an hour or two to peruse the produce—especially if you're here in the glorious summer months. You'll get a unique sense of each individual neighborhood, and be able to interact with some colorful local characters, as well as some of the best local suppliers and farmers. Children have a blast at farmers' markets, too—there's often a bluegrass band playing, cooking demonstrations, and samples galore.

HELPFUL HINTS

Be sure to check online ahead of time to find out about the farmers' market you're planning to visit—there are more than we have room to list, and each one offers a special slice of neighborhood life and character. Dogs are allowed only at some of the markets. It's smart to bring a large basket or a reusable bag to carry your goods.

FAVORITE MARKETS

The **Ballard Farmers' Market** is open every Sunday, rain or shine, from 10 am to 3 pm at Ballard Avenue, between 20th Avenue NW and N.W. Market Street. Loads of vendors—selling anything from eggs, apples, and greens to candles and hats—set up colorful, welcoming tents and stands. *www.ballard-farmersmarket.wordpress.com*

The **University District Market Farmers' Market** is open every Saturday from 9 am to 2 pm, on University Way between N.E. 50th Street and N.E. 52nd Street. An understated elegance pervades here, with flowers and fine cheeses and meats. Come summertime, more than 60 farmers and vendors set up their goods, including a small food court with a selection of ready-to-eat foods. *www.seattlefarmersmarkets.org*

The **West Seattle Farmers' Market** is open every Sunday from 10 am to 2 pm, and is located in the heart of the "West Seattle Junction" at California Avenue SW and S.W. Alaska Street. Going south on I–5, take the West Seattle Bridge exit, then continue to Fauntleroy Way. At the fourth light (S.W. Alaska), take a right. Fruit, vegetables, herbs, greens, cheeses, free-range chicken, cut flowers, and plants fill the tents here. *www.seattlefarmersmarkets.org*

The **Columbia City Farmers' Market** is open on Wednesday, late spring through early fall, from 3 pm to 7 pm, at 37th Avenue South and South Edmunds. This southern neighborhood is absolutely darling—hit up the market for eggs, nuts, grains, poultry, berries, jams and more. *www.seattlefarmersmarkets.org*

The **Broadway Farmers' Market** on Capitol Hill is open every Sunday, late spring through late fall, from 11 am to 3 pm, in front of Seattle Central Community College at Broadway and Pine. This small and lively market sports fresh produce, plus music, samples, and plenty of cut flowers. *www.seattlefarmersmarkets.org*

There are also market listings in the Seattle Shopping reviews.

PARKING AND PLANNING

It's a good idea to arrive at any neighborhood farmers' market prepared to deal with lots of people. Many of the best markets in the city are set in calm areas that have plenty of residential streets nearby that have free parking, though you may need to walk a few blocks from your spot. Be sure to check street signs, as an increasing number of residential areas are seeing pay machines (though parking is always free on Sunday). Check online to find the market that is closest to you—part of the fun can be arriving on foot, as so many locals do. If you're staying Downtown, and have already hit up Pike Place Market, we recommend taking the light-rail up to Capitol Hill, and making your way on foot to the Broadway Farmers' market—then you can wind your way back downhill to the Downtown core, or jump on the bus or into a cab. Cal Anderson Park, between Pine and Denny at 11th, is a good place to eat your berries and plan the rest of the day.

Updated by
Naomi Tomky

Thanks to inventive chefs, first-rate local produce, adventurous diners, and a bold entrepreneurial spirit, Seattle has become one of the culinary capitals of the nation. Fearless young chefs have stepped in and raised the bar. Fresh and often foraged produce, local seafood, and imaginative techniques make the quality of local cuisine even higher.

Seattle's dining scene has been stoked like a wildfire by culinary rock stars who compete on shows like *Iron Chef, Top Chef,* and regularly dominate "best of" lists. Seattle chefs have won big in the prestigious James Beard competition, with Renee Erickson of Bateau, Walrus and the Carpenter, and the Whale Wins taking the "Best Chef Northwest" title in 2016 and creative genius Edouardo Jordan named one of *Food and Wine Magazine*'s "Best New Chefs." The city is particularly strong on new American, Japanese, and Vietnamese cuisines. Chefs continuously fine-tune what can best be called Pacific Northwest cuisine, which features fresh, local ingredients, including anything from nettles and mushrooms foraged in nearby forests; colorful berries, apples, and cherries grown by Washington State farmers; and outstanding seafood from the cold northern waters of the Pacific Ocean, like wild salmon, halibut, oysters, Dungeness crab, and geoduck. Seattle boasts quite a few outstanding bakeries, too, whose breads and desserts you'll see touted on many menus.

Seattle is also seeing a resurgence in American comfort food, often with a gourmet twist, as well as gastropub fare, which can mean anything from divine burgers on locally baked ciabatta rolls to grilled foie gras with brioche toast. But innovation still reigns supreme: local salmon cooked sous vide and accompanied with pickled kimchi or fresh-picked peas can be just as common as aspic spiked with sake and reindeer meat. Many menus feature fusion cuisine or pages of small-plate offerings, and even high-end chefs are dabbling in casual ventures like pop-up eateries or gourmet food trucks. Many, if not most, of the top chefs own their businesses as well, and in recent years they've spread their talents around, operating two or three complementary ventures (or, in Ethan Stowell's case, more than a dozen and counting, while Tom Douglas has nearly 20, plus a cooking school and farm). The trend toward informality and simplicity particularly plays out when it comes to dessert; most neighborhoods boast branches of at least one of the city's popular, independently owned cupcake, doughnut, or ice-cream shops. Regardless of the format or focus, one thing's for sure: chefs are highlighting their inventions with the top-notch ingredients that make Pacific Northwest cooking famous.

PLANNING

MEALTIMES

Many of Seattle's better restaurants serve only dinner and are closed Sunday; quite a few are closed Monday. (Monday is also typically the head chef's day off, so might not be the best day for a onetime visit.) Many restaurants that serve lunch during the week do not do so on weekends, though they may offer brunch, which is increasingly popular in Seattle. Unless otherwise noted, the restaurants listed are open daily for lunch and dinner. Seattle restaurants generally serve food until 10 or 11 pm, Sunday through Thursday—in a new era for a city that once shut down early, there's now a choice of excellent food as late as 2 am on Friday and Saturday, particularly on nightlife-heavy Capitol Hill. Great breakfast menus are easier to come by on weekends than midweek; consequently, if you know where to go *(see our listings)* you can get terrific pastries and breads at a bakery—and, of course, you'll find amazing coffee everywhere.

RESERVATIONS

Seattleites dine out often, so reservations are always a good idea. Restaurant reviews note only where they are required or not accepted. Reservations can sometimes be made a day in advance, but you'll have better luck if you make them a week or two ahead—or more at the most popular restaurants. If you've just arrived in town and heard about a popular restaurant, it doesn't hurt to call—you may be able to get a reservation for midweek when even hot restaurants don't always reach capacity, and some of the ultrapopular spots save a few tables for walk-ins.

SMOKING

Smoking in restaurants and bars is prohibited in Washington State.

TIPPING

Most Seattleites tip around 18%. You should leave 20% if the service was outstanding, or the server or kitchen fulfilled special requests. As Seattle's minimum wage rises, some restaurants have implemented a service fee instead of expecting a traditional tip, while a 18%–20% gratuity will automatically be added to bills for larger parties—be sure to check your receipt before adding a tip, or ask your server.

BEST BETS FOR SEATTLE DINING

With so many restaurants to choose from, how to decide where to eat? Fodor's writers and editors have selected their favorite restaurants by price, cuisine, and experience in the Best Bets lists. Fodor's Choice properties represent the "best of the best" in every price category. Other favorites are listed by price category, cuisine, and experience.

Fodor's Choice ★

Altura, $$$$
Bar Melusine, $$$$
Café Juanita, $$$$
Cafe Munir, $$
Cascina Spinasse, $$$
Delancey, $$
Dino's Tomato Pie, $$
Eden Hill, $$$$
Il Corvo, $
La Marzocco Showroom & Cafe, $
Lark, $$$
Manolin, $$$
Marination Ma Kai, $
Matt's in the Market, $$$$
Revel, $$
Salumi, $
Staple & Fancy, $$$
Sushi Kashiba, $$$$
Vif, $

Best By Price

$

Dick's Drive-In
Dough Zone Dumpling House
Il Corvo
Marination Ma Kai
Salumi
Uneeda Burger
Xi'an Noodles

$$

Brimmer & Heeltap
Cafe Munir
Café Presse
Delancey
Dino's Tomato Pie
Kisaku
Le Pichet
Ma'ono
Omega Ouzeri
Revel

$$$

Lark
Manolin
Staple & Fancy

$$$$

Altura
Café Juanita
Canlis
Eden Hill

Best By Cuisine

ASIAN

Dough Zone, $
Little Uncle, $
Revel, $$
Tamarind Tree, $$

FRENCH

Bastille, $$
Le Pichet, $$

ITALIAN

Café Juanita, $$$$
Cascina Spinasse, $$$
Il Corvo, $

JAPANESE

Kisaku, $$
Maneki, $
Sushi Kashiba, $$$$

MEDITERRANEAN

Cafe Munir, $$
Lola, $$$
Omega Ouzeri, $$$

NEW AMERICAN

Eden Hill, $$$$
Lark, $$$
Ma'ono, $$
Poppy, $$$
Pacific Northwest
Canlis, $$$$
Matt's in the Market, $$$$
Vestal, $$$$

SEAFOOD

Manolin, $$$

RockCreek Seafood & Spirits, $$$
Taylor Shellfish Oyster Bar, $$

STEAK HOUSE

John Howie Steak, $$$$
Metropolitan Grill, $$$$

Best by Experience

BRUNCH

Brimmer & Heeltap, $$
Café Presse, $$
Fat Hen, $$
Vif, $

COFFEEHOUSE

La Marzocco Showroom & Cafe, $
Milstead & Co., $
Slate Coffee Bar, $
Victrola Coffee, $

LATE-NIGHT DINING

Café Presse, $$
Dino's Tomato Pie, $$
Tavolàta, $$

MOST ROMANTIC

Canlis, $$$$
Eden Hill, $$$$
Lark, $$$
Serafina, $$$

WINE LIST

Altura, $$$$
Café Juanita, $$$$
Canlis, $$$$

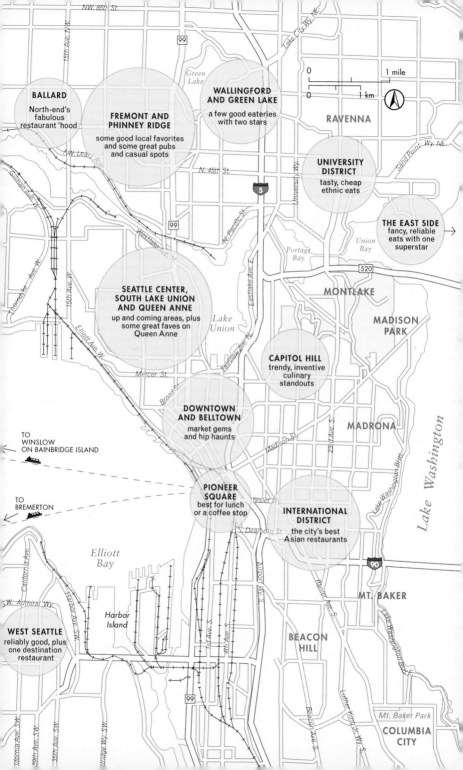

WHAT IT COSTS

If you're watching your budget, be sure to ask the price of daily specials recited by the waiter. The charge for specials at some restaurants can be noticeably out of line with the other prices on the menu. And beware of the $10 bottle of water; ask for tap water instead.

Many restaurants offer great lunch deals with special menus at lower prices designed to give customers a true taste of the place. Early-evening and late-night happy hours, complete with cheap drinks and satisfying food offerings, are a long-standing and beloved local tradition.

Credit cards are widely accepted, and even the smallest places and food trucks will take them.

WHAT IT COSTS AT DINNER			
$	$$	$$$	$$$$
RESTAURANTS under $17	$17–$24	$25–$32	over $32

Price per person for a median main course or equivalent combination of smaller dishes. Note: if a restaurant offers only prix-fixe (set-price) meals, it has been given the price category that reflects the full prix-fixe price.

WHAT TO WEAR

Seattle dining is very informal. It's almost a little too informal—though the city's lack of pretension is one of its charms, residents are trying harder on the fashion front, and it shows. Almost no restaurants require jackets and ties; however, business casual is usually a safe way to go if you're off to a spendy or trendy restaurant. We mention dress only when men are required to wear a jacket or a jacket and tie.

WINE, BEER, AND SPIRITS

The liquor laws in the state of Washington were once stringent, but a voter-approved privatization initiative in 2011 loosened them up. Spirits, once sold only in state-run liquor stores, are now widely available in supermarkets and other privately run stores that are (with a few exceptions) larger than 10,000 square feet. Generally, the variety of wines and specialty beers sold in most grocery stores is quite astounding, with many mirroring the restaurant world's commitment to locally produced ingredients. Additionally, thanks to changes in distillery laws, Washington is also seeing a resurgence in craft distilleries, which are brewing high-quality gin, vodka, whiskey, and other spirits.

WITH KIDS

Although it's unusual to see children in the dining rooms of Seattle's most elite restaurants, dining with youngsters in the city does not have to mean culinary exile. Many of the restaurants are excellent choices for families.

RESTAURANT AND COFFEEHOUSE REVIEWS

Listed alphabetically within neighborhoods. Use the coordinate (1:B2) at the end of each listing to locate a site on the Seattle Dining and Lodging Atlas at the end of this chapter.

DOWNTOWN AND BELLTOWN

After a day of exploring the shopping, museums, sights, galleries, and parks in these two adjacent neighborhoods, what could be better than a perfect meal? Luckily, this area is filled with a wide range of eateries, from a charming French bistro near Pike Place Market called Le Pichet and exciting Seattle sushi spot Sushi Kashiba to rustic-chic Italian at Tavolàta, plus plenty of favorites from local star-chef Tom Douglas, including his acclaimed Lola, Serious Pie, and Palace Kitchen eateries.

DOWNTOWN

$ SICHUAN 🍴 **Country Dough.** After introducing Seattle to the wonders of Sichuanese cuisine at a variety of restaurants around town in the last few decades, chef Cheng Biao Yang has settled into his smallest space yet, where he serves a pared-down menu of Chinese street foods. The hand-shaved noodles, flatbread sandwiches, and Chinese crepes (known as *jian bing* in Chinese) form the backbone of the menu, each dough-based specialty customizable with various stews, meats, and spicy sauces. **Known for:** flatbread sandwiches; street food. [$] *Average main: $8* ✉ *1916 Pike Pl., #14, Downtown* ✥ *Walk through building entrance and to back, Country Dough is on your right* ☎ *206/728–2598* 🌐 *www.countrydough.com* ⏲ *No dinner* ✥ *1:D2.*

$ FAST FOOD Fodor's Choice ★ 🍴 **Ellenos Real Greek Yogurt.** When people walk by the Pike Place Market booth, they might think they're passing a gelato stand from the artful display, but in fact Ellenos is serving up the best (and best-looking) yogurt in the city—and possibly the country. Thicker and smoother than most commercial Greek yogurts, the Australian-Greek family behind the brand uses local milk and a slow culturing process to create their nearly ice-cream–like product. **Known for:** creamy yogurt; beautiful display. [$] *Average main: $3* ✉ *1500 Pike Pl., Downtown* ☎ *206/535–7562* 🌐 *www.ellenos.com* ⏲ *No dinner* ✥ *1:D3.*

$$$ AMERICAN 🍴 **FareStart.** A project of the nationally lauded FareStart job-training program, this eatery in a sleek, dramatic space on Virginia Street serves an American-style lunch of sandwiches, burgers, mac-and-cheese, and fries during the week, as well as rotating specials. The kitchen is staffed by formerly homeless men and women (the servers are not) and the spirit of community outreach runs deep. **Known for:** business lunches; guest-chef dinners. [$] *Average main: $30* ✉ *700 Virginia St., Downtown* ☎ *206/267–7601* 🌐 *www.farestart.org* ⏲ *No lunch weekends, no dinner Fri.–Wed.* ✥ *1:E1.*

$$ FRENCH 🍴 **Le Pichet.** Slate tabletops, a tile floor, and a rolled-zinc bar will transport you out of Downtown Seattle and into the charming 6th arrondissement. The menu is heartbreakingly French: at lunch there are rustic pâtés and *jambon et fromage* (ham-and-cheese) sandwiches on crusty baguettes; dinner sees homemade sausages, daily fish specials, and steak tartare.

Known for: charcuterie; wine. $ *Average main: $18* ✉ *1933 1st Ave., Downtown* ☎ *206/256–1499* ⊕ *www.lepichetseattle.com* ✛ *1:D2.*

$$$

AMERICAN

✕ **Lecosho.** Matt Janke (formerly of Matt's in the Market) doesn't have his name on the marquee at this Downtown restaurant a few blocks from his old stomping grounds, but he and business partner Jill Buchanan still prepare modern, hearty, soul-satisfying dishes that rely on ingredients from Pike Place Market. Lecosho's motto is "food we like"—they say the name is Chinook for "swine," and that means a menu heavy on the likes of house-made charcuterie and sausage, guanciale with pan-seared salmon, and a pork chop served with a side of parsnip puree, pancetta, and salsa verde. **Known for:** Northwest cooking; meat. $ *Average main: $28* ✉ *89 University St., Downtown* ☎ *206/623–2101* ⊕ *www.lecosho.com* ☉ *No lunch weekends* ✛ *1:D3.*

$$$$

PACIFIC NORTHWEST

Fodor'sChoice

★

✕ **Matt's in the Market.** One of the most beloved of Pike Place Market's restaurants, Matt's is now owned by Dan Bugge, who continues to value intimate dining, fresh ingredients, and superb service. You can perch at the bar for pints and the signature deviled eggs or be seated at a table—complete with vases filled with flowers from the market—for a seasonal menu that synthesizes the best picks from the restaurant's produce vendors and an excellent wine list. **Known for:** view; seafood. $ *Average main: $35* ✉ *94 Pike St., Downtown* ☎ *206/467–7909* ⊕ *www.mattsinthemarket.com* ☉ *Closed Sun.* ✛ *1:D3.*

$$$$

STEAKHOUSE

✕ **Metropolitan Grill.** This is a favorite lunch spot for the professional crowd but it's not for timid eaters: custom dry-aged mesquite-grilled steaks—arguably the best in Seattle—are huge and come with baked potatoes, mashed potatoes, or roasted root veggies. Even the veal chop is extra thick. **Known for:** big steaks; classic service. $ *Average main: $72* ✉ *820 2nd Ave., Downtown* ☎ *206/624–3287* ⊕ *www.themetropolitangrill.com* ☉ *No lunch weekends* ✛ *1:E4.*

$$$

ITALIAN

✕ **The Pink Door.** With its Post Alley entrance and meager signage, the Pink Door's speakeasy vibe draws Pike Place Market regulars almost as much as its savory, seasonal Italian food does. ■ **TIP**➔ **In warm months, outdoor dining in Seattle doesn't get much better than the ample deck here, with its shaded grape arbor and views of Elliott Bay.** The food is good, and the pappardelle *al ràgu Bolognese* (with slow-simmered meat sauce) and cioppino are standout entrées, but people come here mostly for the atmosphere. The staff is saucy and irreverent, and cabaret acts regularly perform on a small corner stage in the lounge. **Known for:** patio; view; pasta. $ *Average main: $25* ✉ *1919 Post Alley, Downtown* ☎ *206/443–3241* ⊕ *www.thepinkdoor. net* ☉ *No lunch Sun.* ✛ *1:D2.*

$$$$

SUSHI

Fodor'sChoice

★

✕ **Sushi Kashiba.** After decades spent earning a reputation as one of Seattle's top sushi chefs, Shiro Kashiba opened his own spot in a location as iconic as his skill with seafood deserves. Diners in the spare-but-elegant Pike Place Market space can opt for the *omakase* (chef's choice) selection of the best fish from around the world and just up the street, or order from the menu of Japanese classics and sashimi. **Known for:** omakase; fresh fish. $ *Average main: $85* ✉ *86 Pine St., Suite 1, Downtown* ✛ *Inn at the Market* ☎ *206/441–8844* ⊕ *www.sushikashiba.com* ☉ *No lunch* ✛ *1:D3.*

CLOSE UP

Coffee Culture

Seattle may forever be known as the birthplace of Starbucks, but to really understand the coffee culture—and to get a great cup of coffee—visit one of the numerous independent shops and local minichains, several of which roast their own beans on-site. A Seattleite's relationship with coffee ranges from grabbing the daily quick fix in the morning to spending half the day at a local shop where every barista knows their name (and coffee order), reading, chatting with friends, or tapping away on a laptop. Many coffee shops pull double duty as art galleries, and some of them even pull double duty as good art galleries. Occasionally, shops feature hard-to-get coffees at special "cupping" events, which take on the structure and feel of wine tastings.

These days, there are more independent roasters and shops than ever. Like its sister city, Portland, Seattle is a hot spot for entrepreneurial spirit—it's this energy, mixed with a passion for local and organic ingredients, that has raised the bar on everything artisanal.

Seattle's independent coffee shops rule the roast here. Their ardent commitment to creating premium artisanal blends from small batches of beans is what truly defines the scene. The moment you take your first sip of an expertly executed cappuccino at a coffeehouse such as Caffé Vita or Espresso Vivace you realize that the drink is never an afterthought here. Perfectly roasted beans ground to specification and pulled into espresso shots using dual-boiler machines and velvety steamed milk are de rigueur. In most restaurants, your coffee is likely to be a personal French press filled with a brew roasted just a few blocks away.

LATTE ART

Latte art is a given in Seattle. Designs vary by barista, but the most common flourish is the rosetta, which resembles a delicate fern. Here's how it's done: 1. The Base: A latte consists of a shot (or two) of espresso and hot, frothy milk. 2. The Pour: First the shot is poured. The milk pitcher gets a few gentle swirls and taps (to burst the largest bubbles), then the milk is poured at a steady pace into the center of the tilted cup. 3. The Shake: When the cup's about three-quarters full, the milk is streamed with tiny side-to-side strokes up and down the cup's center line. The "leaves" will start to fan out. 4. The Top: When the cup's almost full, the milk is drawn toward the bottom. With the last stroke the "stem" is drawn through the center of the leaves.

BELLTOWN

$$$ PACIFIC NORTHWEST 🍴 **Dahlia Lounge.** Romantic Dahlia Lounge has the valentine-red walls and deep booths you may be looking for—it's been working its magic on Seattle since 1989. It's cozy and then some, but the food plays its part, too. **Known for:** seafood; doughnuts. [$] *Average main: $29* ✉ *2001 4th Ave., Belltown* ☎ *206/682–4142* 🌐 *www.tomdouglas.com* ✥ *1:D1.*

$$$ MEDITERRANEAN 🍴 **Lola.** Tom Douglas dishes out his signature Northwest style, spiked with Greek and Mediterranean touches—another huge success for the local celebrity chef. Try a sensational tagine of Northwest seafood; a

variety of meat kebabs; and scrumptious spreads including hummus, tzatziki, and *harissa* (a red-pepper concoction). **Known for:** Greek food; breakfast; doughnuts. [$] *Average main: $25* ✉ *2000 4th Ave., Belltown* ☎ *206/441–1430* ⊕ *1:D1.*

$ BAKERY 🍴 **Macrina Bakery.** One of Seattle's favorite bakeries is also popular for breakfast and brunch and an excellent place to take a delicious break on your way to or from the Olympic Sculpture Park. With its perfectly executed breads and pastries—from Nutella brioche and ginger cookies to almond croissants and dark-chocolate, sugar-dusted brownies—it's become a true Belltown institution. **Known for:** baguettes; pastries. [$] *Average main: $7* ✉ *2408 1st Ave., Belltown* ☎ *206/448–4032* 🌐 *www.macrinabakery.com* ⊕ *1:B1.*

$$$ PACIFIC NORTHWEST 🍴 **Palace Kitchen.** The star of this chic yet convivial Tom Douglas eatery may be the 45-foot bar, but the real show takes place in the giant open kitchen at the back. Wood-grilled chicken wings, olive poppers, Penn Cove mussels, roast-pork ravioli, and a nightly selection of cheeses vie for your attention on the ever-changing menu of small plates. **Known for:** late-night dining; burger. [$] *Average main: $25* ✉ *2030 5th Ave., Belltown* ☎ *206/448–2001* 🌐 *www.tomdouglas.com* 🕒 *No lunch* ⊕ *1:D1.*

$$ PIZZA 🍴 **Serious Pie.** Serious artisanal pizzas are worth the wait here—and you will wait, at this teeny-tiny Belltown restaurant. Famed local restaurateur Tom Douglas delivers chewy, buttery crusts anchored by such toppings as fresh arugula, guanciale (cured pork jowl), and a soft egg; or Meyer lemon, chili, and buffalo mozzarella. **Known for:** fun atmosphere; egg pizza. [$] *Average main: $18* ✉ *316 Virginia, Belltown* ☎ *206/838–7388* 🌐 *www.tomdouglas.com* ⊕ *1:D1.*

$$ ITALIAN 🍴 **Tavolàta.** This Belltown favorite is helmed by superstar-chef Ethan Stowell (also of Anchovies & Olives and How to Cook a Wolf). Serving up Italian goodness by the plateful in an industrial-chic bi-level space, Tavolàta is a decidedly lively, loud, and delicious night out on the town. **Known for:** community table; pasta. [$] *Average main: $20* ✉ *2323 2nd Ave., Belltown* ☎ *206/838–8008* 🌐 *www.tavolata.com* ⊕ *1:C1.*

SEATTLE CENTER, SOUTH LAKE UNION, AND QUEEN ANNE

The areas north of Downtown and Belltown are the city's latest culinary destinations. You certainly won't go hungry after rocking out at the Experience Music Project, ascending the Space Needle, or shopping at the REI megastore. This is a very large area, so keep that in mind when you're planning your mealtimes. In Queen Anne, friendly neighborhood haunts are the norm, but a few standouts, such as How to Cook a Wolf, Eden Hill, and destination-restaurant Canlis, up the ante. The arrival of Amazon.com headquarters to South Lake Union has transformed the industrial neighborhood into a veritable restaurant destination.

SWEET TREATS

Seattle is already known for coffee. Now how about a slice of pie with it—or a cupcake or an ice-cream cone? These are a few of our favorites among the city's growing number of sweet spots:

PIE

Pie is so old-fashioned that it's become trendy again, at places like Pie in Fremont, at Pie Bar on Capitol Hill, on the 314 Pie truck, and at A La Mode on Phinney Ridge and in West Seattle.

A La Mode ☎ 206/383–3796 ✉ Multiple locations

Pie ☎ 206/436–8590 ✉ 3515 Fremont Ave. N, between 35th and 36th St., Seattle Center

314 Pie Truck ⊕ www.314pieseattle. com for locations and schedule

CUPCAKES

Seattle cupcake fans are as loyal to their favorite shops as the city's baseball fans are to their Mariners. Trophy Cupcakes and Cupcake Royale, both with several locations around Seattle and the Eastside, are the prime contenders (Trophy has more elegant specialty flavors, while Royale favors local ingredients and grown-up options like the Boozy Rumball).

Cupcake Royale ⊕ www.cupcakeroyale.com ☎ 206/883–7656 ✉ Multiple locations

Trophy Cupcakes ⊕ www.trophycupcakes.com ☎ 206/632–7020 ✉ Multiple locations

Yellow Leaf ⊕ www.theyellowleafcupcake.com ☎ 206/441–4240 ✉ 2209 4th Ave., Belltown

DOUGHNUTS

Top Pot, the high-end doughnut shop with several locations in Seattle and on the Eastside, once warranted a snack stop by President Barack Obama, but vegans swear by the three locations of Mighty-O Donuts, which are organic. If you're visiting Pike Place Market, Daily Dozen Doughnut has adorable, made-while-you-watch minidoughnuts dusted in powdered sugar.

Daily Dozen Doughnut ☎ 206/467–7769 ✉ Pike Place Market, Downtown

Mighty-O Donuts ⊕ www.mightyo. com ☎ 206/547–0335 ✉ Multiple locations

ICE CREAM

For ice cream, top spots include Molly Moon Ice Cream, with six locations around town favoring locally grown and organic ingredients in tempting and trendy combinations like balsamic strawberry and salted licorice. D'Ambrosio Gelato in Ballard, Bellevue, and on Capitol Hill serves unbeatably authentic Italian gelato—don't miss the pistachio. And Full Tilt Ice Cream in Ballard, Columbia City, the University District, and White Center provides flavors inspired by global ingredients like Thai iced tea and horchata—plus Mexican *paletas* (ice pops) and vegan ice cream.

D'Ambrosio Gelato ⊕ www.dambrosiogelato.com ☎ 206/328–4285 ✉ Multiple locations

Molly Moon Ice Cream ⊕ www.mollymoonicecream.com ☎ 206/708–7947 ✉ Multiple locations

Full Tilt Ice Cream ☎ 206/297–3000 ✉ Multiple locations

SOUTH LAKE UNION

$ × **Brave Horse Tavern.** Watch out when the Amazon.com offices in South
AMERICAN Lake Union empty out for the day, because the seats at this Tom Douglas eatery fill up fast with techies craving big, fresh, soft pretzels—some
made into sandwiches, some just dipped in a selection of house-made
mustards—along with burgers, fish-and-chips, and a long beer list that
offers the perfect accompaniments to a game of shuffleboard. The long
wooden tables are quieter at other times, so stop in for eggy brunches
where the produce might come from Douglas's farm in Eastern Washington. **Known for:** beer, pretzels; good for groups. $ *Average main:*
$12 ⊠ *310 Terry Ave. N, South Lake Union* ☎ *206/971–0717* ⊕ *www.*
bravehorsetavern.com ✛ *2:D5.*

$ × **Espresso Vivace.** A cozy and large outpost of the famed Capitol Hill
CAFÉ roaster, the Vivace coffee shrine in South Lake Union is right across
from the REI megastore and amid a growing number of new apartment
buildings and offices. Grab a seat, order an expertly prepared espresso
beverage, and munch on a small variety of snacks—this is a perfect
stop after an exhausting jaunt through REI and before you head out to
the next adventure. **Known for:** cafe Nicos; espresso. $ *Average main:*
$3 ⊠ *227 Yale Ave. N, South Lake Union* ☎ *206/388–5164* ⊕ *www.*
espressovivace.com ✛ *2:E5.*

$ × **Great State Burger.** This new spin on the classic American burger shop
BURGER manages to be both an ode to the Northwest and an example of how
FAMILY fast food can be done right. Organic, grass-fed beef is broken down and
ground in-house, organic milk shakes come in seasonal flavors featuring
Washington fruit, and the crinkle-cut french fries feel like a nostalgic
nod to childhood. **Known for:** organic burgers; local ingredients. $ *Av-*
erage main: $7 ⊠ *2014 7th Ave., South Lake Union* ☎ *206/775–7880*
⊕ *www.greatstateburger.com* ✛ *2:D6.*

$ × **Serious Pie & Biscuit.** Hefty, fresh-baked biscuits come with equally
CAFÉ hefty fillings at the downstairs counter, while the rest of the space is
dedicated to the South Lake Union branch of Tom Douglas's Serious
Pie pizzeria. The crisp, crunchy fried chicken in a biscuit is worth the
caloric wallop, as are fried green tomatoes and bacon on a biscuit.
Known for: biscuits; pizza; wine. $ *Average main: $8* ⊠ *401 Westlake*
Ave. N, South Lake Union ☎ *206/436–0050* ⊕ *www.seriouspieseattle.*
com/westlake ☯ *No dinner* ✛ *2:D5.*

$$$$ × **Vestal.** The Northwest's bounty serves as inspiration for prolific local
PACIFIC chef Joshua Henderson at his highest-end spot. Matsutake mushrooms
NORTHWEST from the forest, salmon collar from the sea, and duck from local farms
pepper the menu, which combines traditional cooking techniques
such as fermentation and hearth roasting with a thoroughly modern
aesthetic for one of the most beautiful, comprehensively Northwest
meals in town. **Known for:** hearth-cooked foods; Northwest ingredients. $ *Average main: $50* ⊠ *513 Westlake Ave. N, South Lake Union*
☎ *206/456–2660* ⊕ *www.vestalseattle.com* ☯ *No lunch. Closed Sun.*
and Mon. ✛ *2:D4.*

QUEEN ANNE

$$$$ PACIFIC NORTHWEST 🍴 **Canlis Restaurant.** Canlis has been setting the standard for opulent dining in Seattle since the 1950s and although there are no longer kimono-clad waitresses, the food, the wine, the practically clairvoyant service, and the views overlooking Lake Union are still remarkable. Executive chef Brady Williams (formerly of New York's acclaimed Roberta's and Blanca) maintains the restaurant's signature insistence on the finest meat and the freshest produce, but he has also refreshed the menu—which offers traditional multicourse and tasting options. **Known for:** view; service; wine. [$] *Average main: $48* ✉ *2576 Aurora Ave. N, Queen Anne* ☎ *206/283–3313* 🌐 *www.canlis.com* 🕒 *Closed Sun. No lunch* 👔 *Jacket required* ✥ *3:E6.*

$$$$ MODERN AMERICAN Fodor's Choice ★ 🍴 **Eden Hill.** This tiny, 24-seat restaurant quietly turns out some of the most exciting and innovative food in the city. With patterned wallpaper, a location on the serene side of Queen Anne, chalkboard menus, and tables cozied into wide windows, it's the perfect place to lean in close to someone special over a series of small plates. **Known for:** pig-head candy bar; tasting menu; romance. [$] *Average main: $38* ✉ *2209 Queen Anne Ave. N, Queen Anne* ☎ *206/708–6836* 🌐 *www.edenhillrestaurant.com* 🕒 *No lunch. Closed Mon.* ✥ *2:A1.*

$$ ITALIAN 🍴 **How to Cook a Wolf.** This sleek eatery—complete with loads of trendy young couples perched at its tables—"pays homage to M.F.K. Fisher and her philosophy of taking simple ingredients and transforming them into culinary splendor." As you would expect then, fresh, artisanal ingredients are the focus. **Known for:** small plates; pasta. [$] *Average main: $16* ✉ *2208 Queen Anne Ave. N, Queen Anne* ☎ *206/838–8090* 🌐 *www.ethanstowellrestaurants.com* 🕒 *No lunch* ✥ *2:A1.*

$ CAFÉ Fodor's Choice ★ 🍴 **La Marzocco Cafe & Showroom.** Though better known for making espresso machines than espresso, La Marzocco brings a sprawling open café, gorgeous light, and incredible coffee and coffeemakers to Seattle Center. Sharing space with Seattle's cherished public radio station, KEXP, the café brings in a different roaster—their drinks, experts, and style—each month. **Known for:** coffee; music. [$] *Average main: $3* ✉ *KEXP Seattle Center Campus, 472 1st Ave N, Lower Queen Anne* ☎ *206/388–3500* 🌐 *www.lamarzoccousa.com/locations/* 🕒 *No dinner* ✥ *2:A4.*

$ AMERICAN 🍴 **Seattle Center Armory.** A complete remodel has changed the Seattle Center food court from an only-if-you're-desperate stop into a quick-bite destination worth a visit even if you're not passing through for a museum exhibit or concert. Several high-quality indie restaurants have erected walk-up windows or shops here, from skillet burgers to Montreal-style bagels at Eltana. **Known for:** beautiful space; quick service; variety. [$] *Average main: $8* ✉ *305 Harrison St., Queen Anne* ☎ *206/684–7200* 🌐 *www.seattlecenter.com* ✥ *2:B5.*

PIONEER SQUARE

Pioneer Square is quickly catching up to its culinary destination neighbors, the International District and Downtown. There are some quirky and reliable lunch spots here—Salumi is a city treasure—and there are some top-notch, authentic coffeehouses. There are also several old-school Italian eateries that Seattle locals still love, especially Il Terrazo Carmine.

$ ✕ **Il Corvo.** It may be a Pioneer Square hole-in-the-wall, but Il Corvo
ITALIAN   serves up some of the best pasta in town. Experienced chef Mike
Fodor's Choice   Easton left the cooking line at higher-end restaurants to found this
★   lunch-only (11 am to 3 pm), cash-only collection of family-style
tables where he prepares a few inexpensive handmade dishes each
day using antique pasta makers and artisanal, seasonal ingredients—
perhaps squid-ink perciatelli with anchovy-toasted bread crumbs or
pappardelle *alla Bolognese.* **Known for:** house-made pasta; affordable prices. Ⓢ *Average main: $9* ✉ *217 James St., Pioneer Square*
☎ *206/538–0999* ⊕ *www.ilcorvopasta.com* ⏱ *Closed weekends. No
dinner* ✛ *1:F5.*

$$$ ✕ **Il Terrazzo Carmine.** Ceiling-to-floor draperies lend the dining room
ITALIAN   understated dignity, and intoxicating aromas waft from the kitchen.
The chef blends Tuscan-style and regional southern Italian cooking to
create soul-satisfying dishes such as veal osso buco, homemade ravioli,
linguine *alle vongole,* and eggplant Parmesan. **Known for:** elegant space;
classic Italian food. Ⓢ *Average main: $30* ✉ *411 1st Ave. S, Pioneer
Square* ☎ *206/467–7797* ⊕ *www.ilterrazzocarmine.com* ⏱ *Closed Sun.,
no lunch Sat.* ✛ *1:E6.*

$ ✕ **Salumi Cured Meats.** The lines are long for hearty, unforgettable sand-
ITALIAN   wiches filled with superior house-cured meats and all other sorts of
Fodor's Choice   goodies at this shoebox shop owned by Gina Batali—sister of famed
★   New York chef Mario Batali—and founded by their dad Armandino.
The oxtail sandwich special is unbeatable, but if it's unavailable or
sold out (as specials often are by the lunchtime peak) order a salami,
bresaola, porchetta, meatball, sausage, or lamb prosciutto sandwich
with onions, peppers, cheese, and olive oil. **Known for:** cured meats;
meatballs. Ⓢ *Average main: $10* ✉ *309 3rd Ave. S, Pioneer Square*
☎ *206/621–8772* ⊕ *www.salumicuredmeats.com* ⏱ *Closed weekends.
Take-out only, limited hrs. on Mon. No dinner* ✛ *1:F5.*

$ ✕ **Taylor Shellfish Oyster Bar.** Oysters don't get any fresher than this:
PACIFIC   Taylor, a fifth-generation, family-owned company, opened its own
NORTHWEST   restaurant in order to serve their products in the manner most befit-
Fodor's Choice   ting such pristine shellfish. The simple preparations—raw, cooked, and
★   chilled—are all designed to best show off the seafood with light broths
and sauces and a few accoutrements. **Known for:** fresh seafood; expert
shucking. Ⓢ *Average main: $15* ✉ *410 Occidental Ave., Pioneer Square*
☎ *206/501–4060* ⊕ *www.taylorshellfishfarms.com* ✛ *1:F6.*

$ ✕ **Zeitgeist Cafe.** A colorful local favorite among coffee shops: even Seat-
CAFÉ   tleites who don't haunt Pioneer Square will happily hunt for parking to
spend a few hours here. In one of Pioneer Square's great brick buildings,
with high ceilings and a few artfully exposed ducts and pipes, Zeitgeist
has a simple, classy look that's the perfect backdrop for the frequent art
shows held in this space. **Known for:** great place to work; art. Ⓢ *Aver-
age main: $6* ✉ *171 S. Jackson St., Pioneer Square* ☎ *206/583–0497*
⊕ *www.zeitgeistcoffee.com* ✛ *1:F6.*

INTERNATIONAL DISTRICT

A favorite culinary destination for its many varied Asian restaurants—from dim sum palaces to hole-in-the-wall noodle shops, the International District (I.D.) is a cultural destination. The Uwajimaya superstore and the Wing Luke Museum both warrant a visit before you settle in for an amazing—and spicy—meal here.

$ VIETNAMESE 🍴 **Green Leaf Vietnamese Restaurant.** Locals pack this friendly café for the expansive menu of fresh, well-prepared Vietnamese staples. The quality of the food—the spring rolls, *báhn xèo* (the Vietnamese version of an omelet), and lemongrass chicken are just a few standouts—and reasonable prices would be enough to make it an instant I.D. favorite. **Known for:** báhn xèo; spring rolls. [$] *Average main: $11* ✉ *418 8th Ave. S, International District* ☎ *206/340–1388* 🌐 *www.greenleaftaste.com* ✣ *1:H6.*

$ CHINESE 🍴 **Jade Garden.** Dim sum enthusiasts, take note: this is the spot for fluffy barbecue pork buns, walnut shrimp, chive dumplings, congee, and sticky rice. There's no doubt that the waits are long and the atmosphere is lacking, but when you're craving dim sum (served 9 am to 3 pm daily) this is the place to go. **Known for:** dim sum; dumplings; waits. [$] *Average main: $9* ✉ *424 7th Ave. S, at King St., International District* ☎ *206/622–8181* ✣ *1:H6.*

$$ CHINESE 🍴 **Little Sheep Mongolian Hot Pot.** This Chinese chain brings their cook-it-yourself soup to Seattle with all of the choice that experienced hot-pot eaters want and all of the introduction newcomers might need. The steaming pots of soup filled with herbs and spices (available in both spicy and plain) provide the perfect antidote for Seattle's gray winter weather. **Known for:** all you can eat; variety. [$] *Average main: $23* ✉ *609 S. Weller St., International District* ☎ *206/623–6700* 🌐 *www.littlesheephotpot.com* 💳 *No credit cards* ✣ *1:G6.*

$ JAPANESE 🍴 **Maneki Japanese Restaurant.** The oldest Japanese restaurant in Seattle, Maneki is no longer a hidden gem that caters to in-the-know locals and chefs, but that doesn't mean the food is any less authentic. Though the James Beard American Classic winner serves good sushi, it's better known for the home-style Japanese dishes, which can be ordered as small plates, and accompanied with sake. **Known for:** home-style dishes; sushi. [$] *Average main: $14* ✉ *304 6th Ave. S, International District* ☎ *206/622–2631* 🌐 *www.manekirestaurant.com* 🕓 *Closed Mon. No lunch* ✣ *1:G6.*

$ ASIAN 🍴 **Panama Hotel Tea and Coffee Shop.** On the ground floor of the historic Panama Hotel is a serene teahouse with tons of personality and a subtle Asian flair that reflects its former life as a Japanese bathhouse. The space is lovely, with exposed-brick walls, shiny, hardwood floors, and black-and-white photos of old Seattle (many of them relating to the history of the city's Japanese immigrants). **Known for:** historic ambience; tea. [$] *Average main: $3* ✉ *607 S. Main St., International District* ☎ *206/515–4000* 🌐 *www.panamahotelseattle.com* ✣ *1:G5.*

$ CHINESE 🍴 **Sichuanese Cuisine Restaurant.** For cheap and greasy but oh-so-good Szechuan cooking, head to this hole-in-the-wall in the Asian Plaza strip mall east of I–5. The atmosphere is forgettable, but the service is friendly and the food here is just about as authentic as it gets. **Known for:** noodles; spicy food. [$] *Average main: $6* ✉ *1048 S. Jackson St., International District* ☎ *206/720–1690* 🌐 *www.sichuan.cwok.com* ✣ *1:H6.*

$$ VIETNAMESE

🍴 **Tamarind Tree.** Wildly popular with savvy diners from all across the city, this Vietnamese haunt on the eastern side of the I.D. *really* doesn't look like much from the outside, especially because the entrance is through a grungy parking lot (which it shares with Sichuanese Cuisine restaurant), but once you're inside, the elegantly simple, large, and warm space is extremely welcoming. The food is the main draw—try the spring rolls, which are stuffed with fresh herbs, fried tofu, peanuts, coconut, jicama, and carrots; authentic bánh xèo; spicy pho; the signature "seven courses of beef"; and, to finish, grilled banana cake with warm coconut milk. **Known for:** spring rolls; cocktails. [$] *Average main: $21* ✉ *1036 S. Jackson St., International District* ☎ *206/860–1404* 🌐 *www.tamarindtreerestaurant.com* ✥ *1:H6.*

$ ASIAN

🍴 **Uwajimaya Village Food Court.** Not only an outstanding grocery and gift shop, Uwajimaya also has a hoppin' food court offering a quick tour of Asian cuisines at lunch-counter prices. For Japanese or Chinese, Yummy House Bakery will start you off with Hong Kong–style pastries, while the deli offers sushi, teriyaki, and barbecued duck; for Vietnamese food, try the fresh spring rolls, served with hot chili sauce, at Saigon Bistro; and Shilla has Korean grilled beef and kimchi stew. **Known for:** variety; affordability. [$] *Average main: $8* ✉ *600 5th Ave. S, International District* ☎ *206/624–6248* 🌐 *www.uwajimaya.com/* ✥ *1:G6.*

CAPITOL HILL AND MADISON PARK

CAPITOL HILL

Capitol Hill has become Seattle's major culinary destination. The greatest concentration of restaurants is in and around the Pike–Pine Corridor—Pike and Pine Streets running from Melrose Avenue to 15th Avenue. Überhip gastropubs like Quinn's and all-day cafés like Oddfellows are all the rage, as are smaller, posh new American and Italian-inspired eateries like Lark, Anchovies & Olives, and Cascina Spinasse. On the northern end of Broadway, Poppy is a delicious departure from standard menus, with its Indian-inspired *thali* (small amounts of different dish preparations served in small compartments on a large platter), while a wide variety of coffeehouses make the Hill downright destination-worthy.

$$$$ ITALIAN

Fodor's Choice ★

🍴 **Altura.** A hand-carved cedar angel statue watches over diners at this lively spot, where chef-owner Nathan Lockwood lends a Northwest focus to Italian cuisine. The set tasting menu weaves rare, intriguing, and fascinating local and global ingredients into classic Italian techniques. **Known for:** tasting menu; interesting ingredients. [$] *Average main: $137* ✉ *617 Broadway E, Capitol Hill* ☎ *206/402–6749* 🌐 *www.alturarestaurant.com* ⏲ *Closed Sun. and Mon. No lunch* ✥ *2:F4.*

$$ SEAFOOD

🍴 **Anchovies & Olives.** Artful lighting, an exposed kitchen, a well-edited Italian and Northwest wine list, and a lively small bar are the backdrop for elegant seafood dishes at this sophisticated Ethan Stowell restaurant on the ground floor of a residential high-rise at the eastern end of the Pike–Pine Corridor. Appetizer plates and crudos are small and easily shared, while mains focus on seasonal fish. **Known for:** seafood; pasta. [$] *Average main: $24* ✉ *1550 15th Ave., at Pine St., Capitol Hill* ☎ *206/838–8080* 🌐 *ethanstowellrestaurants.com/anchoviesandolives* ⏲ *No lunch* ✥ *2:H6.*

$$$$ SEAFOOD Fodor's Choice ★ 🍴 **Bar Melusine.** Renee Erickson, 2016 James Beard Award winner for best chef in the Northwest, takes inspiration from France's Atlantic coast and transforms it into a cool, marble-topped ode to Northwest seafood. The menu offers seafood, both raw and creatively cooked, like the fried fish skin as well as meaty continental classics like steak tartare and a burger. **Known for:** oysters; pretty space. [$] *Average main: $37* ✉ *1060 E. Union St., Capitol Hill* ☎ *206/900–8808* 🌐 *www.barmelusine.com* 🕐 *No lunch* ✥ *2:G6.*

$ FRENCH 🍴 **Café Presse.** Two distinct rooms create plenty of space at this French bistro just off the Pike–Pine Corridor, where you can get such Parisian fare as pressed chicken with greens; a *croque madame*; mussels with french fries; pan-roasted quail with sautéed potatoes and apples; and simple cheese platters with slices of baguette. This is the spot to order some red table wine and people-watch. **Known for:** chicken; french fries; magazine rack. [$] *Average main: $15* ✉ *1117 12th Ave., Capitol Hill* ☎ *206/709–7674* 🌐 *www.cafepresseseattle.com* ✥ *2:G6.*

$ CAFÉ 🍴 **Caffé Vita.** Though it's now a certifiable mini-empire with locations throughout Seattle and in other cities, Caffé Vita's roasting operations, and indeed its heart and soul, are located right in Capitol Hill's Pike–Pine Corridor. The super-savvy owner also owns Via Tribunali pizzeria and several other local hot spots—and there's no doubt he knows how to tap into the gritty Seattle energy. **Known for:** good place to work; coffee. [$] *Average main: $3* ✉ *1005 E. Pike St., Capitol Hill* ☎ *206/709–4440* 🌐 *www.caffevita.com* ✥ *2:G6.*

$$$ ITALIAN Fodor's Choice ★ 🍴 **Cascina Spinasse.** Squeeze into this postage-stamp-size eatery with its cream-colored lace curtains and true Italian soul—and come hungry, because chef Stuart Lane knows how to make pasta. It's made fresh daily and comes with such sauces and fillings as short rib ragu, eggplant and anchovies, or simply, as in their signature dish, dressed in butter and sage. *Secondi* options can range from braised pork belly with cabbage to stewed venison served over polenta. **Known for:** hand-made pasta; amaro. [$] *Average main: $26* ✉ *1531 14th Ave., Capitol Hill* ☎ *206/251–7673* 🌐 *www.spinasse.com* 🕐 *Closed Tues. No lunch* ✥ *2:G6.*

$ BAKERY 🍴 **Crumble & Flake Patisserie.** Long a creative and renowned fine-dining pastry chef, Neil Robertson found his true calling when he opened up this tiny but exciting bakery. His restaurant training and baker brain combine to impress with his sweet spins on classics and detailed re-creations of traditional French baked goods, which earned him a semi-finalist award in the James Beard awards and a spot in the heart of Seattleites. **Known for:** smoked paprika croissants. [$] *Average main: $3* ✉ *1500 E. Olive Way, Capitol Hill* ☎ *206/329–1804* 🌐 *www.crumbleandflake.com* 🕐 *Closed Mon. and Tues. No dinner* ✥ *2:F5.*

$ BURGER 🍴 **Dick's.** This local chain of hamburger drive-ins with iconic orange signage has changed little since the 1950s. The fries are hand-cut, the shakes are hand-dipped (made with hard ice cream), and the burgers hit the spot. **Known for:** affordability; burgers. [$] *Average main: $3* ✉ *115 Broadway E, Capitol Hill* ☎ *206/323–1300* 🌐 *www.ddir.com* ✥ *2:F5.*

$ PIZZA Fodor's Choice ★ 🍴 **Dino's Tomato Pie.** Long hailed as the creator of Seattle's best pizza at his first shop, Delancey, Brandon Petit perhaps even improves on his previous recipe as he re-creates the neighborhood joints of his New Jersey childhood. The thick, crisp corners of the square Sicilian pies caramelize in the hot oven into what is practically pizza candy, while lovers of traditional round pizza will enjoy the char on the classics. **Known for:** square pizza; creative cocktails. [$] *Average main: $15* ✉ *1524 E. Olive Way, Capitol Hill* ☎ *206/403–1742* 🌐 *www.dinostomatopie.com* 🕒 *No lunch* ✥ *2:F5.*

$ AMERICAN 🍴 **Kurt Farm Shop.** Few ice creams in the world go as directly from cow to cone as those of Kurt Farm Shop: Kurt Timmermeister milks his Jersey cows each morning for a smooth, rich, and incredibly fresh scoop. His Jersey cream base flavor combines with both traditional and innovative flavors from his own farm, including nocino, Sichuan peppercorn, and carrot. **Known for:** creative flavors; farm-fresh ingredients. [$] *Average main: $5* ✉ *1424 11th Ave., Capitol Hill* 🌐 *www.kurtwoodfarms.com/kurt-farm-shop* ✥ *2:G6.*

$$$ MODERN AMERICAN Fodor's Choice ★ 🍴 **Lark.** The Central Agency Building, a converted 1917 warehouse with 25-foot ceilings, is the setting for mouthwateringly delicious small plates to share and seasonally inspired main dishes—you'll want to sample as much as possible. The expert servers can help you choose from an impressive wine list, and will happily help you decide from a menu divided into cheese; vegetables and grains; charcuterie; fish; meat; and, of course, dessert. **Known for:** small plates; local ingredients. [$] *Average main: $30* ✉ *952 E. Seneca St., Capitol Hill* ☎ *206/323–5275* 🌐 *www.larkseattle.com* 🕒 *Closed Mon. No lunch* ✥ *2:F6.*

$$$ VIETNAMESE 🍴 **Monsoon.** With an elegant bar and laid-back roof deck, this serene Vietnamese restaurant on a tree-lined residential stretch of Capitol Hill is a better bet than ever. Upscale fare blends Vietnamese and Pacific Northwest elements, including wild gulf prawns with lemongrass, catfish clay pot with fresh coconut juice and green onion, and lamb with fermented soybeans and sweet onions. **Known for:** crab; wine. [$] *Average main: $25* ✉ *615 19th Ave. E, Capitol Hill* ☎ *206/325–2111* 🌐 *www.monsoonrestaurants.com* ✥ *2:H4.*

$$ MODERN AMERICAN 🍴 **Oddfellows Cafe + Bar.** Smack in the center of the Pike–Pine universe, this huge, ultrahip space anchoring the Oddfellows Building, across from Cal Anderson Park, serves good (and sometimes inspired) American food from morning coffee to late-night drinks. The day might start with breakfast biscuits and thick brioche French toast; later on you can order the "Oddball" sandwich of meatballs in marinara sauce with provolone and Parmesan and roasted free-range chicken. **Known for:** baked goods; drinks. [$] *Average main: $20* ✉ *1525 10th Ave., Capitol Hill* ☎ *206/325–0807* 🌐 *www.oddfellowscafe.com* ✥ *2:F6.*

$$ GREEK 🍴 **Omega Ouzeri.** Open the door into Greece, be welcomed by the white-washed walls, blond-wood tables, bold-blue chairs, and most importantly, by the open kitchen full of grilling and olive oil. Unique twists on classic Greek dishes marry tomato jam with meatballs, and watermelon salad with grilled halloumi cheese. **Known for:** seafood; Greek spirits. [$] *Average main: $22* ✉ *1529 14th Ave., Capitol Hill* ☎ *206/257–4515* 🌐 *www.omegaouzeri.com* 🕒 *No lunch* 💳 *No credit cards* ✥ *2:G6.*

$$$
MODERN
AMERICAN

✕ **Poppy.** Jerry Traunfeld's bright, airy restaurant on the northern end of Broadway is a feast for the senses, with funky design details, friendly staff, and a happening bar area. Start with one of the many interesting cocktails and an order of eggplant fries with sea salt and honey; then peruse the menu, which offers small plates and thali of various sizes— the idea is inspired by the Indian thali meal, in which a selection of different dishes is served in small compartments on a large platter, though the food here is mainly seasonal new American cuisine with occasional Asian accents. **Known for:** thali plates; cocktails; Indian spices. ⓢ *Average main: $30* ✉ *622 Broadway E, Capitol Hill* ☎ *206/324–1108* ⊕ *www.poppyseattle.com* ☾ *No lunch* ✛ *2:F4.*

Quinn's. Capitol Hill's original gastropub has friendly bartenders, an *amazing* selection of beers on tap (with the West Coast and Belgium heavily represented), an extensive list of whiskey, and an edgy menu of good food, which you can enjoy at the long bar or at a table on either of the two floors of the industrial-chic space. Spicy fried peanuts and country-style rabbit pâté are good ways to start—then you can choose from Painted Hills beef tartare with pumpernickel crisps, perfect marrow bones with baguette and citrus jam, or a cheese plate. Heartier mains, like the signature wild boar sloppy Joe are available at dinnertime. A pared-down pub menu is also available from 3 pm to midnight or later. The folks here take their libations seriously, so feel free to chat up the bartenders about their favorites. ✉ *1001 E. Pike St., Capitol Hill* ☎ *206/325–7711* ⊕ *www.quinnspubseattle.com* ☾ *No lunch* 🍴 *Reservations not accepted* ✛ *2:G6.*

$$$
ITALIAN

✕ **Serafina osteria & enoteca.** To many loyal patrons, Serafina is *the* perfect neighborhood restaurant: burnt-sienna walls topped by a forest-green ceiling convey the feeling of a lush garden villa—a sense heightened by the small sheltered courtyard out back. Menu highlights include grilled eggplant rolled with ricotta and basil; asparagus with an egg and truffle oil; and gnocchi with rotating ingredients such as mushrooms, nettle, or beef cheeks. **Known for:** live music on some nights; eggplant rolls. ⓢ *Average main: $29* ✉ *2043 Eastlake Ave. E, Capitol Hill* ☎ *206/323–0807* ⊕ *www.serafinaseattle.com* ☾ *No lunch Sat.* ✛ *2:E1.*

$$$
MODERN
AMERICAN

✕ **Sitka & Spruce.** James Beard Award–winner Matthew Dillon helms this popular restaurant at Capitol Hill's Melrose Market; it's romantic, chic, friendly, and cutting-edge all at once. Diners choose from seasonally rotating offerings such as king bolete mushrooms with blistered fava beans, whole baby turnips in tarragon with house-made yogurt with za'atar spice, and deliciously tender charcoal-grilled chicken served with rye berries grown in nearby Winthrop. **Known for:** small plates; vegetables; wood-fired dishes. ⓢ *Average main: $29* ✉ *1531 Melrose Ave., Capitol Hill* ☎ *206/324–0662* ⊕ *www.sitkaandspruce.com* ✛ *2:E6.*

$
AMERICAN

✕ **Skillet Diner.** Diner fare takes a modern turn on Capitol Hill at this stylishly retro, brick-and-mortar version of one of the city's pioneering food trucks. Skillet's hot, strong coffee is made with beans from neighboring Caffé Vita, while their burgers are ridiculously savory, on a beef tallow bun, topped with signature "bacon jam" and blue cheese (max out the decadence with a side of cheesy poutine). **Known for:** bacon jam; burgers; fried chicken. ⓢ *Average main: $14* ✉ *1400 E. Union, Capitol Hill* ☎ *206/512–2000* ⊕ *www.skilletstreetfood.com* ✛ *2:G6.*

$ ✕**Starbucks Reserve Roastery & Tasting Room.** You could call it a coffee
CAFÉ amusement park for its many ways to keep audiences entertained, but
the sprawling combination café and showroom is deadly serious about
its beans. Fans of the chain, and the coffee curious, will find lots to taste
and explore here in 15,000 square feet of coffee culture. **Known for:**
personal attention; great space. $ *Average main: $3* ✉ *1124 Pike St.,
Capitol Hill* ☎ *206/624–0173* ⊕ *www.roastery.starbucks.com* ✛ *2:E6.*

$$ ✕**Stateside.** Low lights, ceiling fans, and palm-patterned wallpaper com-
VIETNAMESE bine with weathered gold fixtures to evoke a sense of Vietnam with
nearly the same precision as the chef's rendition of *bun cha Hanoi.* The
setting transports, while the food impresses: great Vietnamese food isn't
hard to find around town, but chef Eric Johnson brings an outsider's
playfulness to the cuisine—as well as a pedigree at Michelin-starred
restaurants. Vietnamese coffee finds its way into popsicles and tropical
cocktails find their way into coconuts, but what's most impressive is
the sheer amount of flavor—through technique, herbs, and spices—that
Johnson packs into each of his dishes. **Known for:** great ambience;
bun cha Hanoi. $ *Average main: $24* ✉ *300 E. Pike St., Suite 1200,
Capitol Hill* ☎ *206/557–7273* ⊕ *www.statesideseattle.com* ⊗ *No lunch
weekdays* ✛ *2:E6.*

$ ✕**Stumptown Coffee Roasters.** This hip Portland powerhouse is one of the
CAFÉ West Coast's most well-known coffee-roasting operations and Seattle
simply loves the stuff. There's good reason: the coffee is divine, and the
vibe, while überhip, isn't too cool for school. **Known for:** good coffee;
laid-back vibe. $ *Average main: $3* ✉ *1115 12th Ave., Capitol Hill*
☎ *206/860–2937* ⊕ *www.stumptowncoffee.com* ✛ *2:G6.*

$$$$ ✕**Sushi Kappo Tamura.** The seafood is as blindingly fresh as one would
SEAFOOD hope for at a Seattle sushi bar, but chef Taichi Kitamura ups the ante
by adding seasonal and Northwest touches to the meals at his sophis-
ticated restaurant—such as pork loin from sustainable Skagit River
Ranch with organic watercress. Order a series of small plates at the
blond-wood tables, like oysters from nearby Totten Inlet in ponzu
sauce, or impeccable spot prawns in soy-butter sauce—or put yourself
in Kitamura's more-than-capable hands for omakase (chef's choice) at
the 13-seat bar. **Known for:** high-quality fish; creative sushi. $ *Aver-
age main: $39* ✉ *2968 Eastlake Ave. E, Capitol Hill* ☎ *206/547–0937*
⊕ *www.sushikappotamura.com* ✛ *2:F1.*

$$ ✕**Via Tribunali.** This dark, moody, and very happening pizza spot on Pike
PIZZA Street is a reliable place for a fun pizza feast—they churn Neapolitan-
style pizzas from the wood-burning stove so quickly that it may take
you by surprise. Fresh, large salads—such as the di Parma, with arugula and Parmigiano-Reggiano, and the Tonno, with mozzarella, cherry
tomatoes, tuna, and olives—and a vast variety of pizza toppings make
this a crowd-pleaser. **Known for:** pizza margherita; hot scene. $ *Aver-
age main: $17* ✉ *913 Pike St., Capitol Hill* ☎ *206/322–9234* ⊕ *www.
viatribunali.com* ⊗ *No lunch* ✛ *2:F6.*

$ ✕**Victrola Coffee Roasters.** Victrola is one of the most loved of Capitol
CAFÉ Hill's many coffeehouses, and it's easy to see why: the sizable space is
lovely—the walls are hung with artwork by local painters and photographers—the coffee and pastries are fantastic, the baristas are skillful,

and everyone, from soccer moms to indie rockers, is made to feel like this neighborhood spot exists just for them. If 15th Avenue East is too far off the beaten path for you, there are also branches at 310 East Pike Street (206/462–6259), between Melrose and Bellevue, as well as in Beacon Hill. **Known for:** espresso; fresh-roasted beans. $ *Average main: $3* ✉ *411 15th Ave. E, Capitol Hill* ☎ *206/462–6259* ⊕ *www.victrolacoffee.com* ✛ *2:G4.*

MADISON PARK

$ ✕ **Café Flora.** The vegetarian and vegan menu changes frequently at

VEGETARIAN Café Flora, but the chefs tend to keep things simple, with dishes like

FAMILY black-bean burgers topped with spicy aioli, polenta with leeks and spinach, and the popular "Oaxaca tacos" (corn tortillas filled with potatoes and four types of cheese). You can eat in the Atrium, which has a stone fountain, skylight, and garden-style café tables and chairs, or try the weekday happy hour in the bar or on the garden patio. **Known for:** vegan fare; brunch. $ *Average main: $15* ✉ *2901 E. Madison St., Madison Park* ☎ *206/325–9100* ⊕ *www.cafeflora.com* ✛ *2:H5.*

$ ✕ **Little Uncle.** On a busy arterial near the southeastern edge of Capitol

THAI Hill, this tiny storefront is small but mighty: its owners could work—

Fodor's Choice and, in fact, have worked—the line in far more luxurious kitchens.

★ Wiley Frank (formerly of Lark) and his wife Poncharee Kounpungchart ("PK") toured PK's native Thailand for a year, soaking up street food recipes, before founding this haven for exceptional pad thai made with local tofu, tender morsels of braised beef cheek stuffed into steamed buns, and other fresh, spicy specials. **Known for:** kaho soi; street food. $ *Average main: $12* ✉ *1523 E. Madison St., #101, Madison Park* ☎ *206/549–6507* ⊕ *www.littleuncleseattle.com* ⊗ *Closed Sun. and Mon.* ✛ *2:H6.*

FREMONT AND PHINNEY RIDGE

Friendly neighborhood joints, Thai restaurants, good pubs, and a few swankier eateries worth making the trek to the northern part of the city round out the options in these quirky adjacent neighborhoods. Fremont, in particular, has a bumpin' evening scene, with scenesters filling the tables. Phinney Ridge, farther up the hill, is more laid-back and quiet, with mostly family-friendly spots and a few beloved gems.

FREMONT

$$ ✕ **Joule.** Married chef-owners Rachel Yang and Seif Chirchi have wowed

KOREAN Seattle diners with their French-fusion spins on Asian cuisine here and at nearby Revel. Joule's nouvelle take on a Korean steak house serves meat options like Wagyu bavette steak with truffled pine nuts and short rib with Kalbi and grilled kimchi. Nonmeat menu items include Chinese broccoli with walnut pesto and mackerel with green curry cilantro crust and black currant, while a weekend brunch buffet goes slightly more mainstream with a fruit and pastry buffet, as well as entrées like oatmeal-stuffed porchetta. **Known for:** brunch buffet; Korean-sauced steaks. $ *Average main: $21* ✉ *3506 Stone Way N, Fremont* ☎ *206/632–1913* ⊕ *www.joulerestaurant.com* ⊗ *No lunch* ✛ *3:E5.*

$$$ SEAFOOD Fodor's Choice ★ 🍴 **Manolin.** Walking into the light-filled dining room of Manolin, with its horseshoe-shape bar framing the open kitchen, transports you straight to the sea. Blue tiles, the wood-fired oven in the center, the cool marble bar, and the seafood-laden menu all bring diners to the ambiguous maritime destination, where ceviches are inspired by coastal Mexico, plantain chips come from the Caribbean, smoked salmon has vaguely Scandinavian flavors, and the squid with black rice and ginger is as if from Asia, all mingling on the menu. **Known for:** ceviche; cocktails. [$] *Average main: $28* ✉ *3621 Stone Way N, Fremont* ☎ *206/294–3331* 🌐 *www.manolin-seattle.com* 🕓 *No lunch. Closed Mon.* ▭ *No credit cards* ✥ *3:E5.*

$ CAFÉ 🍴 **Milstead & Co.** Seattle's premier multiroaster café would be a parody of coffee culture if it weren't so good at what it does: curate a lineup of the country's best coffees and pour them expertly in a variety of methods. Baristas here coach customers through the process of picking a bean (origin, type, and roast) and method, so this is not the place to come for a quick caffeine hit. **Known for:** knowledgeable staff; variety of beans. [$] *Average main: $4* ✉ *900 N. 34th St., Fremont* ☎ *206/659–4814* 🌐 *www.milsteadandco.com* ✥ *3:E5.*

$ ASIAN FUSION Fodor's Choice ★ 🍴 **Revel.** Adventurous enough for the most committed gourmands but accessible enough to be a neighborhood lunchtime favorite, Revel starts with Korean street food and shakes it up with a variety of influences, from French to Americana. Noodle dishes at this popular, sleek spot (try for a counter seat overlooking the open kitchen) might feature smoked tea noodles with roast duck or seaweed noodles with Dungeness crab, while irresistibly spicy dumplings might be stuffed with bites of short ribs, shallots, and scallions, or perhaps chickpeas, roasted cauliflower, and mustard yogurt. **Known for:** rice bowl; creative dumplings. [$] *Average main: $16* ✉ *403 N. 36th St., Fremont* ☎ *206/547–2040* 🌐 *www.revelseattle.com* ✥ *3:D5.*

$$$ SEAFOOD 🍴 **RockCreek.** A temple to seafood, this is the restaurant that locals want to bring visitors to: an example of the casual way seafood weaves into all sorts of dishes when you live so close to such bounty. The mix of appetizers, oyster shooters, small plates, and full entrées makes the long menu something of an epic adventure filled with fresh local, domestic, and global fish—from local oysters to Hawaiian tuna, Norwegian mackerel, back to black cod from Washington's own Neah Bay. **Known for:** seafood; fun atmosphere. [$] *Average main: $28* ✉ *4300 Fremont Ave. N, Fremont* ☎ *206/557–7732* 🌐 *www.rockcreekseattle.com* 🕓 *No lunch weekdays* ✥ *3:D4.*

$ BURGER FAMILY 🍴 **Uneeda Burger.** A casual burger shack from a fine-dining chef means flavor and execution that are always on point. The controlled chaos of this family-friendly joint can make it hard to get a table on sunny days, but the lines and wait are worth it for the perfectly cooked burgers. **Known for:** family-friendly; patio; burgers. [$] *Average main: $8.50* ✉ *4302 Fremont Avenue N, Fremont* ☎ *206/547–2600* 🌐 *www.uneedaburger.com* ✥ *3:D4.*

$ BISTRO Fodor's Choice ★ 🍴 **Vif.** Part coffee shop, part casual snack restaurant, and part wine retailer, Vif is all magic. The brainchild of a former pastry chef and wine director of one of Seattle's bygone restaurants, the menu brings the kind of nuance and skill that you'd expect from a pastry chef, but the elegance of a wine expert. **Known for:** wine; snacks. [$] *Average*

CLOSE UP

Regional Flavors of the Pacific Northwest

Seattle is a food lover's city, and enjoys easy access to an incredible bounty of foods from land and sea, from wild Dungeness crab and line-caught halibut to foraged stinging nettles and brightly colored apples. Many Seattleites tend kitchen gardens, hunt and fish, trap crabs, dig clams, harvest berries in season, and cross the mountains to pick fruit in the Wenatchee and Yakima valleys.

Gathering fresh foods at the source has honed local palates: Seattleites know—by taste, smell, and touch—when foods are fresh and at their peak. Wild salmon, in particular, has played an important role in local cuisine, as have halibut, oysters, Dungeness crab, prawns, mussels, scallops, geoduck and razor clams, as well as blackberries, huckleberries, fiddlehead ferns, chanterelle and morel mushrooms, and wild greens.

It is an absolute passion of Seattle's chefs to find and use organic ingredients from local farms, orchards, and dairies. (Some even grow their own produce on rooftop gardens or large-scale farms.) Asparagus, tomatoes, and hot peppers arrive from Yakima Valley; sweet onions from Walla Walla; apricots and pears from Wenatchee; apples from Lake Chelan and beyond. Lamb and beef come from dryland pastures, while clams and oysters are harvested from tidal flats in Samish Bay, the Hood Canal, Totten Inlet, and Willapa Bay. Pike Place Market and local farmers' markets are major meeting places for high-quality ingredients from across the state.

Local chefs' obsession with the freshest seasonal ingredients may make it difficult to get the same dish twice—especially at top-notch restaurants, where menus usually change seasonally, if not daily. No Northwest meal is complete, of course, without a bottle of wine from a regional winery, ale from a local microbrewery, or cocktail featuring a locally distilled spirit.

3

main: $8 ✉ *4401 Fremont Ave. N, Fremont* ☎ *206/557–7357* 🌐 *www.vifseattle.com* 🕑 *No dinner. Closed Mon.* ⊕ *3:D4.*

$$$ SEAFOOD 🍴 **Westward.** It's hard to beat the view from the Adirondack chairs around the oyster-shell-lined fire pit that sits on Westward's private lakefront, but the spacious restaurant does its best. But unlike so many restaurants with a view, Westward makes food that matches the scenery, both in style and quality; featuring Northwest seafood with Mediterranean flavors. **Known for:** outdoor dining; seafood; wood-fired dishes. [$] *Average main: $26* ✉ *2501 N. Northlake Way, Fremont* ☎ *206/552–8215* 🌐 *www.westwardseattle.com* 🕑 *No lunch weekdays* ⊕ *3:F5.*

PHINNEY RIDGE

$ BAKERY Fodor's Choice ★ 🍴 **Coyle's Bakeshop.** One of the city's neighborhood charmers, this beloved bakery churns out the best of French, British, and American pastry traditions, as well as their own unique treats. Mornings mean the espresso bar is busy and the croissants are flying off the shelves, while midday offers light salads, quiches, and their savory signature, the cretzel—a buttery, crisp, pretzel-knotted treat. **Known for:** cretzels; cake. [$] *Average main: $4* ✉ *8300 Greenwood Ave. N, Greenwood* ☎ *206/257–4736* 🌐 *www.coylesbakeshop.com* 🕑 *No dinner* ⊕ *3:D1.*

BALLARD

Ballard is the north end's answer to Capitol Hill when it comes to edgy, innovative, and delicious dining. Restaurants have taken a cue from the beloved year-round farmers' market (held every Sunday, rain or shine, from 10 to 3 along historic Ballard Avenue NW), and fresh produce, local ingredients, and top-notch quality are de rigueur here. There's sure a lot to choose from—savor anything from chewy slices at local pizza darling Delancey to pristine Northwest oysters at the Walrus and the Carpenter.

$$ ✕ **Bastille.** A trendy, high-design French brasserie mecca for hip folks
FRENCH   seeking out reliably delicious French cuisine, Bastille is one of the more popular spots in Ballard. Snazzy diners sip simple house cocktails and munch on delicious steak frites, moules frites, local oysters, and well-executed daily fish specials such as Washington-caught salmon. **Known for:** steak frites; boisterous atmosphere; cocktails. $ *Average main: $22* ✉ *5307 Ballard Ave. NW, Ballard* ☎ *206/453–5014* ⊕ *www.bastilleseattle.com* ☾ *No lunch* ✛ *3:A3.*

$$ ✕ **Brimmer & Heeltap.** This stunningly beautiful gastropub is the quintes-
ASIAN FUSION   sential neighborhood restaurant, built on warm service and consistently great food. Seated in the white wooden chairs or on the bold turquoise benches, to eat here is to be welcomed into the dining room of a long-lost friend. **Known for:** brunch; patio; creative Asian-infused dishes. $ *Average main: $17* ✉ *425 N.W. Market St., Ballard* ☎ *206/420–2534* ⊕ *www.brimmerandheeltap.com* ☾ *No lunch weekdays. Closed Tues.* ▭ *No credit cards* ✛ *3:C3.*

$ ✕ **Café Besalu.** A slice of France here in Ballard, this small, casual bakery
BAKERY   gets patrons from across the entire city, thanks to its *I-swear-I'm-in-Paris* croissants—they are buttery, flaky perfection. Weekend lines are long, but if you score a table, you'll be in heaven. **Known for:** croissants; jam. $ *Average main: $8* ✉ *5909 24th Ave. NW, Ballard* ☎ *206/789–1463* ⊕ *www.cafebesalu.com* ☾ *Closed Mon. and Tues.* ✛ *3:A2.*

$$ ✕ **Cafe Munir.** Perhaps the best-kept secret in the city, this neighborhood
LEBANESE   Lebanese joint is adorable and affordable. Whitewashed walls sparsely
Fodor'sChoice   populated by old-world art match the white tablecloths, which are
★   topped with intricate metal candleholders. **Known for:** hummus with lamb; whiskey. $ *Average main: $17* ✉ *2408 N.W. 80th St., Ballard* ☎ *206/783–4190* ⊕ *www.cafemunir.blogspot.com* ☾ *No lunch* ✛ *3:B1.*

$ ✕ **Delancey.** Brandon Pettit spent years developing his thin-but-chewy
PIZZA   pizza crust, and the final product has made him a contender for the
Fodor'sChoice   city's best pies. Pettit himself is occasionally manning the wood-fired
★   oven at this sweetly sophisticated little spot north of downtown Ballard that he owns with partner Molly Wizenberg (author of the popular "Orangette" food blog). **Known for:** quality pizza toppings; desserts. $ *Average main: $16* ✉ *1415 N.W. 70th St., Ballard* ☎ *206/838–1960* ⊕ *www.delanceyseattle.com* ☾ *Closed Mon. No lunch* ✛ *3:B1.*

$ ✕ **The Fat Hen.** An Instagram-perfect brunch spot, this Ballard charmer
CONTEMPORARY   deals in trends like avocado toast, and classic comforts like Benedicts
Fodor'sChoice   and cheesy egg bakes. The light-filled café offers house-made baked
★   goods and coffee to start—and for diners waiting in the sometimes epic lines—from the marble countertop. **Known for:** brunch; egg

bakes; ricotta toast. $ *Average main: $9* ⌧ *1418 N.W. 70th St., Ballard* ☎ *206/782–5422* ⊕ *www.thefathenseattle.com* ⊙ *No dinner. Closed Mon.* ✛ *3:B1.*

$ ✕ **Hot Cakes.** A few savory dishes are available at this Ballard "cak-
CAFÉ ery," but consider passing on the chicken potpie in favor of the grilled chocolate sandwich. Autumn Martin, formerly head chocolatier at Theo Chocolate, specializes in creative, high-quality desserts (including vegan options) such as a "s'mores" molten chocolate cake with house-made marshmallows and caramel, and cookies with house-smoked chocolate chips. **Known for:** molten chocolate cakes; extravagant shakes. $ *Average main: $9* ⌧ *5427 Ballard Ave. NW, Ballard* ☎ *206/420–3431* ⊕ *www.getyourhotcakes.com* ✛ *3:A3.*

$ ✕ **La Carta de Oaxaca.** True to its name, this low-key, bustling Ballard
MEXICAN favorite serves traditional Mexican cooking with Oaxacan accents. The *mole negro* is a must, served with chicken or pork; another standout is the *albondigas* (a spicy vegetable soup with meatballs). **Known for:** margaritas; albondigas; mole. $ *Average main: $15* ⌧ *5431 Ballard Ave. NW, Ballard* ☎ *206/782–8722* ⊕ *www.lacartadeoaxaca.com* ⊙ *Closed Sun. No lunch Mon.* ✛ *3:A3.*

$$ ✕ **Pestle Rock.** Convincing Seattleites to forgo their pad thai in favor of
THAI the spicy, herb-filled Isan cuisine of northern Thailand was a tough battle, but with a sleek, modern restaurant, skillful cooking, and plenty of peppers, Pestle Rock succeeded handily. Today, the tables are filled with locals knowingly ordering the house-made sausage, the coconut-milk curry noodles called kao soi, and pungent papaya salads, all filled with local ingredients such as wild salmon, Dungeness crab, and thoughtfully sourced meats. **Known for:** chicken wings; kao soi. $ *Average main: $17* ⌧ *2305 N.W. Market St., Ballard* ☎ *206/466–6671* ⊕ *www. pestlerock.com* ⊙ *Closed Tues.* ▭ *No credit cards* ✛ *3:A3.*

$$$$ ✕ **Ray's Boathouse.** The view of Shilshole Bay might be the main draw
SEAFOOD here, but the seafood is also fresh and well prepared. Perennial favorites include grilled salmon, Kasu sake–marinated sablefish, Dungeness crab, and regional oysters on the half shell. **Known for:** seafood; view. $ *Average main: $43* ⌧ *6049 Seaview Ave. NW, Ballard* ☎ *206/789–3770* ⊕ *www.rays.com* ✛ *3:A2.*

$ ✕ **Slate Coffee Bar.** In a city full of amazing coffee shops, Slate elevates
CAFÉ the arts of roasting, brewing, and serving. With a focus on flavor, they roast beans lightly enough to highlight unique characteristics (if you love your Starbucks dark roast, this is not the place for you). **Known for:** deconstructed espresso; light-roasted beans. $ *Average main: $4* ⌧ *5413 6th Ave. NW, Ballard* ✛ *3:C3.*

$$$ ✕ **Staple & Fancy.** The "Staple" side of this Ethan Stowell restaurant at
MODERN ITALIAN the south end of Ballard Avenue might mean ethereal gnocchi served
Fodor's Choice with corn and chanterelles, or a whole grilled branzino. But visitors to
★ the glam, remodeled, historic brick building are best served by going "Fancy," meaning the chef's choice dinner where diners are asked about allergies and food preferences, then presented with several courses (technically four, but the appetizer usually consists of a few different plates) of whatever the cooks are playing with on the line that night—cured meats, salads made with exotic greens, handmade pastas, seasonal

desserts. **Known for:** multicourse menu; pasta. [$] *Average main: $30* ✉ *4739 Ballard Ave. NW, Ballard* ☎ *206/789–1200* 🌐 *www.ethanstowellrestaurants.com* ⏲ *No lunch* ✣ *3:A4.*

$$$ ITALIAN 🍴 **Stoneburner.** Stylish and swimming in light, the oak paneling, dark accents, and wide windows onto bustling Ballard Avenue give this quasi-Italian joint an exciting vibe. The menu keeps one foot firmly rooted in Italy, with sections for pizza and pasta on the menu full of Mediterranean sensibilities. **Known for:** family-friendly; brunch; pizzas. [$] *Average main: $25* ✉ *5214 Ballard Ave. NW, Ballard* ☎ *206/695–2051* 🌐 *www.stoneburnerseattle.com* ⏲ *No lunch weekdays* ✣ *3:A3.*

$$$ SEAFOOD 🍴 **The Walrus and the Carpenter.** Chef-owner Renee Erickson was inspired by the casual oyster bars of Paris to open this bustling shoebox of a restaurant on the south end of Ballard Avenue (in the rear of a historic brick building, behind Staple & Fancy). Seats fill fast at the zinc bar and the scattered tall tables where seafood fans slurp on fresh-shucked kusshis and shigokus and other local oysters, but the menu also offers refined small plates like grilled sardines with shallots and walnuts or roasted greengage plums in cream. **Known for:** oysters; small plates. [$] *Average main: $27* ✉ *4743 Ballard Ave. NW, Ballard* ☎ *206/395–9227* 🌐 *www.thewalrusbar.com* ✣ *3:A4.*

WALLINGFORD AND GREEN LAKE

With everything from taco shops to ice cream, Trinidadian cuisine to prix-fixe dining, Wallingford has blossomed into a dining destination. James Beard (and *Iron Chef*) winner Maria Hines owns Tilth on 45th, a standout higher-end spot. With Kisaku as the anchor, this part of town has become something of a Japanese restaurant row. Look for sushi spots from cheap and decent to spectacular and ramen shops with deep, savory broths.

WALLINGFORD

$$$$ MODERN AMERICAN 🍴 **Art of the Table.** Small, pricey, but utterly unforgettable, the Art of the Table is a constantly changing tour de force where you're sure to experience an inspired meal. Friday and Saturday are a communal-dining experience with a prix-fixe menu; Wednesday, Thursday, and Sunday there is an à la carte menu in addition to the prix fixe. **Known for:** tasting menu; local ingredients. [$] *Average main: $95* ✉ *1054 N. 39th St., Wallingford* ☎ *206/282–0942* 🌐 *www.artofthetable.net* ⏲ *Closed Mon. and Tues. No lunch* ✣ *3:E5.*

$$$ SEAFOOD FAMILY 🍴 **Ivar's Salmon House.** This long dining room facing Lake Union has original Northwest Indian artwork collected by the restaurant's namesake founder. It's touristy, often gimmicky, and always packed, but it's also great Seattle fun—a real institution, in a building designed as a loose replica of a traditional longhouse. **Known for:** views; brunch buffet; salmon. [$] *Average main: $30* ✉ *401 N.E. Northlake Way, Wallingford* ☎ *206/632–0767* 🌐 *www.ivars.com* ✣ *3:G5.*

$$$ MODERN AMERICAN 🍴 **Tilth.** A certified organic restaurant by the much-lauded Maria Hines, Tilth serves up wonderful, inventive dishes that can be had as small plates or full entrées—the mini–duck burgers, seasonally inspired risottos, and wild salmon deserve special mention, and there's a vegan menu

CLOSE UP

Dining with Kids

Seattle is just as serious about its food as it is about ensuring that no visiting parent leaves town without knowing why. Here are some picks you and your kids will enjoy.

Café Flora, Capitol Hill. Local families love this vegetarian spot a short drive from the top of Capitol Hill—brunches are particularly fun.

Cafe Munir, Ballard. Later, this intimate, gorgeous spot turns romantic, but until about 7:30 pm, kids rule the roost, squealing with joy as they're allowed to eat hummus with their hands.

Delancey, Ballard. What kind of kid could turn down pizza this good? None, and neither can their parents, which is why this place stays packed with families.

Dough Zone Dumpling House, Bellevue. Consider the in-house dumpling makers live entertainment, and the oodles of noodles the perfect meal to keep kids happy.

Kidd Valley. Burgers, fries, shakes, and more in an indestructible fast-food restaurant that has branches in Queen Anne (on Queen Anne Avenue), Greenlake, and the University District.

Marination Ma Kai, West Seattle. Bright colors, fun food, and endless flavors of Hawaiian shave ice should keep the wee ones grinning.

Uneeda Burger, Fremont. A classic, casual burger joint that has as many options for grown-up tastes as it does for the little ones.

as well. The Craftsman house on Wallingford's busy commercial strip has been lovingly spruced up with leaf-green paint and local artwork. **Known for:** small plates; organic ingredients; brunch. [$] *Average main: $28* ✉ *1411 N. 45th St., Wallingford* ☎ *206/633–0801* 🌐 *www.tilthrestaurant.com* 🕒 *No lunch* ✥ *3:E4.*

GREEN LAKE

$$ JAPANESE 🍴 **Kisaku.** One of the most outstanding sushi restaurants in Seattle is quietly nestled in Green Lake—and the diners come in droves. Fresh sushi is the mainstay, along with signature rolls such as the Green Lake variety, with salmon, flying fish eggs, asparagus, avocado, and marinated seaweed, or the Wallingford, with yellowtail, green onion, cucumber, radish, sprouts, and flying fish eggs. **Known for:** omakase; family-friendly. [$] *Average main: $20* ✉ *2101 N. 55th St., Green Lake* ☎ *206/545–9050* 🌐 *www.kisaku.com* 🕒 *Closed Tues. No lunch Sun.* ✥ *3:F3.*

UNIVERSITY DISTRICT

The "U-District" is great for cheap eats from around the world but falls short on fine dining. It's worth strolling up and down The Ave (University Way NE) to see if anything beckons to you before settling on a spot. There are some popular brunch spots scattered about, too.

$ MEXICAN 🍴 **Agua Verde Café and Paddle Club.** Baja California Mexican cuisine and a laid-back vibe define this casual spot that's done up in bright, beachy colors and has a lively deck come summertime. Regulars swear by the

3

fresh fish tacos and *mangodillas* (quesadillas with mango and poblano chilies). **Known for:** views; fish tacos; margaritas. $ *Average main: $14* ✉ *1303 N.E. Boat St., University District* ☎ *206/545–8570* ⊕ *www.aguaverde.com* ✛ *3:H5.*

$$
BRAZILIAN

✕ **Tempero Do Brasil.** A festive taste of Brazil, Tempero serves satisfying cod, prawn, and halibut dishes simmered in coconut-based sauces, or for a larger meal, try *bife grelhado* (charbroiled Argentine steak); all entrées arrive with moist, chewy, long-grain rice and black beans. Finish with cold passion-fruit mousse and strong dark coffee. **Known for:** cozy setting; live music some nights; home-style cuisine. $ *Average main: $22* ✉ *5628 University Way NE, University District* ☎ *206/523–6229* ⊕ *www.temperodobrasil.net* ☾ *Closed Mon. No lunch* ✛ *3:H3.*

$
CHINESE

✕ **Xi'an Noodles.** Diners here sometimes find their meal interrupted by the soft thumping noise for which the chewy, ropy noodles the restaurant specializes in are named. *Biang biang* noodles are made by slapping strands of dough against the hard counter, which elongates them without toughening the dough. The wide strands come in a number of dishes, along with other preparations from the eponymous city. **Known for:** hand-pulled noodles; spicy food. $ *Average main: $7* ✉ *5259 University Way NE, University District* ☎ *206/522–8888* ✛ *3:H3.*

WEST SEATTLE

West Seattle is enough of a trek from Seattle's central neighborhoods that some restaurants have, historically, had a hard time filling their seats. Luckily, West Seattleites love to eat out, and a new culinary energy is taking hold, making even gourmands from Ballard make the trek. The real superstar here is Ma'ono (formerly known as Spring Hill), but plenty of other neighborhood joints are top-notch and inviting. A walk up and down California Avenue will offer up plenty of choices.

$
CAFÉ

✕ **Bakery Nouveau.** Widely considered one of the best bakeries in the city, Bakery Nouveau has perfected many things, including cakes, croissants, and tarts. Their chocolate cake, in particular, makes us swoon, though twice-baked almond croissants are so good you might think you're in France when you take a bite—and owner William Leaman did lead a U.S. team to victory in France's Coupe du Monde de la Boulangerie. **Known for:** breads; croissants; macarons. $ *Average main: $6* ✉ *4737 California Ave. SW, West Seattle* ☎ *206/923–0534* ⊕ *www.bakerynouveau.com* ✛ *1:E6.*

$$
PACIFIC NORTHWEST
Fodor's Choice
★

✕ **Ma'ono Fried Chicken & Whiskey.** A quietly hip vibe pervades this culinary beacon in West Seattle, where the vast bar surrounds an open kitchen. Diners of all stripes relish the Hawaiian spin on fresh and high-quality Pacific Northwest bounty. **Known for:** fried chicken; whiskey. $ *Average main: $18* ✉ *4437 California Ave. SW, West Seattle* ☎ *206/935–1075* ⊕ *www.maono.springhillnorthwest.com* ☾ *No lunch weekdays* ✛ *1:E6.*

$
HAWAIIAN
Fodor's Choice
★

✕ **Marination Ma Kai.** The best view of Downtown comes at a most affordable price: the brightly colored Adirondack chairs outside this Korean-Hawaiian fish shack offer a panoramic view of the entire Downtown area. Inside, you'll find tacos filled with Korean beef or "sexy tofu," Spam slider sandwiches, and a classic fish-and-chips—served with kimchi tartar sauce. **Known for:** views; Spam sliders; shave ice. $ *Average main: $10* ✉ *1660 Harbor Ave. SW, West Seattle* ☎ *206/328–8226* ⊕ *www.marinationmobile.com* ☾ *Breakfast Fri.–Sun. only* ▤ *No credit cards* ⊹ *1:E6.*

$$$$ ✕ **Salty's on Alki.** It's undeniably touristy, but the views simply can't
SEAFOOD be beat on a summer afternoon. Famed for its Sunday and holiday brunches and view of Seattle's skyline across the harbor, Salty's offers more in the way of quantity than quality—and sometimes a bit too much of its namesake ingredient—but it's a couple of steps up from the mainstream seafood chains. **Known for:** views; brunch buffet. $ *Average main: $40* ✉ *1936 Harbor Ave. SW, just past port complex, West Seattle* ☎ *206/937–1600* ⊕ *www.saltys.com* ⊹ *1:E6.*

THE EASTSIDE

Bellevue, Kirkland, and Woodinville are theoretically easy to get to from Downtown Seattle: the 520 (toll bridge) and I–90 bridges both are accessible from I–5. However, traffic is always an issue and grinds to a halt during rush hour. Don't plan a culinary expedition unless you already plan to visit this side of things—unless, of course, you have reservations at Café Juanita, the beloved and critically acclaimed restaurant that is more than worth the trek.

$$$$ ✕ **Café Juanita.** There are so many ways for a pricey "destination restau-
ITALIAN rant" to go overboard, making itself nothing more than a special-occa-
Fodor'sChoice sion spectacle, but Café Juanita manages to get everything just right.
★ This Kirkland space, remodeled in 2015, is refined without being overly posh, and the food—much of which has a northern Italian influence—is also perfectly balanced. **Known for:** service; tasting menus. $ *Average main: $45* ✉ *9702 N.E. 120th Pl., Kirkland* ☎ *425/823–1505* ⊕ *www. cafejuanita.com* ☾ *Closed Mon. No lunch* ⊹ *3:H6.*

$$ ✕ **Din Tai Fung.** Watch dumplings being pleated by hand through the
CHINESE large glass windows in the waiting area for this restaurant on the sec-
ond floor of Lincoln Square mall—it's a good thing the sight is so entertaining, because there's often a long wait. The *xiao long bao*, or "soup dumplings," are morsels of meat tucked into dough wrappers along with a slurp of broth, and are the famous attraction at Din Tai Fung, a U.S. branch of the famed Taipei-based chain. **Known for:** soup dumplings; rice cakes; pork chop. $ *Average main: $19* ✉ *700 Bellevue Way, Lincoln Square Mall, Bellevue* ☎ *425/698–1095* ⊕ *www. dintaifungusa.com* ⊹ *3:H3.*

$ ✕ **Dough Zone Dumpling House.** This place lives up to its name, serving
CHINESE freshly made carb-filled delights of many types: noodles, flatbreads, crepes, and dumplings. Hearty northern Chinese foods are carefully crafted in view of diners. **Known for:** soup dumplings; noodles. $ *Average main: $8* ✉ *15920 N.E. 8th St., #3, Bellevue* ☎ *425/641–8000* ⊹ *3:H6.*

$$$$ ✕ **The Herbfarm.** You might consider fasting before dining at the Herb-
PACIFIC farm. It's prix-fixe only and you'll get nine courses—dinner takes at
NORTHWEST least four hours and includes six fine wines (you might also want to

arrange for transportation there and back). **Known for:** tasting menu; farm tours. $ *Average main: $240* ✉ *14590 N.E. 145th St., Woodinville* ☎ *425/485–5300* ⊕ *www.theherbfarm.com* ☉ *Closed Mon.–Wed. No lunch* ✛ *3:H6.*

$$$$

STEAKHOUSE

✕ **John Howie Steak.** An upscale Northwest steak house in the Shops at the Bravern, John Howie is well-known for its USDA Prime 28-day, 35-day, and 42-day custom-aged, American Wagyu beef from Snake River Farms. Steaks are tender, juicy, and perfectly executed and salmon is always available. **Known for:** steak; sandwiches. $ *Average main: $45* ✉ *11111 N.E. 8th St., Shops at the Bravern, Bellevue* ☎ *425/440–0880* ⊕ *www.johnhowiesteak.com* ☉ *No lunch weekends* ✛ *3:H6.*

$$$

VIETNAMESE

✕ **Monsoon East.** The Eastside sibling of Capitol Hill's darling Vietnamese eatery is utterly polished and sleek—and much fancier than the original restaurant. The Vietnamese dishes are the favorites: diners love the *bo la lot* beef, crispy drunken chicken, catfish clay pot, and barbecued hoisin pork ribs. **Known for:** wine; drunken chicken. $ *Average main: $25* ✉ *10245 Main St., Bellevue* ☎ *425/635–1112* ⊕ *www.monsooneast.com* ✛ *3:H6.*

DINING AND LODGING MAP ATLAS

KEY

- □ *Hotels*
- ■ *Restaurants*
- ✥ *following reviews indicates a map-grid coordinate*

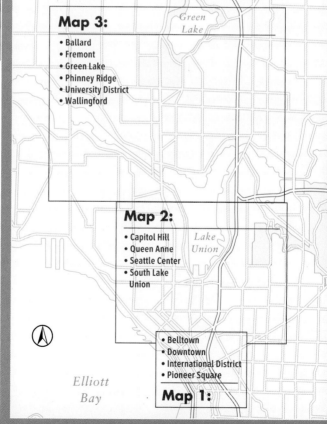

Map 3:
• Ballard
• Fremont
• Green Lake
• Phinney Ridge
• University District
• Wallingford
Green Lake
Map 2:
• Capitol Hill
• Queen Anne
• Seattle Center
• South Lake Union
Lake Union
• Belltown
• Downtown
• International District
• Pioneer Square
Map 1:
Elliott Bay

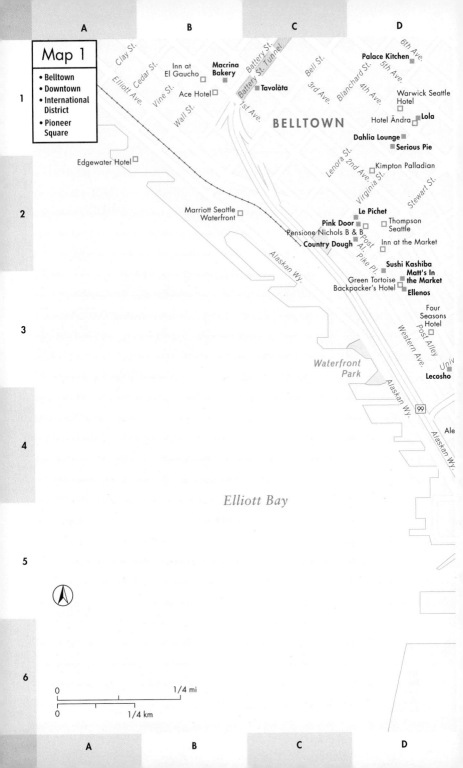

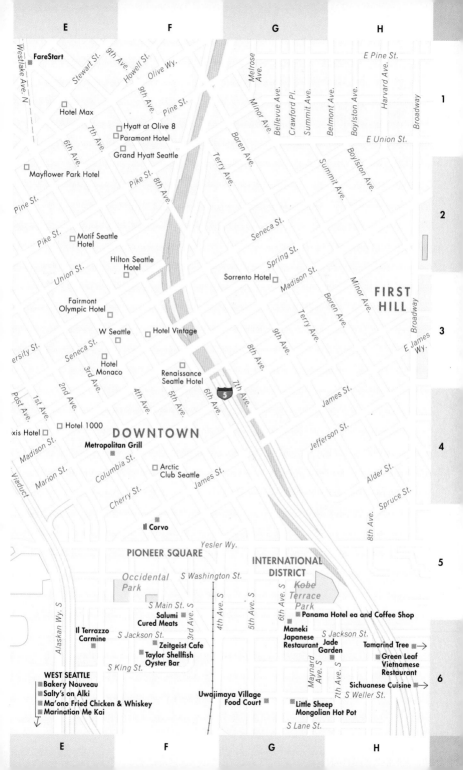

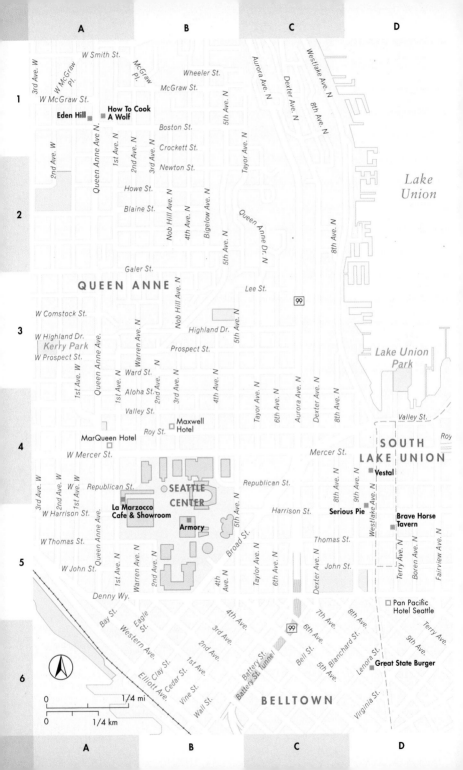

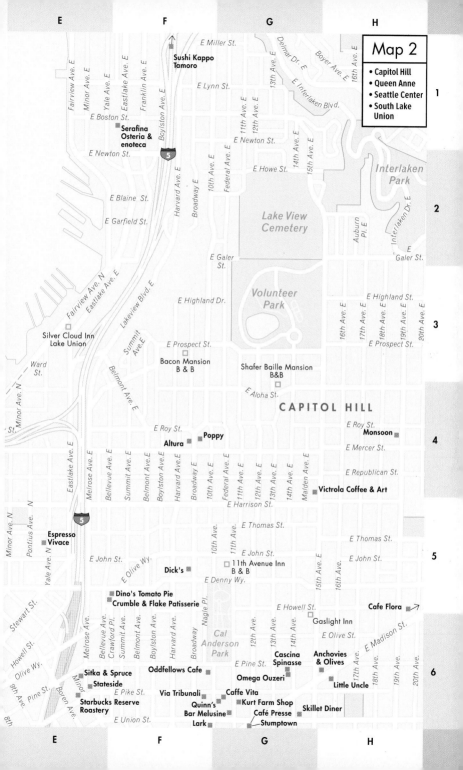

Map 2

- Capitol Hill
- Queen Anne
- Seattle Center
- South Lake Union

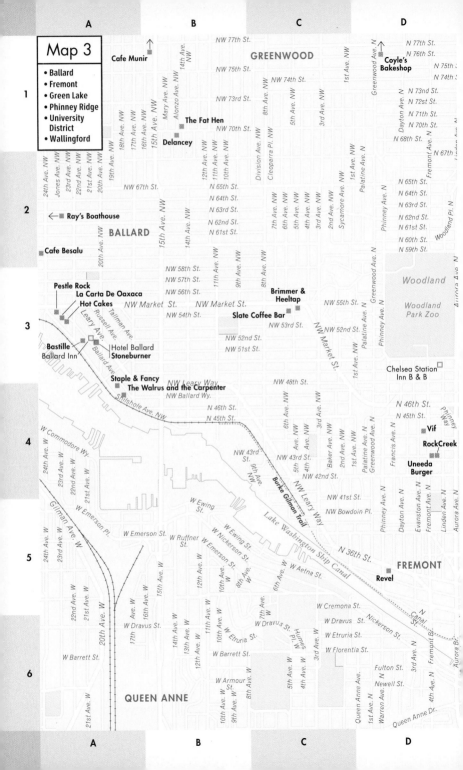

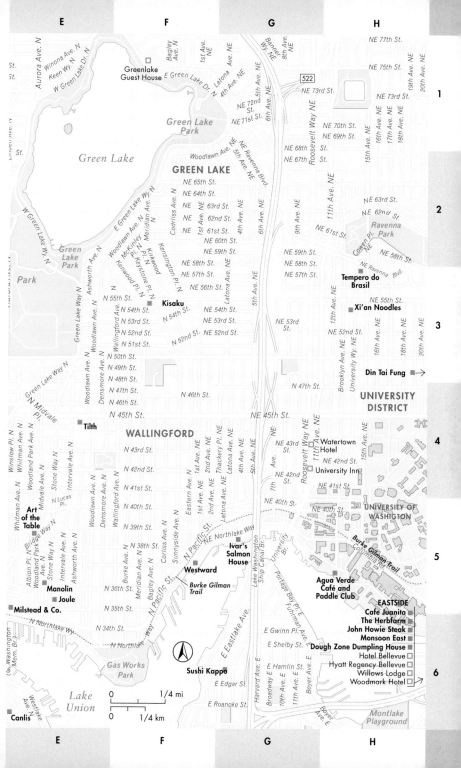

Restaurants

Agua Verde Café and Paddle Club, 3:H5
Altura, 2:F4
Anchovies & Olvies, 2:H6
Art of the Table, 3:E5
Bakery Nouveau, 1:E6
Bar Melusine, 2:G6
Bastille, 3:A3
Brave Horse Tavern, 2:D5
Brimmer & Heeltap, 3:C3
Café Besalu, 3:A2
Café Flora, 2:H5
Café Juanita, 3:H6
Café Munir, 3:B1
Café Presse, 2:G6
Caffé Vita, 2:G6
Canlis Restaurant, 3:E6
Cascina Spinasse, 2:G6
Country Dough, 1:D2
Coyle's Bakeshop, 3:D1
Crumble & Flake, 2:F5
Dahlia Lounge, 1:D1
Delancey, 3:B1
Dick's, 2:F5
Din Tai Fung, 3:H3
Dino's Tomato Pie, 2:F5
Dough Zone Dumpling House, 3:H6
Eden Hill, 2:A1
Ellenos Real Greek Yogurt, 1:D3
Espresso Vivace, 2:E5
FareStart, 1:E1
Great State Burger, 2:D6
Green Leaf Vietnamese Restaurant, 1:H6
Hot Cakes, 3:A3
How to Cook a Wolf, 2:A1

Il Corvo, 1:F5
Il Terrazzo Carmine, 1:E6
Ivar's Salmon House, 3:G5
Jade Garden, 1:H6
John Howie Steak, 3:H6
Joule, 3:E5
Kisaku, 3:F3
Kurt Farm Shop, 2:G6
La Carta de Oaxaca, 3:A3
La Marzocco Café & Showroom, 2:A4
Lark, 2:F6
Le Pichet, 1:D2
Lecosho, 1:D3
Little Sheep Mongolian Hot Pot, 1:G6
Little Uncle, 2:H6
Lola, 1:D1
Ma'ono Fried Chicken & Whiskey, 1:E6
Macrina Bakery, 1:B1
Maneki Japanese Restaurant, 1:G6
Manolin, 3:E5
Marination Ma Kai, 1:E6
Matt's in the Market, 1:D3
Metropolitan Grill, 1:E4
Milstead & Co., 3:E5
Monsoon East, 3:H6
Monsoon, 2:H4
Oddfellows Café + Bar, 2:F6
Omega Ouzeri, 2:G6
Palace Kitchen, 1:D1
Panama Hotel Tea and Coffee Shop, 1:G5
Pestle Rock, 3:A3
Poppy, 2:F4
Quinn's, 2:G6

Ray's Boathouse, 3:A2
Revel, 3:D5
RockCreek, 3:D4
Salty's on Alki, 1:E6
Salumi Cured Meats, 1:F5
Seattle Center Armory, 2:B5
Serafina osteria & enoteca, 2:E1
Serious Pie, 1:D1
Sichuanese Cuisine Restaurant, 1:H6
Sitka & Spruce, 2:E6
Skillet Diner, 2:G6
Slate Coffee Bar, 3:C3
Staple & Fancy, 3:A4
Starbucks Reserve Roastery & Tasting Room, 2:E6
Stateside, 2:E6
Stoneburner, 3:A3
Stumptown Coffee Roasters, 2:G6
Sushi Kappo Tamura, 2:F1
Sushi Kashiba, 1:D3
Tamarind Tree, 1:H6
Tavolàta, 1:C1
Taylor Shellfish Oyster Bar, 1:F6
Tempero Do Brasil, 3:H3
The Fat Hen, 3:B1
The Herbfarm, 3:H6
The Pink Door, 1:D2
The Walrus and the Carpenter, 3:A4
Tilth, 3:E4
Uneeda Burger, 3:D4
Uwajimaya Village Food Court, 1:G6
Vestal, 2:D4

Via Tribunali, 2:F6
Victrola Coffee, 2:G4
Vif, 3:D4
Westward, 3:F5
Xi'an Noodles, 3:H3
Zeitgeist Café, 1:F6

Hotels

11th Avenue Inn Seattle Bed & Breakfast, 2:G5
Ace Hotel, 1:B1
Alexis Hotel, 1:E4
Ballard Inn, 3:A3
Chelsea Station Inn Bed & Breakfast, 3:D3
Four Seasons Hotel Seattle, 1:D3
Gaslight Inn, 2:G6
Grand Hyatt Seattle, 1:F2
Green Tortoise Back-packer's Hotel, 1:D3
Greenlake Guest House, 3:F1
Hilton Seattle, 1:F3
Hotel 1000, 1:E4
Hotel Andra, 1:D1
Hotel Ballard, 3:A3
Hotel Max, 1:E1
Hotel Monaco, 1:E3
Hotel Vintage, 1:F3
Hyatt at Olive 8, 1:F1
Hyatt Regency Bellevue, 3:H6
Inn at El Gaucho, 1:B1
Inn at the Market, 1:D2
Kimpton Palladian Hotel, 1:D2
MarQueen Hotel, 2:A4
Marriott Seattle Water-front, 1:B2

Mayflower Park Hotel, 1:E2
Motif Seattle Hotel, 1:E2
Pan Pacific Hotel Seattle, 2:D5
Pensione Nichols Bed & Breakfast, 1:D2
Renaissance Seattle Hotel, 1:F3
Shafer Baillie Mansion Bed & Breakfast, 2:G4
Silver Cloud Inn Lake Union, 2:E3
Sorrento Hotel, 1:G3
The Arctic Club Seattle, 1:F4
The Bacon Mansion Bed and Breakfast, 2:F3
The Edgewater, 1:A2
The Fairmont Olympic Hotel, 1:E3
The Hotel Bellevue, 3:H6
The Maxwell Hotel, 2:B4
The Paramount Hotel, 1:E1
Thompson Seattle, 1:D2
University Inn, 3:G4
W Seattle, 1:F3
Warwick Seattle Hotel, 1:D1
Watertown Hotel, 3:G4
Willows Lodge, 3:H6
Woodmark Hotel, 3:H6

WHERE TO STAY

Updated by
AnnaMaria
Stephens

Much like the eclectic city itself, Seattle's lodging offers something for everyone. There are grand, ornate vintage hotels; sleek and elegant modern properties; green hotels with yoga studios and enough bamboo for an army of pandas; and cozy bed-and-breakfasts with sweet bedspreads and home-cooked breakfasts.

Travelers who appreciate the anonymity of high-rise chains can comfortably stay here, while guests who want to feel like family can find the perfect boutique inn to lay their heads.

Two of the newest properties on the scene affirm Seattle's growing status as a world-class city: the Thompson Seattle, a boutique hotel with floor-to-ceiling windows that overlook Pike Place Market and Elliott Bay, and the Kimpton Palladian, a stylish and sophisticated urban retreat in a landmark 1910 building. Meanwhile, a pair of the city's most classic and sought-after Downtown digs have recently undergone dramatic modern transformations: the Fairmont Olympic and the Inn at the Market. A number of other tried-and-true hotels have upped the ante as new competition looms, a boon for visitors to this booming city.

Unfortunately, there's no getting around the fact that staying in Seattle is expensive. Unless you're willing to sleep in a hostel, expect to pay at least $130–$200 a night for basic accommodations anywhere in-city. Budget travelers will want to look outside the Downtown core, or try to finagle deals from online booking sites. And as always, the devil is in the details: parking fees, charges for Wi-Fi, and additional costs for view rooms can bump nightly rates $100 or more. As travelers have felt the squeeze, some hotels have responded with lower prices, special packages, and sensible extras, like free parking or meal vouchers. Many hotel bars and restaurants are also offering happy hours, sometimes twice a day, with an emphasis on food as well as cocktails.

WHERE SHOULD I STAY?

	Neighborhood Vibe	Pros	Cons
Downtown and Belltown	Downtown is central, with the hottest hotels with water views. If you're a fan of galleries and bars, stay in Belltown.	A day in Downtown and Belltown can take you from the Seattle Art Museum to Pike Place Market.	Parking can be pricey and hard to come by. This is not your spot if you want quiet, relaxing respite.
Seattle Center, South Lake Union, and Queen Anne	Queen Anne boasts great water views and easy access to Downtown. South Lake Union can feel industrial.	Seattle Center's many festivals (such as Bumbershoot) means you'll have a ringside seat.	If you're mostly focused on seeing the key Downtown sights or have limited mobility, parking can be difficult.
Capitol Hill	One of Seattle's oldest and quirkiest neighborhoods, Capitol Hill has cozy accommodations.	A great place to stay if you want to mingle with creative locals in great bookstores and cafés.	If you're uncomfortable with the pierced, tattooed, or GLBT set, look elsewhere.
Fremont	From the Woodland Park Zoo to the Locks, funky Fremont is an excellent jumping-off point.	This quintessential Seattle 'hood is a short trek from Downtown and has restaurants and shops.	The only lodging to be found here are B&Bs—book ahead.
Green Lake	Laid-back and wonderfully situated near the Woodland Park Zoo and Gas Works Park.	Outdoorsy types will love the proximity to Green Lake, a great place to stroll or jog.	You won't find anything trendy here, and, after a few days, you'll have seen everything.
University District	It offers everything you'd expect from a college area—from bookstores to ethnic food.	If you're renting a car, this area offers centrality with a lower price tag.	Homeless and college kids populate University Avenue ("The Ave"). Not much in the way of sightseeing.
West Seattle	In summer, West Seattle can feel a lot like Southern California: It's a fun place to stay.	Alki Beach and Lincoln Park are fun, plus great restaurants and shopping on California Ave.	You'll need a car to stay in this very removed 'hood. The only way in or out is over a bridge.
The Eastside	Proximity to high-end malls, Woodinville wineries, and Microsoft.	Woodinville is wine HQ; Kirkland offers cute boutiques; and Bellevue is a shopping mecca.	If you're here to experience Seattle, stick to the city. Traffic is a total nightmare.

And with all the convention and cruise travelers, high season can mean a scramble to find anything in the center of town. Never fear, though—most of the neighborhoods have relatively quick access to Downtown; a couple, like Queen Anne, South Lake Union, and Capitol Hill, are a quick walk away, and many hotels offer free shuttles to the core. Take a deep breath, book ahead, and aim high—you never know what sort of deals you might find.

PLANNING

CONSTRUCTION CONCERNS

Seattle is experiencing record growth, and projects in progress can be found throughout the metro area. It's worth inquiring about such things while booking and asking how local construction projects may affect the views, noise levels, and traffic situations around your hotel.

FACILITIES

In the past, air-conditioning was never a deal-breaker—mild summers and cool evenings made it unnecessary. However, recent heat waves have sent many residents running to the nearest movie theater for relief. If you require air-conditioning, make sure your room has it in summer. In another surprising trend for such a tech city, many hotels, particularly the chains, charge for Wi-Fi, and a handful only offer wired Internet. You can skirt the issue at some properties by joining their "clubs," but be sure and check the Wi-Fi policy if it's important to you.

LODGING STRATEGY

Where should we stay? With so many Seattle hotels, it may seem like a daunting question. But fret not—our expert writers and editors have done most of the legwork. The selections here represent the best this city has to offer—from the best budget-friendly B&Bs to the sleekest designer hotels. Scan "Best Bets" for top recommendations by price and experience. Or find a review quickly in the listings. Search by neighborhood, then alphabetically.

MONEY-SAVING TIPS

The best way to save? Travel off-season. Amazing deals at the hottest properties can be had in spring (and sometimes even in early June). Weather is more hit-or-miss this time of year than in July or August, but there are often many beautiful dry days. Rates drop dramatically again once October rolls around. Mild, picture-perfect fall days are a well-kept secret here—hiking's often good until the end of the month and the Cascades get some beautiful fall colors.

But you probably want to see the city in its late-summer glory. In that case, good luck to you. Lodging-wise, there isn't much of an upside to Seattle's high season—the best you can do is book as far in advance as possible and stay out of the Downtown core. Midweek prices may be lower than weekend rates, but don't count on it (in business hotels, the opposite is true). You'll always save more with multinight stays, particularly at B&Bs, which often have unofficial policies of giving discounts to long-term guests. The best collection of good deals is on Capitol Hill because most of its properties are B&Bs; the Queen Anne and Lake Union neighborhoods also turn up some good deals and are much closer to Downtown than the U-District, which is the other neighborhood that has a decent selection of midrange properties.

Another lodging possibility growing in popularity is to book stays in private furnished residences through Airbnb or VRBO. You'll have your pick of neighborhoods and get to experience Seattle more like a local. With choices ranging from tiny studio apartments to spacious multibedroom houses, Airbnb and VRBO make an especially appealing and often more affordable option for families and small groups.

NEED A
RESERVATION? It is imperative to book in advance for July and August, especially if you want to stay in one of the in-demand budget properties or at any bed-and-breakfast. Some B&Bs start to fill up their summer slots by March or April. The best water-view rooms in Downtown luxury hotels are often gone by mid-February. You aren't likely to have trouble booking a room the rest of the year as long as your visit doesn't coincide with major conventions or arts or sporting events. The other exception is the U-District—if your stay coincides with graduation in June or the start of school in late September, you'll want to book early. B&Bs around the city fill up quickly, but it's always worth giving them a call to see what's available. Because they encourage longer stays, you may be able to get a last-minute room for a night or two to bridge the gaps that pop up as long-term guests turn over. In this case, you're doing the B&B a favor and may get a discounted rate.

PARKING Parking in Seattle is expensive, especially Downtown. Expect to pay between $30 and $60 a day, even at hotels that cost more than $300 a night. Many properties have a valet option, and a handful allow valet parking only. A few hotels offer complimentary parking—you'll find more options out of the city center. Metered street parking is common citywide and, like Downtown, street spots come with time limits—you won't be able to leave your car in one spot for more than a couple of hours during the day. Overnight, metered street parking is free, but you'll likely have to move your car by 8 am.

PRICES

Seattle's peak season is May through September, with August at the pinnacle. Prices throughout the city skyrocket then; some are nearly double what they are in low season.

The lodgings listed are the cream of the crop in each price category. Prices in the reviews are the lowest cost of a standard double room in high season; they do not take into account discounts or package deals you may find on consolidator websites.

WHAT IT COSTS FOR TWO PEOPLE			
$	$$	$$$	$$$$
Hotels	under $186	$186–$250	$251–$350	over $350

Prices reflect the rack rate of a standard double room for two people in high season, excluding the 12% (for hotels with fewer than 60 rooms) or 15.6% (for hotels with more than 60 rooms) city and state taxes. Check online for off-season rates and special deals or discounts.

SMOKING

The city has banned smoking in most public places, including all restaurants and bars, and the new and pervasive trend is for hotels to be completely smoke-free. It's now extremely difficult to find smoking rooms; puffers may want to reconsider upgrading to that balcony room.

DOWNTOWN AND BELLTOWN

Use the coordinate (1:B2) at the end of each listing to locate a site on the Seattle Dining and Lodging Atlas preceding this chapter.

DOWNTOWN

Downtown has the greatest concentration of hotels, many of which are new or updated high-end high-rises, though there are also several boutique hotels and midrange properties in historic buildings. There aren't many budget properties in the area. All Downtown hotels are convenient (and within walking distance) to many major sights—including the Seattle Art Museum, Pike Place Market, and the Olympic Sculpture Park. Although the waterfront is an integral part of Downtown, there are surprisingly few hotels directly on the water. Many high-rises have water views, but make sure to specify that you want a room with a view.

$$ HOTEL **Alexis Hotel.** Two historic buildings near the waterfront use exposed brick, walls of windows, and nouveau-baroque touches to appeal to aesthetes and modern romantics, and ornate leather chairs and wood-burning fireplaces recall a different era. **Pros:** great service; close to waterfront; unique, beautiful rooms; suites aren't prohibitively expensive. **Cons:** small lobby; not entirely soundproofed against old building and city noise; some rooms can be a bit dark. [$] *Rooms from: $229* ✉ *1007 1st Ave., Downtown* ☎ *206/624–4844, 888/850–1155* 🌐 *www.alexishotel.com* 🛏 *88 rooms, 33 suites* 🍴 *No meals* ✥ 1:E4.

$$$ HOTEL Fodor's Choice ★ **The Arctic Club Seattle.** From the Alaskan-marble-sheathed foyer and the antique walrus heads to the Northern Lights Dome room with its leaded-glass ceiling to explorer-chic touches like steamer trunks for bedside tables, the Arctic Club pays homage to an era of gold-rush opulence (the early 1900s building was once a gentlemen's club). **Pros:** cool, unique property; great staff; light-rail and bus lines just outside the door. **Cons:** not in the heart of Downtown; rooms are a bit dark; style may be off-putting for travelers who like modern hotels; charge for Wi-Fi. [$] *Rooms from: $275* ✉ *700 3rd Ave., Downtown* ☎ *206/340–0340, 800/445–8667* 🌐 *thearcticclubseattle.com* 🛏 *118 rooms, 2 suites* 🍴 *No meals* ✥ 1:F4.

$$$$ HOTEL FAMILY Fodor's Choice ★ **The Fairmont Olympic Hotel.** With marble floors, soaring ceilings, massive chandeliers, and sweeping staircases, the lobby of this hotel personifies old-world elegance, while guest rooms have a modern twist. **Pros:** great location; excellent service; fabulous on-site dining and amenities. **Cons:** not much in the way of views; a lot of construction nearby. [$] *Rooms from: $379* ✉ *411 University St., Downtown* ☎ *206/621–1700, 888/363–5022* 🌐 *www.fairmont.com/seattle* 🛏 *232 rooms, 218 suites* 🍴 *No meals* ✥ 1:E3.

$$$$ HOTEL FAMILY Fodor's Choice ★ **Four Seasons Hotel Seattle.** Just south of the Pike Place Market and steps from the Seattle Art Museum, this Downtown gem is polished and elegant, with Eastern accents and plush furnishings in comfortable living spaces in which Pacific Northwest materials, such as stone and fine hardwoods, take center stage. **Pros:** fantastic location with amazing water views; large rooms with luxurious bathrooms with

deep soaking tubs; lovely spa. **Cons:** Four Seasons regulars might not click with this modern take on the brand; street-side rooms not entirely soundproofed; some room views are partially obscured by industrial sites. $ *Rooms from: $679* ✉ *99 Union St., Downtown* ☎ *206/749–7000, 800/332–3442* 🌐 *www.fourseasons.com/seattle* 🛏 *134 rooms,13 suites* 🍴 *No meals* ✥ 1:D3.

$$ HOTEL **Grand Hyatt Seattle.** Adjacent to the Washington State Convention Center, this view-centric hotel appeals to business travelers or conventioneers who want a dependable Hyatt-level stay in a great downtown location. **Pros:** spectacular views; central location; large bathrooms; on-site brand-name restaurants. **Cons:** charges for services in Business Center and Wi-Fi; traffic noise; there's no proper lounge. $ *Rooms from: $239* ✉ *721 Pine St., Downtown* ☎ *206/774–1234* 🌐 *www.grandseattle.hyatt.com* 🛏 *317 rooms, 108 suites* 🍴 *No meals* ✥ 1:F2.

$ HOTEL **Green Tortoise Backpacker's Hotel.** This Seattle institution is still considered by many to be the best deal in town—and even if you don't own a backpack and the word "hostel" gives you the heebie-jeebies, the impressive cleanliness makes the Tortoise an option for anyone on a budget who doesn't mind sacrificing a little privacy. **Pros:** cheapest lodging in town; great place to make instant friends from around the globe; across the street from Pike Place Market; great bike rental program; free day storage. **Cons:** street noise; thin walls; if you don't like the communal experience this isn't for you; no a/c; no elevator. $ *Rooms from: $34* ✉ *105½ Pike St., Downtown* ☎ *206/340–1222* 🌐 *www.greentortoise.net* 🛏 *30 rooms without en suite bath* 🍴 *Breakfast* ✥ 1:D3.

$$$ HOTEL **Hilton Seattle.** Just west of I–5, the Hilton Seattle is a popular site for meetings, conventions, and the summer cruise set. **Pros:** great location; children up to age eight stay free; helpful staff; clean rooms; comfortable beds. **Cons:** overpriced for what you get; small bathrooms. $ *Rooms from: $269* ✉ *1301 6th Ave., Downtown* ☎ *206/624–0500, 800/426–0535* 🌐 *www.thehiltonseattle.com* 🛏 *237 rooms, 3 suites* 🍴 *No meals* ✥ 1:F3.

$$$ HOTEL **Hotel Max.** Hip and art-forward, the Hotel Max (for "Maximalism") blends artsy decor with punchy minimalism for an architect-office effect—albeit one with cushy trimmings. **Pros:** cool artwork; late check-out time available; nice staff. **Cons:** tiny rooms and elevator; no views; traffic noise, thin walls, and late-night revelers; older and larger travelers may not be comfortable here. $ *Rooms from: $275* ✉ *620 Stewart St., Downtown* ☎ *866/833–6299, 866/833–6299* 🌐 *www.hotelmaxseattle.com* 🛏 *163 rooms* 🍴 *No meals* ✥ 1:E1.

$$ HOTEL FAMILY Fodor's Choice ★ **Hotel Monaco.** It only takes one glimpse of the gorgeous modern-global lobby to know that this stylish boutique hotel in the heart of Downtown is a standout, and rooms carry on the image, with a palette of soft reds and gunmetal grays, beds topped with Frette linens, floor-to-ceiling drapes in a Turkish motif, and floor lamps that recall telescopes. **Pros:** near Pike Place Market and the Space Needle; welcoming public spaces; daily hosted wine reception with savory snacks. **Cons:** some street-facing rooms can be a little noisy; small gym. $ *Rooms from: $249* ✉ *1101 4th Ave., Downtown* ☎ *206/621–1770,*

4

800/715–6513 ⊕ *www.monaco-seattle.com* 🛏 *152 rooms, 37 suites* ⏐⊙⏐ *No meals* ✛ *1:F3.*

$$$$
HOTEL
FAMILY
Fodor's Choice
★

🍴 **Hotel 1000.** Chic and modern yet warm and inviting, these luxurious tech-savvy rooms are full of surprising touches, including large soaking tubs that fill from the ceiling—and a cute yellow rubber ducky and bubbles for bath time. **Pros:** useful high-tech gadgets; virtual golf club and spa; hotel is hip without being alienating. **Cons:** rooms can be dark; a small percentage of rooms without views look out on a cement wall. Ⓢ *Rooms from: $445* ✉ *1000 1st Ave., Downtown* ☎ *206/957–1000, 877/315–1088* ⊕ *www.hotel1000seattle.com* 🛏 *101 rooms, 19 suites* ⏐⊙⏐ *No meals* ✛ *1:E4.*

$$
HOTEL

🍴 **Hotel Vintage.** Each of the stylish rooms—some of which boast marvelous views of Seattle's iconic public library—feature a vineyard-inspired palette of burgundy, taupe, and green hues, with a focus on unique interior design. **Pros:** friendly staff; beautiful, quiet rooms; caters to wine lovers; close to shopping, theaters, and the Convention Center. **Cons:** a short-but-steep uphill walk from Downtown could be tough on some travelers; small lobby; small bathrooms. Ⓢ *Rooms from: $249* ✉ *1100 5th Ave., Downtown* ☎ *206/624–8000, 800/853–3914* ⊕ *www. hotelvintage-seattle.com* 🛏 *124 rooms, 1 suite* ⏐⊙⏐ *No meals* ✛ *1:F3.*

$$$$
HOTEL
Fodor's Choice
★

🍴 **Hyatt at Olive 8.** In a city known for environmental responsibility, being the greenest hotel in town is no small feat, and green is rarely this chic—rooms have floor-to-ceiling windows flooding the place with light along with enviro touches like dual-flush toilets, fresh-air vents, and low-flow showerheads. **Pros:** central location; superb amenities; environmental responsibility; wonderful spa. **Cons:** standard rooms have showers only; guests complain of hallway and traffic noise; translucent glass bathroom doors offer little privacy; fee for Wi-Fi. Ⓢ *Rooms from: $359* ✉ *1635 8th Ave., Downtown* ☎ *206/695–1234, 800/233–1234* ⊕ *www.olive8.hyatt.com* 🛏 *331 rooms, 15 suites* ⏐⊙⏐ *No meals* ✛ *1:F1.*

$$$$
HOTEL
Fodor's Choice
★

🍴 **Inn at the Market.** From its heart-stopping views to the fabulous location just steps from Pike Place Market, this is a place you'll want to visit again and again. **Pros:** outstanding views from most rooms; half a block from Pike Place Market; fantastic service; complimentary town-car service for Downtown locations. **Cons:** little common space; being in the heart of the action means some street noise. Ⓢ *Rooms from: $390* ✉ *86 Pine St., Downtown* ☎ *206/443–3600, 800/446–4484* ⊕ *www. innatthemarket.com* 🛏 *63 rooms, 7 suites* ⏐⊙⏐ *No meals* ✛ *1:D2.*

$$
HOTEL
Fodor's Choice
★

🍴 **Mayflower Park Hotel.** Comfortable, old-world charm in the center of the action comes with sturdy antiques, Asian accents, brass fixtures, and florals. **Pros:** central Downtown location; quiet; good value; direct connection to the airport via light-rail and Seattle Center via the Monorail; great service. **Cons:** rooms are small; no pool. Ⓢ *Rooms from: $229* ✉ *405 Olive Way, Downtown* ☎ *206/623–8700, 800/426–5100* ⊕ *www. mayflowerpark.com* 🛏 *160 rooms, 29 suites* ⏐⊙⏐ *No meals* ✛ *1:E2.*

$$$
HOTEL

🍴 **Motif Seattle Hotel.** With a hip vibe and signature design motifs updated yearly by a different local designer, this stylish urban property has a boutique feel despite its large size. **Pros:** in the heart of Downtown; great views in some upper-floor rooms; several cool communal spaces. **Cons:** rooms near terrace can be loud; small bathrooms; service can be slow and mediocre. § *Rooms from: $329 ⊠ 1415 5th Ave., Downtown* ☎ *206/971–8015 ⤶ 319 rooms, 10 suites* ✚ *1:E2.*

$$ ⛫ **The Paramount Hotel.** Good value meets great location at this solid,
HOTEL comfortable boutique hotel. **Pros:** good value; excellent location; great
Fodor'sChoice staff; popular on-site restaurant. **Cons:** not much in the way of ameni-
★ ties; tiny fitness center; small lobby. § *Rooms from: $240 ⊠ 724 Pine St., Downtown* ☎ *206/292–9500* ⊕ *www.paramounthotelseattle.com* ⤶ *144 rooms, 2 suites* ⦿ *No meals* ✚ *1:E1.*

$ ⛫ **Pensione Nichols Bed & Breakfast.** Once the favored lodging of Alan
B&B/INN Ginsberg and other beat poets, this is one of the most affordable and
unique options in Downtown Seattle. **Pros:** great views; good value for
location. **Cons:** shared bathrooms; some traffic noise; staff not always
available; lots of stairs. § *Rooms from: $180 ⊠ 1923 1st Ave., Down-town* ☎ *206/441–7125* ⊕ *www.pensionenichols.com* ⤶ *10 rooms with-out private bath, 2 suites* ⦿ *Breakfast* ✚ *1:D2.*

$$$ ⛫ **Renaissance Seattle Hotel.** A bit of a walk uphill from Downtown,
HOTEL this high-rise has a calm feel to it, with contemporary decor and invit-
ing common areas. **Pros:** great views; helpful staff; comfy beds; the
pool at the rooftop health club; good deals are often available online.
Cons: freeway noise; some visitors won't enjoy the walk uphill; not
much happening in the area at night; charge for Wi-Fi. § *Rooms from: $349 ⊠ 515 Madison St., Downtown* ☎ *206/583–0300, 800/546–9184* ⊕ *www.renaissanceseattle.com* ⤶ *463 rooms, 90 executive suites* ⦿ *No meals* ✚ *1:F3.*

$$$$ ⛫ **Sorrento Hotel.** Opened in 1909 for the Alaska-Yukon-Pacific Exposi-
HOTEL tion, the Sorrento features carved wood moldings, period fixtures, and
Fodor'sChoice restored antique furniture. **Pros:** serene and classy; fantastic service;
★ great restaurant; fabulous beds; free Downtown car service. **Cons:** not
central; rooms are a bit small (though corner suites are commodious).
§ *Rooms from: $424 ⊠ 900 Madison St., First Hill* ☎ *206/622–6400, 800/426–1265* ⊕ *www.hotelsorrento.com* ⤶ *34 rooms, 42 suites* ⦿ *No meals* ✚ *1:G3.*

$$$ ⛫ **Thompson Seattle.** Designed by local starchitects Olson Kundig, the
HOTEL 12-story Thompson Seattle is the most stylish newcomer to Seattle's hotel
Fodor'sChoice scene, with a contemporary glass exterior and sophisticated guest rooms
★ that feature floor-to-ceiling windows, hardwood floors, a crisp white-
and-navy palette, and leather and smoked-glass accents. **Pros:** perfect
for the style obsessed; very close to Pike Place Market; top-notch on-site
dining and drinks. **Cons:** blazing afternoon sun in some rooms; some
small rooms; floor beneath rooftop bar can be noisy. § *Rooms from: $279 ⊠ 110 Stewart St., Downtown* ☎ *206/623–4600* ⊕ *www.thomp-sonhotels.com/hotels/thompson-seattle* ⤶ *151 rooms, 7 suites* ✚ *1:D2.*

$$$$ ⛫ **W Seattle.** The W Seattle has a distinct "urban lodge" vibe, with
HOTEL guest rooms that feature a palette of Seattle-inspired grays and blues
accented by bright pops of color, as well as headboards made from
floor-to-ceiling backlit wood stacks and Northwest touches like plaid
pillows and Pendleton-pattern wallpaper. **Pros:** lively bar and restaurant; comfortable beds; good location; hip Northwest decor. **Cons:** self-
consciously trendy; service is hit-and-miss; charge for Wi-Fi; outrageous
room service prices. § *Rooms from: $371 ⊠ 1112 4th Ave., Downtown*

☎ 206/264–6000, 877/946–8357 🌐 www.wseattle.com 🛏 424 rooms, 9 suites 🍴 No meals ✥ 1:F3.

BELLTOWN

Belltown, slightly north and within walking distance of Downtown, has some of the city's trendiest hotels. It's a great place to stay if you plan to hit the bars and clubs in the neighborhood. Belltown hotels are convenient (and within walking distance) to many major sights—including the Seattle Art Museum, Pike Place Market, and the Olympic Sculpture Park.

$ HOTEL Fodor's Choice ★ 🏨 **Ace Hotel.** The Ace is a dream come true for both penny-pinching hipsters and folks who appreciate unique minimalist decor, with such touches in the rooms as army-surplus blankets, industrial metal sinks, and street art breaking up any notion of austerity; the cheapest rooms share bathrooms, which have enormous showers. **Pros:** ultratrendy but with some of the most affordable rates in town; good place to meet other travelers; free Wi-Fi. **Cons:** half the rooms have shared bathrooms; not for people who want pampering; neighborhood rife with panhandlers; lots of stairs to get to lobby. [$] *Rooms from: $129* ✉ *2423 1st Ave., Belltown* ☎ *206/448–4721* 🌐 *www.acehotel.com* 🛏 *14 standard rooms, 14 deluxe rooms* 🍴 *No meals* ✥ 1:B1.

$$$$ HOTEL 🏨 **The Edgewater.** Literally perched over Elliott Bay, the rustic-chic Edgewater has spectacular west-facing views of ferries and sailboats, seals and seabirds, and the distant Olympic Mountains. **Pros:** unparalleled views; great upscale seafood restaurant; inviting public lounge area; complimentary bikes. **Cons:** overpriced; standard rooms are small; visitors complain of spotty service and thin walls; charge for Wi-Fi. [$] *Rooms from: $399* ✉ *Pier 67, 2411 Alaskan Way, Belltown* ☎ *206/728–7000, 800/624–0670* 🌐 *www.edgewaterhotel.com* 🛏 *213 rooms, 10 suites* 🍴 *No meals* ✥ 1:A2.

$$$ HOTEL Fodor's Choice ★ 🏨 **Hotel Ändra.** Scandinavian sensibility and clean, modern lines define this sophisticated hotel on the edge of Belltown, where rooms have dark fabrics and woods, with a few bright accents and geometric prints. **Pros:** hangout-worthy lobby lounge; hip vibe; excellent service; spacious rooms. **Cons:** some street noise; not family-friendly. [$] *Rooms from: $295* ✉ *2000 4th Ave., Belltown* ☎ *206/448–8600, 877/448–8600* 🌐 *www.hotelandra.com* 🛏 *93 rooms, 4 studios, 22 suites* 🍴 *No meals* ✥ 1:D1.

$$ B&B/INN Fodor's Choice ★ 🏨 **Inn at El Gaucho.** Hollywood Rat Pack enthusiasts will want to move right in to these swank, retro-style suites done in dark wood with buttery leather furniture. **Pros:** unique aesthetic; some rooms have great views; location; warm, helpful staff. **Cons:** steep stairs with no elevator; some rooms only have showers; no outdoor spaces; rooms are (purposely) dark; no on-site fitness center. [$] *Rooms from: $249* ✉ *2505 1st Ave., Belltown* ☎ *206/728–1133, 866/354–2824* 🌐 *www.elgaucho.com* 🛏 *17 suites* 🍴 *No meals* ✥ 1:B1.

$$ HOTEL 🏨 **Kimpton Palladian Hotel.** The popular and reliable Kimpton brand nails it again with the Palladian, a hip new hotel in a 1910 Belltown landmark. **Pros:** tons of style; a short walk from Pike Place Market; reliable

Staying with Kids

Traveling with kids can be a challenge, from hauling their gear to finding a spot for them to sleep in cramped hotel rooms. Don't let that stop you, though. Children are welcome at most Seattle hotels; some even cater to your munchkins with kid-friendly treats and amenities. While most hotels in Seattle allow children under a certain age to stay in their parents' room at no extra charge, others charge for them as extra adults, so be sure to find out the cutoff age for children's discounts. Cribs are usually available upon request, and hotel staff can assist you in finding a reputable babysitter. Always let hotel staff know you'll be traveling with children when you book your room—most love the chance to treat your tots and will appreciate the advance warning. Here are a few of our favorite kid-friendly lodging options:

Stylish tots will love the kid-size animal-print robes at **Hotel Monaco**, while the toy chest in the lobby will keep them occupied. They might also get a kick out of having a pet goldfish on loan for the duration of their stay.

Watertown Hotel pampers children with their complimentary "Ala Cart" program—goody carts stocked with games, movies, and art supplies. Families will also love their free bike rentals and fresh cupcakes. (University District)

The **Silver Cloud** hotels are all suitable for families, especially the one on Lake Union. (South Lake Union)

Some of the loveliest (and most expensive) hotels also cater to young ones:

The **Fairmont Olympic Hotel** has a swimming pool and offers outstanding children's treats, such as milk and cookies, kid-friendly movies (popcorn included!), and child-size bathrobes. (Downtown)

Tweens and teens will love the virtual golf club and Xbox suites at **Hotel 1000**, while more Zen youngsters can luxuriate in child-size robes for the hotel's kid spa treatments. (Downtown)

Both the **Pan Pacific Hotel Seattle** in South Lake Union and Downtown's **Four Seasons Hotel Seattle** greet small guests with a stuffed toy on their beds, while the Four Seasons also pampers kids with mini-robes, children's videos, and baby bath products. (South Lake Union and Downtown)

For longer stays, consider renting a family-friendly private residence through **Airbnb** or **VRBO**—having multiple bedrooms and a well-stocked kitchen are perks when traveling with kids.

---

and design-minded brand. **Cons:** rooms are on the small side; awkward bathroom layout; street and construction noise. $ *Rooms from: $229* ✉ *2000 2nd Ave., Belltown* ☎ *206/448–1111* ⊕ *www.palladianhotel. com* ➽ *85 rooms, 12 suites* ✛ 1:D2.

$$$ 🏨 **Marriott Seattle Waterfront.** With views of Elliott Bay from most rooms
HOTEL   (half have small Juliet balconies), proximity to the cruise terminals, comfy beds, and a great location near the tourist spots and the financial district, this property is a hot spot for groups and cruise travelers. **Pros:** relaxing lobby invites lounging; elevator takes you directly to Pike Place Market. **Cons:** service isn't consistent; train noise; expensive restaurant and bar; no Wi-Fi in rooms; it's an uphill walk to most

sites; especially expensive valet parking. [$] *Rooms from: $339* ✉ *2100 Alaskan Way, (between Piers 62/63 and Pier 66), Belltown* ☎ *206/443–5000, 800/455–8254* 🌐 *www.marriott.com/seawf* 🛏 *345 rooms, 13 suites* 🍴 *No meals* ✥ 1:B2.

$$$ HOTEL 🏨 **Warwick Seattle Hotel.** Space Needle views, vintage charm, and family-friendly service abound at this renovated classic hotel in Belltown. **Pros:** great location and views; Juliet balconies in most rooms; heated indoor pool and whirlpool. **Cons:** charge for Wi-Fi; small fitness room. [$] *Rooms from: $270* ✉ *401 Lenora St., Belltown* ☎ *206/443–4300, 206/443–4300* 🌐 *www.warwickwa.com* 🛏 *226 rooms, 4 suites* 🍴 *No meals* ✥ 1:D1.

SOUTH LAKE UNION AND QUEEN ANNE

SOUTH LAKE UNION

The South Lake Union area is going through a rather radical transformation. For years it was an industrial, forgotten part of town with few businesses or restaurants. With several high-profile companies moving in (including Amazon, which has such a major presence that the neighborhood is nicknamed Amazonia) SLU is rapidly becoming a hub of new condos, business high-rises, and amenity development. Though the variety of lodging options currently underwhelms, several new hotels are slated to be built in coming years. And while it bustles during the workweek with throngs of badged techies staring at their phones, parts of South Lake Union can seem like a ghost town during the evening and weekends. Stay here and you'll be close to both Downtown and Capitol Hill.

$$$ HOTEL Fodor's Choice ★ 🏨 **Pan Pacific Hotel Seattle.** One of the best-looking hotels in Seattle is a chic treat for travelers, from the attractive and comfortable modern rooms to the impressive views of the Space Needle and Lake Union. **Pros:** no touristy vibe like Downtown hotels; feels more luxurious than it costs; award-winning sustainability efforts. **Cons:** long walk to Downtown (though streetcar access and the hotel's free car service help with that); bathroom design isn't the most private. [$] *Rooms from: $285* ✉ *2125 Terry Ave., South Lake Union* ☎ *206/264–8111* 🌐 *www.panpacific.com/seattle* 🛏 *131 rooms, 22 suites* 🍴 *No meals* ✥ 2:D5.

$$$ HOTEL FAMILY 🏨 **Silver Cloud Inn Lake Union.** With views of Lake Union, free parking, and family-friendly services, this property offers great value for guests looking to explore more of Seattle than just Downtown. **Pros:** indoor pool; free parking, Wi-Fi, and shuttle service; free yummy breakfasts. **Cons:** not within walking distance of major sights; feels like a business hotel. [$] *Rooms from: $269* ✉ *1150 Fairview Ave. N, South Lake Union* ☎ *206/447–9500, 800/330–5812* 🌐 *www.silvercloud.com/SeattleLakeUnion* 🛏 *184 rooms* 🍴 *Breakfast* ✥ 2:E3.

QUEEN ANNE

Queen Anne is a large, mostly residential neighborhood spread out over a large hill just to the north of Belltown and close to Seattle Center. Upper Queen Anne is posh, quiet, and gorgeous. Lower Queen Anne,

CLOSE UP

Going Green

It takes much more than a recycling program to make a hotel "green," and although few properties in Seattle are doing everything right, a handful of local luxury hotels have expanded the industry's definition of eco-friendly.

Hyatt at Olive 8
The first LEED-certified (Leadership in Energy and Environmental Design) hotel in Seattle, the Hyatt at Olive 8 was built from the ground up with sustainability in mind. From the demolition of the previous building and the painstaking construction of a green roof to details like naturally antimicrobial wool carpeting and dual-flush toilets, this hotel and residence (the upper floors are condos) is healthier for the planet and guests alike. *(Downtown)*

Pan Pacific Hotel Seattle
Motion detectors make sure heating and a/c units don't run when there's no one in the room. All toilets are dual-flush European models that save on the hotel's water consumption. *(South Lake Union)*

The Fairmont Olympic Hotel
The Fairmont has a wide-reaching Green Partnership program in which all hotel employees are educated to help the hotel conserve water and energy. Initiatives range from recycling and composting programs to more inventive programs like capturing condensation from the hotel's steam heating to be used in the washing machines. Eco-friendly weddings and meetings are available. Guest's hybrid vehicles get free valet parking. *(Downtown)*

Kimpton Properties
Kimpton, whose Seattle hotels include Hotel Monaco, Hotel Vintage Park, the Palladian, and the Alexis Hotel, has a far-reaching approach. Recycling, towel and linen reuse, and energy-conservation and water-conservation schemes are standard here, and the company uses environmentally friendly cleaning products in all its properties. Guests also enjoy fair-trade coffee, organic snacks in the minibar, local and organic restaurant fare, and eco-friendly bath products. *(Downtown)*

where all the lodging options lie, is very walkable to Belltown, Downtown, and Seattle Center—but it's considerably less elegant than the top of the hill. You can find better deals here than in most of Downtown—and you'll still be close to everything.

$$ HOTEL **MarQueen Hotel.** Fans of historic boutique hotels will love this reasonably priced 1918 brick property at the foot of Queen Anne Hill. **Pros:** in-room kitchens and living room areas; charming; free Wi-Fi and complimentary breakfast; proximity to Seattle Center. **Cons:** street-side rooms can be loud; housekeeping not always consistent; no elevator. [$] *Rooms from: $239* ✉ *600 Queen Anne Ave. N, Queen Anne* ☎ *206/282–7407, 888/445–3076* 🌐 *www.marqueen.com* 🛏 *51 rooms, 7 suites* 🍴 *Breakfast* ⊕ 2:A4.

$$ HOTEL **The Maxwell Hotel.** Colorful and funky rooms, with argyle-print chairs and outlines of chandeliers painted on the walls, are *the* choice for visitors frequenting the Seattle Center for opera or the ballet, or going to Teatro Zinzanni, whose huge, colorful tent is just steps from the hotel. **Pros:** free parking and shuttle; complimentary bikes; some rooms have

great views of the Space Needle. **Cons:** hotel is on a busy street; pool and gym are tiny; guests complain of low water pressure. [$] *Rooms from: $219* ✉ *300 Roy St., Queen Anne* ☎ *206/286–0629, 866/866–7977* 🌐 *www.themaxwellhotel.com* 🛏 *139 rooms* 🍴 *No meals* ✥ 2:B4.

CAPITOL HILL

For travelers looking to experience a real Seattle neighborhood, Capitol Hill is a terrific option. Close to Downtown, but with a unique scene of its own, "the Hill" offers character-rich bed-and-breakfasts in old mansions and oversized Craftsmans, run with flare by thoughtful proprietors. Airbnb also has a wealth of offerings in this hip neighborhood. Though many of the Hill's residents appear to be hipsters, pierced and tattooed baristas, and intellectual dilettantes, anyone of any age or background is welcome here if you come with an open mind. Seattle's historically LGBT neighborhood is chock-full of live-music venues, true foodie establishments, and little retail gems. While the Pike–Pine Corridor and much of Broadway are alive until the wee hours, most of the neighborhood's lodging spots are set in quiet, tree-lined side streets off the main drags. Most B&Bs require multinight stays.

$ B&B/INN FAMILY 🏨 **The Bacon Mansion Bed and Breakfast.** Serene and traditional, this 1909 Tudor home is surrounded by opulent gardens and is near both Volunteer Park and Broadway—and it also has two suites that welcome children and/or pets. **Pros:** quiet, relaxing retreat; knowledgeable owner; lovely patio and porch; great for families. **Cons:** no a/c; rooms could use updating; breakfasts are on the light side. [$] *Rooms from: $184* ✉ *959 Broadway E, at E. Prospect St., Capitol Hill* ☎ *206/329–1864, 800/240–1864* 🌐 *www.baconmansion.com* 🛏 *11 rooms, 9 with bath; 2 suites* 🍴 *Breakfast* ✥ 2:F3.

$ B&B/INN Fodor's Choice ★ 🏨 **11th Avenue Inn Seattle Bed & Breakfast.** The closest B&B to Downtown offers all the charm of a classic bed-and-breakfast (exquisitely styled with antique beds and Oriental rugs) with the convenience of being near the action. **Pros:** unpretentious take on classic B&B; free on-site parking; oozes vintage charm; wonderful owner and staff. **Cons:** although most guests are courteous, sound does carry in old houses; no kids under 12; minimum three-night stay. [$] *Rooms from: $169* ✉ *121 11th Ave. E, Capitol Hill* ☎ *206/720–7161* 🌐 *www.11thavenueinn.com* 🛏 *9 rooms* 🍴 *Breakfast* ✥ 2:G5.

$ B&B/INN 🏨 **Gaslight Inn.** Rooms here range from a crow's nest with peeled-log furniture and Navajo-print fabrics to a more traditional suite with Arts and Crafts–style furnishings, a fireplace, and stained-glass windows. **Pros:** great art collection; house and rooms are quite spacious; in-ground heated pool; free Wi-Fi. **Cons:** breakfast is unimpressive; street parking not always easy to find; minimum two-night stay. [$] *Rooms from: $168* ✉ *1727 15th Ave., Capitol Hill* ☎ *206/325–3654* 🌐 *www.*

LODGING ALTERNATIVES

B&BS AND HOME RENTALS

There are many tiny B&Bs scattered throughout Seattle—especially in northern areas such as Fremont, Ballard, Wallingford, Phinney Ridge, Green Lake, and the University District. If you are looking for the microlodging experience, check out 🌐 *www.seattlebedandbreakfast.com*. Renting an apartment or a house will give you access to Seattle neighborhoods that don't have a lot of traditional lodging accommodations. A furnished rental can save you money, especially if you're traveling with a group.

Airbnb 🌐 *www.airbnb.com*

Sea to Sky Rentals 🌐 *www.seatoskyrentals.com*

Seattle Bed and Breakfast 🌐 *www.seattlebedandbreakfast.com*

Vacation Rentals by Owner (VRBO) 🌐 *www.vrbo.com*

gaslight-inn.com 🛏 *6 rooms with private bath; 2 rooms with shared bath* 🍴 *Breakfast* ✥ 2:G6.

$$ B&B/INN Fodor's Choice ★ 🏨 **Shafer Baillie Mansion Bed & Breakfast.** The opulent guest rooms and suites on the second floor are large, with private baths, antique furnishings, Oriental rugs, huge windows, and lush details like ornate four-poster beds; third-floor rooms, while lovely, have a more contemporary country feel, but still have private baths and large windows. **Pros:** wonderful staff; great interior and exterior common spaces; free Wi-Fi; location. **Cons:** no elevator and the walk to the third floor might be hard for some guests; while children are allowed, some guests say the mansion isn't kid-friendly; three-night minimum stay during summer weekends; two nights otherwise. [$] *Rooms from: $199* ✉ *907 14th Ave. E, Sea-Tac* ☎ *800/985–4654* 🌐 *www.sbmansion.com* 🛏 *6 rooms, 2 suites* 🍴 *Breakfast* ✥ 2:G4.

FREMONT

This charming north-end neighborhood is a short drive from Downtown. If you don't mind being in a self-contained spot far away from most attractions, this is a good bet, because there are restaurants, shops, and lovely walking galore. Fremont is close to Ballard, Phinney Ridge, and Green Lake; the closest attractions are the Ballard Locks, the Woodland Park Zoo, and Green Lake's lively park.

$$$ B&B/INN Fodor's Choice ★ 🏨 **Chelsea Station Inn Bed & Breakfast.** The four 900-square-foot suites in this 1920s brick colonial have distressed hardwood floors with colorful rugs, decorative fireplaces, sleeper sofas, contemporary furnishings, and a soft, modern color palette, and are a convenient and luxurious jumping-off point for all the north end has to offer. **Pros:** great, unobtrusive host; huge rooms and 1½ bathrooms per suite; fabulous breakfasts and complimentary snacks. **Cons:** far from Downtown; no TVs; no elevator. [$] *Rooms from: $287* ✉ *4915 Linden Ave. N, Fremont*

☎ *206/547–6077* 🌐 *www.chelseastationinn.com* 🛏 *4 suites* 🍴 *Breakfast* ⊕ 3:D3.

BALLARD

Ballard has a real neighborhood vibe, so staying here is a good way to feel like a local, though it can feel a bit cut off from Downtown. There's a good restaurant and nightlife scene in this part of town.

$ B&B/INN **Ballard Inn.** Travelers seeking an authentic Seattle neighborhood experience will fall hard for this charming budget-friendly inn right in the heart of Ballard, tucked between coffee shops, trendy boutiques, and restaurants. **Pros:** friendly staff; free Wi-Fi; comfy beds. **Cons:** no elevator (ask for a room on main floor if stairs are an issue); no in-room phone; thin walls and street noise; no children under 18. [$] *Rooms from: $129* ✉ *5300 Ballard Ave. NW, Ballard* ☎ *206/789–5011* 🌐 *www.ballardinnseattle.com* 🛏 *12 rooms without private baths, 4 suites* 🍴 *No meals* ⊕ 3:A3.

$$$ HOTEL Fodor's Choice ★ **Hotel Ballard.** In the heart of historic Ballard, surrounded by shops and restaurants, this chic boutique hotel features a modern take on baroque style, with gilded mirrors and sumptuous carpeting and furnishings in every room. **Pros:** close to Ballard attractions; friendly service; inexpensive parking by Seattle standards; free access to one of the city's best gyms. **Cons:** a bit isolated from Downtown; some street noise at night, especially on weekends; rooftop event space can be disruptive for guests. [$] *Rooms from: $319* ✉ *5216 Ballard Ave NW, Ballard* ☎ *206/789–5012* 🌐 *www.hotelballardseattle.com* 🛏 *18 rooms, 11 suites* ⊕ 3:A3.

GREEN LAKE

An upbeat, leafy park with a walking loop around a lake, several small commercial stretches with cafés and restaurants, and a relaxed residential vibe make Green Lake a no-fuss option that is well out of the Downtown core.

$$ B&B/INN Fodor's Choice ★ **Greenlake Guest House.** Outdoorsy types, visitors who want to stay in a low-key residential area, and anyone who wants to feel pampered and refreshed will enjoy this lovely B&B across the street from beautiful Green Lake. **Pros:** views; thoughtful amenities and wonderful hosts; can accommodate kids over four years old; short walk to restaurants. **Cons:** 5 miles from Downtown; on a busy street. [$] *Rooms from: $229* ✉ *7630 E. Green Lake Dr. N, Green Lake* ☎ *206/729–8700, 866/355–8700* 🌐 *www.greenlakeguesthouse.com* 🛏 *5 rooms* 🍴 *Breakfast* ⊕ 3:F1.

UNIVERSITY DISTRICT

Seattleites have a love-hate relationship with the University District. On one hand, you'll find some reasonably priced, decent accommodations here, thanks to the many parents visiting their kids at the University of Washington (UW). On the other hand, the areas closest to the main drag, University Avenue (the Ave) can feel both college-y and gritty. One plus of staying close to the Ave is the plethora of cheap ethnic restaurants. You'll also enjoy access to the city's largest farmers' market on Saturdays as well as the UW's Henry Art Gallery and the Burke Museum. The area on the other side of the campus, closest to the upscale open-air mall University Village, is nicer and more residential but inconvenient to the rest of the city. In terms of location, the U-District hotels listed offer fairly quick commutes to both Downtown and Capitol Hill.

$$ 🖥 **University Inn.** This impeccably maintained inn has earned its popu-
HOTEL larity by steadfastly offering clean, friendly lodging in a city where the
FAMILY price for a room is liable to cause sticker shock. **Pros:** great value; free shuttle and parking; friendly staff. **Cons:** not as nice as the Watertown next door; pool is a little cold; panhandlers in the area; not close to many tourist attractions. Ⓢ *Rooms from: $199* ✉ *4140 Roosevelt Way NE, University District* ☏ *206/632–5055, 800/733–3855* ⊕ *www.universityinnseattle.com* 🛏 *102 rooms* 🍽 *Breakfast* ✛ 3:G4.

$$ 🖥 **Watertown Hotel.** Assorted amenities make this University District
HOTEL hotel a great deal, including inexpensive parking ($15), free Wi-Fi,
FAMILY an afternoon reception with coffee and freshly baked cupcakes, and complimentary shuttle service to Downtown, area attractions, and hospitals. **Pros:** free shuttle service; complimentary bikes and laundry; on-site café; pool access. **Cons:** street noise in some rooms; panhandlers in the area; not as close to attractions as other hotels. Ⓢ *Rooms from: $209* ✉ *4242 Roosevelt Way NE, University District* ☏ *206/826–4242, 206/826–4242* ⊕ *www.watertownseattle.com* 🛏 *100 rooms* 🍽 *No meals* ✛ 3:G4.

THE EASTSIDE

The Eastside suburbs have a few high-end properties of note, especially the first-rate Willows Lodge. There are also quite a few midpriced chain hotels, but we don't list them—unless you have business in the area or plan to spend a lot of time out here, it's really not worth staying this far from Downtown Seattle.

$$$ 🖥 **The Hotel Bellevue.** Fitness buffs will particularly enjoy the perks of this
HOTEL architectural jewel in downtown Bellevue because guests have use of
FAMILY the Bellevue Club's 200,000-square-foot private athletic club—though the luxurious rooms will please even travelers whose most strenuous form of exercise is lifting the remote. **Pros:** amazing gym and pools; indoor and outdoor tennis courts; complimentary town-car service to area shopping; good on-site restaurant. **Cons:** outside of downtown Bellevue; hotel can feel a bit corporate; books up well in advance. Ⓢ *Rooms from: $325* ✉ *11200 S.E. 6th St., Bellevue* ☏ *425/454–4424, 800/579–1110* ⊕ *www.thehotelbellevue.com* 🛏 *64 rooms, 3 suites* 🍽 *No meals* ✛ 3:H6.

$$ 🖥 **Hyatt Regency Bellevue.** Near Bellevue Square and other downtown
HOTEL Bellevue shopping centers, the Hyatt looks like any other sleek high-rise but its interior is adorned with huge displays of fresh flowers and elegant touches such as marble floors and a grand piano. **Pros:** free parking on weekends; great location in the heart of Bellevue; great staff. **Cons:** readers complain of spotty housekeeping; charges for Wi-Fi and

business center. [$] *Rooms from: $209* ✉ *900 Bellevue Way NE, Bellevue* ☎ *425/462–1234* 🌐 *www.bellevue.hyatt.com* 🛏 *677 rooms, 55 suites* 🍴 *No meals* ⊕ 3:H6.

$$$$ HOTEL Fodor's Choice ★ 🏨 **Willows Lodge.** Timbers salvaged from a 19th-century warehouse are rustic counterpoints to sleek, modern design of this elegant spa hotel in the heart of Woodinville wine country. **Pros:** a truly romantic getaway; great for foodies and wine people; lovely spa; impeccable service. **Cons:** not really for families; far from Downtown; rooms a bit dark. [$] *Rooms from: $459* ✉ *14580 N.E. 145th St., Woodinville* ☎ *425/424–3900, 877/424–3930* 🌐 *www.willowslodge.com* 🛏 *77 rooms, 7 suites* 🍴 *No meals* ⊕ 3:H6.

$$ HOTEL 🏨 **Woodmark Hotel.** Daily boat tours, waterside views, and complimentary kayak usage make this Kirkland hotel and yacht club, just 9 miles from Seattle on the shores of Lake Washington, a great bet. **Pros:** great staff; boat tours, paddle boarding, and kayak rentals; free late-night snacks. **Cons:** rooms not facing the water have rotten views of an office park; wedding weekends can get a bit lively. [$] *Rooms from: $249* ✉ *1200 Carillon Point, Kirkland* ☎ *425/822–3700, 800/822–3700* 🌐 *www.thewoodmark.com* 🛏 *79 rooms, 21 suites* 🍴 *No meals* ⊕ 3:H6.

NIGHTLIFE AND PERFORMING ARTS

Updated by
Conor Risch

Seattle's amazing musical legacy is well-known, but there's more to the arts and nightlife scenes than live music. In fact, these days, there are far more swanky bars and inventive pubs than music venues in the city.

To put it bluntly, Seattle's a dynamite place to drink. You can sip overly ambitious and ridiculously named specialty cocktails in trendy lounges, get a lesson from an enthusiastic sommelier in a wine bar or restaurant, or swill cheap beer on the patio of a dive bar. Though some places have very specific demographics, most Seattle bars are egalitarian, drawing loyal regulars of all ages.

The music scene is still kicking—there's something going on every night of the week in nearly every genre of music. The city's dynamic theater scene is a highly regarded proving ground for Broadway, and the Seattle International Film Festival draws the finest in world cinema. The ethereal Marion Oliver McCaw Hall is a first-class venue for opera and ballet, and Benaroya Hall, with its outstanding acoustics, is an elegant premier symphony hall. Families enjoy the Children's Theatre, the Northwest Puppet Center, and the many summertime folk art and music festivals.

In addition to its bars, Downtown and Belltown in particular have notable restaurants with separate bar areas. Most restaurants have impressive bar menus, and food is often served until 11 pm, midnight, or even 1 am in some spots.

PLANNING

NIGHTLIFE PLANNER
GETTING AROUND
Many Seattleites rely on Uber or Lyft to get around when they aren't driving. If you don't use these apps, program the numbers for the city's cab companies into your cell phone. Unless you have a designated driver or are not venturing too far from your hotel, you will need them. (Expect longer waits for pickups on Friday and Saturday nights.) Though you'll probably be able to hail cabs on the street in even the

THE BEST OF SEATTLE'S NIGHTLIFE

BEST HOTEL BARS
BoKa, Hotel 1000, Downtown

The Nest, Thompson, Downtown

Oliver's, Mayflower Hotel, Downtown

BEST DIVE BARS
Linda's, Capitol Hill

Whisky Bar, Belltown

BEST COCKTAIL BARS
Essex, Ballard

Oliver's, Downtown

Sun Liquor Lounge, Capitol Hill

Zig Zag Café, Downtown

BEST BEER BARS & BREWERIES
Brouwer's, Fremont

Collins Pub, Pioneer Square

Elysian Brewing Company, Capitol Hill

Quinn's, Capitol Hill

BEST DANCE CLUBS
Century Ballroom, Capitol Hill

Contour, Pioneer Square

Emerald City Soul Club, various locations

BEST GAY AND LESBIAN BARS
Pony, Capitol Hill

BEST SMALL MUSIC VENUES
The Crocodile, Belltown

Jewelbox Theater at the Rendezvous, Belltown

Showbox, Downtown

The Sunset, Ballard

Triple Door, Downtown

quieter sections of Downtown, you'll have trouble finding empty cabs in Capitol Hill, Belltown, and in north-end neighborhoods like Ballard and Fremont. You can also take advantage of the recent additions of light-rail stations that connect downtown to Capitol Hill and the University District, but the routes are limited.

If you are driving around, exercise caution on the roads, especially when the bars start to let out. Unfortunately, drunk driving is far too common here, as so many people rely on their cars to get around, and public transportation becomes even less frequent late at night.

Parking in Belltown is a nightmare on weekend nights. The neighborhood has ample pay lots, but even those fill up, and finding a space on the street requires either a miracle or a lot of circling. Capitol Hill and Ballard are also tough, though at least the former has a few parking garages and pay lots in the Pike–Pine Corridor.

INFORMATION
For detailed music, art, and nightlife listings, as well as hot tips and suggestions for the week's events, check out *The Stranger* (⊕ *www.thestranger.com*) and *Seattle Weekly* (⊕ *www.seattleweekly.com*). Pick them up at delis and coffeehouses throughout the city. Friday editions of the *Seattle Times* include weekend pullout sections detailing arts and entertainment events.

MUSIC FESTIVALS

Music fans have a lot to look forward to throughout the year in Seattle. Here's a taste of some of the festivals and events that are worth planning a trip around:

Ballard Jazz Festival (⊕ *www.ballardjazzfestival.com*; May).

Bumbershoot (⊕ *www.bumbershoot.org*; September).

Capitol Hill Block Party (⊕ *www.capitolhillblockparty.com*; late July).

Decibel Festival (⊕ *www.dbfestival.com*; September).

Earshot Jazz Festival (⊕ *www.earshot.org*; mid-October to early November).

Northwest Folklife (⊕ *www.nwfolklife.org*; June).

Seattle Chamber Music Society Concert Series (⊕ *www.seattlechambermusic. org*; July/January).

Seattle Improvised Music Festival ⊕ *www.seattleimprovisedmusic.us*; February).

SMOKE WON'T GET IN YOUR EYES

Smoking—of all substances, cannabis included—is prohibited in restaurants, bars, and clubs (the smoking ban covers all public places and workplaces). You're not supposed to smoke within 25 feet of any door or window connected to a public place, although this is difficult to enforce in the more congested nightlife areas.

TICKETS AND COVER CHARGES

Tickets for high-profile performances range from $15 to more than $200; fringe-theater plays and performance-art events range from $5 to $25. The Seattle Symphony offers half-price tickets to seniors and students one hour before scheduled performances. Teens can sign up for Seattle's free Teen Tix program (⊕ *www.teentix.org*) to get $5 tickets to many of the top theaters, museums, and other arts venues throughout the city. Cover charges at nonticketed music venues range from $5 to $12. Tickets for major events can be purchased through a venue's website or at its box office; Sonic Boom record stores *(Shopping)* also sell tickets to select music venues like The Crocodile and Neumos, as well as to some music festivals. ■ TIP→ Major online ticket retailers are Ticketmaster (⊕ *www.ticketmaster.com*) ■ TIP→ and Brown Paper Tickets (☎ *800/838–3006* ⊕ *www.brownpapertickets.com*).

NIGHTLIFE

Every neighborhood has a little bit of everything, save for dance clubs, which are in short supply and mostly concentrated in Pioneer Square and Belltown. The number of bars in each neighborhood increases greatly if you take into account all of the stellar restaurants that also have happening bar scenes—in some cases the line between restaurant and nightspot is quite blurred. The happy-hour scene is positively bumpin' in Seattle; bars, lounges, gastropubs, breweries, sushi spots, hotel bars, and restaurants alike often have one, or even two, happy hours per night, often from 3 to 6 and again after 10. It's definitely worth calling or checking a restaurant's website to find out about happy-hour details. Many favorite restaurants—especially those on Capitol Hill and in Ballard and Belltown—have alluring bar areas that rival the most popular watering holes in the same locales.

If jazz is your thing, check out the Seattle Jazz Vespers, held the first Sunday of every month at the Seattle First Baptist Church (corner of Harvard Avenue and Seneca Street ⊕ *www.seattlefirstbaptist.org*) starting at 6 pm. The event lasts about 1½ hours, with outstanding musicians playing two sets; the church's pastor gives a brief sermon between sets.

DOWNTOWN AND BELLTOWN

DOWNTOWN

Downtown is a great place for anyone looking to dress up a bit and hit glam hotel bars, classy lounges, and wine bars where you don't have to be under the age of 30 to fit in. Downtown also has a smattering of pubs popular with the happy-hour crowd. Barhopping Downtown may require several taxi rides, as things can be a bit spread out, but cabs can actually be hailed on the street in this part of town.

5

BARS AND LOUNGES

Alibi Room. Well-dressed locals head to this hard-to-find wood-paneled bar to sip double martinis while taking in views of Elliott Bay or studying the scripts, handbills, and movie posters that line the walls. The lower level is more crowded and casual. It's an ever-cool yet low-key, intimate place. Stop by for a drink or a meal, or stay to listen and dance to live music. Happy hour—daily from 11:30 am to 6 pm—is quiet and a good respite from the Market. ⊠ *85 Pike St., in Post Alley, at Pike Place Market, Downtown* ☎ *206/623–3180* ⊕ *www.seattlealibi.com.*

BoKa Restaurant + Bar. Featuring creative cocktails, addictive burgers, a posh clientele, and a sublimely sleek interior with mood lighting, graphic art pieces, and booth seating, Boka Restaurant + Bar, part of Hotel 1000, is worth checking out for its happy hour (2:30 to 6 daily). ⊠ *1010 1st Ave., Downtown* ☎ *206/357–9000* ⊕ *www.bokaseattle.com.*

The Diller Room. Occupying the former lobby of the historic Diller Hotel, which was built in 1890, the Diller Room is a charming, worn-around-the-edges spot for cocktails in downtown, across the street from the Seattle Art Museum. Exposed brick, mismatched crystal chandeliers, a beat-up white tile floor, and a vintage neon Diller Hotel sign above the wood bar provide the atmosphere. The drink menu includes cocktails and a section devoted to tallboys. Happy hour runs 2–7 pm every day, and the food menu offers various sliders, pizzas, and bar snacks. ⊠ *1224 1st Ave., Downtown* ☎ *206/467–4042* ⊕ *www.dillerroom.com.*

Heartwood Provisions. From the arcing bar at Heartwood Provisions, you can look through tall windows onto Spring Street as you sip house cocktails, wine, or beer, and eat upscale bar food in a room that combines wood and light to beautiful effect. Nightly cocktail hours, which run 3–6 pm daily and from 10 pm to close Tuesday–Saturday, offer a handful of discounted cocktails, beer and wine specials, and a burger. ⊠ *1103 1st Ave., Downtown* ☎ *206/582–3505* ⊕ *www.heartwoodsea.com.*

Oliver's. The most important question here: Shaken or stirred? This bar in the Mayflower Park Hotel is famous for its martinis. In fact, having a cocktail here is like having afternoon tea in some other parts of the world. Wing chairs, low tables, and lots of natural light make it easy to relax after a hectic day. The likes of Frank Sinatra or Billie Holiday may be playing in the background; expect an unfussy crowd of regulars, hotel guests, and older Manhattan-sippers who appreciate old-school elegance. ⊠ *405 Olive Way, Downtown* ☎ *206/623–8700* ⊕ *oliverstwistseattle.com.*

The Nest at Thompson Seattle. One look at the unobstructed views of Elliott Bay and you might forget why you came to this beautiful rooftop bar at the Thompson hotel—the carefully crafted cocktails and tasty snacks are nearly beside the point. On a clear evening, the outdoor deck, with ample seating and fireplaces, is the perfect spot to gaze across Puget Sound at the Olympic Mountains. This place gets busy, though, so reservations—available for parties of 4–20 guests—are a good idea. ⊠ *110 Stewart St., Downtown* ☎ *206/623–4600* ⊕ *www.thompsonhotels.com/hotels/thompson-seattle/eat-and-drink/the-nest.*

Purple Café and Wine Bar. Wine lovers come for the massive selection—the menu boasts 90 wines by the glass and some 600 bottles—but this place deserves props for its design, too. Despite the cavernous quality of the space and floor-to-ceiling windows, all eyes are immediately drawn to the 20-foot tower ringed by a spiral staircase that showcases thousands of bottles. Full lunch and dinner menus feature American and Pacific Northwest fare—the lobster mac 'n' cheese is especially tasty—and servers know their ideal pairings. ⊠ *1225 4th Ave., Downtown* ☎ *206/829–2280* ⊕ *www.thepurplecafe.com.*

Trace. The W Hotel's bar, adjoining the restaurant of the same name, gives you a chance to enjoy the hotel's signature design style even if you haven't booked a room here. You'll certainly feel fabulous sipping a costly but well-poured martini among the other chic patrons. Definitely dress up, and come prepared for a scene if it's a weekend night. Kick back and enjoy table service on the couches in the lobby, or pull up to the bar during happy hour, which runs 4–7 pm, Monday–Saturday, and 4 pm–midnight on Sunday. There's a bar menu that includes sushi, and there's a limited late-night menu 11–1 am on Friday and Saturday night. ⊠ *1112 4th Ave., Downtown* ☎ *206/264–6000* ⊕ *www.whotels.com/Seattle.*

Fodor's Choice ★ **Zig Zag Café.** A mixed crowd of mostly locals hunts out this unique spot at Pike Place Market's Street Hill Climb (a nearly hidden stairwell leading down to the piers). In addition to pouring a perfect martini, Zig Zag features a revolving cast of memorable cocktails. A Mediterranean-inspired food menu offers plenty of tasty bites to accompany the excellent cocktails. A small patio is the place to be on a summery happy-hour evening. Zig Zag is friendly—retro without being obnoxiously ironic—and very Seattle, with the occasional live music show to boot. ⊠ *1501 Western Ave., Downtown* ☎ *206/625–1146* ⊕ *zigzagseattle.com.*

CLOSE UP

Suds Appeal

Seattle loves its beer, and for good reason. America's ever-burgeoning craft-beer scene owes this city a big debt. In 1981, RedHook Ale Brewery became one of the country's first microbreweries, and Seattle's love affair with the good stuff hasn't faltered since.

Craft beer aficionados will find plenty of spots for sampling local brews as well as the best imports from around the country and the world; nearly every neighborhood worth its weight boasts a great beer bar or two, and brewery taprooms abound.

People here take beer every drop as seriously as oenophiles at a wine bar. If you have any questions, your bartender—or the guy on the barstool next to you—is sure to have plenty of suggestions. Keep in mind that every May brings Seattle Beer Week (⊕ *seattlebeerweek.com*), with events all over town.

5

BREWPUBS

The Pike Brewing Company. True to its location, you might find more tourists than locals at the Pike Brewing Company, though it is popular with the Downtown after-work crowd. The cavernous bar and restaurant, operated by the brewers of the Pike Place Pale Ale, also houses the Seattle Microbrewery Museum and an excellent shop with home-brewing supplies. Pints of beer are cold and satisfying—the pale ale and the Kilt Lifter Scottish ale have been local favorites for more than two decades. ⊠ *1415 1st Ave., Downtown* ☎ *206/622–6044* ⊕ *www. pikebrewing.com.*

Pyramid Alehouse. The loud and festive Pyramid brews a top-notch Hefeweizen and an apricot ale that tastes much better than it sounds. Madhouse doesn't even begin to describe this place when it hosts concerts or during games at Safeco Field or CenturyLink Field, so if you're looking for quiet and immediate seating, make sure your visit doesn't coincide with either. The brewery, which is just south of Pioneer Square, offers tours daily at 4 pm. ⊠ *1201 1st Ave. S, SoDo* ☎ *206/682–3377* ⊕ *www.pyramidbrew.com.*

COMEDY CLUBS

Unexpected Productions Improv. Unexpected Productions Improv, adjacent to Pike Place Market, hosts tons of different improv events; shows may have holiday or seasonal themes or be done in the style of a certain TV or film genre like sci-fi or noir. On Friday and Saturday at 10:30, the troupe presents the long-running "TheatreSports" show, in which the skits are based entirely on audience suggestions. ⊠ *Market Theater, 1428 Post Alley, Downtown* ☎ *206/587–2414* ⊕ *www.unexpectedproductions.org.*

MUSIC CLUBS

Dimitriou's Jazz Alley. Seattleites dress up to see nationally known jazz artists at Dimitriou's. The cabaret-style theater, where intimate tables for two surround the stage, runs shows nightly. Those with reservations for cocktails or dinner, served during the first set, receive priority seating. ⊠ *2033 6th Ave., Downtown* ☎ *206/441–9729* ⊕ *www.jazzalley.com.*

Owl N' Thistle Irish Pub. This affable pub near Pike Place Market presents acoustic folk music on a small stage in a cavernous room. It's often loaded with regulars, who appreciate the well-drawn pints of Guinness, the talent, and the Tuesday-night jazz jam. ⊠ *808 Post Ave., Downtown* ☎ *206/621–7777* ⊕ *www.owlnthistle.com.*

Showbox. Just across from Pike Place Market, this venue—which turned 75 in 2014—is a great spot to see some pretty big-name acts. The room's small enough that you don't feel like you're miles away from the performers, and the terraced bar areas flanking the main floor provide some relief if you don't want to join the crush in front of the stage. Another branch, **Showbox SoDo** (*1700 1st Avenue South, SoDo*), is named for its location south of Downtown; the converted warehouse, larger than the original, features big national acts, but has little of the charm of the original. ⊠ *1426 1st Ave., Downtown* ☎ *888/929–7849* ⊕ *www. showboxpresents.com.*

The Triple Door. Despite its reputation as a rock club for thirty- and forty-somethings, the Triple Door has an interesting lineup that often appeals to younger patrons, too. You'll see more world music and jazz here than alternative music, and the half-moon booths that make up the majority of the seating in the main room are more cabaret than rock. ⊠ *216 Union St., Downtown* ☎ *206/838–4333* ⊕ *www.thetripledoor.net.*

BELLTOWN

Belltown can be an absolute madhouse on weekends. That said, there are some lovely spaces here, a few of which stay relatively low-key even during the Saturday-night crush, as well as some quirky old neighborhood dives left over from Belltown's former life. (Speaking of which, although the city is working to keep the streets clear of panhandlers and drug dealers, Belltown can get gritty late at night around the Pike–Pine Corridor, so stick to busy, well-lit areas. In recent years, the police have beefed up their presence to cut back on crime in the neighborhood.)

BARS AND LOUNGES

Bathtub Gin & Co. The speakeasy trend has produced some lovely, intimate bars, including this one, which is reached via a wooden door in an alley next to the Humphrey Apartments (it's actually in the basement of the building). The tiny, shabby-chic bar is a very laid-back spot to settle into a couch for a few drinks. Note that despite being a pain in the neck to find, the bar still attracts the hard-partying Belltown crowd on weekends, so go midweek for maximum serenity. ⊠ *2205 2nd Ave., Belltown* ☎ *206/728–6069* ⊕ *bathtubginseattle.com.*

Black Bottle. This sleek and sexy gastro-tavern makes the northern reaches of Belltown look good. The interior is simple but stylish, with black chairs and tables and shiny wood floors. It gets crowded on nights and weekends with a laid-back but often dressed-up clientele. A small selection of beers on tap and a solid wine list (with Washington, Oregon, California, and beyond well represented) will help you wash down the sustainably sourced pub snacks, including house-smoked wild boar ribs, pork belly with kimchi, and oysters on the half shell. ⊠ *2600 1st Ave., Belltown* ☎ *206/441–1500* ⊕ *www.blackbottleseattle.com.*

Clever Bottle. In a raw space that resembles an artist's studio with a bar built into it, this low-key, candlelit craft cocktail spot draws a local crowd for tasty drinks featuring house-made ingredients, a small but solid wine list, and local draft and bottled beer. There's a great list of nonalcoholic mixed drinks, and the staff coax tasty bites out of a small kitchen. Happy hour runs 5–7 pm Tuesday through Saturday. ✉ *2222 2nd Ave., Suite 100, Belltown* ☎ *206/915–2220* ⊕ *www.cleverbottle.com.*

List. A Belltown favorite for great happy-hour deals, this hip, dimly lit space has a come-hither glow thanks to red and white backlighting. An all-day happy hour on Sunday and Monday means you get half off the yummy food menu (local clams, Angus beef burgers, bacon-wrapped prawns, spicy calamari), plus $15 bottles of wine. ✉ *2226 1st Ave., Belltown* ☎ *206/441–1000* ⊕ *www.listbelltown.com.*

The Rendezvous Restaurant and Lounge. It opened in 1926 as an elite screening room for film stars and moguls. Since then, Rendezvous has done time as both a porn theater and a much-loved dive bar, but it's been spruced up just enough to suit the new wave of wealthy locals without alienating everyone else. An old-time feel and the great calendar of events at the bar's Jewelbox Theater (live music, film, burlesque shows) set it apart from the neighborhood's string of cookie-cutter trendy spots. The food is nothing to write home about, but the atmosphere is chilled out and fun. ✉ *2322 2nd Ave., Belltown* ☎ *206/441–5823* ⊕ *www.therendezvous.rocks.*

Rob Roy. With its deep selection of dark liquor, low-light ambience, and black leather walls, Rob Roy is a serious-but-inviting cocktail bar. Their original concoctions change four to five times a year, and include drinks like a Saffron Sandalwood Sour. They also feature nonalcoholic cocktails for teetotalers and designated drivers. Meatballs and a breakfast sandwich decorate a limited food menu, which is half-off during a daily 4–7 pm happy hour that also features drink specials. They also have Tiki Night every Monday. ✉ *2332 2nd Ave., Belltown* ☎ *206/956–8423* ⊕ *www.robroyseattle.com.*

Shorty's. It may be one of the dingiest bars in Belltown, but Shorty's is a bright spot in a neighborhood where most bars serve $10 drinks. Along with a come-as-you-are atmosphere, the grown-up arcade features pinball machines and video games, cheap beer and hot dogs, and lots of no-frills fun. ✉ *2222 2nd Ave., Belltown* ☎ *206/441–5449* ⊕ *www.shortydog.com.*

Umi Sake House. Choose from a wide selection of sake and sake-based cocktails in a space designed to look like someone shoehorned a real *izakaya* (a sake house that also serves substantial snacks) into a Belltown building—there's even an enclosed patio, which they refer to as the "porch," and a tatami room that can be reserved for larger parties. The sushi is good, and there's a very long happy hour offered at one of the bar areas. Umi is less of a meat market than some Belltown spots—unless you're here late on a Friday or Saturday night. ✉ *2230 1st Ave., Belltown* ☎ *206/374–8717* ⊕ *www.umisakehouse.com.*

The Whisky Bar. One of Belltown's reigning dive bars has recently relocated to a new space but maintained the same jaw-dropping selection of whisky, bourbon, and rye. They also have 24 beers on tap, mostly from West Coast brewers, and a bottle list with beers from around the world. The food menu includes sliders, a burger, and a scotch egg among other snacks and small plates. Daily happy hour runs from when they open the doors—noon on weekends, 2 pm weekdays—until 7 pm. ⊠ *2122 2nd Ave., Belltown* ☎ *206/443–4490* ⊕ *www.thewhiskybar.com.*

MUSIC CLUBS

Fodor's Choice
★
The Crocodile. The heart and soul of Seattle's music scene since 1991 has hosted the likes of Nirvana, Pearl Jam, and Mudhoney, along with countless other bands. There's a reason *Rolling Stone* once called the 525-person Crocodile one of the best small clubs in America. Nightly shows are complemented by cheap beer on tap and pizza at the Back Bar. All hail the Croc! ⊠ *2200 2nd Ave., Belltown* ☎ *206/441–7416* ⊕ *www.thecrocodile.com.*

Tula's. Less of a production (and expense) than Dimitriou's, Tula's offers a similar lineup of more traditional favorites as well as top-notch local and national acts. The intimate space hosts weekly Latin jazz and big-band jazz jams and often showcases vocal artists. ⊠ *2214 2nd Ave., Belltown* ☎ *206/443–4221* ⊕ *www.tulas.com.*

SEATTLE CENTER, SOUTH LAKE UNION, AND QUEEN ANNE

SOUTH LAKE UNION

DANCE CLUBS

Kremwerk. This "queer-centric" club that combines modern fixtures and an industrial space is known for electronic music and theatrical performances that draw fun crowds. Tickets to shows by local and out-of-town DJs, musicians, and multidisciplinary artists are often available in advance for discounted prices. ⊠ *1809 Minor Ave., South Lake Union* ☎ *206/682–2935* ⊕ *www.kremwerk.com.*

Re-Bar. A loyal following enjoys cabaret shows, weekend stage performances, and great DJs at this combination bar, theater, dance club, and art space. It's extremely friendly to all persuasions; it also has a reputation for playing good house music, but there are lots of different theme nights, including an '80s night and a B movie–music mashup. Every fourth Saturday of the month Re-Bar hosts Cherry, a popular lesbian dance party. ⊠ *1114 Howell St., South Lake Union* ☎ *206/233–9873* ⊕ *www.rebarseattle.com.*

QUEEN ANNE

Queen Anne is a diffuse and mostly residential neighborhood, and there's no real center to its nightlife. Some of the bars we list here are on the top of Queen Anne's formidable hill, but most are on the lower reaches, near Seattle Center and Key Arena. *Definitely check a map if you're on foot and planning an early-evening drink.*

BARS AND LOUNGES

The Masonry. One of the best bars in Seattle for craft beer, The Masonry also happens to have great Neapolitan-style pizzas and other brick-oven goodies. Brewer dinners and beer events, good music, and a bottle list full of limited releases from top breweries are other highlights. There are also ciders and wine on draft. ⊠ *20 Roy St., Lower Queen Anne* ☎ *206/453–4375* ⊕ *www.themasonryseattle.com.*

The Sitting Room. With its European-café vibe and excellent mixed drinks, The Sitting Room lures residents of both the lower and upper parts of Queen Anne. It's quite an accomplishment to get those two very different demographics to agree on anything, but this sweet, relaxed little spot has done it with its eclectic furniture, zinc bar, sexy lighting, and friendly staff. ⊠ *108 W. Roy St., Queen Anne* ☎ *206/285–2830* ⊕ *www. the-sitting-room.com.*

Solo. This spot has a lot going on: it's part tapas bar, part art gallery, part screening room, and part music venue, where up-and-coming indie musicians perform on a small stage. The cutting-edge local artwork and music bring in a lot of Seattle's hipsters, but the bar's location near the Seattle Center and its reputation for excellent, reasonably priced tapas mean that folks without tattoos often wander in, too. ⊠ *200 Roy St., Queen Anne* ☎ *206/213–0080* ⊕ *www.solo-bar.com.*

BREWPUBS

McMenamins. McMenamins is part of the same Portland-based brewpub chain as Six Arms on Capitol Hill, with the same brands on tap. It's a total zoo when Seattle Center events let out, but at other times it's a respectable watering hole. ⊠ *200 Roy St., Queen Anne* ☎ *206/285–4722* ⊕ *www.mcmenamins.com.*

MUSIC CLUBS

Teatro ZinZanni. There's dinner theater, and then there's Seattle's famous, over-the-top—and totally entertaining—five-course feast with a circus on the side. Featuring vaudeville, comedy, music, and dance, the themed shows change every few months, but ZinZanni, in the heart of Seattle Center, remains a reliable favorite for locals and tourists alike. Tickets start at $99. ⊠ *222 Mercer St., Queen Anne* ☎ *206/802–0015* ⊕ *www. zinzanni.com.*

PIONEER SQUARE

Pioneer Square is changing. The area is still home to dance clubs that attract a very young crowd, many of whom come in from the suburbs. But with new offices opening, and new bars, restaurants, and coffee shops catering to after-work and sports crowds, Pioneer Square is a place worth visiting. As always, First Thursdays attracts a more varied crowd participating in the art walk. Galleries provide another focal point, and an additional reason to spend the evening here.

Despite the development, transients and drug use remain a part of the Pioneer Square scene, and it can feel unsafe at times. On weekends, disturbances from the hard-partying crowd make this a less-attractive neighborhood for some.

BARS AND LOUNGES

Collins Pub. The best beer bar in Pioneer Square features 22 rotating taps of Northwest (including Boundary Bay, Chuckanut, and Anacortes) and California beers and a long list of bottles from the region. Its upscale pub menu features local and seasonal ingredients. ✉ *526 2nd Ave., Pioneer Square* ☎ *206/623–1016* ⊕ *www.thecollinspub.com.*

Good Bar. This bright, high-ceilinged space in a historic building in Pioneer Square still features the safe doors of the former Japanese Commercial Bank that once occupied the building. Postwork crowds and some pregaming sports fans mix at the U-shape marble bar and few small tables during a daily 4–7 pm happy hour. There's a rotating list of classic cocktails, newly developed libations featuring house-made infusions, and a beer and wine list. Small plates like pork terrine, wings, and sardines come out of an open kitchen. ✉ *240 2nd Ave. S, Pioneer Square* ☎ *206/624–2337* ⊕ *www.goodbarseattle.com.*

Sake Nomi. Whether you're a novice or expert, you'll appreciate the authentic offerings here. The shop and tasting bar is open until 10 pm Tuesday through Saturday and from noon to 6 on Sunday. Don't be shy— have a seat, try a few of the rotating samples, and ask a lot of questions. Sake can be served up in a variety of temperatures and styles. ✉ *76 S. Washington St., Pioneer Square* ☎ *206/467–7253* ⊕ *www.sakenomi.us.*

COMEDY CLUBS

The Comedy Underground. Beneath Swannie's Sports Bar & Grill, this club puts on stand-up comedy, open-mike sessions, and comedy competitions nightly at 8:30. ✉ *109 S. Washington St., Pioneer Square* ☎ *206/628–0303* ⊕ *www.comedyunderground.com.*

DANCE CLUBS

Contour. If you're not ready to quit partying when Seattle's bars shut at 2, then head here; this small club is famous for after-hours events that keep the doors open until 7 am. There are regular nights for deep house and Nu Disco; '80s industrial and goth; Top 40 and throwback hits; and reggae on Sunday. ✉ *807 1st Ave., Pioneer Square* ☎ *206/447–7704* ⊕ *www.clubcontour.com.*

Trinity. This multilevel, multiroom club plays hip-hop, reggae, disco, and Top 40. It gets packed on weekends—arrive early to avoid lines or to snag a table for some late-night snacks. This is the most appealing and interesting of the Pioneer Square megaclubs—in terms of decor, anyway. ✉ *111 Yesler Way, Pioneer Square* ☎ *206/447–4140* ⊕ *www. trinitynightclub.com.*

CAPITOL HILL

Capitol Hill has a lot of music venues and interesting watering holes— it's one of the city's best areas for nightlife. The Pike–Pine Corridor was always base camp for hipsters drinking Pabst out of the can, but the changing face of the neighborhood has brought some edgy, upscale gastropubs and appearance-conscious lounges. The Hill is also the center of the city's gay and lesbian community, with the majority of gay bars and dance clubs along Pike, Pine, and Broadway. A short stretch of 15th Avenue around East Republican Street is another mini–nightlife district, which is a bit more subdued.

As with Downtown, most of the neighborhood's restaurants double as nightspots. Quinn's (on Pike Street) and Smith (on 15th Avenue), for example, both get kudos for tasty food but are also notable as drinking spots (in Quinn's case for its excellent beer list).

BARS AND LOUNGES

Artusi. Sit at the white tile bar—or on the patio on a sunny day—of this Italian cocktail bar and order delicious antipasti and desserts to go with expertly prepared drinks. Beer selection is limited, but Artusi has great wine options. Make it to the daily 5–7 pm happy hour, or the 10 pm–close late-night happy hour on Friday and Saturday, if you can. ✉ *1535 14th Ave., Capitol Hill* ☎ *206/678–2516* ⊕ *www.artusibar.com.*

Barca. A large space with velvet-lined booths and dark lighting, Barca has mood to spare. There is plenty of bar space early on in the evening and a mezzanine with ample seating, too. Because they can tout the largest vodka selection in the state at their Vodka Bar, as well as a renowned menu of mixed drinks, the bar fills up relatively early with young patrons. As the evening unfolds, it becomes a frenzy of drinking, merrymaking, and people-watching. ✉ *1510 11th Ave., Capitol Hill* ☎ *206/325–8263* ⊕ *www.barcaseattle.com.*

Bitter/Raw. Walk through the excellent Lark restaurant and up the stairs to this small, quiet bar that serves up great craft cocktails, charcuterie, oysters, and crudo. In addition to the Bitter/Raw goodies that you can watch the chef prepare as your sip your drink, you can also order from the full Lark menu and wine list, which will be tough to resist. ✉ *952 E. Seneca St., Capitol Hill* ☎ *206/323–5275* ⊕ *www.larkseattle.com/bitter-raw.*

Hopvine Pub. A neighborhood institution, Hopvine is a no-frills pub with solid pub grub and about a dozen local beers on tap. This is a favorite spot for locals in this slightly out-of-the-way neighborhood—it's not Pike–Pine central, but instead it's on 15th, closer to Volunteer Park. There's an open-mike night on Wednesday and trivia night on most Tuesdays. Note that it serves beer and wine only. ✉ *507 15th Ave. E, Capitol Hill* ☎ *206/328–3120* ⊕ *www.3pubs.com/Hopvine.html.*

Linda's Tavern. Welcome to one of the Hill's iconic dives—and not just because it was allegedly the last place Kurt Cobain was seen alive. The interior has a vaguely Western theme, but the patrons are pure Capitol Hill indie-rockers and hipsters. The bartenders are friendly, the burgers are good (brunch is even better), and the always-packed patio is one of the liveliest places to grab a happy-hour drink. ✉ *707 E. Pine St., Capitol Hill* ☎ *206/325–1220* ⊕ *www.lindastavern.com.*

Oddfellows. Oddfellows anchors a 19th-century building, a former Oddfellows Lodge, that also houses the Century Ballroom, Tin Table, and Elliott Bay Books. It doubles as a bar on weekends, and there's a pleasant, small outdoor space, too. The vibe is hipster-chic; grab a seat at one of the large communal tables and hit up the small but quirky cocktail list. Steak, porchetta sandwiches, soups, salads, bread pudding, and more are on offer, as well. ✉ *1525 10th Ave., Capitol Hill* ☎ *206/325–0807* ⊕ *www.oddfellowscafe.com.*

The Pine Box. The clever name is just one reason to visit this beer hall housed in a former funeral home on the corner of Pine Street. The churchlike interior is stately, with soaring ceilings, dark woodwork, and custom furniture made from huge Douglas fir timbers found in the basement—they were supposedly used to shelve coffins many years ago. The place is rumored to be haunted, but that doesn't stop a trendy crowd from congregating to sample from 30-plus taps of craft beer and a menu of wood-fired pizza and meatballs and pulled-pork tacos. Or get your morning drink on at the weekend brunch. ⊠ *1600 Melrose Ave., Capitol Hill* ☎ *206/588–0375* ⊕ *www.pineboxbar.com.*

Poco Wine + Spirits. Poco Wine + Spirits deserves accolades just for taking one of the least interesting architectural spaces out there—the oddly proportioned retail space of a condo complex—and making it into a sophisticated parallel universe where a friendly crowd lounges on couches and huddles around two small bars to enjoy a competent menu of artisanal Northwest wines, cocktails, and tapas. A selection of subtle fruit wines is a nice surprise. Happy hour runs 4–6:30 pm, and again 10–midnight, Sunday–Thursday. ⊠ *1408 E. Pine St., Capitol Hill* ☎ *206/322–9463* ⊕ *www.pocowineandspirits.com.*

Revolver. Revolver stands out from a row of bars on this crowded block of Capitol Hill with a vinyl-only music policy, classic cocktails, draft beer, and "drop shots" (shots dropped into soda or beer). ⊠ *1514 E. Olive Way, Capitol Hill* ☎ *206/860–7000* ⊕ *www.revolverbarseattle.com.*

Smith. Great for people-watching and very Capitol Hill, Smith is a large, dark space with portraits of ex-presidents and taxidermied birds all over the walls, plus a mixture of booth seating and large communal tables. A bit outside the Pike-Pine heart, and filled to brimming with tattooed hipsters on weekends, this is a superfriendly and inviting space with a very solid menu of food (including a top-notch burger and sweet-potato fries) and a full bar. Beer selection is small but good, and the cocktail list is decent. ⊠ *332 15th Ave. E, Capitol Hill* ☎ *206/709–1099* ⊕ *www. smithseattle.com.*

Fodor'sChoice **Sun Liquor Lounge.** If you adore creative handcrafted cocktails, add this
★ intimate Capitol Hill haunt to your must-visit list. Friendly bartenders sling exceptional drinks mixed with fresh-squeezed juices and house-made ingredients like shrubs—flavorful "drinking vinegars" that first became popular in colonial America—and aromatic bitters. They even make and sell their own hooch. A few years ago, Sun Liquor opened a nearby distillery, which produces the company's flagship Hedge Trimmer Gin, among others. ∎ **TIP➔ The lounge is a much cozier place to hang out, but the same specialty cocktails are served up at the distillery, along with a lunch menu (512 East Pike).** ⊠ *607 Summit Ave. E, Capitol Hill* ☎ *206/860–1130* ⊕ *www.sunliquor.com.*

Tavern Law. Take a trip back in time to the golden age of cocktails before Prohibition and the speakeasies that followed it. Tavern Law is dark and tucked away, and houses a "secret" upstairs area (accessed, if there's room available, by picking up the phone next to the old bank-vault door). And the drinks are impeccably made, often with surprising ingredients. ⊠ *1406 12th Ave., Capitol Hill* ☎ *206/322–9734* ⊕ *www.tavernlaw.com.*

The Tin Table. Upstairs from Oddfellows and across from Cal Anderson Park, the Tin Table is a welcoming little lounge with lots of exposed brick and a long, glossy bar. Its happy hour (3 to 6) is very popular, and so is the Chimay that's on tap. It's also beloved for its good food, like dynamite steak frites. Try the "floozy burger" (with caramelized onion, bacon, cheese, and shoestring fries) and a creative cocktail. ⊠ *915 E. Pine St., Capitol Hill* ☎ *206/320–8458* ⊕ *www.thetintable.com.*

BILLIARDS

Garage Billiards. Built in 1928, this former auto-repair shop is now a large, happening, chrome-and-vinyl pool hall, restaurant, and bar. The large garage doors are thrown wide open on warm evenings, making it a pleasurable alternative to other, more cramped places. There are 18 tournament pool tables and a small bowling alley, and you must be 21 to enter the bowling and billiards areas. ⊠ *1130 Broadway Ave., Capitol Hill* ☎ *206/322–2296* ⊕ *www.garagebilliards.com.*

BREWPUBS

Elysian Brewing Company. Worn booths and tables are scattered across the bi-level warehouse space of this Capitol Hill mainstay, where the beers are a good representation of the thriving brewing scene in the Northwest. Always on tap are the hop-heavy Immortal IPA, the rich Perseus Porter, and the crisp Elysian Fields Pale Ale. The food (burgers, fish tacos, sandwiches, salads) is decent, too. This is a favorite of Seattleites and Capitol Hill residents and a laid-back alternative to the more trendy haunts and lounges in the area. ⊠ *1221 E. Pike St., Capitol Hill* ☎ *206/860–1920* ⊕ *www.elysianbrewing.com.*

Quinn's. Capitol Hill's original gastropub has friendly bartenders, an *amazing* selection of beers on tap (with the West Coast and Belgium heavily represented), an extensive list of whiskey, and an edgy menu of good food, which you can enjoy at the long bar or at a table on either of the two floors of the industrial-chic space. Spicy fried peanuts and country-style rabbit pâté are good ways to start—then you can choose from Painted Hills beef tartare with pumpernickel crisps, perfect marrow bones with baguette and citrus jam, or a cheese plate. Heartier mains, like the signature wild boar sloppy Joe are available at dinnertime. A pared-down pub menu is also available from 3 pm to midnight or later. The folks here take their libations seriously, so feel free to chat up the bartenders about their favorites. ⊠ *1001 E. Pike St., Capitol Hill* ☎ *206/325–7711* ⊕ *www.quinnspubseattle.com* ⊗ *No lunch* ⌲ *Reservations not accepted.*

Six Arms. Named for the six-armed Indian dancer on its logo, this spacious and popular brewpub has 17 house and craft beers on tap. Two that stand out are the medium-bodied Hammerhead and the Terminator Stout. As you head back to the restrooms, note the fermenting tanks painted with amusing murals. ⊠ *300 E. Pike St., Capitol Hill* ☎ *206/223–1698* ⊕ *www.mcmenamins.com.*

DANCE CLUBS

The Baltic Room. It's the little dance club that could: a classy piano bar–turned–art deco cocktail lounge that's still popular after quite a few years on the scene—and that still manages to get Seattleites of all stripes to take a few turns on the dance floor. Dress up a bit, but keep it comfortable. Along with top-notch DJs, skillful rock and blues acts entertain from a small stage. The compact dance floor gets crowded—a little too crowded—on weekends. ⊠ *1207 E. Pine St., Capitol Hill* ☎ *206/625–4444* ⊕ *balticroom.com.*

Century Ballroom. This is an elegant place for dinner and dancing, with a polished, 2,000-square-foot dance floor. Salsa and swing events often include lessons in the cover charge. The Tin Table, the restaurant-bar across the hall, is excellent. There's a bachata social on Wednesday, salsa on Thursday, Friday, and Saturday, and swing on Sunday. ⊠ *915 E. Pine St., 2nd fl., Capitol Hill* ☎ *206/324–7263* ⊕ *www.centuryballroom.com.*

GAY AND LESBIAN SPOTS

Gay City. An inclusive gathering space for Seattle's LGBTQ community, Gay City hosts regular parties, variety shows, and music and theater events at this space that also tests for HIV and sexually transmitted diseases as part of its mission to promote health and wellness. ⊠ *517 E. Pike St., Capitol Hill* ☎ *206/860–6969* ⊕ *www.gaycity.org.*

Madison Pub. Regulars shoot pool, hang out with groups of friends, and chat up the friendly bartenders at this laid-back, anti-scenester joint. ⊠ *1315 E. Madison St., Capitol Hill* ☎ *206/325–6537* ⊕ *www.madisonpub.com.*

Neighbours. In business since 1983, Neighbours is an institution thanks in part to its drag shows, great theme DJ nights, and relaxed atmosphere (everyone, including the straightest of the straights, seems to feel welcome here). It's no longer the center of the gay and lesbian scene, but the dance floor and the rest of this large club is still usually packed Thursday through Saturday. ⊠ *1509 Broadway, Capitol Hill* ☎ *206/324–5358* ⊕ *www.neighboursnightclub.com.*

Pony. The original and short-lived Pony, which got bulldozed along with the rest of the 500 block of Pine Street, was notorious for wild fun. The current incarnation, just a bit more polished and with an amazing patio, retains some of the former space's decorating touches (vintage nude photos). There's a small dance floor and a mix of gays, lesbians, and their friends. ⊠ *1221 E. Madison St., Central District* ☎ *206/324–2854* ⊕ *www.ponyseattle.com.*

Wildrose. Seattle's only dedicated lesbian bar draws a mob nearly every night. The crowd at weeknight karaoke is fun and good-natured, cheering for pretty much anyone. Weekends are raucous, so grab a window table early and settle in for perpetual ladies' night. ⊠ *1021 E. Pike St., Capitol Hill* ☎ *206/324–9210* ⊕ *www.thewildrosebar.com.*

MUSIC CLUBS

Neumos. One of the grunge era's iconic clubs (when it was Moe's) has managed to reclaim its status as a staple of the Seattle rock scene, despite being closed for a six-year stretch. And it is a great rock venue: acoustics are excellent, and the roster of cutting-edge indie rock bands is one of the best in the city. Other genres of music are also represented among the acts coming through Neumos. Their intimate downstairs venue, Barboza, often brings in great, lesser-known acts. ⊠ *925 E. Pike St., Capitol Hill* ☎ *206/709–9467* ⊕ *www.neumos.com.*

FREMONT AND PHINNEY RIDGE

FREMONT

Fremont has quite a few bars lining its main commercial drag of North 36th Street, including a few spots for live music. Unfortunately, Fremont suffers from Dr. Jekyll and Mr. Hyde syndrome. During the week, almost any of its simple bars is a fine place to grab a quiet drink with a friend. Come Friday night, however, the neighborhood can transform into an extended frat party—so consider yourself warned.

BARS AND LOUNGES

Brouwer's. It may look like a trendy Gothic castle, but in fact this is heaven for Belgian-beer lovers. A converted warehouse is home to a top selection of suds, which are provided by the owners of Seattle's best specialty-beer shop, Bottleworks. Brouwer's serves plenty of German and American/Northwest beers, too, as well as English, Czech, and Polish selections. Surprisingly good sandwiches, frites, and Belgian specialties help to lay a pre-imbibing foundation (remember that most Belgian beers have a higher alcohol content). Before settling on a seat downstairs, check out the balcony and the cozy parlor room. ☒ *400 N. 35th St., Fremont* ☎ *206/267–2437* ⊕ *www.brouwerscafe.com.*

Chuck's Hop Shop. Were it not for the picnic tables and rotating food trucks routinely parked outside, this place might look like just another corner convenience store. In fact, that's precisely what it used to be before owner Chuck transformed it into one of North Seattle's favorite spots for sampling craft beer and hanging out for hours. With nearly 40 taps, Chuck's features an especially good selection of IPAs and ciders on draft, many of local origin. Families love this extremely kid-friendly spot—there's an ice-cream counter, ample seating, and a stack of board games inside—and so do the dogs that get plenty of head pats and a big cookie, if you ask. Chuck's also offers a huge selection of bottled beers from all over the world, including gluten- and alcohol-free options. Sticking to the Capitol Hill area? Chuck's now has a second location (2001 East Union Street). ☒ *656 N.W. 85th St., Greenwood* ☎ *206/297–6212* ⊕ *www.chucks85th.com.*

Fremont Brewing. Founded in 2008, Fremont Brewing makes small-batch pale ales using organic hops. Locals (including their kids and dogs) crowd into the communal tables at the Urban Beer Garden, which includes both indoor and outdoor space, and a fireplace. Lines for beer move quickly, and visitors are encouraged to order or bring in outside food, though the brewery provides free pretzels and apples to snack on. ☒ *1050 N. 34th St., Fremont* ☎ *206/420–2407* ⊕ *www. fremontbrewing.com.*

The George & Dragon Pub. Beloved by locals, this divey English pub attracts grizzled old Brits watching soccer, hipsters looking for cheap beer and whiskey, a frat crowd that clogs up the front patio area on weekends, and know-it-alls hoping to crush the competition at the popular Tuesday quiz night. Major soccer events like the World Cup bring in huge crowds. ☒ *206 N. 36th St., Fremont* ☎ *206/545–6864* ⊕ *www.georgeanddragonpub.com.*

Quoin. Even if you're not staying for dinner at the neighboring Revel— a Korean-fusion restaurant that's won raves for its dumplings, rice, and noodle dishes—this sliver of a bar is worth a visit, and you can order food from next door. Bartenders make a fantastic cocktail, and it offers a much more intimate and stylish experience than other Fremont spots. There's also an outdoor deck with bench seating around a fire pit. Happy hour runs 4–6 pm daily. ⊠ *403 N. 36th St., Fremont* ☎ *206/547–2040.*

BREWPUBS

Hale's Ales. One of the city's oldest craft breweries, opened in 1983, produces unique English-style ales, cask-conditioned ales, and nitrogen-conditioned cream ales, plus a popular Mongoose IPA. The pub serves a full menu and has a great view of the fermenting room. Order a taster's flight if you want to try everything. ⊠ *4301 Leary Way NW, Fremont* ☎ *206/706–1544* ⊕ *www.halesbrewery.com.*

PHINNEY RIDGE

Phinney Ridge is a predominantly residential neighborhood with a few nightlife options if you're in the area.

BARS AND LOUNGES

Oliver's Twist. Down the street from the Woodland Park Zoo, Oliver's Twist is a welcoming spot with cozy leather booths and tons of local art on the walls. Drinks are expertly poured with house-made shrubs and syrups, and the tapas menu includes tasty snacks (garlic truffle popcorn, grilled cheese and tomato soup). It makes for a fun evening slightly off the beaten path, especially during the happy hour, 5–7 Monday through Thursday and 4–6 on Friday and Saturday. There's a second location in Magnolia, as well. ⊠ *6822 Greenwood Ave. N, Phinney Ridge* ☎ *206/706–6673* ⊕ *www.oliverstwistseattle.com.*

BREWPUBS

Naked City Taphouse. This bar has its own small brewery, so expect to see a few of its ales and stouts. The rest of the 48 taps are dedicated to their peers. Pub grub is simple, local, and organic. The beer garden is decorated with murals, and there's also a screening room where they host occasional events. ⊠ *8564 Greenwood Ave. N, Phinney Ridge* ☎ *206/838–6299* ⊕ *drink.nakedcity.beer.*

BALLARD

On weekends, Ballard rivals Capitol Hill in popularity. There are at least a dozen bars and restaurants on Ballard Avenue alone. The neighborhood has quickly evolved from a few pubs full of old salts to a bustling nightlife district that has equal parts average-Joe bars, trendy haunts, music spots, wine bars, and Belltown-style lounges.

BARS AND LOUNGES

Barnacle. Part of the Sea Creatures mini-empire led by chef Renee Erickson, Barnacle is a narrow bar adjacent to the popular Walrus and Carpenter restaurant. It invariably collects people waiting for tables, but with a beautiful copper-topped bar, tiled walls, and plates of oysters, cured meats, and fish to go with the apertivos, it's a great place to drink and snack even if you aren't planning to dine next door. ⊠ *4743 Ballard Ave. NW, Ballard* ☎ *206/706–3379* ⊕ *www.thebarnaclebar.com.*

Bastille. This French bistro is one of the neighborhood's most attractive spots to sip. First, there's the 45-foot zinc bar in the main dining room. Then there's the Back Bar, which is cozy, dimly lighted, with salvaged antique wood paneling and prints. On warm evenings, there's also the partially enclosed patio that looks out onto Ballard Avenue. Specialty cocktails are popular, and the wine list is extensive (though a bit overpriced). The bar menu lets you sample favorites like the lamb burger and *moules frites.* ⊠ *5307 Ballard Ave. NW, Ballard* ☎ *206/453–5014* ⊕ *www.bastilleseattle.com.*

Essex. Removed from bustling Ballard on a quiet street, Essex boasts craft cocktails, a handful of which are served on tap. The rotating cocktails often include house-made ingredients or are barrel aged. A solid wine list and local beer selections are also available, as are charcuterie plates, salads, snacks, desserts, and a burger, which they only serve on Sunday. ⊠ *1421 N.W. 70th St., Ballard* ☎ *206/724–0471* ⊕ *www. essexbarseattle.com.*

Hazlewood. The hipster quotient is high at this tiny, bi-level space around the corner from the Ballard Avenue hubbub. The space is Victorian-drawing-room chic but very short on furniture—don't come here if the prospect of standing all night turns you off. Hazlewood has a long list of specialty cocktails, and although they're not the best in the city, there is real skill behind the bar. Hazlewood can be frustrating—sometimes it's just too crowded—but it's worth peeking in on the way to or from dinner. If you hit it at the right low-key moment, it can be the best bar in Ballard. ⊠ *2311 N.W. Market St., Ballard* ☎ *206/783–0478.*

King's Hardware. Brought to you by the owner of Linda's Tavern in Capitol Hill, King's Hardware has the same ironic rustic decor, the same great patio space, and the same cachet with hipsters. It also has great burgers. This place gets packed to the rafters on weekends—if you want the same scene with fewer crowds, go two doors down to Hattie's Hat, which was the reigning spot until King's showed up. ⊠ *5225 Ballard Ave. NW, Ballard* ☎ *206/782–0027* ⊕ *www.kingsballard.com.*

The Noble Fir. A rotating selection of great beer, cider, and wine and a truly varied crowd are just part of the appeal of this popular bar. Like many (most?) Seattleites, the husband-and-wife owners are outdoorsy—and it shows in the rustic-modern interior, which includes a library-like seating area stocked with large trail maps, as well as hundreds of travel books. The Noble Fir serves a few simple snacks, like cheese, charcuterie, fish, and vegan and vegetarian options, in case you feel like settling in and planning your next big adventure. ⊠ *5316 Ballard Ave., Ballard* ☎ *206/420–7425* ⊕ *www.thenoblefir.com.*

Ocho. Blink and you'll miss it, and that would be a shame, because this tiny corner hot spot crafts some of the finest cocktails in town. Dimly lit and loud, Ocho only has a few tables and bar seats, and it fills up fast with a mixed crowd that flocks here for the drinks and top-notch Spanish tapas. It's usually possible to snag a table without a wait during the weekend happy hour from noon to 6. Come summer, the slender sidewalk patio is an ideal spot for soaking up the sun and people-watching. ⊠ *2325 N.W. Market St., Ballard* ☎ *206/784–0699.*

The Peoples Pub. Head to this Ballard institution to see what locals love about this unpretentious neighborhood. The pub (a dining room and a separate bar in the back) isn't much to look at—a lot of wood paneling, simple wood tables and chairs, and some unfortunate floral upholstery—but it has a *Prost*-worthy selection of German beers and one delicious fried pickle. True to its name, Peoples draws an interesting cross section of the neighborhood, from the young and trendy to old-school fishermen. ⊠ *5429 Ballard Ave. NW, Ballard* ☎ *206/783–6521* ⊕ *www.peoplespub.com.*

Stoneburner. Settle into a leather, high-backed stool at the beautiful, wood bar at Stoneburner, the Mediterranean restaurant at Hotel Ballard, and enjoy classic cocktails, fizzes, sours, craft beer, and the full restaurant menu. Happy hour, 3–5 pm daily, is a great time to visit for great prices on the delicious pizzas coming out of the stone oven, but the bar stays open after the kitchen closes. ⊠ *5214 Ballard Ave. NW* ☎ *206/695–2051* ⊕ *www.stoneburnerseattle.com.*

Stoup. Stoup is a great starting point for exploring Ballard's excellent craft-beer scene. A good-size tap room and patio area are family-friendly, and a rotating roster of food trucks provide eats to beer enthusiasts sipping staples like the Citra IPA and Mosaic Pale Ale, as well as new and experimental brews. Reuben's Brews, Peddler Brewing Company, and other brewery taprooms are close by for those looking to sample a variety. ⊠ *1108 N.W. 52nd St., Ballard* ☎ *206/457–5524.*

MUSIC CLUBS

Conor Byrne Pub. You might actually hear an Irish accent or two at Conor Byrne Pub, along with live folk, roots, alt-country, bluegrass, and traditional Irish music. There's live music almost every night of the week and great beer (including the obligatory Guinness on tap) at this laid-back pub. ⊠ *1540 Ballard Ave. NW, Ballard* ☎ *206/784–3640* ⊕ *www.conorbyrnepub.com.*

Egan's Ballard Jam House. A neighborhood spot rather than an overpriced tourist trap, this small jazz club and restaurant is devoted to music education for local high schoolers during the day and performances from local and touring acts in the evenings. ⊠ *1707 N.W. Market St., Ballard* ☎ *206/789–1621* ⊕ *www.ballardjamhouse.com.*

Sunset Tavern. A Chinese restaurant-turned-bar, Sunset Tavern attracts just about everyone: punks, college students, postgrad nomads, neighborhood old-timers. They come for the ever-changing eclectic music acts. There's also a bar in front, Betty's Room, where you can grab a drink before the show. ⊠ *5433 Ballard Ave. NW, Ballard* ☎ *206/784–4880* ⊕ *www.sunsettavern.com.*

Tractor Tavern. Seattle's top spot for roots music and alt-country has a large, dimly lighted hall with all the right touches—wagon-wheel fixtures, exposed-brick walls, and a cheery staff. The sound system is outstanding. ⊠ *5213 Ballard Ave. NW, Ballard* ☎ *206/789–3599* ⊕ *www.tractortavern.com.*

WALLINGFORD AND GREEN LAKE

WALLINGFORD

MUSIC CLUBS

SeaMonster Lounge. With its low lighting and wall of very secluded booths, SeaMonster makes the tame Wallingford neighborhood just a little bit sexier. The space is tiny—the "stage" is more like a holding pen sandwiched between the bar and a few tables—but that just makes it all the more intimate and friendly. The bar presents high-quality local acts, mainly of the jazz and funk variety. ⊠ *2202 N. 45th St., Wallingford* ☎ *206/992–1120* ⊕ *www.seamonsterlounge.com.*

GREEN LAKE

Green Lake is mostly residential neighborhood with a few worth-a-visit options if you happen to be in the vicinity.

BARS AND LOUNGES

Über Tavern. At what many serious aficionados claim may be one of the best beer bars on the planet, there's a constantly changing lineup of drafts—everything from Belgian imports to hop-heavy California DIPAs (double IPAs)—as well as a big list of bottles from around the globe. A digital menu shows what's on tap (and what's almost out) and there are Scrabble and checkerboards built into the bar tables—perfect for lazy afternoons. Über doesn't offer food, but you're free to order from a stack of takeout menus. ⊠ *7517 Aurora Ave. N, Green Lake* ☎ *206/782–2337* ⊕ *www.uberbier.com.*

MUSIC CLUBS

The Little Red Hen. Bring your cowboy boots and hats to this honky-tonk, which is inexplicably located in one of Seattle's most gentrified and generic neighborhoods. Live country bands take the stage most nights; there are free country- and line-dancing classes on Sunday, Monday, and Tuesday nights. Don't expect anything fancy—this place has not been sanitized for tourists. ⊠ *7115 Woodlawn Ave. NE, Green Lake* ☎ *206/522–1168* ⊕ *www.littleredhen.com.*

UNIVERSITY DISTRICT

The U-District doesn't offer much of interest unless you're taking your new fake ID out for a spin. With the exception of jazz club Lucid *(Music Venues)* and the District Lounge in the Hotel Deca, most U-District haunts fall firmly in the pub category and are filled with students on weekends. If you don't want to drink, you'll have better luck: the neighborhood has a comedy club, a few theater troupes, and several good movie theaters, including beloved art house Grand Illusion Cinema *(Film).*

BARS AND BREWPUBS

Big Time Brewery. With its neat brick walls, polished wood floors, and vintage memorabilia, Big Time Brewery is one of the best places in the U-District for a quiet beer away from the frenetic college scene. The brewery offers more than a dozen beers on tap, including cask ales; tours of the adjacent brewery tell the whole story. Skip the mediocre pub grub. ⊠ *4133 University Way NE, University District* ☎ *206/545–4509* ⊕ *www.bigtimebrewery.com.*

COMEDY CLUBS

Jet City Improv. Seattle's best improv group fuses quick wit with music and games, and the audience often provides input on what the skits should be. Shows, which are all ages, are on every Friday and Saturday at 10:30; there are also eight shows on most Saturdays. ⊠ *5510 University Way, University District* ☎ *206/352–8291* ⊕ *www.jetcity-improv.com.*

PERFORMING ARTS

The high-tech boom created an enthusiastic and philanthropic audience for Seattle's arts community, which continues to grow. The gorgeous Benaroya Hall is a national benchmark for acoustic design. Its main tenant is the Seattle Symphony. At the Seattle Center, the ethereal Marion Oliver McCaw Hall combines Northwest hues and hanging screens in colorful light shows accompanying performances by the Seattle Opera and the Pacific Northwest Ballet.

Although the city's music scene has lost some of its shine after Portland became the go-to city for indie rock, music is still a main form of entertainment here. This very literate city also supports a full calendar of readings, lectures, and writing workshops.

The Seattle International Film Festival gets a lot of attention, but the city also hosts numerous smaller festivals throughout the year. The most popular include **STIFF** (Seattle's True Independent Film Festival; ⊕ *www.trueindependent.org*) in June; the **Children's Film Festival** (⊕ *www.childrensfilmfestivalseattle.nwfilmforum.org/*), held at the Northwest Film Forum in January; and the **Seattle Lesbian and Gay Film Festival** (⊕ *www.threedollarbillcinema.org*) in October.

BELLEVUE

ARTS CENTER

The Theatre at Meydenbauer Center. Children's theater troupes, Ballet Bellevue, Bellevue City Opera, the Bellevue Civic Theater, and other groups perform here, where the equipment is state-of-the-art and the acoustics are excellent. ⊠ *11100 N.E. 6th St., Bellevue* ☎ *425/637–1020* ⊕ *www.meydenbauer.com.*

BELLTOWN

FILM

Big Picture. Enjoy the same first-run films that are playing down the street at the multiplex—minus the crowds, screaming kids, and sensory overload—at the Big Picture. This small, elegant theater has a full bar (you can order refills during the screening), and it's 21 and older only. ⊠ *2505 1st Ave., Belltown* ☎ *206/256–0572* ⊕ *www.thebigpicture.net.*

Fodor'sChoice ★ **Cinerama.** This 1963 cinema, scooped up and restored by Microsoft billionaire Paul Allen, seamlessly blends the luxury of the theater with high technology. Behind a standard-size movie screen sits an

CLOSE UP

Musical Seattle

Seattle buzzes with music energy—and has for years. The symphony gave its first performance in 1903. The Cornish College of the Arts, which has an extensive music program, was founded in 1914. As early as 1918, a vibrant jazz scene was developing in the Central District.

Clubs clustered around Jackson Street and 12th Avenue attracted big names like Jelly Roll Morton, Duke Ellington, and Charlie Parker. Quincy Jones and Ray Charles both started their careers at the tail end of the city's jazz era—Jones was a Seattle native and Charles moved here at age 17. The jazz scene peaked in the early '50s, though it received a fleeting boost again in the late '80s and early '90s after guitarist Bill Frisell and keyboardist-composer Wayne Horvitz moved here from New York.

The '60s and '70s brought soul, garage rock, and punk to the city. The Wailers were an influential group with a national hit "Tall Cool One." Legendary rock band Heart was gigging around Seattle in the mid-'70s. Jimi Hendrix grew up in Seattle and attended Garfield High School, which today produces one of the nation's top high-school jazz ensembles. Although Hendrix wouldn't become famous until he left his hometown, Seattle still holds this rock icon dear.

Seattle's best-known contribution—grunge—started in the late 1980s. By 1992, with local bands Nirvana, Pearl Jam, and Soundgarden gracing nearly every rock fan's album collection in the nation, *Rolling Stone* dubbed Seattle "the new Liverpool." By the mid-'90s, Seattleites were starting to move away from the movement that put the city on the map; Kurt Cobain's suicide in 1994 felt to many like the last nail in the coffin of the grunge scene. However, Sub Pop Records, the major independent label that was instrumental in the grunge scene, continues to flourish. KEXP, the local nonprofit radio station, is an integral part of the music scene in Seattle, hosting concerts at its home at Seattle Center, and organizing and promoting music events throughout the city.

In 1988, rapper Sir Mix-a-Lot released *Swass*, with its memorable hit "Baby's Got Back." In the '90s, Seattle's hip-hop scene belonged to the b-boys, with the Oldominion Crew and the Massive Monkees being the major players.

FUN FACTS

■ The University of Washington has one of the nation's best ethnomusicology archives: 10,000 recordings and more than 250 instruments from around the globe.

■ Gypsy Rose Lee, the burlesque dancer whose life inspired the musical *Gypsy*, was born in Seattle.

■ Hole, Bikini Kill, and Sleater-Kinney are all from Olympia, the state capital. If you drive south on I-5, you'll see an exit for Sleater-Kinney Road—the band got its name from the road, not the other way around.

5

enormous, 30-foot by 90-foot restored curved panel—one of only three in the world—used to screen old three-strip films like *How the West Was Won*, as well as 70-millimeter presentations of *2001: A Space Odyssey*. The sight lines throughout are amazing. Rear-window captioning, assistive listening devices, audio narration, wheelchair access, and other amenities ensure that everyone has an outstanding experience. ⊠ *2100 4th Ave., Belltown* ☎ *206/448–6680* ⊕ *www. cinerama.com.*

THEATER

Theater Schmeater. As if you couldn't tell by the name, Theater Schmeater is one of Seattle's zanier fringe theaters. Productions—live reenactments of *Twilight Zone* episodes, radical reinterpretations of Chekhov—are hit-or-miss, but there have been enough hits to garner the company a lot of respect. One of the theater's missions is to inspire the next generation of performers, so kids 18 and under get in free. ⊠ *2125 3rd Ave., Belltown* ☎ *206/324–5801* ⊕ *www. schmeater.org.*

CAPITOL HILL

ARTS CENTERS

PONCHO Concert Hall. Distinguished jazz, dance, and other groups all perform at this concert venue at Cornish College of the Arts. It also hosts solid student productions. ⊠ *710 E. Roy St., Capitol Hill* ☎ *206/325–6500* ⊕ *www.cornish.edu/performance_venues/.*

FILM

Egyptian Theater. Head to this art deco movie palace, a former Masonic temple, for first-run films. ⊠ *805 E. Pine St., at Broadway, Capitol Hill* ☎ *206/324–9996* ⊕ *www.siff.net/egyptian-theatre.*

Northwest Film Forum. A cornerstone of the city's independent film scene, its two screening rooms screen classic repertory, cult hits, experimental films, and documentaries. ⊠ *1515 12th Ave., Capitol Hill* ☎ *206/329–2629* ⊕ *www.nwfilmforum.org.*

READINGS AND LECTURES

Elliott Bay Book Company Reading Series. The famed bookstore presents a popular series of renowned local, national, and international author readings in a cozy, basement room next to a café. Events are free, but tickets are often required. ⊠ *1521 10th Ave., Capitol Hill* ☎ *206/624–6600* ⊕ *www.elliottbaybook.com.*

CENTRAL DISTRICT

FILM

Central Cinema. If you're tired of 40-ounce Cokes and $10 popcorn with neon-yellow butter and wish that moviegoing could be a little more elegant, check out Central Cinema. The first few rows of this charming, friendly little theater consist of diner-style booths—before the movie starts a waiter takes orders for delicious pizzas, salads, and snacks (including popcorn with inventive toppings like curry or brewer's yeast); your food is delivered unobtrusively during the first few minutes of the movie. Wash it down with a normal-size soda, a cup of coffee, or better yet a cocktail or a glass of wine or beer. You won't find first-run films here, but the theater shows a great mix of favorites (*Hairspray* and *E.T.*) and local indie and experimental films. ⊠ *1411 21st Ave., Central District* ☎ *206/328–3230* ⊕ *www. central-cinema.com.*

DOWNTOWN

ARTS CENTERS

Benaroya Hall. The acoustics are good from every one of the main hall's 2,500 seats—great news if you want to check out the Seattle Symphony, which is based here, or any of a number of world-class speakers, musicians, and other performers who appear here throughout the year. The four-story lobby has a curved glass facade that makes intermissions almost as impressive as performances. ⊠ *200 University St.* ☎ *206/215– 4800* ⊕ *www.seattlesymphony.org/benaroya.*

CLASSICAL MUSIC

Fodor's Choice
★

Seattle Symphony. The symphony performs under the direction of Ludovic Morlot from September through June in the stunning Benaroya Hall. The group has been nominated for numerous Grammy Awards and is well regarded nationally and internationally. ⊠ *Benaroya Hall, 200 University St., Downtown* ☎ *206/215–4747* ⊕ *www. seattlesymphony.org.*

THEATER

A Contemporary Theatre (*ACT*). Dedicated to launching exciting works by emerging dramatists, the Contemporary has four staging areas, including a theater-in-the-round and an intimate downstairs space for small shows. The season runs from April to November. ⊠ *700 Union St., Downtown* ☎ *206/292–7676* ⊕ *www.acttheatre.org.*

The 5th Avenue Theatre. Even if you don't plan on seeing anything here, this Asian fantasia is worth a peek—it's one of the most beautiful venues in the world. The 5th Avenue Theatre opened in 1926 as a silent-movie house and vaudeville stage, complete with a giant pipe organ and ushers who dressed as cowboys and pirates. Today it has its own theater company, which stages lavish productions October through May. At other times it hosts concerts, lectures, and films. ⊠ *1308 5th Ave., Downtown* ☎ *206/625–1900* ⊕ *www.5thavenue.org.*

Moore Theater. Built in 1907, Seattle's oldest theater still hosts off-Broadway performances and music events, including jazz concerts, instrumental duets, hard-rock bookings, and pop-music shows. The venerable hall was featured in Pearl Jam's video for "Even Flow," and many of the big grunge music acts of Seattle's early-'90s rock heyday performed here. ⊠ *1932 2nd Ave., Downtown* ☎ *206/682–1414* ⊕ *www.stgpresents.org/moore.*

Paramount Theatre. Built in 1928 as a venue for early talkies and vaudeville acts, this lovely beaux arts movie palace—which features an original Wurlitzer theater pipe organ—now mostly hosts concerts, as well as the occasional comedy, dance, or Broadway event. Seattle Theatre Group (STG Presents) also operates the Moore and the Neptune, both old Seattle theaters with terrific music-and-beyond lineups. ✉ *907 Pine St., Downtown* ☎ *206/682–1414* ⊕ *www.stgpresents.org.*

READINGS AND LECTURES

Town Hall. Christian Scientists occupied the Roman-revival-style Town Hall for decades, and attending lectures here can still make you feel a little starchy. Town Hall hosts scores of events in its spacious yet intimate Great Hall, chief among them talks and panel discussions with leading politicians, authors, scientists, and academics. ✉ *1119 8th Ave., Downtown* ☎ *206/652–4255* ⊕ *www.townhallseattle.org.*

QUEEN ANNE

ARTS CENTERS

Marion Oliver McCaw Hall. The home of the Seattle Opera and the Pacific Northwest Ballet is an opulent, glass-enclosed structure reflecting the skies and the Space Needle nearby. The facility houses two auditoriums and a four-story main lobby area where several artworks are on display. A programmed light art installation by Leni Schwendinger displays outside McCaw Hall in the Kreielsheimer Promenade. ✉ *321 Mercer St., Lower Queen Anne* ☎ *206/389–7676, 206/733–9725* ⊕ *www. mccawhall.com.*

Seattle Center. Several of the Seattle Center's halls are used for theater, opera, dance, music, and performance art. Public radio station KEXP frequently hosts concerts in their home on the Seattle Center campus, and the Center is also the site of Labor Day weekend's Bumbershoot Festival, which celebrates music and the arts. ✉ *305 Harrison St., Queen Anne* ☎ *206/684–7200* ⊕ *www.seattlecenter.org.*

THEATER

Cornish Playhouse at Seattle Center. This performance and education venue run by the Cornish College of the Arts hosts public music and theater programs, produced by students and professionals, throughout the year in a 470-seat auditorium on the Seattle Center Campus. ✉ *Seattle Center, 201 Mercer St., Queen Anne* ☎ *206/315–5776* ⊕ *www.cornish. edu/playhouse.*

Seattle Children's Theatre. Top-notch productions of new works join adaptations from classic children's literature here. After the show, actors come out to answer questions and explain how the tricks are done. ✉ *201 Thomas St., Lower Queen Anne* ☎ *206/441–3322* ⊕ *www.sct.org.*

Seattle Repertory Theater. During its September-through-April season, the Seattle Repertory Theater brings new and classic plays to life. Adoring fans flock to new takes on choice classics as well as works fresh from the New York stage. You can preorder your drinks from the Rotunda Bar for intermission, or linger after the show at Café at the Rep, for drinks, coffee, and dessert. ✉ *155 Mercer St., Lower Queen Anne* ☎ *206/443–2222* ⊕ *www.seattlerep.org.*

DANCE

On the Boards. Since 1978, On the Boards has been presenting contemporary dance performances, as well as theater, music, and multimedia events. The main subscription series runs from September through May, but events are scheduled nearly every weekend year-round. ✉ *100 W. Roy St., Lower Queen Anne* ☎ *206/217–9886* ⊕ *www. ontheboards.org.*

Pacific Northwest Ballet. The lineup of Seattle's resident ballet company and school includes works from celebrated contemporary choreographers as well as a mix of classic and international productions (think *Swan Lake* and *Carmina Burana*). Fans of *Swan Lake* and *The Nutcracker* can rest assured that those timeless productions are still part of the company's repertoire. Its season runs from September through June. ✉ *McCaw Hall at Seattle Center, 301 Mercer St., Lower Queen Anne* ☎ *206/441–2424* ⊕ *www.pnb.org.*

OPERA

Seattle Opera. Housed in the beautiful Marion Oliver McCaw Hall, the opera stages productions from August through May. Evening-event guests are treated to a light show from 30-foot hanging scrims above an outdoor piazza. ✉ *McCaw Hall at Seattle Center, 321 Mercer St., Lower Queen Anne* ☎ *206/389–7676* ⊕ *www.seattleopera.org.*

UNIVERSITY DISTRICT

DANCE

Meany Hall for the Performing Arts. National and international companies perform October through May at the University of Washington's Meany Hall. The emphasis is on modern and jazz dance. ✉ *1313 N.E. 41st St., University District* ☎ *206/543–4880* ⊕ *www.meanycenter.org.*

FILM

The Grand Illusion Cinema. Seattle's longest-running independent movie house was a tiny screening room in the 1930s. It's still tiny, but it's also an outstanding and unique home for independent and art films that feels as comfortable as a home theater. ✉ *1403 N.E. 50th St., University District* ☎ *206/523–3935* ⊕ *www.grandillusioncinema.org.*

Seattle International Film Festival. Seattle has several wonderful film festivals, but the Seattle International Film Festival is the biggest, taking place over several weeks from mid-May to mid-June. Though some highly anticipated events sell out, last-minute and day-of tickets are usually available. ✉ *Seattle* ☎ *206/464–5830* ⊕ *www.siff.net.*

READINGS AND LECTURES

University Book Store. Free readings by best-selling authors and academics are the attraction here. The second-floor space is rich with book stacks, perfect for browsing afterward. Tickets, some free, are required, and they go quickly. ✉ *4326 University Way NE, University District* ☎ *206/634–3400* ⊕ *www.bookstore.washington.edu.*

THEATER

The Neptune Theatre. A cultural hub for the nearby University of Washington since opening in 1921, this striking Renaissance-revival theater is operated by STG Presents, which also runs the Paramount and Moore. The lineup—mostly music with a smattering of performing arts—includes a mix of emerging and well-established acts. ✉ *1303 N.E. 45th St., University District* ☎ *206/682–1414* ⊕ *www.stgpresents.org.*

Northwest Puppet Center. Keeping its stories lively and brief (45 minutes), and encouraging kids to sprawl on the floor, this troupe uses marionettes to dramatize folktales. Puppet workshops are available. ✉ *9123 15th Ave. NE, University District* ☎ *206/523–2579* ⊕ *www. nwpuppet.org.*

SHOPPING

DOWNTOWN AND BELLTOWN

Where else can you shop with scenic mountain and water views, serenading seagulls, and the low hum of ferries pulling into port? Shopping Seattle's core is as good as it gets, with high-end designers and tiny mom-and-pop shops, one of the oldest public markets in the country, and a seemingly endless supply of coffee shops.

(Above) Sundries from Watson Kennedy Fine Living (Opposite page bottom) Freshly made doughnuts (Opposite page top) Macrina Bakery

Put on some comfy shoes and get ready to explore. You could shop all day here and hit only a fraction of the stores. With no shortage of either national chains or independent specialty shops, this area has a little something for everyone—from outdoor gear to imported perfume—all in a walkable area in the heart of the city. Start in Downtown to hit the high-end stores and the city's most beloved landmark—Pike Place Market. Browse the market stalls filled with local honey, flower bouquets, and fresh produce, then hit the antiques stores, jewelry boutiques, and gift shops in and around the market. After you've exhausted the Downtown core, head just north to Belltown, where you'll find clothiers and specialty shops tucked between art galleries and restaurants.

BEST TIME TO GO

The summer cruise season brings thousands of visitors to Downtown Seattle, so expect packed sidewalks in the warm months. Spring and fall are less crowded, and come winter it will mostly be you and the locals, if you're willing to brave the weather. Whatever the season, stick to daytime—Pike Place Market closes at 6 pm most days, and Belltown is choked with barhoppers when night falls.

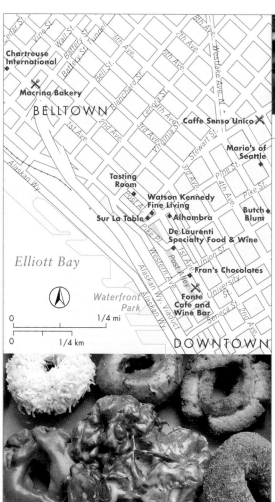

REFUELING

Caffe Senso Unico. Amazing sandwiches, croissants, and coffee. ⊠ *622 Olive Way* ☎ *206/264–7611.*

Fonte Cafe and Wine Bar. A one-stop shop for all your needs, whether that's an espresso brewed with freshly roasted coffee beans or a glass of rosé and local cheese plate. ⊠ *1321 1st Ave.* ☎ *206/777–6193* ⊕ *www.cafefonte.com.*

Macrina Bakery. Sit down with a slice of Sardinian flatbread, Nutella brioche, or a raisin twist—or more elaborate lunch options. ⊠ *2408 1st Ave.* ☎ *206/448–4032* ⊕ *www.macrinabakery.com.*

BEST FOR...

CHIC CLOTHING
Alhambra: This high-end bohemian boutique features global designers.

Butch Blum: Nearly everything in this store will increase your style quotient.

Mario's of Seattle: Looks are classic at this high-end designer shop.

ITEMS FOR THE HOME
Chartreuse International: Modern standout pieces to add to your home.

Sur La Table: Hard-to-find kitchen tools you can't get elsewhere.

Watson Kennedy Fine Living: Lovely dishes, linens, bath soaps, and treasures galore.

TREATS AND WINE
DeLaurenti Specialty Food Markets: Nosh on panini or pizza while you browse the cheese, meat, and wine.

Fran's Chocolates: Sample treats like salted caramels and raspberry-infused truffles.

The Tasting Room: Local wines perfect for a picnic.

CAPITOL HILL

Like a rum-soaked tiramisu, Capitol Hill is wonderfully layered and steeped in both character and intrigue—you never know what you might encounter. Take a breath and bite into the Hill with an open mind and a sense of adventure. It's delicious.

(Above) Cupcake Royal (Opposite page bottom) Espresso Vivace (Opposite page top) Elliot Bay Book Company

Capitol Hill presents an interesting juxtaposition of old and new, rich and poor. Fabulous Edwardian mansions mingle with brick apartments and low-income housing—and the shopping reflects this blend of income and interests. You'll find dollar stores half a block from museum-quality antiques galleries, and egalitarian bookstores next to boutiques with sky-high prices. During the day, the Pike–Pine Corridor is a hotbed of great independent shopping and sleepy coffee shops, although at night this strip pulses with live music, dance clubs, street food, and high-end dining. Broadway is a mixed bag of the cool and the tacky—if time is limited, stick to Pike–Pine.

BEST TIME TO GO

It's best to wrap up before 5 pm if you're here only to shop. The Hill comes alive as night falls, and you'll have to push through dinner crowds.

If, however, you want to experience Pike–Pine in all its glory, stick around and take advantage of the late hours many stores keep in this strip—many stay open until 7 pm and some don't close until midnight.

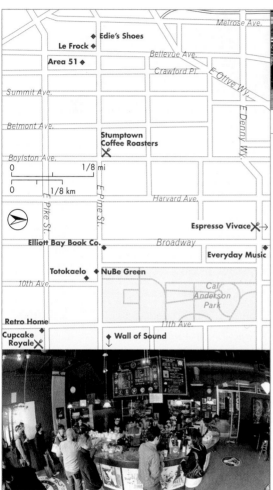

BEST FOR...

BOOKS AND MUSIC

Elliott Bay Book Company: Books and more books. If you want it, they probably have it.

Everyday Music: A huge selection of used music in a store open until midnight.

Wall of Sound: A wide variety of new and used records.

CLOTHES AND FOOTWEAR

Edie's Shoes: Comfy, trendy, get-you-noticed shoes for men and women.

Le Frock: Vintage Chanel and new Gucci are packed into this classy consignment shop.

Totokaelo: Innovative high fashion for men and women.

QUIRKY GIFTS

Area 51: Score fun coffee mugs or midcentury side tables.

NuBe Green: Environmentally friendly home goods.

Retro Home: Everything from figurines to midcentury-modern furniture.

REFUELING

Cupcake Royale. Try the cupcake of the month or flavors like the peppermint patty and the tiramisu, made with Stumptown coffee. ✉ 1111 E. Pike St., between 11th Ave. and 12th Ave. ☎ 206/328–6544 ⊕ www.cupcakeroyale.com.

Espresso Vivace. At one of the city's original kings of coffee, the espresso is as pretty as it is divine. ✉ 532 Broadway Ave. E, at E. Roy St. ☎ 206/860–2722 ⊕ www.espressovivace.com.

Stumptown Coffee Roasters. Yep, it's a Portland import, but Seattleites have swallowed their pride with this one, as the coffee is just too good to ignore. ✉ 616 E. Pine St., between Belmont Ave. and Boylston Ave. ☎ 206/329–0115 ⊕ www.stumptowncoffee.com.

Updated by
Lauren Kelley

Seattleites are sometimes scorned for their fashion sense (polar fleece, sport sandals, and socks—oh my!), but as the city has grown and enough money has percolated through the ranks of retail, the city's style barometer has made a steady creep upward. Bibliophiles, foodies, wine aficionados, and design-centrists will also find plenty of shopping opportunities—Seattle is a hotbed of unique, independent shops stocking one-of-a-kind treasures.

Shopping in Seattle is something best done gradually. Don't expect to find it all in one or two days worth of blitz shopping tours. Downtown is the only area that allows for easy daylong shopping excursions. Within a few blocks along 4th and 5th Avenues, you'll find the standard chains (The Gap, Urban Outfitters, H&M, Anthropologie, Sephora, Old Navy), along with Nike's flagship store, and a few more glamorous high-end stores, some featuring well-known designers like Gucci. Downtown is also where you'll find department stores like Nordstrom, Macy's, and Barneys New York. Belltown and Pioneer Square are also easy areas to patrol—most stores of note are within a few blocks.

To find many of the stores that are truly special to Seattle—such as boutiques featuring handmade frocks from local designers, independent record stores run by encyclopedic-minded music geeks, cozy used-book shops that smell of paper and worn wood shelves—you'll have to branch out to Capitol Hill, Queen Anne, and northern neighborhoods like Ballard. Shopping these areas will give you a better feel for the character of the city and its quirky inhabitants, all while you score that new dress or nab gifts for your friends.

And don't forget about Seattle's culinary bounty, which includes the stalls at Pike Place Market; the flagship Sur La Table, which stocks every kitchen gadget known to man; and the city's various weekly farmers' markets, where you'll find enough locally made, artisanal offerings to fill a suitcase or two.

PLANNER

SHOPPING PLANNER
BUSINESS HOURS

Malls and major national retailers keep pretty reliable hours, generally 9:30 am–9 pm; with antiques shops and independent stores, however, anything goes. Many businesses close Monday; some close Sunday as well, and others may close for one day midweek. Small boutiques rarely open before 11 am or noon and often close up shop by 5 or 6 pm. If you have your heart set on visiting a particular shop, call ahead to confirm its hours.

GO VINTAGE

Seattle boasts some of the best secondhand shopping in the country. There are plenty of trendy consignment and used-clothing shops like Buffalo Exchange, and Crossroads Trading Co. on Capitol Hill and in the U-District, where each shirt and jacket has been carefully screened by the store's tastemakers; vintage shops like Red Light and the Fremont Vintage Mall, where nearly every item is a one-of-a-kind find from the days of yore; and straight-up thrift shops like Goodwill and Salvation Army. If you're a fan of bargain prices and unique finds, and you enjoy the thrill of the hunt, take a chance on these shops. You never know what you might find.

DOWNTOWN

Much of the Downtown core is given over to chains, but shoppers from towns without their own J.Crew and Ann Taylor will be pleased with the ample offering of reliable retail. Louis Vuitton, Gucci, Anthropologie, and Brooks Brothers anchor the area around 5th Avenue. You'll find Nordstrom's lovely flagship store here, and an outdoor urban atmosphere of street musicians, panhandlers, and the bustle of industry, making for an enjoyable, walkable retail experience. Independent gems are scattered throughout, particularly in and around Pike Place Market and along Western Avenue—although for a greater concentration of indie stores, head to Capitol Hill, Belltown, or the northern neighborhoods. Downtown is a great area for wandering, browsing, and people-watching along the way, but we've listed the shops that are worth a special visit.

Best shopping: 4th, 5th, and 6th Avenues between Pine and Spring Streets, and 1st Avenue between Virginia and Madison Streets.

ANTIQUES AND COLLECTIBLES

Seattle Antiques Market. For antiques lovers, this market should not be missed. A funky warehouse offering everything from modern furniture to gemstones and bicycles, there is an unmistakable charm that keeps Seattleites coming back. Parking is tricky, so if you are already shopping in Pike Place Market, we recommend soaking up the fresh salty breeze and walking to this hidden gem. ✉ *1400 Alaskan Way* ☎ *206/623–6115* ⊕ *www.seattleantiquesmarket.com.*

BOOKS AND PRINTED MATERIAL

Metsker Maps of Seattle. Whether you're searching for a laminated pocket map of Seattle or a world map made up of music notes, stop here for a massive selection of books, globes, charts, atlases, antique reproduction maps, and local satellite images. Don't let the store's location in the middle of Pike Place Market fool you: this is a Seattle institution, not a tourist trap. ⊠ *1511 1st Ave., Downtown* ☎ *206/623–8747* ⊕ *www.metskers.com.*

Zanadu Comics. One of the oldest and best comic-book stores in a city with close to 70 comics shops, Zanadu Comics specializes in "alternative," small-press, local, and self-published comics and graphic novels. They also carry mainstream titles alongside copies of harder-to-find titles like Joe Sacco's *Footnotes in Gaza.* ⊠ *1923 3rd Ave., Downtown* ☎ *206/443–1316* ⊕ *www.zanaducomics.com.*

CLOTHING

Alhambra. Sophisticated, casual, and devastatingly feminine, this pricey boutique delivers quality, European-style looks for women of all ages. Pop into the Moorish-inspired shop for a party dress, elegant jewelry, or separates, and be sure to check out the house line, designed by the owners. ⊠ *101 Pine St., Downtown* ☎ *206/621–9571* ⊕ *www. alhambrastyle.com.*

Baby & Co. There's nothing childish about this sophisticated fashion house. A longtime Seattle favorite, Baby and Co. dresses women in urban-lifestyle looks by designers such as Girbaud, Rundholz, High, and Lilith. Edgy, asymmetrical frocks; jackets; and sweaters with graphic prints come in butter-soft linens, wool, jersey, and crepe. You'll pay a lot for the privilege of being ahead of the trends. ⊠ *1936 1st Ave., Downtown* ☎ *206/448–4077* ⊕ *www.babyandco.us.*

Butch Blum. The attentive staff at this decidedly upscale retailer for men and women gives expert guidance on creations by Giorgio Armani, Ermenegildo Zegna, Bluemarine, and Luciano Barbera—just to drop a few names. This is a fabulous spot for pricey but gorgeous men's suits—with a tailor on-site, too. ⊠ *1408 5th Ave. N, Downtown* ☎ *206/622–5760* ⊕ *www.butchblum.com.*

Endless Knot. An alternative to the high-end designers that are scattered throughout Downtown Seattle's shopping haven, this women's clothing store offers on-trend options that won't break the bank. From dresses to coats to accessories galore, this perfectly manicured boutique is a gold mine. ⊠ *2300 1st Ave.* ☎ *206/448–0355* ⊕ *www. endlessknotseattle.com.*

Ian. The hottest contemporary American sportswear and premium denim for men and women can be found at Ian, where the clientele is young and the clothes are very now. With a service-oriented staff and the latest looks from J Brand, Life/After/Denim, Cheap Monday, Spiewak, and Civilianaire, this is a good bet for tidy hipsters who've moved beyond thrift-store finds. ⊠ *1913 2nd Ave., Downtown* ☎ *206/441–4055* ⊕ *www.ianshop.com.*

CLOSE UP

Top Areas to Shop in Seattle

Shopping becomes decidedly less fun when it involves driving around in circles for parking. You're better off limiting your all-day shopping tours to one of several key areas than planning to do a citywide search for a particular item. The following areas have the greatest concentration of shops and the greatest variety.

5th and 6th Avenues, Downtown. Depending on where you're staying, you may not need to drive to this area, but if you do, the parking garage at Pacific Place mall (at 600 Pine Street) always seems to have a space somewhere (it also has valet parking). Tackling either Pacific Place or the four blocks of 5th and 6th Avenues between Olive Way and University Street will keep you very busy for a day.

1st Avenue, Belltown. From Wall Street to Pine Street, you'll find clothing boutiques, shoe stores, and some sleek home and architectural design stores. 1st Avenue and Pike Street brings you to the Pike Place Market. There are numerous pay parking lots on both 1st and 2nd Avenues.

Pioneer Square. Walk or bus here if you can. Art galleries are the main draw, along with some home-decor and rug shops. If you do drive, many pay lots in the neighborhood participate in the "Parking Around the Square" program, which works with

local businesses to offer shoppers validated parking; the website ⊕ www.pioneersquare.org lists the lots and stores that offer it.

International District. Parking in the I.D. can be hit or miss depending on the time of day. It's best if you can walk here from Downtown or take a quick bus ride over. If you do drive, go directly to the Uwajimaya parking lot. They validate for purchases, and it's a safe bet you'll be buying something there. It's too fun to resist.

Pike–Pine Corridor, Capitol Hill. The best shopping in the Hill is on Pike and Pine Streets between Melrose Avenue and 10th Avenue E. Most of the stores are on Pike Street; Pine's best offerings are clustered on the western end of the avenue between Melrose and Summit. There are pay lots on Pike Street (near Broadway) and one on Summit by East Olive Way (next to the Starbucks).

Fremont and Ballard. Start in Fremont's small retail center, which is mostly along 36th Street. You may be able to snag street parking. After you've exhausted Fremont's shops, it's an easy drive over to Ballard. Ballard Avenue and N.W. Market Street are chockablock with great boutiques. Finding parking in Ballard can be tricky on weekends, but it's usually possible.

Mario's. Known for fabulous service and designer labels, this high-end boutique treats every client like a superstar. Men shop the ground floor for Armani, Etro, and Zegna; women ascend the ornate staircase for Prada, Emilio Pucci, and Lanvin. A freestanding Hugo Boss boutique sells the sharpest tuxedos in town. ⊠ *1513 6th Ave., Downtown* ☎ *206/223–1461* ⊕ *www.marios.com.*

Nancy Meyer Fine Lingerie. Elegant European lingerie designs by La Perla, Fleur of England, Sonia Rykiel, and others fill every nook and cranny of this tiny shop. The prices are sky-high, but these are exquisite underpinnings. ⊠ *1318 5th Ave., Downtown* ☎ *800/605–5098* ⊕ *www. nancymeyer.com.*

DEPARTMENT STORES

Fodor'sChoice   **Barneys New York.** You'll find this slice of the Big Apple anchoring
★   Pacific Place Shopping Center, across from "Nordies." Barneys' two floors are filled with übertrendy designer lines like 3.1 Philip Lim, Alexander Wang, Marc Jacobs, and Christian Louboutin. Our favorite goods are right by the entryway: top-of-the-line makeup (by the likes of Shu Uemura), fragrances (Comme des Garçons never ceases to amaze), and baubles, including stackable rings encrusted with tiny gemstones. ⊠ *600 Pine St., Downtown* ☎ *206/622–6300* ⊕ *www. barneys.com.*

Macy's. This Downtown retail giant is a reliable source for clothing, housewares, cosmetics, and furniture, and it's just a stone's throw from Nordstrom and Pacific Place. Every year, the store's entryway on 4th and Pine is bedecked with a giant retro star that lights up on Thanksgiving weekend and into the holidays. ⊠ *1601 3rd Ave., Downtown* ☎ *206/506–6000* ⊕ *www.macys.com.*

Fodor'sChoice   **Nordstrom.** Seattle's own retail giant sells quality clothing, accesso-
★   ries, cosmetics, jewelry, and lots of shoes—in keeping with its roots in footwear—including many hard-to-find sizes. Peruse the various floors for anything from trendy jeans to lingerie to goods for the home. A sky bridge on the store's fourth floor will take you to Pacific Place Shopping Center. Deservedly renowned for its impeccable customer service, the busy Downtown flagship has a concierge desk and valet parking. ■TIP➔ The Nordstrom Rack store at 1st Avenue and Spring Street, close to Pike Place Market, has great deals on marked-down items. ⊠ *500 Pine St., Downtown* ☎ *206/628–2111* ⊕ *shop. nordstrom.com.*

GIFTS AND HOME DECOR

Sur La Table. Need a brass-plated medieval French duck press? You've come to the right place. Culinary artists and foodies have flocked to this popular Pike Place Market destination since 1972. The chain's flagship shop is packed to the rafters with many thousands of kitchen items, including an exclusive line of copper cookware, endless shelves of baking equipment, tabletop accessories, cookbooks, and a formidable display of knives. ⊠ *84 Pine St., Downtown* ☎ *206/448–2244* ⊕ *www.surlatable.com.*

Watson Kennedy Fine Living. This small store in the courtyard of the Inn at the Market is worth a visit just for how heavenly it smells. With a lovely line of artisanal jewelry, luxurious bath products, and enticing—and often aromatic—gifts, it makes for a relaxing stop in the Pike Place tour. A standout favorite? Seattle-based fragrance brand Antica Farmacista—their line of luxury reed diffusers will leave you wanting every scent. Watson Kennedy's sister store is located on 1st Avenue and Spring Street (Watson Kennedy Fine Home) and includes vintage furniture, tableware, gourmet foods, and its own line of beeswax candles. ⊠ *86 Pine St., Downtown* ☏ *206/443–6281* ⊕ *www.watsonkennedy.com.*

> ### FURNITURE ROW
>
> You're probably not planning to browse for armchairs and coffee tables while on vacation, but if you're in the market for such things, Western Avenue between Union and Seneca Streets has several high-end home-furnishings showrooms, which make up an informal and stylish "Furniture Row."

JEWELRY

Turgeon Raine Jewelers. Offering an art-forward take on gems and jewelry in a spacious contemporary gallery, Turgeon Raine employs only staff with a design background—you can work with them to create a one-of-a-kind piece, or pick from house-made items on display. It's also Washington's exclusive representative for Patek Philippe watches. ⊠ *1407 5th Ave., Downtown* ☏ *206/447–9488* ⊕ *www.turgeonraine.com.*

SHOES

A Mano. The store's name means "by hand," and that ethos of handmade, high-quality craftsmanship seems soaked into the very (exposed brick) walls of this charming shop. A small selection of shoes from all over the world, along with some jewelry and handbags from local designers can be found here—all of it lovingly selected and much of it unique. ⊠ *1115 1st Ave., Downtown* ☏ *206/292–1767* ⊕ *www.shopamano.com.*

John Fluevog Shoes. You'll find the store's own brand of fun and funky boots, chunky leather shoes, and urbanized wooden sandals here in men's and women's styles. ⊠ *205 Pine St., Downtown* ☏ *206/441–1065* ⊕ *www.fluevog.com.*

SPAS

Gene Juarez Salons & Spas. With both a lively hair and nail salon and a more tranquil retreat for massage and skin treatments, Gene Juarez (in Downtown and Bellevue and elsewhere) offers one-stop shopping. The skin-care menu is long and inventive; massage techniques stick to the classics like deep tissue, shiatsu, and reflexology, with Hawaiian healing and hot-stone methods thrown in for good measure. The spa also offers a full menu of men's treatments, including hide-the-gray hair coloring and pedicures. ⊠ *607 Pine St., Downtown* ☏ *206/326–6000* ⊕ *www.genejuarez.com.*

Ummelina International Day Spa. Hand-carved Japanese doors open into this tranquil and luxurious, Asian-influenced spa. Relax beneath a warm waterfall shower, take a steamy, scented sauna, or submit to a mud wrap or smoothing body scrub. The three-hour Equator package for couples includes all this and more. Linger over the experience with a cup of house-blended tea. ⊠ *1525 4th Ave., Downtown* ☎ *206/624–1370* ⊕ *www.ummelina.com.*

WINE AND SPECIALTY FOODS

Fodor'sChoice
★ **DeLaurenti Specialty Food and Wine.** Attention foodies: clear out your hotel minibars and make room for delectable treats from DeLaurenti. And, if you're planning any picnics, swing by here first. Imported meats and cheeses crowd the deli cases, and packaged delicacies pack the aisles. Stock up on hard-to-find items like truffle-infused olive oil or excellent Italian vintages from the wine shop upstairs. Spring travelers will also want to stop by DeLaurenti's nosh nirvana, called Cheesefest, in May. ⊠ *Pike Place Market, 1435 1st Ave., Downtown* ☎ *206/622–0141* ⊕ *www.delaurenti.com.*

Fodor'sChoice
★ **Fran's Chocolates.** A Seattle institution (helmed by Fran Bigelow) has been making quality chocolates for decades. Its world-famous salted caramels are transcendent—a much-noted favorite of the Obama family, in fact—as are delectable truffles, which are spiked with oolong tea, single-malt whiskey, or raspberry, among other flavors. This shop is housed in the Four Seasons on 1st Avenue—how very elegant, indeed! ⊠ *1325 1st Ave., Downtown* ☎ *206/682–0168* ⊕ *www.franschocolates.com.*

Pike and Western Wine Shop. These folks have spent nearly four decades carving out a reputation as one of the best wine markets in the city. With more than 1,000 wines personally selected from the Pacific Northwest and around the world, this shop offers expert advice from friendly salespeople. ⊠ *1934 Pike Pl., Downtown* ☎ *206/441–1307* ⊕ *www. pikeandwestern.com.*

Sotto Voce Inc. This Italian-inspired local company has taken savory infusions to the next level with its assortment of "made from scratch" oils and vinegars. Each bottle is produced by hand, from flavoring to filling and labeling. Tastings are encouraged at the Pike Place Market storefront. The red-chili-and-horseradish-infused olive oil and the lemon-, tarragon-, and dill-infused balsamic vinegar are the perfect Pacific Northwest mementos you can enjoy in your own home for many meals to come. ⊠ *1532 Pike Pl.* ☎ *206/624–9998* ⊕ *www.sottovoce.com.*

The Tasting Room. When you're ready for a break from sightseeing, make a detour into this relaxing tasting room and wine store in the northern end of Post Alley. Several Washington State boutique wineries are represented; most of the bottles are handcrafted and/or reserve vintages. Taste the offerings, then buy a bottle or two—you can sit and enjoy your pick in the wine bar without paying for corkage. ⊠ *1924 Post Alley, Downtown* ☎ *206/770–9463* ⊕ *www.winesofwashington.com.*

World Spice Merchants. Many of the city's best chefs get their herbs, spices, and salts at this aromatic shop under Pike Place Market. Many teas are also available. ⊠ *1509 Western Ave., Downtown* ☎ *206/682–7274* ⊕ *www.worldspice.com.*

CLOSE UP

Seattle Souvenirs

FOOD AND DRINK

The Tasting Room in Pike Place Market's Post Alley is a great spot for local wines.

Pick up delectable fair-trade chocolates from **Theo Chocolate** in Fremont.

Visit Pike Place Market for a bag of famous chocolate-covered cherries by **Chukar Cherries** (✉ *1529 Pike Pl., Downtown* ☎ *206/623-8043* ⊕ *www.chukar.com*), then stop into **Fran's Chocolates** on 1st Avenue for famous sea-salt caramels.

Seafood isn't the easiest thing to bring home, but if you go to **Pike Place Fish Market** (at Pike Place Market), the friendly, fish-flinging experts here can ship your purchase across the country for you.

To bring home some coffee beans, pop into a coffee shop—most offer whole or ground coffee by the bag. Many coffee shops roast their own brands, including **Caffe Vita, Victrola, Stumptown Coffee, Herkimer Coffee, Lighthouse Roasters, Cafe Vita**, and **Caffe Fiore**.

MUSIC AND LITERATURE

Staff recommendations at **Sonic Boom Records** will help you discover the Northwest's up-and-coming musicians. **Elliott Bay Book Company** has a good, well-organized selection of local literature and history books, with handwritten staff recommendations to help you pick out the real gems.

SPORTS STUFF

Seattle Team Shop. The Seattle Team Shop has your Seahawks, Sounders, and Mariners needs covered. ✉ *1029 Occidental Ave. S, SoDo* ☎ *206/621-1880* ⊕ *www.seattleteams.com.*

The Pro Shop. Official shop for all your Seattle-sports-fan needs, including merchandise from the NFL Seahawks and MLS Sounders. ✉ *410 Pike St.* ☎ *206/467-3115* ⊕ *www.seahawks.com/proshop.*

T-SHIRTS

Destee-Nation. Before you buy a teenage relative—or anyone else for that matter—an oversize T-shirt that says "Seattle!" head up to Fremont's Destee-Nation for one that's a lot more distinctive. ✉ *3412 Evanston Ave. N, Fremont* ☎ *206/324-9403* ⊕ *www.desteenation.com.*

6

BELLTOWN

Stroll along 1st Avenue to find an eclectic mix of high-end clothing boutiques, custom tailoring shops, artsy gift stores, and gritty standouts. Many local, independent designers are represented here, although the clothing tends to be more upmarket than the crafty, DIY goods offered in Capitol Hill or Ballard.

Best shopping: Along 1st Avenue between Cedar and Virginia Streets.

BOOKS

★

Peter Miller Architectural & Design Books and Supplies. Aesthetes and architects haunt this shop, which is stocked floor to ceiling with all things design. Rare, international architecture, art, and design books mingle with high-end products from Alessi and Iittala; sleek notebooks, bags, portfolios, and drawing tools round out the collection. This is a great shop for quirky, unforgettable gifts, like a Black Dot sketchbook, an Arne Jacobsen wall clock, or an aerodynamic umbrella. ⊠ *2326 2nd Ave., Belltown* ☎ *206/441–4114* ⊕ *www.petermiller.com.*

CLOTHING

Gian DeCaro Sartoria. There is nothing quite like a bespoke suit to make a man look like a million bucks, and luckily, Gian DeCaro's offerings don't cost anywhere near that much. The suits may be pricey, but DeCaro is one of the best tailor-designers around, counting local and visiting celebrities among his well-dressed clientele. For the rest of us, his shop is also stocked with elegant ties, cuff links, and other accessories, as well as some ready-to-wear clothing in luxurious fabrics. ⊠ *2025 1st Ave., Suite D, Belltown* ☎ *206/448–2812* ⊕ *www.giandecaro.com.*

Kuhlman. This tiny store on the same hip block as the Ace Hotel has a careful selection of urban street wear that includes hard-to-find designers like Nudie Jeans Co., Barbour, and Fred Perry—it's sophisticated while still maintaining an edge. Kuhlman is best known for creating custom clothing, often from superb European and Japanese fabrics. ⊠ *2419 1st Ave., Belltown* ☎ *206/441–1999* ⊕ *www.kuhlmanseattle.com.*

Moorea Seal. Are accessories your Achilles' heel? Then look no further than the chic, trendy Moorea Seal. With its modern, airy storefront offering everything from booties to boho-chic handbags, Moorea pledges 7% of all proceeds to benefit nonprofits supporting environmental issues and women's causes. Shop till you drop with these great prices, and do some good while you're at it. ⊠ *2523 3rd Ave.* ⊹ *Between Wall St. and Vine St.* ☎ *206/728–2523* ⊕ *www.mooreaseal.com.*

GIFTS AND HOME DECOR

Chartreuse International. Savvy collectors shop here for authentic mid-century-modern furniture and accessories by Harry Bertoia, Arne Jacobsen, Isamu Noguchi, and other luminaries. The store also stocks new goods by Alessi, Kartell, and other modern designers. ⊠ *2609 1st Ave., Belltown* ☎ *877/328–4844* ⊕ *www.modchartreuse.com.*

MUSIC

Singles Going Steady. If punk rock is more to you than anarchy symbols sewn on Target sweatshirts, then stop here. Punk and its myriad subgenres on CD and vinyl are specialties, though they also stock rockabilly, indie rock, and hip-hop. It's a nice foil to the city's indie-rock-dominated record shops, and a good reminder that Belltown is still more eclectic than its rising rents may indicate. ⊠ *2219 2nd Ave., Belltown* ☎ *206/441–7396.*

OUTDOOR CLOTHING

Patagonia. If the person next to you on the bus isn't wearing North Face, he or she is probably clad in Patagonia. This popular and durable brand excels at functional outdoor wear—made with earth-friendly materials such as hemp and organic cotton—as well as technical clothing hip enough for mountaineers or urban hikers. The line of whimsically patterned fleece wear for children is particularly cute. ⊠ *2100 1st Ave., Belltown* ☎ *206/622–9700* ⊕ *www.patagonia.com.*

> **NOVEL NEEDLE**
>
> **SpaceBase Gift Shop.** The SpaceBase Gift Shop has the city's ultimate icon, the Space Needle, rendered in endless ways. Among the officially licensed goods are bags of Space Needle Noodles, towering wooden pepper grinders, and artsy black T-shirts. ⊠ *400 Broad St., Queen Anne* ☎ *206/905–2100* ⊕ *www.spaceneedle.com.*

SHOES

J. Gilbert Footwear. Wrap your feet in comfort and European styling by designers Thierry Rabotin, Arche, Paul Green, and Robert Clergerie. Along with limited-edition handmade Western boots by Lucchese and Alden, you'll find glove-soft leather jackets and chic, casual clothing. ⊠ *2025 1st Ave., Suite S, Belltown* ☎ *206/441–1182* ⊕ *www.jgilbert-footwear.com.*

SPA

Spa Noir. If you're not into the new-age earthy vibe found in so many day spas, head to Spa Noir, a hip Belltown spot done up in black, red, and gold. The spa specializes in facials, manicures, pedicures, and other beauty treatments, but it also offers a small menu of reasonably priced massage treatments. ⊠ *2120 2nd Ave., Belltown* ☎ *206/448–7600* ⊕ *www.spanoir.net.*

SOUTH LAKE UNION

South Lake Union was once a semiforgotten industrial area. Nowadays, cranes hover over new hotels, high-rise buildings, and Amazon's new campus, while design shops are popping up next to the enormous, trip-worthy flagship REI store. This neighborhood is just east of Seattle Center, whose Space Needle and Experience Music Project museum are on most visitors' itineraries; a walk (especially on a sunny day) from there to the REI store can be quite fun—then you can take the South Lake Union Streetcar (⊕ *www.seattlestreetcar.org*) back to the heart of Downtown.

OUTDOOR EQUIPMENT AND CLOTHING

Fodor'sChoice ★ **REI.** The enormous flagship for Recreational Equipment, Inc. (REI) has an incredible selection of outdoor gear—polar-fleece jackets, wool socks, down vests, hiking boots, raingear, and much more—as well as its own 65-foot climbing wall. The staff is extremely knowledgeable; there always seems to be enough help on hand, even when the store is busy. You can test things out on the mountain-bike test trail or in the simulated rain booth. REI also rents gear such as tents, sleeping bags, skis, snowshoes, and backpacks. Bonus: the outdoor behemoth offers an hour of free parking. ✉ *222 Yale Ave. N, South Lake Union* ☎ *206/223–1944* ⊕ *www.rei.com.*

QUEEN ANNE

There are actually two shopping areas in this hillside neighborhood—the more urban-feeling Lower Queen Anne, near the large Seattle Center campus, and the more neighborhoody Upper Queen Anne, along Queen Anne Avenue North at the top of the hill. West from the Seattle Center along Queen Anne and Mercer Avenues are tiny cafés, antiques, and music stores. The cluster of businesses at the top of the hill includes a bookshop, gift stores, and a heralded wine shop.

Best shopping: Along Queen Anne Avenue North between West Harrison and Roy Streets, and between West Galer and McGraw Streets.

BOOKS AND MUSIC

FAMILY **Queen Anne Book Company.** This beloved Seattle bookstore is well-known for its friendly, knowledgeable staff and extensive book selection. Pop in for children's storytelling sessions on the third Sunday of every month, or browse at night and catch one of the many author events. After you grab your new books, slip into El Diablo, the cute coffee shop adjacent to the bookstore. ✉ *1811 Queen Anne Ave. N, Queen Anne* ☎ *206/283–5624* ⊕ *www.queenannebooks.com.*

CLOTHING

Peridot Boutique. Strapless animal-print pocket dresses, retro gingham tops, and ruffly skirts abound in this contemporary women's boutique in lower Queen Anne. The prices are reasonable, the accessories are abundant, and local designers are represented as well. ✉ *2135 Queen Anne Ave. N, Queen Anne* ☎ *206/687–7130* ⊕ *www.peridotboutique. wordpress.com.*

WINE AND SPECIALTY FOODS

McCarthy & Schiering Wine Merchants. One of the best wine shops in the city is attitude-free and offers an amazing selection of wines from around the world. Check out the selection of local wines to experience the true flavor of the Northwest. ✉ *2401B Queen Anne Ave. N, Queen Anne* ☎ *206/282–8500* ⊕ *www.mccarthyandschiering.com.*

PIONEER SQUARE

Gritty, eccentric, artsy, and fabulous, Pioneer Square is an eclectic blend of what makes Seattle ... Seattle. Although this neighborhood has more than a few tourist traps hiding in its attractive brick buildings, it also has some wonderful clothiers, several bookstores, and a few standouts we're positive you won't find anywhere else, plus many galleries and shops selling high-end furniture and collectibles. *Serious art collectors and gallery-hoppers should peruse the Neighborhoods listings for the galleries in Pioneer Square.* ■ TIP➜ Here we've listed only the shops selling antiques and collectibles, not artwork.

Best shopping: 1st Avenue South between Yesler Way and South Jackson Street, and Occidental Avenue South between South Main and Jackson Streets.

ANTIQUES AND COLLECTIBLES

Chidori Antiques. So packed full of stuff it looks more like a curio shop than a high-end antiques seller, Chidori deals in high-quality Asian antiques, pre-Columbian and primitive art, Japanese paintings, and antiquities from all over the world. ⊠ *108 S. Jackson St., Pioneer Square* ☏ *206/343–7736* ⊕ *www.chidoriantiques.com.*

Flury and Company. View one of the largest collections of vintage prints by the Western photographer Edward S. Curtis, along with Native American antiques, traditional carvings, baskets, jewelry, and tools in a historic space that's as interesting as the store's wares. ⊠ *322 1st Ave. S, Pioneer Square* ☏ *206/587–0260* ⊕ *www.fluryco.com.*

ART AND GIFTS

Agate Designs. Amateur geologists, curious kids, and anyone fascinated by fossils and gems should make a trip to this store that's almost like a museum (but a lot more fun). Between the 500-million-year-old fossils and the 250-pound amethyst geodes, there's no shortage of eye-popping items on display. ⊠ *120 1st Ave. S, Pioneer Square* ☏ *206/621–3063* ⊕ *www.agatedesigns.com.*

Glass House Studio. Seattle's oldest glassblowing studio and gallery lets you watch fearless artisans at work in the "hot shop." Some of the best glass artists in the country work out of this shop, and many of their impressive studio pieces are for sale, along with around 40 other Northwest artists represented by the shop. ⊠ *311 Occidental Ave. S, Pioneer Square* ☏ *206/682–9939* ⊕ *www.glasshouse-studio.com.*

Laguna Pottery. Watch your step as you navigate through this colorful, crowded shop; it's wall-to-wall collectible 20th-century American dinnerware, art pottery, tiles, and garden pieces. There's also a large selection of Heath Ceramics. A stop here will truly make you want to change up your practical dinner go-to dishware for something retro and divine. ⊠ *116 S. Washington St., Pioneer Square* ☏ *206/682–6162* ⊕ *www.lagunapottery.com.*

Northwest Fine Woodworking. For more than 30 years, this artist co-op has showcased a rotating cast of more than 20 Northwest craftspeople in a large, handsome showroom. Even if you're not in the market for new furniture, stop in for a reminder of how much personality wood pieces can have when they're not mass-produced. The store also carries gifts like chess sets and ornate handcrafted kaleidoscopes and more practical household items like wooden bowls and utensils. ⊠ *101 S. Jackson St., Pioneer Square* ☎ *206/625–0542* ⊕ *www.nwfinewoodworking.com.*

BOOKS AND TOYS

Arundel Books. Since 1984, this bastion of bibliophilia has offered new, used, and collectible titles to discerning shoppers. Its shelves are especially strong in art, photography, and graphic design. This eclectic assortment will satisfy both the avid reader and discriminating collector. ⊠ *209 Occidental Ave. S, Pioneer Square* ☎ *206/624–4442* ⊕ *www.arundelbookstores.com.*

FAMILY **Magic Mouse Toys.** Since 1977, this two-story, 7,000-square-foot shop in the heart of Pioneer Square has been supplying families with games, toys, puzzles, tricks, candy, and figurines. They claim a professional child runs this friendly store—and it shows. ⊠ *603 1st Ave., Pioneer Square* ☎ *206/682–8097* ⊕ *www.magicmousetoys.com.*

Wessel & Lieberman Booksellers. Crammed with first editions, antiquarian materials, Pacific Northwest history and literature, Western Americana, poetry, and fine examples of letterpress, this is a bookstore that smells exactly as a bookstore should—like books. There's nothing sterile about this handsomely fitted shop in a historic building. Come for the hard-to-find tomes, and stay for the small-press, local material. ⊠ *209 Occidental Ave. S, Pioneer Square* ☎ *206/682–3545* ⊕ *www.wlbooks.com.*

CLOTHING

Filson. Seattle's flagship Filson store is a shrine to meticulously well-made outdoor wear for men and women. The hunting-lodge-like decor of the space, paired with interesting memorabilia and pricey, made-on-site clothing, makes the drive south of Pioneer Square worth it (we recommend catching a cab, not hoofing it). The attention to detail paid to the plaid vests, oil-treated rain slickers, and fishing outfits borders on the fetishistic. ⊠ *1741 1st Ave. S, Pioneer Square* ☎ *206/622–3147* ⊕ *www.filson.com.*

Ragazzi's Flying Shuttle. For women of a certain age who want to add some whimsy and color to their wardrobe without veering into crazy-cat-lady territory, Ragazzi's offers artisan-crafted, handwoven clothing in bold colors, as well as fun scarves and bold jewelry. Be sure to check out their travel line of washable easy-wear looks, also infused with a whole lot of moxie. ⊠ *607 1st Ave., Pioneer Square* ☎ *206/343–9762* ⊕ *www.ragazzisflyingshuttle.com.*

Utilikilts. If you (or someone you know) is man enough to rock a kilt, then we've got the store for you. The flagship Utilikilts store stocks their own brand of utility-style "manskirts," which you'll see out and about often in Seattle, often paired with rugged combat boots—especially at such outdoor events as Bumbershoot. Pick up a workman's kilt, made from thick duckcloth, with a hammer loop and plenty of pockets for nails and screws; or snag a tuxedo kilt, for those formal occasions when you really want to make a statement. ⊠ *620 1st Ave., Pioneer Square* ☎ *206/282–4226* ⊕ *www.utilikilts.com.*

Velouria. The ultimate antidote to mass-produced, unimaginative women's clothes can be found in this exquisitely feminine shop where independent West Coast designers rule. Much on offer is one of a kind: handmade, '70s-inspired jumpsuits; romantic, demure eyelet dresses; and clever screen-printed tees. Superb bags, delicate jewelry, and fun cards and gifts are also on display. It's worth a look just to check out all the wearable art. ⊠ *145 S. King St., Pioneer Square* ☎ *206/788–0330* ⊕ *shopvelouria.com.*

SHOES

Clementines. This tiny boutique provides a unique collection of shoes, clothing, and accessories from designer brands like Coclico and Arama, The sales personnel create an inviting shopping experience that will leave no room for buyer's remorse. ⊠ *310 Occidental Ave. S* ☎ *206/935–9400* ⊕ *www.clementines.com.*

INTERNATIONAL DISTRICT

Seattle's primarily Asian neighborhood is meant for delicious exploring. Sample tea at Seattle Best Tea, leaf through books at Kinokuniya, check out Asian antiques, and stop for dim sum along the way. Megamarket Uwajimaya *(Neighborhoods)* is the major shopping attraction of the International District, but the rest of the neighborhood is packed with shops worth visiting, too. Wander the neighborhood for bubble tea (milky tea with tapioca pearls), Chinese pastries, jade and gold jewelry, Asian produce, and Eastern herbs and tinctures. Little souvenir shops, dusty and deep, sell plants, Japanese kites, Vietnamese bowls, Chinese slippers, Korean art, and tea or dish sets. ■TIP➔ **The International District is a very short walk from Pioneer Square. Walk east on Jackson Street from Pioneer Square (passing Amtrak's King Street Station), and you're well on your way.**

Best shopping: South Jackson Street to South Lane Street, between 5th and 8th Avenues South.

BOOKS

Kinokuniya Book Stores of America. Japanamaniacs, get thee to this Tokyo-based chain for a huge collection of books, magazines, office supplies, collectibles, clothes, and gifts. Their manga selection is particularly impressive—nearly every title you could want is represented, and they'll happily order anything you don't find in the store. ⊠ *525 S. Weller St., International District* ☎ *206/587–2477* ⊕ *www.kinokuniya.com.*

GIFTS AND HOME DECOR

Kobo at Higo. Housed in what used to be a 75-year-old five-and-dime store, this distinctive gallery has fine ceramics, textiles, and exquisite crafts by Japanese and Northwest artists; you can also see artifacts from the old store. Items range from something as simple as incense from Kyoto to an enormous, painted antique chest. ⌧ *602–608 S. Jackson St., International District* ☎ *206/381–3000* ⊕ *www.koboseattle.com.*

Momo. Right next door to the Kobo gallery is a perky little shop with great gift options, including unique clothing, vials of perfume, plastic sushi magnets, coin purses with personality, canvas bags, quirky jewelry (such as a long chain necklace dangling a wee enamel cupcake at the end), and more. The owner is friendly and fun, and that comes through in this adorable store. ⌧ *600 S. Jackson St., International District* ☎ *206/329–4736* ⊕ *www.momoseattle.com.*

SPECIALTY FOODS

Seattle Best Tea Corporation. If you haven't been introduced to the wonders of Asian tea, you need to make a trip here, where the experience is as enriching as the tea itself. Palette pleasure abounds with their selection of oolong, pouchong, jasmine, and green teas. All the teas are available to try, and you can pick up a cute teapot while you're at it. ⌧ *506 S. King St., International District* ☎ *206/749–9855* ⊕ *www. seattlebesttea.com.*

CAPITOL HILL

If you always make sure that your jeans are on trend, subscribe to *Dwell* magazine, embody the DIY ethos, or just like to people-watch, head to Capitol Hill for some of the best shopping in town. Broadway is popular among college students because of its cheap clothing stores, including standbys Urban Outfitters and American Apparel. The Pike–Pine Corridor holds the majority of the neighborhood's most interesting shops.

Best shopping: East Pike and East Pine Streets between Bellevue Avenue and Madison Avenue East, East Olive Way between Bellevue Avenue East and Broadway East, and Broadway East between East Denny Way and East Roy Street.

BOOKS AND MUSIC

Fodor's Choice ★ **Elliott Bay Book Company.** A major reason to visit this landmark bookstore—formerly a longtime haunt in Pioneer Square, hence the name—is the great selection of Pacific Northwest history books and fiction titles by local authors, complete with handwritten recommendation cards from the knowledgeable staff. A big selection of bargain books, underground parking, lovely skylights, and an appealing café all sweeten the deal—and the hundreds of author events held every year mean that nearly every day is an exciting one for dropping by. ⌧ *1521 10th Ave., Capitol Hill* ☎ *206/624–6600* ⊕ *www.elliottbaybook.com.*

Everyday Music. For a huge selection of used CDs and vinyl, wander over to Everyday Music, where you'll find more than 100,000 titles in stock. They're open until midnight, so you can join the late-night browsers clicking through the stacks after you've had dinner and a few drinks. Just don't blame us if you head home with a Milli Vanilli CD and can't remember why. ✉ *1523 10th Ave., Capitol Hill* ☎ *206/568–3321* ⊕ *www.everydaymusic.com.*

Twice Sold Tales. It's hard to miss this excellent used-book store—simply look for the six-foot neon cat sign—he'll be waving his Cheshire tail. Inside, you'll find five more kitties winding their way through the maze of stacks. Pick up a few tales and take advantage of the 25% discount offered the last two hours of the evening. Be sure to grab a map of all the used bookstores in the city if you're hungry for more. ✉ *1833 Harvard Ave., at Denny, Capitol Hill* ☎ *206/324–2421* ⊕ *www.twicesoldtales.info.*

Wall of Sound. If you're on the hunt for Japanese avant-rock on LP, antiwar spoken word, spiritual reggae with Afro-jazz undertones, or old screen-printed show posters, you've found the place. Obscure, experimental, adventurous, and good? Wall of Sound probably has it. ✉ *315 E. Pine St., Capitol Hill* ☎ *206/441–9880* ⊕ *www.wosound.com.*

CLOTHING

Le Frock. It may look like just another overcrowded consignment shop, but among the racks of Seattle's classiest vintage and consignment store you'll find classic steals for men and women from Burberry, Fendi, Dior, Missoni, and the like. Contemporary looks from Prada, Gucci, and Chanel round out the collection. ✉ *613 E. Pike St., Capitol Hill* ☎ *206/623–5339* ⊕ *www.lefrockonline.com.*

Standard Goods. If you want to get a true sense of Pacific Northwest style, this men's and women's clothing shop embodies it all, from casual plaid button-down shirts to wood-framed sunglasses. Carrying local brands like Filson, Shwood, and Capitol Hill Candles, this trendy local shop sources only quality goods. ✉ *701 E. Pike St., Capitol Hill* ☎ *206/323–0207* ⊕ *www.thestandardgoods.com.*

GIFTS AND HOME DECOR

Kobo. This lovely store sells artisan crafts from studios in Japan and in the Northwest. What's here is similar to what's stocked at the International District branch: tasteful home wares, cute but functional gifts, and quirky pieces of furniture. After a long day of looking at retro and ironic items, this place will cleanse your palate. ✉ *814 E. Roy St., Capitol Hill* ☎ *206/726–0704* ⊕ *www.koboseattle.com.*

NuBe Green. An emphasis on recycled goods and sustainability is the mission of this well-presented store anchoring a corner of the Oddfellows Building. All items are sourced and made in the United States, including linens, candles, glass art, and even dog beds made from old jeans. Our favorite items are by local **Alchemy Goods** (*www.alchemygoods.com*), which recycles bicycle tubes, reclaimed vinyl mesh, and seatbelts into distinctively cool wallets and messenger bags. ✉ *921 E. Pine St., Capitol Hill* ☎ *206/402–4515* ⊕ *www.nubegreen.com.*

Continued on page 234

PIKE PLACE MARKET
Nine Acres of History & Quirky Charm

With more than a century of history tucked into every corner and plenty of local personality, the Market is one spot you can't miss. Office workers hustle past cruise-ship crowds to take a seat at lunch counters that serve anything from pizza to piroshkies to German sausage. Local chefs plan the evening's menu over stacks of fresh, colorful produce. At night, couples stroll in to canoodle by candlelight in tucked-away bars and restaurants. Sure, some residents may bemoan the hordes of visitors, and many Seattleites spend their dollars at a growing number of neighborhood farmers' markets. But the Market is still one of Seattle's best-loved attractions.

The Pike Place Market dates from 1907. In response to anger over rising food prices, the city issued permits for farmers to sell produce from wagons parked at Pike Place. The impromptu public market grew steadily, and in 1921 Frank Goodwin, a hotel owner who had been quietly buying up real estate around Pike Place for a decade, proposed to build a permanent space.

More than 250 businesses, including 90 eateries. Breathtaking views of Elliott Bay. A pedestrian-friendly central shopping arcade that buzzes to life each day beginning at 6:30 AM. Strumming street musicians. Cobblestones, flying fish, and the very first Starbucks. Pike Place Market—the oldest continuously operated public market in the United States and a beloved Seattle icon—covers all the bases.

The Market's vitality ebbed after World War II, with the exodus to the suburbs and the rise of large supermarkets. Both it and the surrounding neighborhoods began to deteriorate. But a group of dedicated residents, led by the late architect Victor Steinbrueck, rallied and voted the Market a Historical Asset in the early 1970s. Years of subsequent restoration turned the Market into what you see today.

Pike Place Market is many buildings built around a central arcade (which is distinguished by its huge red neon sign).

Shops and restaurants fill buildings on Pike Place and Western Avenue. In the main arcade, dozens of booths sell fresh produce, cheese, spices, coffee, crafts, and seafood—which can be packed in dry ice for flights home. Farmers sell high-quality produce that helps to set Seattle's rigorous dining standards. The shopkeepers who rent store spaces sell art, curios, clothing, beads, and more. Most shops cater to tourists, but there are gems to be found.

EXPLORING THE MARKET

TOP EATS

❶ THE PINK DOOR. This adored (and adorable) Italian eatery is tucked into Post Alley. Whimsical decor, very good Italian food (such as the scrumptious *linguine alla vongole*), and weekend cabaret and burlesque make this gem a must-visit.

❷ LE PANIER. It's a self-proclaimed "Very French Bakery" and another Seattle favorite. The pastries are the main draw, but sandwiches on fresh baguettes and stuffed croissants offer more substantial snacks.

❸ PIROSHKY PIROSHKY. Authentic piroshky come in both standard varieties (beef and cheese) and Seattle-influenced ones (smoked salmon with cream cheese). There are plenty of sweet piroshky, too, if you need a sugar fix.

❹ CAMPAGNE. This French favorite and its charming attached café have you covered, whether you want a quick Croque Madame for lunch, a leisurely and delicious weekend brunch, or a white-tablecloth dinner.

❺ BEECHER'S. Artisanal cheeses—and mac-n-cheese to go—make this a spot Seattleites will brave the crowds for.

❻ THREE GIRLS BAKERY. This tiny bakery turns out piles of pastries and sandwiches on their fresh-baked bread (the baked salmon is a favorite).

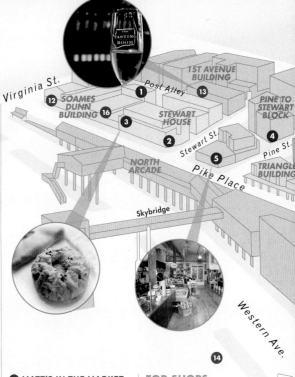

❼ MATT'S IN THE MARKET. Matt's is the best restaurant in the Market, and one of the best in the city. Lunch is casual (try the catfish po'boy), and dinner is elegant, with fresh fish and local produce showcased on the small menu. Reservations are essential.

❽ DAILY DOZEN DONUTS. Mini-donuts are made fresh before your eyes and are a great snack to pick up before you venture into the labyrinth.

❾ MARKET GRILL. This no-frills counter serves up the market's best fish sandwiches and a great clam chowder.

❿ CHUKAR CHERRIES. Look for handmade confections featuring—but not restricted to—local cherries dipped in all sorts of sweet, rich coatings.

TOP SHOPS

⓫ MARKET SPICE TEA. For a tin of the Market's signature tea, Market Spice Blend, which is infused with cinnamon and clove oils, seek out Market Spice shop on the south side of the main arcade.

⓬ PIKE & WESTERN WINE SHOP. The Tasting Room in Post Alley may be a lovely place to sample Washington wines, but Pike and Western is the place where serious oenophiles flock.

⓭ THE TASTING ROOM. With one of the top wine selections in town, the Tasting Room offers Washington wines for the casual collector and the experienced connoisseur. Stop by the bar for

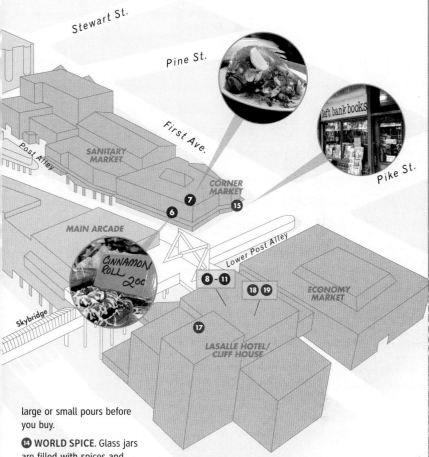

Stewart St.

Pine St.

First Ave.

Post Alley

Pike St.

left bank books

SANITARY MARKET

CORNER MARKET

7

6 **15**

MAIN ARCADE

Lower Post Alley

8-11

18 **19**

ECONOMY MARKET

17

Skybridge

LASALLE HOTEL/ CLIFF HOUSE

large or small pours before you buy.

🄸 **WORLD SPICE.** Glass jars are filled with spices and teas from around the world here: Buy by the ounce or grab a pre-packaged gift set as a souvenir.

🄵 **LEFT BANK BOOKS.** A collective in operation since 1973, this tiny bookshop specializes in political and history titles and alternative literature.

🄶 **THE ORIGINAL STARBUCKS.** At 1912 Pike Place, you'll find the tiny store that opened in 1971 and started

an empire. The shop is definitely more quaint and old-timey than its sleek younger siblings, and it features the original, uncensored (read: bare-breasted) version of the mermaid logo.

🄷 **RACHEL'S GINGER BEER.** The flagship store for Seattle's wildly popular ginger beer serves up delicious variations on its homemade brew, including boozy cocktails.

🄸 **PAPPARDELLE'S PASTA.** There's no type of pasta you could dream up that isn't already in a bin at Pappardelle's.

🄹 **DELAURENTI'S.** This amazing Italian grocery has everything from fancy olive oil to digestifs and wine to meats and fine cheeses.

TOP EXPERIENCES

Pike Place Flowers

Market buskers

Pike Place Fish Co.

FISHMONGERS. There are four spots to visit if you want to see some serious fish: Pike Place Fish Co. (where the fish-throwers are—look for the awestruck crowds); City Fish (the place for fresh crab); Pure Food Fish Market (selling since 1911); and Jack's Fish Spot.

FLOWER STALLS. Flower growers, many of them Hmong immigrants, dot the main arcade. The gorgeous, seasonal bouquets are among the market's biggest draws.

PILES OF PRODUCE. The bounty of the agricultural valleys just outside Seattle is endless. In summer, seek out sweet peaches and Rainier cherries. In fall, look for cider made from Yakima Valley apples. There are dozens of produce vendors, but Sosio's and Manzo Brothers have been around the longest.

BUSKERS. The market has more than 240 street entertainers in any given year; the parade of Pacific Northwest hippie quirkitude is entertainment in itself.

POST ALLEY. There are some great finds in the alley that runs the length of the Market, paralleling First Avenue, from the highbrow (The Tasting Room) to the very lowbrow (the Gum Wall, a wall speckled with discarded gum supposedly left by people waiting in line at the Market Theater).

GHOSTS. If you listen to local lore, Pike Place Market may be the most haunted spot in Seattle. The epicenter seems to be 1921 First Avenue, where Butterworths & Sons Undertakers handled most of Seattle's dead in the early 1900s. You might see visitors sliding flowers into the building's old mail slot.

***SLEEPLESS IN SEATTLE* STOP.** Though it's been more than a decade since Rob Reiner and Tom Hanks discussed dating mores at the bar of The Athenian Inn, tourists still snap pictures of the corner they occupied. Look for the bright red plaque declaring: TOM HANKS SAT HERE.

A DAY AT THE MARKET

6:30 AM Delivery vans and trucks start to fill the narrow streets surrounding Pike Place Market. Vendors with permanent stalls arrive to stack produce, arrange flowers, and shovel ice into bins for displaying salmon, crab, octopus, and other delicacies.

7:30 AM Breakfast is served! ■TIP➔ For freshly made pastries head to Three Girls and Le Panier.

9 AM Craftspeople vying for day stalls sign in and are assigned spots based on seniority.

10 AM Craftspeople set up Down Under —the levels below the main arcade—as the main arcade officially opens. The Heritage Center on Western Avenue opens. Market tours ($10) start at the information booth. ■TIP➔ Make reservations for market tours at least a day in advance; call ☎ 206/774-5249.

11 AM The Market madness begins. In summer, midday crowds make it nearly impossible to walk through the street-level arcades. ■TIP➔ Head Down Under where things are often a bit quieter.

12 PM–2 PM Lunch counters at places like the Athenian Inn and the Market Grill fill up.

Pike Place Market

5 PM Down Under shops close and the cobblestones are hosed down. (The Market closes at 6 PM Mon.–Sat. and 5 PM on Sun.)

7 PM–2 AM Patrons fill the tables at the Alibi Room, Zig Zag Café, the Pink Door, Matt's at the Market, and Maximilien's.

RACHEL THE PIG

Rachel, the 550-lb bronze pig that greets marketgoers at the main entrance on Pike and 1st Avenue, is a popular photo stop. But she's also a giant piggy bank that contributes up to $9,000 per year to the Market Foundation. Rachel was sculpted by Georgia Gerber, of Whidbey Island, and was named for the 750-pound pig that won the 1985 Island County Fair.

PARKING

There are numerous garages in the area, including one affiliated with the market itself (the Public Market Parking Garage at 1531 Western Ave.), at which you can get validated parking from many merchants; some restaurants offer free parking at this garage after 5 PM. You'll also find several pay lots farther south on Western Ave. and north on 1st Ave. Street parking is next to impossible to find midday. From Downtown hotels, the Market is easy to reach on foot or on city buses in the "Ride Free Zone."

MARKETS

Broadway Farmers Market. This small and lively market fills up a parking lot one block east of Broadway; there's fresh produce galore, plus music, samples, and plenty of cut flowers. ⊠ *10th Ave. E, at E. Thomas St., Capitol Hill* ⊕ *www.seattlefarmersmarkets.org.*

Melrose Market. Seattle is famously foodie-friendly, and this historic triangular building packs several of the city's best culinary shops under one roof. Browse and sample artisanal meats, cheeses, shellfish, and liquor, all with locavore leanings. Unlike Pike Place, the relatively pint-size Melrose is more a hipster haunt than a tourist trap: Anthony Bourdain and the Seattle *Top Chef* contestants have been spotted here. ⊠ *1501–1535 Melrose Ave., Capitol Hill* ⊕ *melrosemarketseattle.com.*

SHOES

Edie's Shoes. Supercomfy, effortlessly cool shoes can be found at this small, carefully planned shop. Plop down on the big purple couch and try on trendy but sensible footwear by Camper, Onitsuka Tiger, Biviel, Tretorn, and Tsubo. You won't find any outrageous designs or one-of-a-kind items here, but it does have a great selection of favored brands in perhaps a few more styles than you'd find at Nordstrom. ⊠ *500 E. Pike St., Capitol Hill* ☎ *206/839–1111* ⊕ *www.ediesshoes.com.*

LIKELIHOOD. With designers ranging from Puma X Rihanna to Spalwart, this store has an extensive brand selection that's perfect for the eclectic Capitol Hill neighborhood. With its emphasis on "less is more," the clean, white space creates the illusion of art gallery rather than shoe retailer. They also have a wide variety of apparel and bags. ⊠ *1101 E. Union St.* ☎ *206/257–0577* ⊕ *www.likelihood.us.*

FREMONT

Fremont is full of the sort of stores perfectly suited to browsing and window-shopping—lots of pretty, pricey nonessentials and fun junk shops, in a cute and quirky north-end neighborhood. The weekly summer Sunday market along the waterfront (with free parking nearby) is hit or miss, but worth a look if you're in the area.

Best shopping: Blocks bound by Fremont Place North and Evanston Avenue North to North 34th Street and Aurora Avenue North.

ANTIQUES AND COLLECTIBLES

Fremont Vintage Mall. Goods from about 25 vendors are crammed into every conceivable corner of this bi-level space, so you'll likely score at least something to take home. Clothing, furniture, and collectible art are among the finds, and the dishes, toys, and other cool stuff are fun to look through whether you're a serious collector or just an innocent bystander. The Jive Time Records Annex is also a tenant. It's easy to walk right past this place—look carefully for the door and then proceed down the flight of stairs. ✉ *3419 Fremont Pl. N, Fremont* ☎ *206/548–9140* ⊕ *www.fremontvintagemall.com.*

BOOKS AND MUSIC

Dusty Strings. A Seattle institution since 1979, Dusty Strings has long been delighting folk and roots music lovers with beautifully crafted hammered dulcimers, harps, guitars of all stripes, banjos, ukuleles, and mandolins. The relaxed shop invites hands-on browsing, and the lilting strains of traditional melodies often fill the space. The nonprofit group Victory Music frequently hosts acoustic concerts and workshops in the store—check *www.victorymusic.org* for showtimes. ✉ *3406 Fremont Ave. N, Fremont* ☎ *206/634–1662* ⊕ *www.dustystrings.com.*

Ophelia's Books. With a tiny spiral staircase leading to the basement, and resident cats wandering through the tightly packed aisles, Ophelia's offers a classic used-bookstore experience in an age when so many are disappearing. The owner is well-known for her excellent taste, and it shows—you'll find major titles from well-known authors as well as obscure works and poetry books. Be sure to ask for recommendations—she'll be happy to help. ✉ *3504 Fremont Ave. N, Fremont* ☎ *206/632–3759* ⊕ *www.opheliasbooks.com.*

CLOTHING

Atlas Clothing. Atlas is loaded with previously appreciated shirts, jackets, and tees; stacks of new and vintage denim; must-have sneakers from the '70s and '80s; and tons of accessories. This is not over-the-top costume vintage; visit Red Light Clothing Exchange for that. ✉ *3509 Fremont Ave N, Suite 200, Fremont* ☎ *206/323–0960* ⊕ *www.atlasclothing.net.*

Les Amis. Women whose sartorial leanings go beyond low-rise jeans will adore the sophisticated dresses, gorgeous handknits, and the makings of great work outfits here, much of it from Europe and Japan. Younger fashionistas come here, too, for unique summer skirts and ultrasoft T-shirts. Everyone seems to love the whimsical lingerie collection. Les Amis carries some top designers, such as Dosa, Isabel Marant, and Nanette Lepore. ✉ *3420 Evanston Ave. N, Fremont* ☎ *206/632–2877* ⊕ *www.lesamis-inc.com.*

Show Pony. With a mix of new, used, and locally designed clothing, Show Pony is a great spot to grab reasonably priced girly frocks and fabulous accessories. Especially good is the used/vintage section upstairs, which mostly stocks designer labels. Jewelry, perfume, gifts, and home-decorating items round out the collection. ✉ *702 N. 35th St., Fremont* ☎ *206/706–4188* ⊕ *www.showponyseattle.com.*

GIFTS AND HOME DECOR

Burnt Sugar. If there's a rocket on the roof, then you've found Burnt Sugar—or you've gone too far and are in Cape Canaveral. This hip and funky shop offers a mélange of handbags, greeting cards, soaps, candles, jewelry, toys, children's gifts, and other eclectic baubles you never knew you needed. There's a makeup counter, and half the store is devoted to a small but ultracool selection of women's shoes. ✉ *601 N. 35th St., Fremont* ☏ *888/545–0699* ⊕ *www.burntsugarfrankie.com.*

Essenza. A gurgling stone fountain stands in the center of this light-filled boutique, where airy displays showcase delicately scented European bath products by Santa Maria Novella, Tocca, and Cote Bastide. You'll find the complete line of Fresh cosmetics, handmade bed linens, women's loungewear and lingerie, delicate jewelry, and exquisitely detailed children's clothing. ✉ *615 N. 35th St., Fremont* ☏ *206/547–4895* ⊕ *www.essenza-inc.com.*

PHINNEY RIDGE

Phinney Ridge and its nearby sister neighborhood of Greenwood are north of Fremont and east of Ballard. This is a great destination when you feel like strolling as much as shopping. You can park near the Woodland Park Zoo and walk the length of Phinney Avenue (which becomes Greenwood Avenue farther north). You'll be right near Green Lake and, on a clear day, will be looking out across at the Cascade Mountains to the east, and the Olympics to the west. Sure, the area's a bit spread out, but the stores, coffee shops, and restaurants on this 2-mile stretch are sweet and affordable, and make for a pleasant afternoon.

ANTIQUES AND COLLECTIBLES

Johnson & Johnson Antiques. This family-owned shop provides 1900s American oak furniture in craftsman and mission styles, as well as plenty of other decorating knickknacks. French art deco pieces from the 1930s and 1860s American walnut make their collection distinctive and impressive. Stop in to browse and if something catches your eye; they make shipping easy. ✉ *6820 Greenwood Ave. N* ☏ *206/789–6489* ⊕ *johnsonandjohnsonantiques.com.*

CLOTHING

Frock Shop. The clothing in this light-filled Phinney boutique is so creative and unique looking that you'd swear it was vintage. But everything here is new, and much of it is locally designed. Anything bought is sure to elicit lots of "where did you get that?" squeals. ✉ *6500 Phinney Ave. N, Phinney Ridge* ☏ *206/297–1638* ⊕ *www.shopfrockshop.com.*

NOVELTIES AND GIFTS

FAMILY | **Greenwood Space Travel Supply Co.**
The name of this shop baffled Greenwood residents for months until it was revealed that it was part of 826 Seattle, the amazing national creative-writing program for kids that was founded by novelist Dave Eggers and educator Nínive Calegari in 2002. The small store has kooky items purported to be space-travel essentials (freeze-dried meals), many of which are obvious nods to kitschy science-fiction movies (check out the ray guns). It also carries 826 clothing, and all of the proceeds go to the writing center. ■TIP→ While you're here, check the bulletin board for notices about upcoming events and single-session workshops. Note that this is not a full-blown toy store: go in with a sense of humor and an imagination because much of the cleverness is literary—standard toys and items given ridiculous new names to sound like important instruments of space travel. Everyone will enjoy filling out the hilarious space-traveler screening questionnaires and spaceship accident reports. ⊠ *8414 Greenwood Ave. N, Greenwood* ☎ *206/725–2625* ⊕ *www.greenwoodspacetravelsupply.com.*

> **GREENWOOD**
>
> **Sip & Ship.** If you really fall in love with Greenwood, head to this shop where T-shirts, hoodies, coffee mugs, and other hip accessories are emblazoned with the neighborhood's name. It's a unique one-stop shop where you can buy a gift and have it wrapped, packed, and shipped, while you sip espresso. ⊠ *7511 Greenwood Ave. N, Greenwood* ☎ *206/783–4299* ⊕ *www.sipandship.com.*

The Shop Agora. Greenwood is often called "Greekwood" for its many Greek restaurants. The Shop Agora, just down the way in Phinney Ridge, offers all the ingredients for authentic Mediterranean meals, including imported spices, herbs, olive oil, honey, and jam from Greece, Tunisia, Italy, and Spain. Stop in for fresh (and inexpensive) baklava, dolmas, or truffle popcorn, and browse an extensive wine collection that includes the largest offering of Greek wines in the city. ⊠ *6417-A Phinney Ave. N, Phinney Ridge* ☎ *206/782–5551* ⊕ *www. theshopagora.com/.*

BALLARD

Ballard is the shining star of the north end when it comes to shopping. Packed with cute home stores, great clothing boutiques, locally made gifts, and just about every genre of store imaginable, this neighborhood is a must-visit locale. Their Saturday Farmers' Market is one of the best in the city, and it operates year-round for a dependably fun outing. Pick up smoked salmon, artisanal cheese, and vegan baked goods, and pop into the shops listed here if the rain starts.

Best shopping: Ballard Avenue between 22nd Avenue NW and 20th Avenue NW; N.E. Market Street between 20th and 24th Avenues.

6

BOOKS AND MUSIC

FAMILY **Secret Garden Bookshop.** Named after the Francis Hodgson Burnett classic, this cozy shop has been delighting readers for 34 years. A favorite of teachers, librarians, and parents, the store stocks a wide array of imaginative literature and thoughtful nonfiction for all ages; their children's section is particularly notable. ⊠ *2214 N.W. Market St., Ballard* ☎ *206/789–5006* ⊕ *www.secretgardenbooks.com.*

CLOTHING AND ACCESSORIES

Blackbird. This perfectly stocked and fashion-forward store is a favorite destination for stylish men. With choice clothes from designers such as RVCA, KZO, and Obey, and sharp accessories like wrist cuffs and fedoras, urban menfolk can kick their look up a notch. Ladies will be pleased to see accessories and makeup for women round out the store's collection. Blackbird also has a tiny "apothecary" on nearby Leary Avenue that carries products for the face and hair. ⊠ *2208 N.W. Market St. #320, Ballard* ☎ *206/547–2524* ⊕ *www.blackbirdballard.com.*

FAMILY **Clover.** What's easily the cutest children's store in town carries wonderful handcrafted wooden toys, European figurines, works by local artists, and a variety of swoon-worthy, perfectly crafted little clothes. Even shoppers without children will be smitten—it's hard to resist the vintage French Tintin posters, knit-wool cow dolls, and classic figurines. ⊠ *5333 Ballard Ave. NW, Ballard* ☎ *206/782–0715* ⊕ *www.clovertoys.com.*

Horseshoe. "A little bit country, a little bit rock and roll," Horseshoe offers girlie Western wear and hipster fare in its Ballard digs. Comfy, sassy shirts and dresses are available from designers like Kensie, Prairie Underground, Eva Franco, and Ella Moss. Premium denim, cowboy boots, unique jewelry, hot bags, and frills like Butter London nail polish are among the wares. ⊠ *5344 Ballard Ave. NW, Ballard* ☎ *206/547–9639* ⊕ *www.horseshoeseattle.com.*

GIFTS AND HOME ACCESSORIES

Camelion Design. This reasonably affordable, modern home-accessories store in Ballard is crammed, showroom-style, with furniture, accessories, and gift items that straddle the line between modern, arty, and organic feeling. It's a good place to get living-room envy, order a custom couch, or just pick up an area rug, vase, or picture frame. Camelion also sells jewelry, bath products, greeting cards, and stationery. ⊠ *5330 Ballard Ave. NW, Ballard* ☎ *206/783–7125* ⊕ *www.cameliondesign.com.*

Dandelion Botanical Company. "Apothecary" is the term that this high-end but down-to-earth boutique gift stores uses to describe itself. Its brick walls are lined with hundreds of jars of botanicals—bulk Chinese and ayurvedic herbs, teas, and cooking spices among them. Essential oils, bath salts, and aromatherapy products are also on hand, and most of the items they sell are organic or made of all-natural materials. ⊠ *5424 Ballard Ave. NW, Ballard* ☎ *206/545–8892* ⊕ *www. dandelionbotanical.com.*

Venue. Venue is the chic version of the Made In Washington stores: it stocks only goods made by local artists (some of whom have their studios in the sleek bi-level space), but you won't find any tacky souvenirs here. Watch the designers at work, chat with the staff (most are artists taking shifts), or just browse through artisanal chocolates, custom handbags, handmade soaps, baby wear, and colorful prints and mosaics. ⊠ *5408 22nd Ave. NW, Ballard* ☎ *206/789–3335* ⊕ *www. venueballard.com.*

OUTDOOR CLOTHING AND EQUIPMENT

KAVU. Founded in the Pacific Northwest, KAVU's flagship store in Ballard is an outdoor shopping staple. Loudly printed fleece pullovers, thermal vests, and sturdy duffel bags are just a few items you'll find in this funky shop that feels like REI's cooler kid brother. ⊠ *5419 Ballard Ave. NW, Ballard* ☎ *206/783–0060* ⊕ *www.kavu.com.*

MARKETS

Ballard Farmers Market. Every Sunday, rain or shine, loads of vendors come to Ballard Avenue to set up colorful, welcoming tents and stands to sell produce as well as giftier items like candles and hats. Meanwhile, local buskers entertain foodies and families. ⊠ *Ballard Ave., between 20th Ave. NW and 22nd Ave. NW, Ballard* ⊕ *www.ballard-farmersmarket.wordpress.com.*

SHOES

Market Street Shoes. One of the best all-around shoe stores in town, Market Street stocks so many styles from so many brands that you're likely to find something. Its shoes for men, women, and children skew on the end of Seattle-style comfort, so you'll see sensible picks from Dankso, Born, Camper, Clarks, and Doc Martins, but there are a plenty of fun options by Fluevog, Tsubo, Think!, and Frye, as well. ⊠ *2232 N.W. Market St., Ballard* ☎ *206/783–1670* ⊕ *www.market-streetshoes.com.*

re-souL. Stocking cool but comfortable shoes from Biviel, MOMA, PF Flyers, Cydwoq, and the like, this hip space offers a small selection of crazy fashionable boots, shoes, sneaks, and high heels. In keeping with the "little bit of everything" trend so popular with Seattle boutiques, re-souL also sells great jewelry pieces, as well as usable art pieces from Alessi. They carry both men's and women's shoes and accessories. Everything is a bit pricey, but not excessively so. ⊠ *5319 Ballard Ave. NW, Ballard* ☎ *206/789–7312* ⊕ *www.resoul.com.*

SPA

Habitude Salon, Day Spa and Gallery. Plush furnishings and tropical scents relax you the moment you enter Habitude (in Ballard and Fremont). Indulge in a single treatment or in such packages as Beneath the Spring Thaw Falls (hydrating glow, massage, scalp treatment, sauna, and a spa smoothie). Other offerings include the Hot Rocks detox sauna, Rainforest Steam Shower, and door-to-door town-car service. It's the state's only Aveda Lifestyle spa. ⊠ *2801 N.W. Market St., Ballard* ☎ *206/782–2898* ⊕ *www.habitude.com.*

WALLINGFORD

Wallingford offers a more grown-up selection of shopping than Fremont or Ballard. You won't find trendy clothing boutiques here, and the only scene you're likely to encounter is a pack of knitters congregating at Bad Women Yarn. But with a great selection of independent shops, specialty bookstores, fabulous gift-buying opportunities, and the best beer store in the city, you're likely to have a fun afternoon poking through this neighborhood.

Best shopping: 45th Street between Stone Way and Meridian Avenue.

BEER

Bottleworks. If you love microbrews, then make a pilgrimage to Bottleworks to peruse its massive collection. With around 950 chilled varieties of malty goodness available, including seasonal varieties, vintage bottles, and global rarities, there's a beer for everyone here—as well as a good sampling of mead and cider. ⊠ *1710 N. 45th St., Wallingford* ☎ *206/633–2437* ⊕ *www.bottleworks.com.*

BOOKS AND PRINTED MATERIAL

Open Books. One of only a couple of poetry-only bookstores in the country, this serene space is conducive to hours of browsing; when you're ready to interact, the owners are always happy to answer your questions, make suggestions, or chat about the titles you've selected. There's also a good selection of magazines as well as chapbooks; the emporium also hosts readings. ⊠ *2414 N. 45th St., Wallingford* ☎ *206/633–0811* ⊕ *www.openpoetrybooks.com.*

Wide World Travel Store. One of the first travel-only bookstores in the country, Wide World Travel Store has been outfitting the adventurous since 1976. This is a great place to grab hard-to-find travel guides to just about anywhere, along with trip essentials by Eagle Creek, Klean Kanteen, and more. From travel journals to sporks (a handy cross between spoons and forks), to voltage transformers for overseas trips, they'll either have it or know where to get it. ⊠ *4411 Wallingford Ave. N, Wallingford* ☎ *206/634–3453* ⊕ *www.wideworldtravelstore.com.*

GIFTS AND HOME ACCESSORIES

Fodor'sChoice **Archie McPhee.** If your life is missing a punching-nun puppet, an Edgar
★ Allen Poe action figure, or a bacon-scented air freshener, there's hope. Leave your cares and woes at the door and step into a warehouse of the weird and wonderful. It's nearly impossible to feel bad while perusing stacks of armadillo handbags, demon rubber duckies, handerpants

(don't ask), and homicidal unicorn play sets. Grab a cat-in-a-can to keep you company, or leave with a dramatic chipmunk oil painting. You'll feel better. Trust us. ⊠ *1300 N. 45th St., Wallingford* ☎ *206/297–0240* ⊕ *www.archiemcpheeseattle.com.*

MALL

Wallingford Center. In this quirky shopping center, a converted 1904 schoolhouse, there are 15 resident shops—all of them independent with the exception of Pharmaca, an integrative pharmacy with on-site naturopaths. From cupcakes to contemporary crafts and clothing, there's a lot on offer here. And on Wednesday afternoons from May through September there's a farmers' market in the parking lot. ⊠ *1815 N. 45th St., Wallingford* ☎ *206/547–7246* ⊕ *www.wallingfordcenter.com.*

OUTDOOR CLOTHING

evo. For outdoor gear with an edgy vibe, locals head to evo, which specializes in snow sports gear and also carries a solid selection of hip street clothes for men and women. You'll find everything you need to shred Washington's big mountains in style, from fat powder skis and snowboards with wild graphics to flashy ski jackets and thick woolen beanies. Occupying a two-level space at the Fremont Collective building, evo also has a gallery space that hosts art shows. Traveling with skateboarders? Seattle's only indoor skate park, All Together Skate Park, is right next door. ⊠ *3500 Stone Way N, Fremont* ☎ *206/973–4470* ⊕ *www.evo.com.*

UNIVERSITY DISTRICT

The "U-District" is packed with predictably college-friendly shopping—lots of used clothing, books, trendy footwear, and coffee. Meander down University Way (known to locals as "The Ave") to find the standout shops listed here, and stop at any of the numerous ethnic restaurants to refuel with cheap, decent eats. ■TIP→ **If you're uncomfortable with panhandlers, skateboarding teens, and throngs of university students, bypass this area and head directly down the hill to outdoor shopping mall University Village.**

Best shopping: University Way NE between N.E. 42nd and 47th streets, and University Village at 25th Avenue NE and N.E. 45th Street.

BOOKS

University Book Store. Campus bookstores are usually rip-offs to be endured only by students clutching syllabi, but the University of Washington's store is a big exception to that rule. This enormous resource has a well-stocked general book department in addition to the requisite textbooks. Author events are scheduled all year long. Check out the bargain-book tables and the basement crammed with every art supply imaginable. ⊠ *4326 University Way NE, University District* ☎ *206/634–3400* ⊕ *www.bookstore.washington.edu.*

CLOSE UP

Native American Culture and Crafts

Looking at a map of the Seattle area, you're bound to encounter some unusual names. Enumclaw, for instance. Or Mukilteo, Puyallup, Snohomish, and Tukwila. They're legacies of the dozens of Native American tribes and nations that first occupied the region.

Seattle, in fact, is named after Chief Si'ahl, a leader of the Suquamish and Duwamish tribes. For many thousands of years, Native American tribes have called the Pacific Northwest home—from the salmon-packed waters of the Skagit River to the high country of the Cascade Mountains. The majority of these tribes were subgroups of the Coast Salish peoples, who historically inhabited the entire Puget Sound region from Olympia north to British Columbia.

Tribes residing in and around the Seattle area included Duwamish, Suquamish, Tulalip, Muckleshoot, and Snoqualmie. Each tribe developed complex cultural and artistic traditions, and a regional language—Lushootseed—allowed tribes to trade resources. Today, members of many Seattle-area tribes are keeping their traditions alive: basketry, weaving, and sculpture—including totems—are traditional artistic media of the Coast Salish, and all three arts are still vibrant today. Contemporary Salish artists work in several modern media as well, including painting, studio glass, and printmaking.

Two top activities for experiencing Native culture up close and personal are:

Burke Museum of Natural History and Culture. On the campus of the University of Washington, the Burke Museum of Natural History and Culture houses thousands of Coast Salish artifacts and artworks. The museum's exhibits also feature artwork from farther-flung native tribes, including the Tlingit and Haida of British Columbia and southeast Alaska. ⊠ N.E. 45th St. and 17th Ave. NE, University District ☎ 206/543–5590 ⊕ www.burkemuseum.org.

Tillicum Village. Located on Blake Island, 8 miles west of Seattle in Puget Sound, Tillicum Village offers a combination salmon bake and Native American stage show. Most visitors to the island travel aboard an Argosy Cruise ship; the four-hour tours are offered daily from May through September. Tours depart from Pier 55 on the Seattle waterfront. ⊠ Seattle ☎ 206/622–8687 ⊕ www.argosycruises.com/tillicum-village 🍴 $79.95.

Coast Salish arts and crafts can be found in many museums and galleries around Seattle. Some favorite sites for shopping include:

Seattle Art Museum Store (⊠ 1300 1st Ave., Downtown ☎ 206/654–3100 ⊕ www.seattleartmuseum.org)

Steinbrueck Native Gallery (⊠ 2030 Western Ave., Belltown ☎ 206/441–3821 ⊕ www.steinbruecknativegallery.com)

Stonington Gallery (⊠ 119 S. Jackson St., Pioneer Square ☎ 206/405–4040 ⊕ www.stoningtongallery.com)

CLOTHING

Buffalo Exchange. This big, bright shop of new and recycled fashions is always crowded, and it takes time to browse the stuffed racks—but the rewards are great: the latest looks from all the trend-heavy outfitters along with one-of-a-kind leather jackets and vintage dresses. As with all thrift stores, the selection can be hit or miss, but you can find some pretty great deals on high-quality clothing. Check out their smaller store in Ballard on N.W. Market Street. ⊠ *4530 University Way NE, University District* ☎ *206/545-0175* ⊕ *www.buffaloexchange.com.*

Crossroads Trading Co. Another spot on the used-clothing-store offerings on The Ave, Crossroads Trading Co. carries dependably cute and trendy clothes, bags, and accessories. Their buyers screen each item, so you won't be stuck poring over a rack of stained T-shirts. It's all clean, bright, and fun. A second location can be found on Broadway in Capitol Hill. ⊠ *4300 University Way NE, University District* ☎ *206/632–3111* ⊕ *www.crossroadstrading.com.*

Red Light Vintage and Costume. Nostalgia rules in this cavernous space filled with well-organized, good-quality (and sometimes pricey) vintage and new clothing. Fantasy outfits from decades past—complete with accessories—adorn the dressing rooms. It's a go-to spot for costumers, stylists and thrifters. Fun fact: this funky shop was one of the locations in Macklemore's "Thrift Shop" video. ⊠ *4560 University Way NE, University District* ☎ *206/545-4044* ⊕ *www.redlightvintage.com.*

MALL

University Village. Make a beeline here for fabulous upscale shopping and good restaurants in a pretty, outdoor, tree- and fountain-laden shopping "village." You can have your fill of chains like Williams-Sonoma, Banana Republic, L'Occitane, Hanna Andersson, Crate & Barrel, Sephora, Aveda, Restoration Hardware, H&M, Madewell, Apple, Anthropologie, and Kiehl's. If you get enough of that at home, however, there are a few unique gems among the batch, including the excellent Village Maternity Store, candy wonderland The Confectionery, and local artsy chain Fireworks. Note that parking here is a nightmare, and the atmosphere is slightly snobby. ■ TIP→ **If you're in the mood to brave it, go immediately to the free parking garage, even if it means you have to walk farther.** ⊠ *2623 N.E. University Village St., Suite 7, University District* ☎ *206/523–0622* ⊕ *www.uvillage.com.*

MARKETS

University District Market Farmers Market. An understated elegance pervades this farmers' market, where there are loads of flowers and fine cheeses and meats, as well as a small food court with a yummy selection of ready-to-eat foods. The market's held on Saturday in a parking lot; come summer, more than 60 farmers and vendors set up their goods. ⊠ *University Heights Center for the Community, University Way, at N.E. 50th St., University District* ⊕ *www.seattlefarmersmarkets.org.*

SHOES

Woolly Mammoth. A conservative take on Pacific Northwest footwear, this cozy shop offers brands like Naot, Keen, Dansko, and La Canadienne. The friendly and knowledgeable staff will happily help customers with hard-to-fit feet and help find the perfect shoe. ✉ *4303 University Way NE* ☎ *206/632–3254* ⊕ *www.woollymammothshoes.com.*

THE EASTSIDE

The core of Bellevue's growing shopping district is the Bellevue Collection (Bellevue Square Mall, Lincoln Center, and Bellevue Place) and the sparkling upscale mall called the Bravern. The community's retail strip stretches from Bellevue Square between N.E. 4th and 8th Streets to the community-centered Crossroads Shopping Center several miles to the east.

Best shopping: Bellevue Square and The Shops at the Bravern.

MALLS

Crossroads Shopping Center. Bellevue's most laid-back and least ritzy mall has become something of an old town square to the residential community around it. Midlevel retail, like Old Navy, Dress Barn, and Bed Bath & Beyond surround the open Public Market Stage and community rooms, where there's free live music, story hours, tax workshops, Tai Chi, knitting, and meditation workshops. A giant chessboard and playground are packed with families, and the Crossroads Cinema anchors the southeast corner. If you're hungry, there are more than 20 restaurants, or grab a bite at the farmers' market, Tuesday noon–5, May through October. ✉ *N.E. 8th St. and 156th Ave., Bellevue* ☎ *425/644–1111* ⊕ *www.crossroadsbellevue.com.*

The Shops at the Bravern. If you have some serious cash to burn, the sleek, upscale Bravern might be the Eastside spot for you. With high-end shops like Neiman Marcus, Hermès, Jimmy Choo, Salvatore Ferragamo, and Louis Vuitton, it's tempting to empty your wallet—but save room for a spa treatment at the Elizabeth Arden Red Door Spa or a meal at Northwest favorite Wild Ginger. Valet and complimentary parking (with validation) are available. ✉ *11111 N.E. 8th St., Bellevue* ☎ *425/456–8780* ⊕ *www.thebravern.com.*

7

SPORTS AND
THE OUTDOORS

Updated by
Kade Krichko

The question in Seattle isn't "Do you exercise?" Rather, it's "How do you exercise?" Athleticism is a regular part of most people's lives here, whether it's an afternoon jog, a sunrise rowing session, a lunch-hour bike ride, or an evening game of Frisbee.

The Cascade Mountains, a 60-minute drive east, have trails and peaks for Alpinists of all skill levels. Snoqualmie Pass attracts downhill skiers and snowboarders, and cross-country skiing and snowshoeing are excellent throughout the Cascades. To the west of the city is Puget Sound, where sailors, kayakers, and anglers practice their sports. Lake Union and Lake Washington also provide residents with plenty of boating, kayaking, fishing, and swimming opportunities. Farther west, the Olympic Mountains beckon adventure-seeking souls to their unspoiled wilderness.

Spectator sports are also appreciated here, from the UW Huskies (Go Dawgs!) to the Sonics, Seattle's beloved pro soccer team.

PARKS INFORMATION

King County Parks and Recreation. This agency manages many of the parks outside city limits. ⊠ *201 S. Jackson, Suite 700, Downtown* ☎ *206/477–4527 information* ⊕ *www.kingcounty.gov/services/parks-recreation/parks.*

Seattle Parks and Recreation Department. To find out whether an in-town park baseball diamond or tennis court is available, contact the Seattle Parks and Recreation Department, which is responsible for most of the parks, piers, beaches, playgrounds, and courts within city limits. The department issues permits for events, arranges reservations for facilities, and staffs visitor centers and naturalist programs. ⊠ *100 Dexter Ave. N, Central District* ☎ *206/684–4075* ⊕ *www.seattle.gov/parks.*

Washington State Parks. The state manages several parks and campgrounds in greater Seattle. ⊠ *1111 Israel Rd. SW, Olympia* ☎ *360/902–8844 for general information, 888/226–7688 for campsite reservations* ⊕ *www.parks.wa.gov.*

For Parks and Beaches coverage, see Neighborhoods.

BASEBALL

Seattle Mariners. The Seattle Mariners play at **Safeco Field,** a retractable-roof stadium where there really isn't a bad seat in the house. One local sports columnist referred to the $656 million venue—which finished $100 million over budget—as "the guilty pleasure." You can purchase tickets through Ticketmaster or StubHub; online or by phone from Safeco Field (to be picked up at the Will Call); in person at Safeco's box office (no surcharges), which is open daily 10–6; or from the Mariners team store at 4th Avenue and Stewart Street in Downtown. Priced dynamically based on day and opponent, the cheap seats start at $16; better seats cost $36 to $120, and the best seats go for upward of $500. ⊠ *1250 1st Ave. S, SoDo* ☎ *206/346–4000* ⊕ *seattle.mariners.mlb.com.*

BASKETBALL

Seattle Storm. The WNBA Seattle Storm has its season from May to mid-September. The Storm play at **KeyArena,** on the Seattle Center campus. Tickets cost $10–$126. ⊠ *KeyArena, 305 Harrison St., Downtown* ☎ *206/217–9622* ⊕ *www.wnba.com/storm.*

UW Huskies. Representing Seattle basketball in the Pac-12 Conference, the UW Huskies have made huge strides under the guidance of coach Lorenzo Romar. Along with several conference titles, the team has advanced to the NCAA Sweet Sixteen three times in a decade. The always-tough women's team—which also enjoys a very loyal (and loud) fan base—has advanced to the NCAA tournament several times in recent years, as well. **Alaska Airlines Arena at Hec Edmundson Pavilion,** known locally as "Hec Ed," is where the UW's men's and women's basketball teams play. Tickets are $6–$35. ⊠ *3870 Montlake Blvd. NE, University District* ☎ *206/543–2200* ⊕ *gohuskies.cstv.com.*

BICYCLING

Biking is probably Seattle's most popular sport. Thousands of Seattle-ites bike to work, and even more ride recreationally, especially on weekends. In the past, Seattle hasn't been a particularly bike-friendly city. But in 2007, city government adopted a sweeping Bicycle Master Plan, calling for 118 new miles of bike lanes, 19 miles of bike paths, and countless route signs and lane markings throughout the city by 2017. The plan can't erase the hills, though—only masochists should attempt Queen Anne Hill and Phinney Ridge. Fortunately, all city buses have easy-to-use bike racks (on the front of the buses, below the windshield) and drivers are used to waiting for cyclists to load and unload their bikes. If you're not comfortable biking in urban traffic—and there is a lot of urban traffic to contend with here—you can do a combination bus-and-bike tour of the city or stick to the car-free Burke-Gilman Trail.

Seattle drivers are fairly used to sharing the road with cyclists. With the exception of the occasional road-rager or clueless cell-phone talker, drivers usually leave a generous amount of room when passing; however, there are biking fatalities every year, so be alert and cautious, especially when approaching blind intersections, of which Seattle has many. You must wear a helmet at all times (it's the law) and be sure to lock up your bike—bikes do get stolen, even in quiet residential neighborhoods.

The Seattle Parks Department sponsors Bicycle Sundays on various weekends from May through September. On these Sundays, a 4-mile stretch of Lake Washington Boulevard—from Mt. Baker Beach to Seward Park—is closed to motor vehicles. Many riders continue around the 2-mile loop at Seward Park and back to Mt. Baker Beach to complete a 10-mile, car-free ride. Check with the **Seattle Parks and Recreation Department** (☎ 206/684–4075 ⊕ www.seattle.gov/parks/bicyclesunday) for a complete schedule.

The trail that circles **Green Lake** is popular with cyclists, though runners and walkers can impede fast travel. The city-maintained **Burke-Gilman Trail**, a slightly less congested path, follows an abandoned railroad line 14 miles, roughly following Seattle's waterfront from Ballard to Kenmore, at the north end of Lake Washington. (From there, serious cyclists can continue on the Sammamish River Trail to Marymoor Park in Redmond; in all, the trail spans 42 miles between Seattle and Issaquah.) **Discovery Park** is a very tranquil place to tool around in. **Myrtle Edwards Park**, north of Pier 70, has a two-lane waterfront path for bicycling and running. The **islands of the Puget Sound** are also easily explored by bike (there are rental places by the ferry terminals), though keep in mind that Bainbridge, Whidbey, and the San Juans all have some tough hills.

King County has more than 100 miles of paved and nearly 70 miles of unpaved routes, including the Sammamish River, Interurban, Green River, Cedar River, Snoqualmie Valley, and Soos Creek trails. For more information contact the **King County Parks and Recreation** office (☎ 206/296–4232).

Cascade Bicycle Club. The Cascade Bicycle Club organizes more than 1,000 rides annually for recreational and hard-core bikers. The most famous of its events is the Seattle-to-Portland Bicycle Classic—or, as it's known around the state, the "STP." Cascade offers daily rides in Seattle and the Eastside that range from "superstrenuous" to leisurely, such as the relaxed rides to the Red Hook Brewery in Woodinville. ☎ 206/522–3222 ⊕ www.cascade.org.

Seattle Bicycle Program. The Seattle Bicycle Program was responsible for the creation of the city's multiuse trails (aka bike routes) as well as pedestrian paths and roads with wide shoulders—things, in other words, that benefit bicyclists. The agency's website has downloadable route maps; you can also call the number listed to request a free full-color printed version of the Seattle Bicycling Guide Map. ☎ 206/684–7583 ⊕ www.seattle.gov/transportation/bikeprogram.htm.

Washington Bikes. The state's largest cycling advocacy group is a great source for information. ✉ 314 1st Ave. S, Pioneer Square ☎ 206/224–9252 ⊕ www.wabikes.org.

Continued on page 256

THE BALLARD LOCKS AND SEATTLE'S MANY WATERWAYS

by Nick Horton

DID YOU KNOW?

More than 40,000 commercial vessels, private yachts, sailboats, and even kayaks pass through the Ballard Locks each year.

SEATTLE'S WATERWAYS

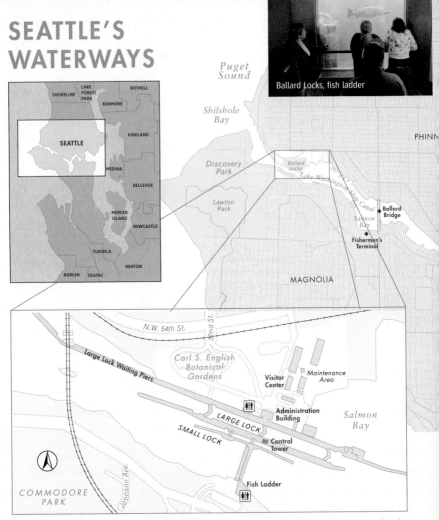

Ballard Locks, fish ladder

Puget Sound

Shilshole Bay

Discovery Park

Lawton Park

Ballard Locks

Lake Washington Ship Canal

Ballard Bridge

Salmon Bay

Fishermen's Terminal

PHINN

MAGNOLIA

N.W. 54th St.

32nd St.

Large Lock Waiting Piers

Carl S. English Botanical Gardens

Visitor Center

Maintenance Area

Administration Building

Salmon Bay

LARGE LOCK

SMALL LOCK

Control Tower

Johnson Ave.

Fish Ladder

COMMODORE PARK

SHORELINE, LAKE FOREST PARK, BOTHELL, KENMORE, KIRKLAND, SEATTLE, MEDINA, BELLEVUE, MERCER ISLAND, NEWCASTLE, TUKWILA, RENTON, BURLEN, SEATAC

From its earliest days as a tribal settlement to its current status as high-tech hub, Seattle has been defined by its lakes, canals, and bays. Everywhere you look there is water: To the west is the deep, chilly saltwater of Puget Sound, and to the east are the welcoming, warmer waters of Lake Washington. Linking the two is the Lake Washington Ship Canal, a bustling marine thoroughfare. This astounding network of waterways plays a vital role in Seattle's daily life, whether it is for livelihood, transport, recreation, or sweet summertime relaxation.

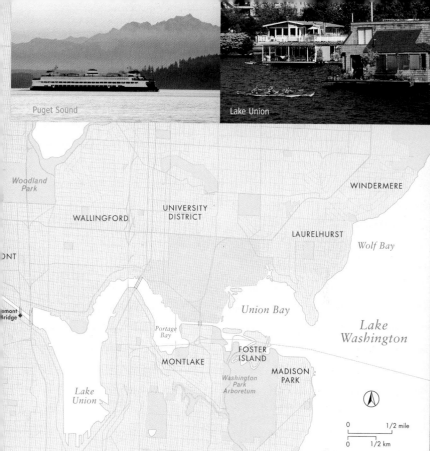

Puget Sound

Lake Union

WINDERMERE

Woodland
Park

WALLINGFORD

UNIVERSITY
DISTRICT

LAURELHURST

Wolf Bay

ONT

emont
Bridge

Union Bay

Lake
Washington

Portage
Bay

FOSTER
ISLAND

MONTLAKE

Washington
Park
Arboretum

MADISON
PARK

Lake
Union

0   1/2 mile

0   1/2 km

Each of Seattle's bodies of water has a unique appeal. At 33 mi in length, **Lake Washington** is the city's largest lake. Come summer, it's a pleasure boater's paradise, often speckled with kayaks, motorboats, sailboats, and multimillion-dollar yachts. Its many beaches become crowded with sunbathers.

From Lake Washington, vessels may travel west via the Lake Washington Ship Canal toward **Lake Union**, a smaller, more urban lake that is the center of the city's maritime industry. The shoreline here is lined by yacht brokerages and shipyards, but Lake Union isn't all business. It hosts weekly sailing regattas and an annual Fourth of July fireworks show. In addition, its northern shores are rife with houseboats—including the home made famous in the film *Sleepless in Seattle*. These live-aboard communities are the dwellings of well-off yuppies, eccentric sailors, and grizzled fishermen alike.

Traveling farther west, the Ship Canal leads vessels under the Fremont and Ballard bridges toward the bustling docks at **Fishermen's Terminal**, home to the city's vibrant fleet of commercial fishing boats. Finally, the canal leads through the **Ballard Locks**—the final step in a miles-long journey to **Puget Sound**, where oceangoing cargo ships sail in and out of Seattle's booming port.

THE BALLARD LOCKS

Hiram M. Chittenden

In the 1850s, when Seattle was founded, Lake Washington and Lake Union were inaccessible from the tantalizingly close Puget Sound. The city's founding fathers—most notably, Thomas Mercer in 1854—began dreaming of a canal that would connect the freshwater lakes and the Sound.

The lure of freshwater moorage and easier transport of timber and coal proved powerful, but it wasn't until 1917 that General Hiram M. Chittenden and the Army Corps of Engineers completed the Lake Washington Ship Canal and the locks that officially bear his name. More than 90 years later, the Ballard Locks, as they are more commonly known, are still going strong. Tens of thousands of boaters pass through the Locks each year, carrying over a million tons of commercial products—including seafood, fuel, and building materials.

THE LOCKS ESSENTIALS

- ✉ 3015 N.W. 54th St., Seattle, WA 98107
- ☎ 206/783-7059 (visitor center)
- 🌐 www.ci.seattle.wa.us/tour/locks.htm (City of Seattle)
- 🕑 Grounds are open 7 AM–9 PM year-round; fish ladder is open 7 AM–8:45 PM year-round; visitor center is open 10 AM–6 PM daily from May 1 through Sept. 30 and Thurs.–Mon. 10 AM–4 PM from Oct. 1 through April 30

Best time to visit: The salmon runs and recreational boat traffic are most active from mid-June through mid-September.

Public transportation from downtown: Metro Route 17 runs from downtown Seattle to Ballard/Sunset Hill, and includes a stop at the Locks. Buses run approximately twice per hour from 5 AM–11 PM. The fare is $2.

Ample public parking ($2/hr) is available at the entrance to the Locks.

The Locks are one of the city's most popular attractions, receiving more than one million visitors annually. Families picnic beneath oak trees in the adjacent 7-acre Carl S. English Botanical Gardens; jazz bands serenade visitors on summer Sundays; and steel-tinted salmon awe spectators as they climb a 21-step fish ladder en route to their freshwater spawning grounds—a heroic journey from the Pacific to the base of the Cascade Mountains. Hummingbirds flit from flower to flower in the nearby gardens, and the occasional sea lion can be spotted to the west of the Locks, snacking on unsuspecting salmon.

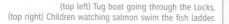

(top left) Tug boat going through the Locks, (top right) Children watching salmon swim the fish ladder.

FISH AT THE LOCKS

Chinook (king): Chinook tend to arrive at the locks in July, with late August being the best time to view them.

Coho (silver): Primetime coho viewing occurs in late September.

Sockeye (red): July is the peak time to view these fish, which gradually turn red as they migrate upstream.

Steelhead: Peak steelhead viewing occurs from mid-February through the end of March.

MIGRATING FISH

In a place where engineering has reshaped the natural landscape, it comes as a surprise that the most alluring and electrifying attraction at the Ballard Locks may be nature itself. Every summer, the fish ladder here flashes to life, and Seattle comes to watch.

Thousands upon thousands of migrating salmon pass through the ladder each year, making their way to freshwater spawning grounds in rivers and lakes throughout the region. They traverse the ladder's 21 steps, headed for the streams of their birth and distant gravel beds that will soon be their graves, as well. But their journey isn't in vain: The salmon carry with them the seeds of the next generation. It's a miraculous and mysterious voyage, and the fish ladder at the Locks is a wonderful place to witness it.

BEST BETS ON SEATTLE'S WATERS

LAKE WASHINGTON

BEACHES: The hands-down favorite sun-and-swim spots in Seattle are **Madison Park** (✉ E. Madison St. and E. Howe St. ☎ 206/684–4075) and **Matthews Beach** (✉ Sand Point Way NE and NE 93rd St. ☎ 206/684–4075).

BEACHSIDE PARK: Seward Park (✉ 5895 Lake Washington Blvd. S ☎ 206/684–4075) is a 300-acre piece of woodland along the Lake's western shore, and is a great spot for eagle-watching and trail walking.

CRUISE IT: Argosy Cruises (✉ 1101 Alaskan Way #201 ☎ 888/623–1445; ⊕ www.argosycruises.com) offers thrice-daily cruises of the lakes, including a peek at the lakeside estate of Microsoft co-founder Bill Gates.

SUMMER FEST: Every summer, Seattleites welcome **Seafair** (⊕ www.seafair.com), a monthlong celebration of the summer, water, and sun. Events include a triathlon, parades, an air show featuring the Blue Angels, and a hydroplane race.

LAKE UNION

LEARN TO PADDLE: South Lake Union's **Center for Wooden Boats** (✉ 1010 Valley Street ☎ 206/382–2628 ⊕ www.cwb.org) is a wonderful resource for all things maritime, including small-boat rental and tours.

RENT A BOAT: Northwest Outdoor Center (✉ 2100 Westlake Ave. N, Suite 101, on West Lake Union ☎ 206/281–9694 ⊕ www.nwoc.com) has a large fleet of rentable kayaks, wetsuits, paddleboards, and more.

QUACK: Ride the **Ducks of Seattle** (✉ 516 Broad St. ☎ 206/441–3825 ⊕ www.ridetheducksofseattle.com) offers 90-minute amphibian-vehicle tours around Seattle; the tour includes a brief cruise in Lake Union.

EAT AND PADDLE: Agua Verde Café and Paddle Club (✉ 1303 NE Boat St. ☎ 206/545–8570 ⊕ www.aguaverde.com), on Portage Bay, just west of Lake Union, rents kayaks by the hour; the upstairs café serves top-notch Mexican-American fare.

PUGET SOUND

RIDE A FERRY: Washington State Ferries (☎ 888/808–7977 ⊕ www.wsdot.wa.gov/ferries) serves twenty ports of call around Puget Sound. The Seattle to Bainbridge Island round trip is a pleasant jaunt from the Downtown area.

CRUISE IT: Argosy Cruises (✉ 1101 Alaskan Way ☎ 888/623–1445 ⊕ www.argosycruises.com) offers sightseeing tours of Puget Sound; some include a trip through the Locks.

GO WEST: West Seattle's **Alki Beach** is a great summertime hangout. **Alki Kayak** Tours (✉ 1660 Harbor Ave SW ☎ 206/953–0237 ⊕ www.kayakalki.com) leads guided sunset tours for beginners and offers rentals to experienced paddlers.

EAT AT RAY'S: At the far western edge of Ballard is **Ray's Boathouse** (✉ 6049 Seaview Ave NW ☎ 206/789–3770 ⊕ www.rays.com). The food is worth the trip, but it's the waterfront location and incredible sunsets that have made this place an institution.

7

(left) Seward Park, (center) kayaking in Lake Union, (right) Seattle Ferry in Puget Sound.

Biking around Seattle is a lovely way to spend an afternoon.

RENTALS

Montlake Bicycle Shop. This shop a mile south of the University of Washington and within easy riding distance of the Burke-Gilman Trail rents mountain bikes, road bikes, basic cruisers, and tandems. Prices range from $50 to $110 for the day, with discounts for longer rentals (credit card hold required). If you find yourself on the Eastside, you can rent a bike from its Kirkland branch. ⊠ *2223 24th Ave. E, Montlake* ☎ *206/329–7333* ⊕ *www.montlakebike.com* ⊠ *Kirkland Bicycle Shop, 208 Kirkland Ave., Kirkland* ☎ *425/828–3800* ⊕ *www.montlakebike.com.*

Pronto Cycle Share. With dozens of stations interspersed throughout the city, Pronto Cycle Share is the easiest way to hop on a bike. For $8, riders can rent a seven-speed road cruiser at one of Pronto's automated stations and drop the bike off at any of the city's other Pronto Cycle locations. The first 30 minutes is included in rental, with $2 for the next 30, and $5 for each 30 after that. Those looking for multiple rides can score a three-day pass for $16. Helmets are also included and can be picked up at each station. ☎ *844/677–6686* ⊕ *www.prontocycleshare.com.*

BOATING AND KAYAKING

Alki Kayak Tours & Adventure Center. For a variety of daylong guided kayak outings—from a Seattle sunset sea kayak tour to an Alki Point lighthouse tour—led by experienced, fun staff, try this great outfitter in West Seattle. In addition to kayaks, you can also rent stand-up paddleboards, skates, fishing boats, and longboards here. Custom sea-kayaking adventures can be set up, too. To rent a kayak without a guide, you must be an experienced kayaker; otherwise, sign up for one of the fascinating guided outings (the popular sunset tour is $69 per person). ✉ *1660 Harbor Ave. SW, West Seattle* ☎ *206/953–0237* ⊕ *kayakalki.com.*

Fodor's Choice ★ **Agua Verde Cafe & Paddle Club.** Start out by renting a kayak and paddling along either the Lake Union shoreline, with its hodgepodge of funky-to-fabulous houseboats and dramatic Downtown vistas, or Union Bay on Lake Washington, with its marshes and cattails. Afterward, take in the lakefront as you wash down some Mexican food (halibut tacos, anyone?) with a margarita. Kayaks and stand-up paddleboards are available March through October and are rented by the hour—$18 for single kayaks, $24 for doubles, and $23 for SUPs. It pays to paddle midweek: the third hour is free on weekdays. ✉ *1303 N.E. Boat St., University District* ☎ *206/545–8570* ⊕ *www.aguaverde.com.*

The Center for Wooden Boats. Located on the southern shore of Lake Union, Seattle's free maritime heritage museum is a bustling community hub. Thousands of Seattleites rent rowboats and small wooden sailboats here every year; the center also offers workshops, demonstrations, and classes. Rentals for nonmembers range from $24 to $40 per hour. There's also a $25 skills-check fee for sailing. Free half-hour guided sails and steamboat rides are offered on Sunday from 11 am to 4 pm (arrive an hour early to reserve a spot). ✉ *1010 Valley St., Lake Union* ☎ *206/382–2628* ⊕ *www.cwb.org.*

Green Lake Boathouse. This shop is the source for canoes, paddleboats, sailboats, kayaks, stand-up paddleboards, and rowboats to take out on Green Lake's calm waters. On beautiful summer afternoons, however, be prepared to spend most of your time dealing with traffic, both in the parking lot and on the water. Fees are $20 an hour for paddleboats, single kayaks, rowboats, and stand-up paddleboards, $30 an hour for sailboats. Don't confuse this place with the Green Lake Small Craft Center, which offers sailing programs but no rentals. ✉ *7351 E. Green Lake Dr. N, Green Lake* ☎ *206/527–0171* ⊕ *www.greenlakeboatrentals.net.*

Moss Bay Rowing Club. Moss Bay rents a variety of rowing craft—including Whitehall pulling boats, wherries, and sliding-seat rowboats—but sailboats are rented only to club members. Single kayaks rent for $16 per hour, doubles go for $22, and stand-up paddleboards are $18 an hour. You can also rent kayaks to take with you on trips outside the city; daily rates are $75 for singles and $100 for doubles. Lessons and sailing tours are also available. ✉ *1001 Fairview Ave. N, Lake Union* ☎ *206/682–2031* ⊕ *www.mossbay.co.*

Northwest Outdoor Center. This center on Lake Union's west side rents one- or two-person kayaks (it also has a few triples) by the hour or day, including equipment and basic or advanced instruction. The hourly rate is $16 for a single and $23 for a double (costs are figured in 10-minute increments after the first hour). For the more vertically inclined, the center also rents out stand-up paddleboards for $18 an hour. In summer, reserve at least three days ahead. NWOC also runs sunset tours near Golden Gardens Park and moonlight tours of Portage Bay. ✉ *2100 Westlake Ave. N, Lake Union* ☎ *206/281–9694* ⊕ *www.nwoc.com.*

Seafair. Seattle's rowdy Seafair festivities, which occur from mid-July through the first Sunday in August, include parades, a marathon, and many other events. The popular air show and hydroplane races are held at Lake Washington near Seward Park. ⊠ *2200 6th Ave., Suite 400* ☏ *206/728–0123* ⊕ *www.seafair.com.*

Seattle Yacht Club. In summer, weekly sailing regattas take place on Lakes Union and Washington. Contact the club for schedules. ⊠ *1807 E Hamlin St.* ☏ *206/325–1000* ⊕ *www.seattleyachtclub.org.*

Waterfront Activities Center. This center, located behind UW's Husky Stadium on Union Bay, rents three-person canoes and four-person rowboats for $10 an hour on weekdays and $12 an hour on weekends from February through October. You can tour the Lake Washington shoreline or take the Montlake Cut portion of the ship canal and explore Lake Union. You can also row to nearby Foster Island and visit the Washington Park Arboretum. ⊠ *3710 Montlake Blvd. NE, University District* ☏ *206/543–9433* ⊕ *depts.washington.edu/ima.*

Yarrow Bay Marina. The marina rents 19- and 22-foot Bayliner runabouts for $110 an hour. Ask about daily rates, as well. ⊠ *5207 Lake Washington Blvd. NE, Kirkland* ☏ *425/822–6066* ⊕ *www.yarrowbaymarina.com.*

FISHING

There's world-class fishing in the Puget Sound from July through September. Local salmon runs have been improving in recent years, and populations of pink (humpy) and coho (silver) salmon are actually booming. Most salmon fishermen fish from small boats throughout the Sound, but shore fishing is also popular throughout the region. Seattle has public piers along Shilshole Bay in Ballard's Golden Gardens Park, and Elliott Bay has public piers at Waterfront Park, near Downtown and Pioneer Square. Shilshole Bay charter-fishing companies offer trips to fish for salmon, rockfish, cod, flounder, and sea bass.

Lake Washington has its share of parks department piers as well. You can fish year-round for rainbow trout, cutthroat trout, and large- and smallmouth bass. Chinook, coho, and steelhead salmon can also be fished, but often are subject to restrictions. Popular piers include the Reverend Murphy Fishing Pier, located at Seward Park, and the East Madison Street dock, located at the far eastern end of East Madison Street.

Additional freshwater fishing can be found at Green Lake, which is stocked with more than 10,000 legal-size rainbow trout each year. Anglers can also vie for brown trout, largemouth bass, yellow perch, and brown bullhead catfish. The parks department maintains three fishing piers along Green Lake's shores: East Green Lake Drive at Latona Avenue NE, West Green Lake Drive North and Stone Avenue North, and West Green Lake Way North, just north of the shell house.

All anglers age 15 and older are required to purchase licenses, which are sold at more than 600 locations throughout the state. Check regulations in the "Sport Fishing Rules" pamphlet (available at most sporting goods stores) when you buy your license. A one-day license for saltwater and freshwater fishing is around $30. Visit ⊕ *fishhunt.dfw.wa.gov* for a list of locations.

Adventure Charters. Adventure Charters takes private groups out on six-person trolling boats to fish for salmon, bottom fish, and crab—depending on the season. The guided trips from Shilshole Bay Marina last for six or seven hours. The price per person is $185; license, tackle, and bait are included, and your fish will be cleaned or filleted and bagged for you. ⊠ *7001 SeaView Ave., Ballard* ☎ *206/789–8245* ⊕ *www.seattlesalmoncharters.com.*

Fish Finders Private Charters. Fish Finders Private Charters takes small groups of two or more out on Puget Sound for guided salmon and ling cod fishing trips. The cost is $225 per person and includes a fishing license. Morning trips last about six hours; afternoon trips are about four hours. All gear, bait, cleaning, and bagging are included in the fee. ⊠ *7001 Seaview Ave. NW, Ballard* ☎ *206/632–2611* ⊕ *www.fishingseattle.com.*

FOOTBALL

Seattle Seahawks. If you heard the earth rumbling on February 2, 2014, it was probably just Seattle. The entire city went nuts when their beloved team trounced the Denver Broncos and won the Super Bowl. Now it's harder than ever to get tix to see the Seattle Seahawks play in their $430 million arena, the state-of-the-art **CenturyLink Field.** Single-game tix go on sale in late July or early August, and all home games sell out quickly. They're expensive, too, leading the NFL in starting prices at $150 for the cheap seats. The average ticket ask-price averages more like $400. Note that traffic and parking are both nightmares on game days; try to take public transportation—or walk the mile from Downtown. **Fun local trivia:** The number 12—look around and you'll see it everywhere—refers to Seattle's "12th Man" phenomenon. The squad consists of 11 players and the fans are the 12th man. Just how serious are the Seahawks fans to earn such a title? The stadium gets so loud that it literally generates earthquakes. ⊠ *800 Occidental Ave. S, SoDo* ☎ *425/203–8000* ⊕ *www.seahawks.com.*

UW Huskies. The UW Huskies are almost as popular as the Seahawks. Home games are at the newly renovated **Husky Stadium,** a U-shape stadium that overlooks Lake Washington, where the Dawgs host some of the best teams in the nation. Tickets, which start around $35, go on sale at the end of July. ⊠ *University of Washington, 3800 Montlake Blvd. NE, University District* ☎ *206/543–2200* ⊕ *gohuskies.cstv.com.*

GOLF

Gold Mountain Golf Complex. Most people make the trek to Bremerton to play the Olympic Course, a beautiful and challenging par 72 that is widely considered the best public course in Washington. The older, less-sculpted Cascade Course is also popular; it's better suited to those new to the game. There are four putting greens, a driving range, and a striking clubhouse with views of the Belfair Valley. Prime-time greens fees are $29 to $45 for the Cascade and $40 to $70 for the Olympic. Carts are $16.50 prior to twilight and $10 after. You can drive all the way to Bremerton via I–5, or you can take the car ferry to Bremerton from Pier 52. The trip will take roughly 1½ hours no matter which way you do it, but the ferry ride (60 minutes) might be a more pleasant way to spend a large part of the journey. Note, however, that the earliest departure time for the ferry is 6 am, so this option won't work for very early tee times. ⊠ *7263 W. Belfair Valley Rd., Bremerton* ☎ *360/415–5433* ⊕ *www.goldmt.com.*

> ## WORK ON YOUR SHORT GAME
>
> **Hotel 1000.** If you don't want to set up a whole day of golfing, head to Hotel 1000 to use their state-of-the-art virtual driving range. Choose from 50 of the world's best courses, including Pinehurst #2 and the Old Course at St. Andrews; private instruction is available. Rates are $50 per two-hour session for up to two people. ⊠ *1000 1st Ave., Downtown* ☎ *206/957–1000* ⊕ *www.hotel1000seattle.com.*

The Golf Club at Newcastle. Probably the best option on the Eastside, this golf complex, which includes a pair of courses and an 18-hole putting green, has views, views, and more views. From the hilly greens you'll see Seattle, the Olympic Mountains, and Lake Washington. The 7,000-yard, par-72 Coal Creek course is the more challenging of the two, though the China Creek course has its challenges and more sections of undisturbed natural areas. This is the Seattle area's most expensive golf club—greens fees for Coal Creek range from $140 to $195 depending on the season; fees for China Creek range from $100 to $140. Newcastle is about 35 minutes from Downtown—if you don't hit traffic. ⊠ *15500 Six Penny La., Newcastle* ☎ *425/793–5566* ⊕ *www.newcastlegolf.com.*

Interbay Family Golf Center. About a 10-minute drive from Downtown, Interbay is the city's most convenient course. It has a wildly popular driving range ($10 for 70 balls, $12 for 108, $15 for 160), a 9-hole executive course ($17 on weekends, $15 on weekdays), and a miniature golf course ($8). The range and miniature golf course are open daily 7 am–10 pm March–October and 7 am–9 pm November–February; the executive course is open dawn to dusk year-round. ⊠ *2501 15th Ave. W, Magnolia* ☎ *206/285–2200* ⊕ *www.premiergc.com/interbay.*

Jefferson Park. This golf complex has views of the city skyline *and* Mt. Rainier. The par-27, 9-hole course has a lighted driving range with heated stalls that's open from dusk until midnight. And the 18-hole, par-72 main course is one of the city's best. Greens fees are $35 on weekends and $30 on weekdays for the 18-hole course; you can play the 9-hole course for $8.50 daily. Carts are $28 and $18, and $6 buys you a bucket of 34 balls at the driving range. You can book tee times online up to 10 days in advance or by phone up to 7 days in advance. ⊠ *4101 Beacon Ave. S., Beacon Hill* ☎ *206/762–4513* ⊕ *www.seattlegolf.com.*

West Seattle Golf Course. This 18-hole course has a reputation for being tough but fair—and for some excellent views of Downtown. Greens fees are $35 on weekdays, $40 on weekends. It's $14 per person for a cart. The front 9 will challenge you, while the back 9 will reward you with views of Elliott Bay and the skyline. ⊠ *4600 35th Ave. SW, West Seattle* ☎ *206/935–5187* ⊕ *www.seattlegolf.com.*

HIKING

If there were ever a state sport of Washington, hiking would be it. The state is blessed with hundreds of miles of beautiful trails; Mt. Rainier National Park alone has enough to keep you busy (and awestruck) for months. If hiking is a high priority for you, and if you have more than a few days in town, your best bet is to grab a hiking book or check out the sites ⊕ *www.wta.org* and ⊕ *www.cooltrails.com*, rent a car, and head out to the Olympics or east to the Cascades. If you have to stay close to the city, don't despair: there are many beautiful walks within town and many gratifying hikes only an hour away.

■ **TIP→** Within Seattle city limits, the best nature trails can be found in Discovery Park, Lincoln Park, Seward Park, and at the Washington Park Arboretum.

Walking the Burke-Gilman Trail from Fremont to its midway point at Matthews Beach Park (north of the U-District) would take several hours and cover more than 7 miles. You'll get a good glimpse of all sides of Seattle; the trail winds through both urban areas and leafier residential areas, and the first part of the walk takes you right along the Lake Washington Ship Canal.

OUTSIDE SEATTLE

Bridle Trails State Park. Though most of the travelers on the trails in this Bellevue park are on horseback, the 28 miles of paths are popular with hikers, too. The 482-acre park consists mostly of lowland forest, with Douglas firs, big-leaf maples, mushrooms, and abundant birdlife being just a few of its features. Note that horses are given the right-of-way on all trails; if you encounter riders, stop and stand to the side until the horses pass. ⊠ *Bridle Trails State Park, Bellevue* ✛ *From Downtown Seattle take I–90 or 520 E and get on I–405 N. Take Exit 17 and turn right onto 116 Ave. NE. Follow that road to park entrance.*

Cougar Mountain Regional Wildland Park. This spectacular park in the "Issaquah Alps" has more than 36 miles of hiking trails and 12 miles of bridle trails within its 3,000-plus acres. The Indian Trail, believed to date back 8,000 years, was part of a trade route that Native Americans used to reach North Bend and the Cascades. Thick pine forests rise to spectacular mountaintop views; there are waterfalls, deep caves, and the remnants of a former mining town. Local residents include deer, black bears, bobcats, bald eagles, and pileated woodpeckers, among many other woodland creatures. ⊠ *18201 S.E. Cougar Mountain Dr., Issaquah* ⊹ *From Downtown Seattle take I–90 E; follow signs to park beyond Issaquah.*

Larrabee State Park. This favorite spot has two lakes, a coastline with tidal pools, and 15 miles of hiking trails. The Interurban Trail, which parallels an old railway line, is perfect for leisurely strolls or trail running. Head up Chuckanut Mountain to reach the lakes and to get great views of the San Juan Islands. ⊠ *245 Chuckanut Dr., Bellingham* ⊹ *Take I–5 N to Exit 231. Turn right onto Chuckanut Dr. and follow that road to park entrance.*

Mt. Si. This thigh-buster is where mountaineers train to climb grueling Mt. Rainier. Mt. Si offers a challenging hike with views of a valley (slightly marred by the suburbs) and the Olympic Mountains in the distance. The main trail to Haystack Basin, 8 miles round-trip, climbs some 4,000 vertical feet, but there are several obvious places to rest or turn around if you'd like to keep the hike to 3 or 4 miles. Note that solitude is in short supply here—this is an extremely popular trail thanks to its proximity to Seattle. On the bright side, it's one of the best places to witness the local hikers and trail runners in all their weird and wonderful splendor. ⊠ *North Bend* ⊹ *Take I–90 E to Exit 31 (toward North Bend). Turn onto North Bend Way and then make left onto Mt. Si Rd. and follow that road to trailhead parking lot* ⊕ *www.mountsi.com.*

Fodor'sChoice   **Snow Lake.** Washington State's most popular wilderness trail may be
★   crowded at times, but the scenery and convenience of this hike make it a classic. Though very rocky in stretches—you'll want to wear sturdy shoes—the 8-mile round-trip sports a relatively modest 1,300-foot elevation gain; the views of the Alpine Lakes Wilderness are well worth the sweat. The glimmering waters of Snow Lake await hikers at the trail's end; summer visitors will find abundant wildflowers, huckleberries, and wild birds. ⊠ *Snoqualmie Pass* ⊹ *Take I–90 E to Exit 52 (toward Snoqualmie Pass West). Turn left (north), cross under freeway, and continue on to trailhead, located in parking lot at Alpental Ski Area* ⊕ *www.wta.org/go-hiking/hikes/snow-lake-1.*

ROCK CLIMBING

REI. Every weekend more than 250 people have a go at REI's Pinnacle, a 65-foot indoor climbing rock. An "open climb" takes place most Wednesdays from 6:30 to 8:30 pm with climbing from 1:30 to 6:30 pm on Friday and 11 am to 7 pm on weekends. It's $25 per person, ages 13 and up, and $15 for members. You can also hone your skills in regularly scheduled classes for children and adults of all skill levels. ⊠ *222 Yale Ave. N, Downtown* ☏ *206/223–1944* ⊕ *www.rei.com.*

Schurman Rock. The nation's first man-made climbing rock was designed in the 1930s by local climbing expert Clark Schurman. Generations of climbers have practiced here, from beginners to rescue teams to such legendary mountaineers as Jim Whittaker, the first American to conquer Mt. Everest. Don't expect something grandiose—the rock is only 25 feet high. It's open for climbs Tuesday–Saturday 10–6. Rappelling classes for kids are offered year-round at Camp Long, which is also the site of the only campground within the city limits. Campers can also rent cabins for $50 a night. ⊠ *Camp Long, 5200 35th Ave. SW, West Seattle* ☎ *206/684–7434* ⊕ *www.seattle.gov/parks/find/centers/camp-long/schurman-rock-at-camp-long.*

Stone Gardens Rock Gym. Beyond the trying-it-out phase? Head here and take a stab at the bouldering routes and top-rope faces. Although there's plenty to challenge the advanced climber, the mellow vibe is a big plus for families, part-timers, and the aspiring novice-to-intermediate crowd. The cost is $17; renting a full equipment package of shoes, harness, and chalk bag costs $10. There are "Climbing 101" classes most evenings for $50. ⊠ *2839 N.W. Market St., Ballard* ☎ *206/781–9828* ⊕ *www.stonegardens.com.*

SKIING AND SNOWBOARDING

Snow sports are one of the few reasons to look forward to winter in Seattle. Ski season usually lasts from late November until late March or early April. A one-day adult lift ticket at an area resort averages around $65; most resorts rent equipment and have restaurants.

Cross-country trails range from undisturbed backcountry routes to groomed resort tracks. To ski on state park trails you must purchase a Sno-Park Pass, available at most sporting goods stores, ski shops, and forest service district offices. Always call ahead for road conditions, which might prevent trail access or require you to put chains on your tires.

Road conditions. ☎ *800/695–7623* ⊕ *wsdot.wa.gov/traffic.*

Ski conditions. ☎ *206/634–0200 Cascade* ⊕ *www.skiwashington.com.*

State Parks Information Center. For information on cross-country trails and trail conditions, contact the State Parks Information Center. ☎ *800/233–0321* ⊕ *www.parks.wa.gov/winter.*

Alpental at the Summit. Part of the Summit at Snoqualmie complex, Alpental attracts advanced skiers to its many long, steep runs. (Giant slalom gold medalist Debbie Armstrong trained here for the 1984 Olympics.) A one-day lift ticket will run you $58–$66; equipment is another $40. The resort is 50 miles from Seattle, but it's right off the highway, so you (mostly) avoid icy mountain roads. ⊠ *Exit 52 off I–90, Snoqualmie Pass* ☎ *425/434–7669* ⊕ *www.summitatsnoqualmie.com.*

Crystal Mountain. Serious skiers and boarders don't mind the 2½-hour drive here (it's about 75 miles from the city). The slopes are challenging, the snow conditions are usually good, and the views of Mt. Rainier are amazing. A gondola whisks riders—and visitors who simply want to check out the views and eat at The Summit—up quickly and comfortably. Lift tickets cost $74 for a full day, $69 for a half day. Full rental packages run $45. There are only three lodging options on or near the mountain (Crystal Mountain Hotels, Crystal Mountain Lodging Suites, and Alta Crystal Resort). They tend to fill up on busy winter weekends, so book ahead if you want to stay the night. ✉ *33914 Crystal Mountain Blvd.* ☎ *360/663–2265, 800/695–7623 road conditions, 888/754–6199 snow report* ⊕ *www.crystalmountainresort.com.*

Hurricane Ridge Ski and Snowboard Area. The cross-country trails here, in Olympic National Park, begin at the lodge and have great views of Mt. Olympus. A small downhill ski and snowboarding area is open weekends and holidays; lift tickets are $12–$35. There's also a tubing/sledding hill. The Hurricane Ridge Visitor Center has a small restaurant, an interpretive center, and restrooms. Admission to the park is $25 per vehicle. Call ahead for road conditions before taking the three-hour drive from Seattle. ✉ *Olympic National Park, 17 miles south of Port Angeles* ☎ *360/565–3100, 360/565–3131 for road reports* ⊕ *www.hurricaneridge.com.*

The Summit at Snoqualmie. Chances are good that any local skier you ask took his or her first run at Snoqualmie, the resort closest to the city. With four ski areas, gentle-to-advanced slopes, rope tows, moseying chairlifts, a snowboard park, and dozens of educational programs, it's the obvious choice for an introduction to the slopes. One-day lift tickets cost $58–$66 for adults; equipment packages are $40 a day. The Nordic Center at Summit East is the starting point for 31 miles of cross-country trails. Guided snowshoe hikes are offered here on Friday and weekends. For Nordic skiers, the $21 trail pass includes two rides on the chairlifts. ✉ *Exit 52 off I–90, Snoqualmie Pass* ☎ *425/434–7669, 206/434–6708 for Nordic center* ⊕ *www.summitatsnoqualmie.com.*

Fodor'sChoice ★ **Whistler Blackcomb.** Whistler, 200 miles north of Seattle, is best done as a three-day weekend trip. (Just make sure your car has chains or snow tires.) And you really can't call yourself a skier here and not go to Whistler at least once. The massive resort is renowned for its nightlife, which is just at the foot of the slopes. When you arrive, you abandon your car outside the village—you can reach the entire hotel/dining/ski area on foot. A one-day adult lift ticket costs about $160 at the window, which includes access to the famous Peak 2 Peak gondola, a hair-raising ride between Whistler and Blackcomb mountains; you'll save if you buy a multiday pass in advance online. The area includes more than 17 miles of cross-country trails, usually open November–March. For diehard skiers and boarders who want an extended season, there's summer skiing on Blackcomb Glacier through July. ✉ *Hwy. 99, Whistler* ☎ *866/218–9690* ⊕ *www.whistlerblackcomb.com.*

TENNIS

Citywide Athletics Office. There are 151 public tennis courts in Seattle's parks. To reserve a court, call the Citywide Athletics Office. The rate for outdoor courts is $8 per hour. Indoor courts are $32. ☎ *206/684–4062* ⊕ *www.seattle.gov/PARKS/tennis.asp.*

SIDE TRIPS
FROM SEATTLE

MT. ST. HELENS

One of the most prominent peaks in the Northwest's rugged Cascade Range, Mount Saint Helens National Volcanic Monument affords visitors an up-close look at the site of the most destructive volcanic blast in U.S. history.

BEST TIME TO GO

It's best to visit from mid-May through late October, as the last section of Spirit Lake Highway, Johnston Ridge Observatory, and many of the park's forest roads are closed the rest of the year. The other visitor centers along the lower sections of the highway are open year-round, but overcast skies typically obscure the mountain's summit in winter.

Just 55 miles northeast of Portland, and 155 miles southeast of Seattle, this once soaring, conical summit stood at 9,667 feet above sea level. Then, on May 18, 1980, a massive eruption launched a 36,000-foot plume of steam and ash into the air and sent nearly 4 million cubic yards of debris through the Toutle and Cowlitz river valleys. The devastating eruption leveled a 230-square-mile area, claiming 57 lives and more than 250 homes. The mountain now stands at 8,365 feet, and a horseshoe-shape crater—most visible from the north—now forms the scarred summit. A modern highway carries travelers to within about 5 miles of the summit, and the surrounding region offers thrilling opportunities for climbing, hiking, and learning about volcanology.

PARK HIGHLIGHTS

Ape Cave. The longest continuous lava tube in the continental United States, Ape Cave is one of the park's outstanding attractions. Two routes traverse the tube. The lower route is an easy hour-long hike; the upper route is more challenging and takes about three hours. It's a good idea to bring a light source (although you can rent lanterns from the headquarters for $5) and warm clothing—temperatures in the cave don't rise above the mid-40s. In high season ranger-led walks are sometimes available; inquire at the **Apes' Headquarters** (*360/449–7800*), off Forest Service Road 8303, 3 miles north of the junction of Forest Roads 83 and 90. Although Ape Cave is open year-round, the headquarters closes from November through April. ⌧ *Cougar* ☎ *360/449–7800* ⊕ *www.fs.usda.gov/giffordpinchot.*

Johnston Ridge Observatory. The visitor center closest to the summit is named for scientist David Johnston, who was killed by the mountain's immense lateral blast, and stands at the end of the park's Spirit Lake Highway. Inside are fascinating exhibits on the mountain's geology, instruments measuring volcanic and seismic activity, and a theater that shows a riveting film that recounts the 1980 eruption. Several short trails afford spectacular views of the summit. ⌧ *2400 Spirit Lake Hwy., Toutle* ☎ *360/274–2140* ⊕ *www.fs.usda.gov/giffordpinchot* ⌦ *$8* ⊗ *Closed mid-May–early Nov.*

Spirit Lake Highway. Officially known as Highway 504, this winding road rises some 4,000 feet from the town of Castle Rock (just off I–5, Exit 49) to within about 5 miles of the Mt. St. Helens summit. Along this road are several visitor centers that interpret the region's geology and geography, and several turnouts afford views of the destruction wrought upon the Toutle and Cowlitz river valleys. Don't miss the **Mt. St. Helens Visitor Center at Silver Lake** (*Hwy. 504, 5 miles east of I–5, 360/274–0962, www.parks.wa.gov*) in Seaquest State Park, which shows video footage of the eruption, contains superb exhibits on the region's geologic beginnings, and houses a scale model of the mountain that you can actually climb through.

STAY THE NIGHT

Mt. St. Helens is in a remote area. You'll find a handful of chain motels in Kelso and Longview, about 10 to 15 miles south.

Patty's Place at 19 Mile House. For a memorable meal midway up Spirit Lake Highway, drop by this rustic roadhouse with a veranda overlooking the North Fork Toutle River—be sure to save room for the fresh-fruit cobblers. **Known for:** fruit cobbers; river setting. ⌧ *9440 Spirit Lake Hwy., Kid Valley* ☎ *360/274–8779* ⊗ *Closed Nov.–Apr.*

Lewis River B&B. In Woodland, 30 miles south of Castle Rock but right on Highway 503, the gateway for approaching great Mount St. Helens hiking from the south, the charming Lewis River B&B is a terrific lodging option. **Pros:** gorgeous, secluded setting; charming decor; delicious and filling breakfasts. **Cons:** a 40-minute drive from beginning of Highway 503. ⌧ *2339 Lewis River Rd., Woodland* ☎ *360/225–8630* ⊕ *www.lewisriverbedandbreakfast.com* ⌦ *7 rooms* ⎟⊙⎟ *Breakfast.*

8

Updated by
AnnaMaria
Stephens

The beauty of Seattle is enough to wow most visitors, but it can't compare to the splendor of the state that surrounds it. You simply must put aside a day or two to venture out to one of the islands of Puget Sound or do a hike or scenic drive in one of the spectacular mountain ranges a few hours outside the city.

If you head west to Olympic National Park, north to North Cascades National Park, or east to the Cascade Range, you can hike, bike, or ski. Two and a half hours southeast of Seattle is majestic Mt. Rainier, the fifth-highest mountain in the contiguous United States. Two hours beyond Rainier, close to the Oregon border, is the Mt. St. Helens National Volcanic Monument. The state-of-the-art visitor centers here show breathtaking views of the crater and lava dome and the spectacular recovery of the areas surrounding the 1980 blast.

You can get a taste of island life on Bainbridge, Whidbey, or Vashon—all easily accessible for day trips—or settle in for a few days on one of the San Juan Islands, where you can hike, kayak, or spot migrating whales and resident sea lions or otters.

Whatever trip you choose to take from Seattle, you'll be amazed at the scenery and wilderness that are immediately evident upon exiting the city. As you leave the city by ferry, the gorgeous Seattle skyline starts to fade as you get closer to the craggy, forested islands. As you drive toward your destination, whether into the Cascade National Park or toward Mt. Rainier, you'll encounter huge evergreen trees surrounding the road.

THE PUGET SOUND ISLANDS

The islands of Puget Sound—particularly Bainbridge, Vashon, and Whidbey—are easy and popular day trips for Seattle visitors, and riding the Washington State ferries is half of the fun. There are a few classic inns and B&Bs in the historic towns of Langley and Coupeville if you want to spend the night. It's definitely worth planning your trip around mealtimes because the islands of Puget Sound have top-notch restaurants serving local foods—including locally grown produce, seafood, and even island-raised beef. On Vashon Island, Sea Breeze farm's restaurant La Boucherie is at the top of the locavore pack; Bainbridge, Whidbey, and the San Juans also have a myriad of small farms and charming restaurants worth a visit. Seafood, of course, is a big draw. Local crab, salmon, and shellfish should be on your not-to-miss list, including the world-renowned Penn Cove mussels from Whidbey Island.

Whidbey Island has the most spectacular natural attractions, but it requires the biggest time commitment to get to (it's 30 miles northwest of Seattle). Bainbridge is the most developed island—it's something of a moneyed bedroom community—with higher-end restaurants and shops supplementing its natural attractions. It's also the easiest to get to—just hop on a ferry from Pier 52 on the Downtown Seattle waterfront. Vashon is the most pastoral of the islands—if you don't like leisurely strolls, beachcombing, or bike rides, you might get bored there quickly. Bainbridge and Whidbey get tons of visitors in summer. Though you'll be able to snag a walk-on spot on the ferry, spaces for cars can fill up, so arrive early. Whidbey is big, so you'll most likely want to tour by car (you can actually drive there, too, as the north end of the island is accessible via Deception Pass), and a car is handy on Bainbridge as well, especially if you want to tour the entire island or visit spectacular Bloedel Reserve. Otherwise, Bainbridge is your best bet if you want to walk on the ferry and tour by foot.

BAINBRIDGE ISLAND

35 mins west of Seattle by ferry.

Of the three main islands in Puget Sound, Bainbridge has by far the largest population of Seattle commuters. Certain parts of the island are dense enough to have rush-hour traffic problems, while other areas retain a semirural, small-town vibe. Longtime residents work hard to keep parks and protected areas out of the hands of condominium builders, and despite the increasing number of stressed-out commuters, the island still has resident artists, craftspeople, and old-timers who can't be bothered to venture into the big city. Though not as dramatic as Whidbey or as idyllic as Vashon, Bainbridge always makes for a pleasant day trip.

The ferry, which departs from the Downtown terminal at Pier 52, drops you off in the charming village of Winslow. Along its compact main street, Winslow Way, it's easy to while away an afternoon among the antiques shops, art galleries, bookstores, and cafés. There are two bike-rental shops in Winslow, too, if you plan on touring the island on two wheels. Getting out of town on a bike can be a bit nerve-racking, as the traffic to and from the ferry terminal is thick, and there aren't a lot of dedicated bike lanes, but you'll soon be on quieter country roads. Be sure to ask for maps at the rental shop, and if you want to avoid the worst of the island's hills, ask the staff to go over your options with you before you set out.

Many of the island's most reliable dining options are in Winslow—or close to it. You'll also find the delightful Town & Country supermarket on the main stretch if you want to pick up some provisions for a picnic, though you can also easily do that in Seattle at the Pike Place Market before you get on the ferry.

GETTING HERE AND AROUND

Unless you're coming from Tacoma or points farther south, or from the Olympic Peninsula, the only way to get to Bainbridge is via the ferry from Pier 52 Downtown. Round-trip fares start at $8.20 per person; round-trip fare for a car and driver is $29.20. Crossing time is 35 minutes. If you confine your visit to the village of Winslow, as many visitors do, then you won't need anything other than a pair of walking shoes. Out on the island, besides driving or biking, the only way to get around is on buses provided by Kitsap Transit. Fares are only $2 one way (ORCA cards accepted), but note that since routed buses are for commuters, they may not drop you off quite at the doorstep of the park or attraction you're headed to. Be sure to study the route map carefully or call Kitsap at least a day in advance of your trip to inquire about their Dial-A-Ride services.

Contacts Bainbridge Chamber of Commerce. ☎ *206/842–3700* ⊕ *www.bainbridgechamber.com.* **Kitsap Transit.** ☎ *800/501–7433* ⊕ *www.kitsaptransit.com.*

VISITOR INFORMATION
EXPLORING

Bainbridge Island Studio Tour. Twice a year (the second weekend in August and the first weekend in December), the island's artists and craftspeople are in the spotlight when they put their best pieces on display for these three-day events, and you can buy anything from watercolors to furniture directly from the artists. Even if you can't make the official studio tours, check out the website, which has maps and information on studios and shops throughout the island, as well as links to artists' websites. Many of the shops have regular hours, and you can easily put together your own tour. ✉ *Bainbridge Island* ⊕ *www.bistudiotour.com.*

Bainbridge Vineyards. Bainbridge Vineyards has 8 acres of grapes that produce small batches of Pinot Noir, Pinot Gris, and Siegerrebe; it's the only winery in the Seattle area that grows all of its own grapes. Fruit wines are made from the seasonal offerings of neighboring farms. It's open for tastings Friday–Sunday noon–5. ✉ *8989 Day Rd. E* ☎ *206/842–9463* ⊕ *www.bainbridgevineyards.com.*

Fodor'sChoice ★ **Bloedel Reserve.** This 150-acre internationally recognized preserve is a stunning mix of natural woodlands and beautifully landscaped gardens—including a moss garden, Japanese garden, a reflection pool, and the impressive former Bloedel estate home. Dazzling rhododendrons and azaleas bloom in spring, and Japanese maples colorfully signal autumn's arrival. Picnicking is not permitted, and you'll want to leave the pooch behind—pets are not allowed on the property, even if they stay in the car. Check the website's events page for special events, lectures, and exhibits. ✉ *7571 N.E. Dolphin Dr., 6 miles west of Winslow, via Hwy. 305* ☎ *206/842–7631* ⊕ *www.bloedelreserve.org* ✍ *$15.*

Woodinville Wineries

Walla Walla wine country is too far to go from Seattle if you've only got a few days. Instead, check out Woodinville's excellent wineries, only about 22 miles from Seattle's city center. You'll need a car unless you sign up for a guided tour. Check out ⊕ www.woodinvillewinecountry.com for a full list of wineries and touring maps. If you plan to spend a day or two in Woodinville, consider picking up a Passport to Woodinville Wine Country for $75. It includes a standard wine tasting at more than 60 participating wineries and tasting rooms (⊕ www.woodinvillewinecountry.com/passport).

WINERIES

There are more than 50 wineries in Woodinville, though most of them don't have tasting rooms. This list provides a good survey, from the big guys to the smallest boutique producers:

Chateau Ste. Michelle is the grande dame of the Woodinville wine scene, and perhaps the most recognizable name nationwide. Guided tours of the winery and grounds (which include a chateau) are available daily there's also a tasting room. Check the website for special events like dinners and concerts. ⊕ www.ste-michelle.com

Columbia Winery is another major player with a grand house anchoring its winery. Columbia's tasting room is open daily for regular tastings and private tastings. ⊕ www.columbiawinery.com

Novelty Hill-Januik is often described as the most Napa-esque experience in Woodinville. The tasting room for these sister wineries is sleek and modern and brick-oven pizza is available on weekends. ⊕ www.noveltyhilljanuik.com

DeLille Cellars is on the list of nearly every fancy restaurant in Seattle. Most recently it's garnered national acclaim for the predominantly cab-sauv blend Chaleur Estate. The Carriage House tasting room, slightly north of the winery, is open daily. ⊕ www.delillecellars.com

Mark Ryan is an indie winery that has earned praise nationwide for its use of mostly Red Mountain AVA grapes—especially for the Dead Horse reds. The winery has a small tasting room open daily. ⊕ www.markryanwinery.com

The Woodinville Warehouse District is a collective of dozens of wineries, breweries and distilleries around Woodinville. Print out a map for a self-guided tour if you want to explore the area ⊕ www.woodinvillewinecountry.com/wine/maps.

DINING AND LODGING

One of the swankiest hotels in the Puget Sound region, **Willows Lodge** (⊕ www.willowslodge.com) is only a few minutes away from the major wineries and next door to destination restaurant the **Herbfarm**. The hotel's restaurant, **The Barking Frog**, is also superb. For a simpler meal with an equally intense focus on wine, check out the Woodinville outpost of the **Purple Café and Wine Bar**.

8

Bloedel Reserve, Bainbridge Island

Fort Ward Park. On the southwest side of the island is this lovely and tranquil 137-acre park. There are 2 miles of hiking trails through forest, a long stretch of (sometimes) sun-drenched rocky beach, several picnic tables, and even a spot for scuba diving. Along with views of the water and the Olympic Mountains, you might be lucky and get a peek of Mt. Rainier—or of the massive sea lions that frequent the near-shore waters. A loop trail through the park is suitable for all ability levels, and will take you past vestiges of the park's previous life as a military installation. ⊠ *Fort Ward Hill Rd. NE* ⊕ *Take Hwy. 305 out of Winslow; turn west on High School Rd. and follow signs to park* ☎ *206/842–3931* ⊕ *www.biparks.org/parksandfacilities/pkftward.html.*

WHERE TO EAT

$ ✕ **Blackbird Bakery.** A great place to grab a cup of coffee and a snack
BAKERY before exploring the island serves up rich pastries and cakes along with quiche, soups, and a good selection of teas and espresso drinks. Though there is some nice window seating that allows you to watch the human parade on Winslow Way, the place gets very crowded, especially when the ferries come in, so you might want to take your order to go. Ⓢ *Average main: $5* ⊠ *210 Winslow Way E, Winslow* ☎ *206/780–1322* ⊕ *www.blackbirdbakery.com* ▭ *No credit cards* ⊘ *No dinner.*

$$ ✕ **Café Nola.** This is the best option on the island for something a little
BISTRO fancier than pub grub or picnic fare. The bistro setting is pleasant, with pale yellow walls, white tablecloths, and jazz music, and there's a small patio area for alfresco dining. Ⓢ *Average main: $22* ⊠ *101 Winslow Way E, Winslow* ☎ *206/842–3822* ⊕ *www.cafenola.com.*

$ ✕ **Harbor Public House.** An 1881 estate home overlooking Eagle Harbor
SEAFOOD was renovated to create this casual pub and restaurant at Winslow's
Harbor Marina, where a complimentary boat tie-up is available for pub
patrons. Local seafood—including steamed mussels, clams, and oyster
sliders—plus burgers, fish-and-chips, and poutine are typical fare, and
there are 12 beers on tap. $ *Average main: $16* ⌧ *231 Parfitt Way SW,
Winslow* ☎ *206/842–0969* ⊕ *www.harbourpub.com.*

VASHON ISLAND

20 mins by ferry from West Seattle.

Vashon is the most peaceful and rural of the islands easily reached from
the city, home to fruit growers, commune-dwelling hippies, rat-race
dropouts, and Seattle commuters.

Biking, beachcombing, picnicking, and kayaking are the main activities here. A tour of the 13-mile-long island will take you down country
lanes and past orchards and lavender farms. There are several artists'
studios and galleries on the island, as well as a small commercial district
in the center of the island, where a farmers' market is a highlight every
Saturday from May to October. The popular Strawberry Festival takes
place every July.

GETTING HERE

Washington State Ferries leave from Fauntleroy in West Seattle
(about 9 miles southwest of Downtown) for the 20-minute ride to
Vashon Island. The ferry docks at the northern tip of the island.
Round-trip fares are $5 per person or $18.60 for a car and driver.
A water taxi also goes to Vashon from Pier 50 on the Seattle waterfront, but it's primarily for commuters, operating only on weekdays
during commuter hours. One-way fares are $5.30. There's limited
bus service on the island; the best way to get around is by car or
by bicycle (bring your own or rent in Seattle. Note that there's the
huge hill as you immediately disembark the ferry dock and head up
to town). The site ⊕ *www.vashonchamber.com* is also a good source
of information.

VISITOR INFORMATION

Vashon-Maury Island Chamber of Commerce. The office is open Monday–
Saturday 10 to 3. ⌧ *17141 Vashon Hwy. SW, across from Ober Park,
Vashon* ☎ *206/463–6217* ⊕ *www.vashonchamber.com.*

EXPLORING

Jensen Point and Burton Acres Park. Vashon has many parks and protected
areas. This park, on the lush Burton Peninsula overlooking Quartermas-
ter Harbor, is home to 64 acres of secluded hiking and horseback-riding
trails. The adjacent Jensen Point, a 4-acre shoreline park, has picnic
tables, a swimming beach, and kayak and paddleboard rentals (May
through September). ⌧ *8900 S.W. Harbor Dr., Vashon* ✛ *From ferry
terminal, take Vashon Hwy. SW to S.W. Burton Dr. and turn left. Turn
left on 97 Ave. SW and follow it around as it becomes S.W. Harbor Dr.*
⊕ *www.vashonparks.org.*

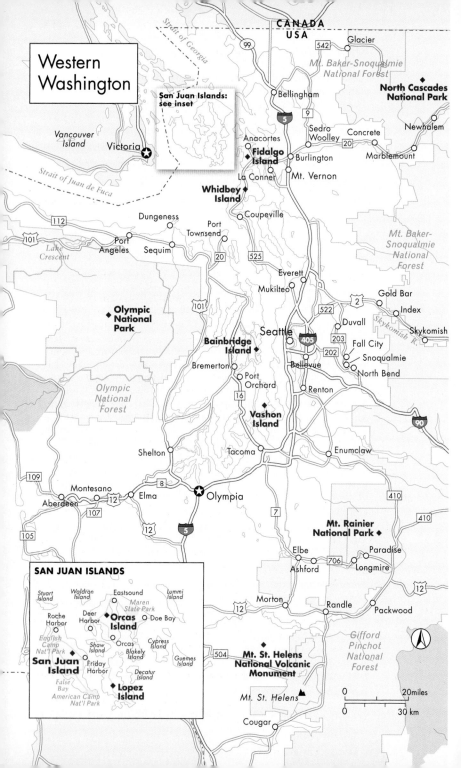

Point Robinson Park. You can stroll along the beach, which is very picturesque thanks to **Point Robinson Lighthouse.** The lighthouse is typically open to the public from noon to 4 on Sunday during the summer; call to arrange a tour or rent out the keeper's quarters by the week. ⊠ *3705 S.W. Pt. Robinson Rd., Vashon* ☎ *206/463–9602* ⊕ *www.vashonparks.org.*

Vashon Allied Arts. The best representative of the island's diverse arts community presents monthly exhibits and events that span all mediums, including dance, chamber music, and art lectures. The gallery's exhibits rotate monthly, featuring local and Northwest artists, and Heron's Nest (17600 Vashon Highway SW, 206/463–5252), the affiliated gift shop in town, is where you'll find fine art and handcrafted items by local artists. ⊠ *19704 Vashon Hwy.* ☎ *206/463–5131* ⊕ *www.vashonalliedarts.org.*

WHERE TO EAT

$$
AMERICAN
✕ **Hardware Store.** This all-day restaurant's unusual name comes from its former life as a mom-and-pop hardware shop—it occupies the oldest commercial building on Vashon, and certainly looks like a relic from the outside. Inside, you'll find a charming restaurant that's a cross between a bistro and an upscale diner. Ⓢ *Average main: $17* ⊠ *17601 Vashon Hwy. SW, Vashon* ☎ *206/463–1800* ⊕ *www.thsrestaurant.com.*

$$$$
FRENCH
✕ **La Boucherie and Sea Breeze Farm.** La Boucherie, the restaurant at the "beyond organic" Sea Breeze Farm, is a much-discussed outpost of local cuisine serving meats, poultry, and produce grown on or very close to the property. As a result, the menu is highly seasonal, but it always highlights Vashon's growers and farmers. Ⓢ *Average main: $125* ⊠ *17635 100th Ave. SW, Vashon* ☎ *206/567–4628* ⊕ *www.seabreezefarm.net.*

$
THAI
Fodor's Choice
★
✕ **May Kitchen + Bar.** Here's another reason for city dwellers to hop a ferry to come to Vashon for dinner. This is where sophisticated foodies swoon over delectable and highly authentic Thai dishes. Ⓢ *Average main: $15* ⊠ *17614 Vashon Hwy. SW, Vashon* ☎ *206/408–7196* ⊕ *www.maykitchen.com* ⊙ *Closed Mon. and Tues. No lunch.*

WHIDBEY ISLAND

20 mins by ferry from Mukilteo (20 miles north of Seattle) to Clinton, at the southern end of Whidbey Island, or drive north 87 miles to Deception Pass at the north end of the island.

Whidbey is a blend of low pastoral hills, evergreen and oak forests, meadows of wildflowers (including some endemic species), sandy beaches, and dramatic bluffs with a few pockets of unfortunate suburban sprawl. It's a great place for a scenic drive, viewing sunsets over the water, taking ridge hikes that give you uninterrupted views of the Strait of Juan de Fuca, walking along miles of rugged seaweed-strewn beaches, and for boating or kayaking along the protected shorelines of Saratoga Passage, Holmes Harbor, Penn Cove, and Skagit Bay.

The best beaches are on the west side, where wooded and wildflower-bedecked bluffs drop steeply to sand or surf—which can cover the beaches at high tide and can be unexpectedly rough on this exposed shore. Both beaches and bluffs have great views of the shipping lanes and the Olympic Mountains. Maxwelton Beach, with its sand, driftwood, and amazing sunsets, is popular with the locals. Possession Point includes a park and a beach, but it's best known for its popular boat launch. West of Coupeville, Ft. Ebey State Park has a sandy spread and an incredible bluff trail; West Beach is a stormy patch north of the fort with mounds of driftwood. At 35 miles long, Whidbey's island vibe is split between north and south; the historic southern and central towns of Langley and Coupeville are quaint and offer the most to do; Clinton (near the ferry terminal) isn't much of a destination, nor is the sprawling Navy town of Oak Harbor farther north. Yet Deception Pass at the island's northern tip offers the most jaw-dropping splendor, so plan enough time to visit both ends of the island. One fun way to see it all is to arrive via the Clinton ferry and drive back to Seattle via Deception Pass, or vice versa.

GETTING HERE

You can reach Whidbey Island by heading north from Seattle on I–5, west on Route 20 onto Fidalgo Island, and south across Deception Pass Bridge. The Deception Pass Bridge links Whidbey to Fidalgo Island. From the bridge it's just a short drive to Anacortes, Fidalgo's main town and the terminus for ferries to the San Juan Islands. It's easier—and more pleasant—to take the 20-minute ferry trip from Mukilteo (30 miles northwest of Seattle) to Clinton, on Whidbey's south end, as long as you don't time your trip on a Friday evening, which could leave you waiting in the car line for hours. Fares are $4.65 per person for walk-ons (round-trip) and $9.75 per car and driver (one way). Be sure to look at a map before choosing your point of entry; the ferry ride may not make sense if your main destination is Deception Pass State Park. Buses on Whidbey Island, provided by Island Transit, are free. Routes are fairly comprehensive, but keep in mind that Whidbey is big—it takes at least 35 minutes just to drive from the southern ferry terminal to the midway point at Coupeville—and if your itinerary is far-reaching, a car is your best bet.

Contact Island Transit. ☎ *800/240–8747* ⊕ *www.islandtransit.org.*

VISITOR INFORMATION

Central Whidbey Chamber of Commerce. The Chamber's website provides a great list of resources, from lodging to shopping, restaurants, and local events. ✉ *107 S. Main St., Coupeville* ☎ *360/678–5434* ⊕ *www. centralwhidbeychamber.com.*

Langley Chamber of Commerce. Start off the "Langley Loop"—an 8-mile scenic driving or biking tour—at the Chamber offices, which will point you in the right direction for South Whidbey's eclectic mix of restaurants, galleries, wineries, and markets. ✉ *208 Anthes Ave., Langley* ☎ *360/221–6765* ⊕ *www.visitlangley.com.*

LANGLEY

The historic village of Langley, 7 miles north of Clinton on Whidbey Island, is above a 50-foot-high bluff overlooking Saratoga Passage, which separates Whidbey from Camano Island. A grassy terrace just above the beach is a great place for viewing birds on the water or in the air. On a clear day you can see Mt. Baker in the distance. Upscale boutiques selling art, glass, jewelry, books, and clothing line 1st and 2nd Streets in the heart of town.

WHERE TO EAT

$$ BISTRO 🍴 **Prima Bistro.** Langley's most popular gathering spot occupies a second-story space on 1st Street, right above the Star Store Grocery. Northwest-inspired French cuisine is the headliner here; classic bistro dishes like steak frites, salade nicoise, and confit of duck leg are favorites. [$] *Average main: $21* ✉ *201½ 1st St., Langley* ☎ *360/221–4060* 🌐 *www.primabistro.com.*

WHERE TO STAY

$$$ B&B/INN Fodor's Choice ★ 🏨 **Inn at Langley.** Perched on a bluff above the beach, this concrete-and-wood Frank Lloyd Wright–inspired structure is just steps from the center of town. **Pros:** island luxury; lovely views; amazing restaurant. **Cons:** some rooms can be on the small side; decor is starting to feel slightly dated. [$] *Rooms from: $335* ✉ *400 1st St., Langley* ☎ *360/221–3033* 🌐 *www.innatlangley.com* 🛏 *28 rooms* 🍽 *Breakfast.*

$$ B&B/INN 🏨 **Saratoga Inn.** At the edge of Langley, this cedar-shake, Nantucket-style inn features cozy decor and fireplaces in every room. **Pros:** breathtaking views; cozy interiors. **Cons:** a bit rustic; some small bathrooms; minimum two-night stay. [$] *Rooms from: $195* ✉ *201 Cascade Ave., Langley* ☎ *360/221–5801, 800/698–2910* 🌐 *www.saratogainnwhidbeyisland.com* 🛏 *15 rooms, 1 carriage house* 🍽 *Breakfast.*

SHOPPING

Brackenwood Gallery. At this gallery known for its fine art and well-known Pacific Northwest artists, you can see pieces by Georgia Gerber, a famed island sculptor whose bronze pieces are regionally famous; Western-themed paintings and prints by Bruce Morrow; exquisite stone sculpture by Sharon Spencer; and Northwest landscape paintings by Pete Jordan. ✉ *302 1st St., Langley* ☎ *360/221–2978* 🌐 *www.brackenwoodgallery.com.*

Moonraker Books. Langley's independent bookshop, an institution since 1972, stocks a wonderful and eclectic array of fiction, nonfiction, cookbooks—and, according to the owners, "books you didn't even know you wanted until you stepped inside." ✉ *209 1st St., Langley* ☎ *360/221–6962.*

Museo. This contemporary fine art gallery focused on Northwest and regional artists is known for its glass art, sculpture, and handcrafted jewelry. Artist receptions are held on the first Saturday of each month from 5 to 7 pm. ✉ *215 1st St., Langley* ☎ *360/221–7737* 🌐 *www.museo.cc.*

GREENBANK

About halfway up Whidbey Island, 14 miles northwest of Langley, is the hamlet of Greenbank, home to a loganberry farm encircled by views of the Olympic and Cascade ranges.

EXPLORING

FAMILY **Greenbank Farm.** You can't miss the huge, chestnut-color, two-story barn with the wine vat out front—the centerpiece to this picturesque, 150-acre property. Greenbank's loganberry wines and dessert wines (for which they are famous) can be sampled daily in the tasting room. The adjacent Whidbey Pies Café creates gourmet sandwiches, soups, and pies, all of which disappear quickly as visitors head for the scattered picnic tables. There's also a specialty cheese shop. Bring your dog (or horse!) and walk the scenic meadow trails. The 1904 barn, which once housed a winery, is now a community center for farmers' markets, concerts, flea markets, and other events, including the famous Loganberry Festival each September. ✉ *765 Wonn Rd., Greenbank* ☎ *360/678–7700* 🌐 *www.greenbankfarm.com* 🎟 *Free.*

Meerkerk Rhododendron Gardens. The 53-acre Meerkerk Rhododendron Gardens contain 1,500 native and hybrid species of rhododendrons and more than 100,000 spring bulbs on 10 acres of display gardens with more than 4 miles of nature trails (a guided tour is available for $10). The flowers are in full bloom in April and May; summer flowers and fall color provide interest later in the year. The 43 remaining acres are kept wild as a nature preserve. Leashed pets are permitted on the gravel paths. ✉ *Hwy. 525 and Resort Rd., Greenbank* ☎ *360/678–1912* 🌐 *www.meerkerkgardens.org* 🎟 *$5.*

WHERE TO STAY

$ B&B/INN 🏨 **Guest House Cottages.** Surrounded by 25 secluded wooded acres, each of these six private cabins, resembling cedar-sided barns with towering stone chimneys, comes with a feather bed, a Jacuzzi, country antiques, a kitchen, and a fireplace. **Pros:** lots of privacy and amenities; good location between Langley and Coupeville. **Cons:** strict cancellation policy of 21 days; basic breakfast foods are provided but you have to make your own. [$] *Rooms from: $165* ✉ *24371 State Rte. 525 E, Christianson Rd., Greenbank* ☎ *360/678–3115, 800/997–3115* 🌐 *www.guesthouselogcottages.com* 🛏 *6 cabins* 🍴 *Some meals.*

COUPEVILLE

Restored Victorian houses grace many of the streets in quiet Coupeville, Washington's second-oldest city, on the south shore of Penn Cove, 12 miles north of Greenbank. It also has one of the largest national historic districts in the state, and has been used for filming movies depicting 19th-century New England villages. Stores above the waterfront have maintained their old-fashioned character. Captain Thomas Coupe founded the town in 1852. His house was built the following year, and other houses and commercial buildings were built in the late 1800s. Even though Coupeville is the island county seat, the town has a laid-back, almost 19th-century air.

EXPLORING

FAMILY Fodor's Choice ★ **Ebey's Landing National Historic Reserve.** The reserve encompasses a sand-and-cobble beach, bluffs with dramatic views down the Strait of Juan de Fuca, two state parks (Ft. Casey and Ft. Ebey; see separate listings), and several privately held pioneer farms homesteaded in the early 1850s. The first and largest reserve of its kind holds nearly 400 nationally registered historic structures (including those located within the town of Coupeville), most of them from the 19th century. Miles of trails lead along the beach and through the woods. Cedar Gulch, south of the main entrance to Ft. Ebey, has a lovely picnic area in a wooded ravine above the beach. ✉ *Coupeville* ✥ *From Hwy. 20, turn south on Main St. in Coupeville. This road turns into Engles Rd. as you head out of town. Turn right on Hill Rd. and follow it to reserve* 🌐 *www.nps.gov/ebla.*

Ft. Casey and Keystone State Park. The 467-acre Ft. Casey State Park, on a bluff overlooking sweeping views of Strait of Juan de Fuca and the Port Townsend ferry landing, was one of three forts (the "Triangle of Death") built after 1890 to protect the entrance to Admiralty Inlet from a naval invasion. Look for the concrete gun emplacement and a couple of 8-inch "disappearing" guns. The charming Admiralty Head Lighthouse Interpretive Center is north of the gunnery emplacements. There are also grassy picnic sites, rocky fishing spots, waterfront campsites, and a boat launch. A Washington State Discover Pass is required ($30/year or $10/day; see *www.discoverpass.wa.gov*). Once you're done exploring the park, take the ferry from here to Port Townsend for a quick side trip or long lunch. ✉ *2 miles west of Rte. 20, Coupeville* ☎ *360/678–4519* 🌐 *www.parks.wa.gov/parks* 🎟 *Discover Pass required; $30/year or $10/day.*

Ft. Ebey State Park. In late May and early June, Ft. Ebey State Park blazes with native rhododendrons. West of Coupeville on Point Partridge, it has 3 miles of shoreline, campsites in the woods, trails to the headlands, a freshwater lake for fishing, World War II gun emplacements, wildflower meadows, spectacular views down the Strait of Juan de Fuca, and miles of hiking and biking trails. A Washington State Discover Pass is required. ✉ *3 miles west of Rte. 20, Coupeville* ☎ *360/678–4636* 🌐 *www.parks.wa.gov* 🎟 *Washington State Discover Pass required ($30/year or $10/day).*

FAMILY **Island County Historical Museum.** Collections include Ice Age relics, mammoth remains, and a strong Native American collection, including cedar dugout canoes. The square-timber **Alexander Blockhouse** outside dates from 1855. Note the squared logs and dovetail joints of the corners—no overlapping log ends. This construction technique was favored by many western Washington pioneers. ✉ *908 N.W. Alexander St., Coupeville* ☎ *360/678–3310* 🎟 *$4.*

WHERE TO EAT AND STAY

$$ PACIFIC NORTHWEST 🍴 **Christopher's on Whidbey.** This warm and casual place is in a house one block from the waterfront. The menu features many Whidbey favorites, including local mussels and clams, and such flavorful fare as raspberry barbecued salmon, bacon-wrapped pork tenderloin with mushrooms, Penn Cove seafood stew, and linguine with a smoked-salmon cream sauce. [$] *Average main: $22* ✉ *103 N.W. Coveland, Coupeville* ☎ *360/678–5480* 🌐 *www.christophersonwhidbey.com* 🕒 *Closed Mon.*

$$$ SEAFOOD Fodor's Choice ★ 🍴 **The Oystercatcher.** A dining destination for foodies from across the Northwest is renowned for its local-inspired cuisine. The simple menu is heavily influenced by fresh, in-season ingredients. [$] *Average main: $30* ✉ *901 Grace St. NW, Coupeville* ☎ *360/678–0683* 🌐 *www.oystercatcherwhidbey.com* 🕒 *Closed Mon. and Tues. No lunch weekdays.*

$ B&B/INN 🏨 **Captain Whidbey Inn.** Over a century old, this venerable historic lodge on a wooded promontory offers a special kind of old-world romance and charm now rarely found, with gleaming log-walled rooms and suites. **Pros:** private cabins with hot tubs; rustic yet comfortable. **Cons:** poor soundproofing in the main motel; shared bathrooms. [$] *Rooms from: $103* ✉ *2072 Captain Whidbey Inn Rd., off Madrona Way, Coupeville* ☎ *360/678–4097, 800/366–4097* 🌐 *www.captainwhidbey.com* 🛏 *29 rooms, 2 suites, 4 cabins.*

This Historic Ferry House is part of Ebey's Landing National Historic Reserve on Whidbey Island.

$
B&B/INN
🏨 **Compass Rose Bed and Breakfast.** Inside this stately 1890 Queen Anne Victorian on the National Register of Historic Places, a veritable museum of art, artifacts, and antiques awaits you. **Pros:** wonderful hosts; great breakfast; full of interesting antiques and collectibles. **Cons:** only two rooms, so it gets booked up fast. $ *Rooms from: $140* ✉ *508 S. Main St., Coupeville* ☎ *360/678–5318, 800/237–3881* ⊕ *www.compassrosebandb.com* ▤ *No credit cards* ⇆ *2 rooms* ⦿ *Breakfast.*

OAK HARBOR

Oak Harbor, about 10 miles north of Coupeville, is the least attractive and least interesting part of Whidbey—it mainly exists to serve the Whidbey Island Naval Air Station, and has none of the historic or pastoral charm of the rest of the island. It is, however, the largest town on the island and the one closest to Deception Pass State Park. If you need to stock up on provisions, you'll find all the big-box stores here, in addition to major supermarkets. In town, the marina, at the east side of the bay, has a picnic area with views of Saratoga Passage and the entrance of Penn Cove.

FAMILY **Deception Pass State Park.** The biggest draw of the park is the historic two-lane Deception Pass Bridge connecting Whidbey Island to Fidalgo Island, about 9 miles north of Oak Harbor. Park the car and walk across in order to get the best views of the dramatic saltwater gorges and churning whirlpools below. Then, spend a few hours walking the 19 miles of rocky shore and beaches, exploring three freshwater lakes, or walking along the many forest and meadow trails. ✉ *Rte. 20, 9 miles north of Oak Harbor, Oak Harbor* ☎ *360/675–2417* ⊕ *www.parks. wa.gov* 🎫 *Daily Discover pass $10 per vehicle; annual $30 (valid at all state parks); campsite fees vary.*

THE SAN JUAN ISLANDS

Updated
by Andrew
Collins

The waters of the Pacific Northwest's Salish Sea, between mainland Washington and Vancouver Island, contain hundreds of islands, some little more than rocky reefs, others rising to nearly 2,500 feet. Among these, the San Juans are considered by many to be the loveliest.

About 100 miles northwest of Seattle, these romantic islands abound with breathtaking rolling pastures, rocky shorelines, and thickly forested ridges, and their quaint villages draw art lovers, foodies, and city folk seeking serenity. Inns are easygoing and well-appointed, and many restaurants are helmed by highly talented chefs emphasizing local ingredients.

Each of the San Juans maintains a distinct character, though all share in the archipelago's blessings of serene farmlands, unspoiled coves, blue-green or gray tidal waters, and radiant light. Offshore, seals haul out on sandbanks and orcas patrol the deep channels. You may see the occasional minke whale frolicking in the kelp, and humpback whales have become increasingly visible around the islands. You'll very rarely spy gray whales, which stick closer Washington's mainland.

There are 172 named islands in the archipelago. Sixty are populated (though most have only a house or two), and 10 are state marine parks, some of which are accessible only to nonmotorized craft—kayakers, canoes, small sailboats—navigating the Cascadia Marine Trail.

The San Juan Islands have valleys and mountains where eagles soar, and forests and leafy glens where the small island deer browse. Even a species of prickly pear cactus (*Opuntia fragilis*) grows here. Beaches can be of sand or shingle (covered in small pebbles). The islands are home to ducks and swans, herons and hawks, otters and whales. The main draw is the great outdoors, but there's plenty to do once you've seen the whales or hiked. Each island, even tiny Lopez, has at least one commercial center, where you'll find shops, restaurants, and history museums. Not surprisingly, many artists take inspiration from the dramatic surroundings, and each island has a collection of galleries; Friday Harbor even has an impressive sculpture park and art museum. Lavender and alpaca farms, spas and yoga studios, a whale museum and lighthouse tours—the San Juans have a little bit of everything.

THE SAN JUAN ISLANDS PLANNER

WHEN TO GO

This part of Washington has a mild, maritime climate. Winter temperatures average in the low 40s, while summer temps hover in the mid 70s. July and August are by far the most popular months to visit the three main islands—they can get busy during this time, with resorts, boating tours, and ferries often at capacity. To beat the crowds and avoid the worst of the wet weather, visit in late spring or early fall—September and early October can be fair and stunningly gorgeous, as can May and early June. Hotel rates are generally lower everywhere during these shoulder seasons—and even lower once often drizzly winter starts.

Orcas, Lopez, and San Juan islands are extremely popular in high season; securing hotel reservations in advance is essential. If you're bringing a car to the islands, be sure to book a ferry reservation well in advance. Or if you're traveling light and plan to stay put in one place in the islands, consider walking or biking on. Lot parking at Anacortes is $10 per day and $40 per week in summer and half that October–April.

FESTIVALS

Orcas Island Chamber Music Festival. This music festival comprises more than two weeks of "classical music with a view" in August. These concerts are immensely popular with chamber-music fans around the Pacific Northwest. ✉ *Orcas Island* ☎ *866/492–0003* ⊕ *www.oicmf.org.*

Savor the San Juans. Autumn has become increasingly popular thanks to the growth of this culinary festival, which runs about six weeks. It consists of an islands-wide series of events and gatherings celebrating local foods and beverages, including farm tours, film screenings, and harvest dinners. ☎ *360/378–3277* ⊕ *www.visitsanjuans.com/savor.*

GETTING HERE AND AROUND

AIR TRAVEL

Port of Friday Harbor is the main San Juan Islands airport, but there are also small airports on Lopez, Shaw, and Orcas Islands. Seaplanes land on the waterfront at Friday Harbor and Roche Harbor on San Juan Island; Rosario Resort, Deer Harbor, and West Sound on Orcas Island; and Fisherman Bay on Lopez Island. Daily scheduled flights link the San Juan Islands with mainland airports at Anacortes, Bellingham, and Lake Washington, Renton, and Boeing Field near Seattle. Some airlines also offer charter services.

If traffic and ferry lines really aren't your thing, consider hopping aboard a seaplane for the quick flight from Seattle. **Kenmore Air** offers several daily departures from Lake Union, Lake Washington, and Boeing Field, and from May through September **Friday Harbor Seaplanes** has up to four daily departures from Renton to Friday Harbor. Flying isn't cheap—around $130–$170 each way—but the scenic, hour-long flight is an experience in itself. Flights on **San Juan Airlines** from Bellingham and Anacortes run about $90 each way.

Air Contacts Friday Harbor Seaplanes. ☎ ⊕ www.fridayharborseaplanes.com. **Kenmore Air.** ☎ 425/486–1257, 866/435–9524 ⊕ www.kenmoreair.com. **San Juan Airlines.** ☎ 800/874–4434 ⊕ www.sanjuanairlines.com.

CAR TRAVEL

Most visitors arrive by car, which is the best way to explore these mostly rural islands comprehensively, especially if you plan on visiting for more than a couple of days. You can also park your car at the Anacortes ferry terminal ($10 per day or $40 per week high season, and half that fall through spring), as fares are cheaper and lines much shorter for passengers without cars. B&B owners can often pick guests up at the ferry terminal by prior arrangement, and you can rely on bikes and occasional taxis or on-island car or moped rentals (on San Juan and Orcas) for getting around. Also, in summer, a shuttle bus makes its way daily around San Juan Island and on weekends on

Orcas and Lopez islands. From Seattle, it's a 90-minute drive via Interstate 5 north and Highway 20 west to reach Anacortes.

Island roads are narrow and often windy, with one or two lanes. Slow down and hug the shoulder when passing another car on a one-lane road. Expect rough patches, some unpaved lanes, deer and rabbits, bicyclists, and other hazards—plus the distractions of sweeping water views. There are a few car-rental agencies on San Juan and Orcas, with daily rates running about $60 to $100 in summer, and as much as 25% less off-season. You'll likely save money renting a car on the mainland, even factoring in the cost of ferry transport (which in high season is about $45 to $65 for a standard vehicle including driver, plus around $14 per passenger, depending on which island you're headed to).

Rental Car Contacts M and W Rental Cars. ⊠ *725 Spring St., Friday Harbor* ☎ *360/376–5266 Orcas, 360/378–2794 San Juan* ⊕ *www.sanjuanauto.com.* **Orcas Island Rental Cars.** ☎ *360/376–7433* ⊕ *www.orcasislandshuttle.com.* **Susie's Mopeds.** ⊠ *125 Nichols St., Friday Harbor* ☎ *360/378–5244, 800/532–0087* ⊕ *www.susiesmopeds.com.*

FERRY TRAVEL

The Washington State Ferries system can become overloaded during peak travel times. Thankfully, the company recently implemented a long-awaited reservations system, which makes it far easier to plan trips and avoid lines. Reservations are highly recommended, especially in summer and on weekends, although a small number of spaces on every sailing are always reserved for standby; always arrive at least 45 minutes ahead of your departure, and as much as two hours ahead at busy times if you don't have a reservation. You'll find information on the Washington State Ferries website on up-to-minute wait times as well as tips on which ferries tend to be the most crowded. It's rarely a problem to get a walk-on spot, although arriving a bit early to ensure you get a ticket is wise. *For more information, see Getting Here and Around in individual islands below.*

Ferry Contacts Washington State Ferries. ⊠ *2100 Ferry Terminal Rd., Anacortes* ☎ *206/464–6400, 888/808–7977* ⊕ *www.wsdot.wa.gov/ferries.*

RESTAURANTS

The San Juans have myriad small farms and restaurants serving local foods and fresh-harvested seafood, and culinary agritourism—visiting local farmers, growers, and chefs at their places of business—is on the rise.

HOTELS

With the exception of Lopez Island, which has just a handful of inns, accommodations in the San Juans are quite varied and tend be plush, if also expensive during the high summer season. Rosario Resort & Spa on Orcas Island and Roche Harbor Resort on San Juan Island are favorite spots for special-occasion splurges, and both islands have seen an influx of either new or luxuriously updated inns in recent years. These places often have perks like lavish breakfasts and on-site outfitters and tour operators. *Hotel reviews have been shortened. For full information, visit Fodors.com.*

The view from Mount Constitution on Orcas Island, the highest point in the San Juans

VISITOR INFORMATION

Look to the San Juan Islands Visitors Bureau for general information on all the islands—the website is very useful.

San Juan Islands Visitors Bureau. ⊠ *The Technology Center, 640 Mullis St., Suites 210–211, Friday Harbor* ☎ *360/378–3277, 888/468–3701* ⊕ *www.visitsanjuans.com.*

LOPEZ ISLAND

45 mins by ferry from Anacortes.

Known affectionately as "Slow-pez," the closest significantly populated island to the mainland is a broad, bay-encircled bit of terrain set amid sparkling blue seas, a place where cabinlike homes are tucked into the woods, and boats are moored in lonely coves. Of the three San Juan Islands with facilities to accommodate overnight visitors, Lopez has the smallest population (approximately 2,200), and with its old orchards, weathered barns, and rolling green pastures, it's the most rustic and least crowded in the archipelago. Gently sloping roads cut wide curves through golden farmlands and trace the edges of pebbly beaches, while peaceful trails wind through thick patches of forest. Sweeping country views make Lopez a favorite year-round biking locale, and except for the long hill up from the ferry docks, most roads and designated bike paths are easy for novices to negotiate.

The only settlement is Lopez Village, really just a cluster of cafés and boutiques, as well as a summer market and outdoor theater, an upscale inn, a visitor information center, and a grocery store. Other attractions—such as seasonal berry-picking farms, small wineries, kitschy galleries, intimate restaurants, and one secluded bed-and-breakfast—are scattered around the island.

GETTING HERE AND AROUND

The Washington State Ferries crossing from Anacortes take about 45 minutes; round-trip peak-season fares are about $14 per person, $45 for a car and driver. One-hour flights from Seattle cost about $130 to $170 each way. You can get around the island by car (bring your own—there are no rentals) or bike; there are bike-rental facilities by the ferry terminal.

ESSENTIALS

Visitor Information **Lopez Island Chamber of Commerce.** ⊠ *Lopez Rd., at Tower Rd., Lopez* ☎ *360/468–4664* ⊕ *www.lopezisland.com.*

EXPLORING

Lopez Island Historical Museum. Artifacts from the region's Native American tribes and early settlers include some impressive ship and small-boat models and maps of local landmarks. You can also listen to fascinating digital recordings of early settlers discussing life on Lopez Island. ⊠ *Weeks Rd. and Washburn Pl., Lopez* ☎ *360/468–2049* ⊕ *www.lopezmuseum.org* 🖭 *Free* ☼ *Closed Mon., Tues., and Oct.–Apr.*

Lopez Island Vineyards. You sample wines from this popular wine-making operation at its tasting room right in the heart of Lopez Village. The vineyards and orchards, which themselves aren't open to the public, yield estate-grown white wines, including Madeleine Angevine and Siegerrebe; sweet wines using raspberries, blackberries, and other local fruits; and a number of reds sourced from eastern Washington's Yakima Valley, including Malbec and Sangiovese. ⊠ *265 Lopez Rd., Lopez* ☎ *360/468–3644* ⊕ *www.lopezislandvineyards.com* 🖭 *Free* ☼ *Closed Sun.–Tues. and late Dec.–mid-Mar., and most weekdays late Mar.–June and Oct.–mid-Dec.*

Fodor's Choice
★ **Shark Reef Sanctuary.** A quiet forest trail along beautiful Shark Reef leads to an isolated headland jutting out above the bay. The sounds of raucous barks and squeals mean you're nearly there, and eventually you may see throngs of seals and seagulls on the rocky islets across from the point. Bring binoculars to spot bald eagles in the trees as you walk, and to view sea otters frolicking in the waves near the shore. The trail starts at the Shark Reef Road parking lot south of the airport, and it's a 15-minute walk to the headland. ⊠ *Shark Reef Rd., Lopez* ✛ *2 miles south of Lopez Island Airport* 🖭 *Free.*

Spencer Spit State Park. Set on a spit along the Cascadia Marine Trail for kayakers, this popular spot for summer camping is on former Native American clamming, crabbing, and fishing grounds. A variety of campsites are available, from primitive tent sites to full hookups. This is one of the few Washington beaches where cars are permitted. ⊠ *521 A. Bakerview Rd., Lopez* ☎ *360/468–2251* ⊕ *www.parks.wa.gov/parks* 🖭 *$10.*

WHERE TO EAT AND STAY

$ ✕ **Haven Kitchen & Bar.** It's the rare kitchen that turns out such region-
AMERICAN ally diverse fare as Native American fry bread with honey, Spam musubi, made-to-order guacamole, and burrata with heirloom plum tomatoes, but this unassuming neighborhood tavern prides itself in offering a little something for everyone. Prices are reasonable, too, and the eclecticism carries through to the well-curated wine, beer, and cocktail lists. **Known for:** Spam musubi appetizer; expansive flower-lined outdoor deck; well-crafted artisanal cocktails. $ *Average main: $14 ⊠ 210 Lopez Rd., Lopez* ☎ *360/468–3272* ⊕ *www.lopezhaven. com* ⊗ *Closed Sun.–Tues.*

$ ✕ **Holly B's Bakery.** Tucked into a small, cabinlike strip of businesses set
BAKERY back from the water, this cozy, wood-paneled bakery has been a source of delicious fresh ham-and-Gruyere croissants, marionberry scones, slices of pizza, and other savory and sweet treats since 1977. Sunny summer mornings bring diners out onto the patio, where kids play and parents relax. **Known for:** ginormous, decadent cinnamon rolls; pizza by the slice; scones flavored with seasonal fruit. $ *Average main: $6 ⊠ Lopez Plaza, 211 Lopez Rd., Lopez* ☎ *360/468–2133* ⊕ *www. hollybsbakery.com* ⊟ *No credit cards* ⊗ *Closed Dec.–Mar. No dinner.*

$ ✕ **Vita's Wildly Delicious.** At this gourmet market and wine shop (open
CAFÉ primarily during the daytime but until 8 pm on Friday), the proprietors create a daily-changing assortment of prepared foods and some made-to-order items, such as Reuben panini sandwiches. Other favorites include Dungeness crab cakes, hearty meat loaf, lobster mac-and-cheese, and an assortment of tempting desserts. **Known for:** Dungeness crab cakes; pretty garden-dining area; gourmet picnic supplies. $ *Average main: $10 ⊠ 77 Village Rd., Lopez* ☎ *360/468–4268* ⊕ *www.vitasonlopez.com* ⊗ *Closed Sun., Mon., and late fall–late spring. No dinner.*

$$ ⚏ **Edenwild Inn.** Thoughtful and friendly owners Anthony and Crys-
B&B/INN tal Rovente operate this large Victorian-style farmhouse surrounded by gardens and framed by Fisherman Bay. Spacious rooms are each painted or papered in different pastel shades and furnished with simple antiques; some have claw-foot tubs and brick fireplaces. **Pros:** bikes and kayaks can be rented on-site; nice breakfast buffet using local produce and homemade baked goods; handy location close to village restaurants. **Cons:** no TVs in rooms. $ *Rooms from: $195 ⊠ 132 Lopez Rd., Lopez* ☎ *360/468–3238* ⊕ *www.edenwildinn.com* ⤳ *9 rooms* ⏐◯⏐ *Breakfast.*

$$ ⚏ **Mackaye Harbor Inn.** This former sea captain's house, built in 1904,
B&B/INN rises two stories above the beach at the southern end of the island and
Fodor'sChoice accommodates guests in cheerfully furnished rooms with golden-oak
★ and brass details and wicker furniture; three have views of MacKaye Harbor. **Pros:** fantastic water views; mountain bikes (free) and kayaks (reasonable daily fee) available; friendly and attentive hosts. **Cons:** on far end of the island; several miles from the ferry terminal and airport; some bathrooms are across the hall from rooms. $ *Rooms from: $175 ⊠ 949 MacKaye Harbor Rd., Lopez* ☎ *360/468–2253, 888/314–6140* ⊕ *www.mackayeharborinn.com* ⤳ *4 rooms, 1 suite* ⏐◯⏐ *Breakfast.*

8

SPORTS AND THE OUTDOORS

BIKING

Bike rental rates start at around $7 an hour and $30 a day. Reservations are recommended, particularly in summer.

Lopez Bicycle Works. At the marina 4 miles from the ferry, this full-service operation can bring bicycles to your door or the ferry. In addition to cruisers and mountain bikes, the shop also rents tandem and recumbent bikes. ⊠ *2847 Fisherman Bay Rd., Lopez* ☎ *360/468–2847* ⊕ *www. lopezbicycleworks.com.*

Village Cycle. This aptly named full-service rental and repair shop is in the heart of Lopez Village. ⊠ *214 Lopez Rd., Lopez* ☎ *360/468–4013* ⊕ *www.villagecycles.net.*

SEA KAYAKING

Cascadia Kayaks. This company rents kayaks for half days or full days The outfitter also organizes half-day, full-day, and two- to three-day guided tours. Hour-long private lessons are available, too, if you need a little coaching before going out on your own. ⊠ *135 Lopez Rd., Lopez* ☎ *360/468–3008* ⊕ *www.cascadiakayaks.com.*

Lopez Island Sea Kayak. Open May–September at Fisherman Bay, this outfitter has a huge selection of kayaks, both plastic and fiberglass touring models. Rentals are by the hour or day, and the company can deliver kayaks to any point on the island for an additional fee. ⊠ *2845 Fisherman Bay Rd., Lopez* ☎ *360/468–2847* ⊕ *www.lopezkayaks.com.*

ORCAS ISLAND

75 mins by ferry from Anacortes.

Orcas Island, the largest of the San Juans, is blessed with wide, pastoral valleys and scenic ridges that rise high above the neighboring waters. (At 2,409 feet, Orcas's Mt. Constitution is the highest peak in the San Juans.) Spanish explorers set foot here in 1791, and the island is actually named for one of these early visitors, Juan Vicente de Güemes Padilla Horcasitas y Aguayo—not for the black-and-white whales that frolic in the surrounding waters. The island was also the home of Native American tribes, whose history is reflected in such places as Pole Pass, where the Lummi people used kelp and cedar-bark nets to catch ducks, and Massacre Bay, where in 1858 a tribe from southeast Alaska attacked a Lummi fishing village.

Today farmers, fishermen, artists, retirees, and summer-home owners make up the population of about 4,500. Houses are spaced far apart, and the island's few hamlets typically have just one major road running through them. Low-key resorts dotting the island's edges are evidence of the thriving local tourism industry, as is the gradual but steady influx of urbane restaurants, boutiques, and even a trendy late-night bar in the main village of Eastsound. The beauty of this island is beyond compare; Orcas is a favorite place for weekend getaways from the Seattle area any time of the year, as well as one of the state's top settings for summer weddings.

The main town on Orcas Island lies at the head of the East Sound channel, which nearly divides the island in two. More than 20 small shops and boutiques here sell jewelry, pottery, and crafts by local artisans, as well as gourmet edibles, from baked goods to chocolates.

GETTING HERE AND AROUND

The Washington State Ferries crossing from Anacortes to Orcas Village, in the island's Westsound area, takes about 75 minutes; peak-season round-trip fares are about $14 per person, $55 for a car and driver. One-hour flights from Seattle cost about $130 to $170 each way. Planes land at Deer Harbor, Eastsound, Westsound, and at the Rosario Resort and Spa.

The best way to get around the island is by car—bikes will do in a pinch, but the hilly, curvy roads that generally lack shoulders make cycling a bit risky. Most resorts and inns offer transfers from the ferry terminal.

ESSENTIALS

Visitor Information Orcas Island Chamber of Commerce & Visitor Center.
✉ *65 N. Beach Rd.* ☎ *360/376–2273* ⊕ *www.orcasislandchamber.com.*

EXPLORING

Moran Museum at Rosario. This 1909 mansion that forms the centerpiece of Rosario Resort was constructed as the vacation home of Seattle shipping magnate and mayor Robert Moran. On the second floor is this fascinating museum that spans several former guest rooms and includes old photos, furniture, and memorabilia related to the Moran family, the resort's history, and the handsome ships built by Moran and his brothers. A highlight is the music room, which contains an incredible two-story 1913 aeolian pipe organ and an ornate, original Tiffany chandelier. Renowned musician Christopher Peacock discusses the resort's history and performs on the 1900 Steinway grand piano daily (except Sunday) at 4 pm in summer, and on Saturday at 4 the rest of the year. The surrounding grounds make for a lovely stroll, which you might combine with lunch or a cocktail in one of the resort's water-view restaurants. ✉ *1400 Rosario Rd.* ☎ *360/376–2222* ⊕ *www. rosarioresort.com/museum* 🎟 *Free.*

NEED A BREAK

✕ **Brown Bear Baking.** You might make it a point to get to this wildly popular village bakery by late morning—come midafternoon, many of the best treats are sold out. Delectables here include flaky almond-coated bear paw pastries, rich croque monsieur sandwiches, hubcap-sized "Sasquatch" cookies, Tuscan olive bread, and moist blueberry muffins. Known for: almond-coated bear paw pastries; alfresco dining on the patio. ✉ *29 N. Beach Rd.* ☎ *360/855–7456* ⊕ *www.facebook.com/brownbearbaking.*

FAMILY
Fodor's Choice
★

Moran State Park. This pristine patch of wilderness comprises 5,252 acres of hilly, old-growth forests dotted with sparkling lakes, in the middle of which rises the island's highest point, 2,409-foot Mt. Constitution. A drive to the summit affords exhilarating views of the islands, the Cascades, the Olympics, and Vancouver Island, and avid hikers enjoy the strenuous but stunning 7-mile round-trip trek from rippling Mountain Lake to the summit (some 38 miles of trails traverse the

8

entire park). The observation tower on the summit was built by the Civilian Conservation Corps in the 1930s. In summer, you can rent boats to paddle around beautiful Cascade Lake. ✉ *Mt. Constitution Rd.* ☎ *360/376–2326* 🌐 *www.parks.wa.gov/parks* 🎟 *$10.*

Orcas Island Historical Museum. Surrounded by Eastsound's lively shops and cafés, this museum comprises several reassembled and relocated late-19th-century pioneer cabins. An impressive collection of more than 6,000 photographs, documents, and artifacts tells the story of the island's Native American and Anglo history, and in an oral-history exhibit longtime residents of the island talk about how the community has evolved over the decades. The museum also operates the 1888 Crow Valley Schoolhouse, which is open on summer Wednesdays and Saturdays; call the museum for hours and directions. ✉ *181 N. Beach Rd.* ☎ *360/376–4849* 🌐 *www.orcasmuseum.org* 🎟 *$5* ⏲ *Closed Oct.–May, Sun.–Tues.*

Fodor's Choice ★ **Turtleback Mountain Preserve.** A more peaceful, less crowded hiking and wildlife-watching alternative to Moran State Park, this 1,576-acre expanse of rugged ridges, wildflower-strewn meadows, temperate rain forest, and lush wetlands is one of the natural wonders of the archipelago. Because the San Juan County Land Bank purchased this land in 2006, it will be preserved forever for the public to enjoy. There are 8 miles of well-groomed trails, including a steep trek up to 1,519-foot-elevation Raven Ridge and a windy hike to Turtlehead Point, a soaring bluff with spectacular views west of San Juan Island and Vancouver Island beyond that—it's an amazing place to watch the sunset. You can access the preserve either from the North Trailhead, which is just 3 miles southwest of Eastsound on Crow Valley Road, or the South Trailhead, which is 3 miles northeast of Deer Harbor off Wild Rose Lane—check the website for a trail map and detailed directions. ✉ *North Trailhead parking, Crow Valley Rd., just south of Crow Valley Schoolhouse* ☎ *360/378–4402* 🌐 *www.sjclandbank.org/turtle_back.html* 🎟 *Free.*

WHERE TO EAT

$$ PACIFIC NORTHWEST Fodor's Choice ★ 🍴 **Doe Bay Cafe.** Most of the tables in this warmly rustic dining room at Doe Bay Resort overlook the tranquil body of water for which the café is named. This is a popular stop for brunch or dinner before or after hiking or biking in nearby Moran State Park—starting your day off with smoked-salmon Benedict with Calabrian-chili hollandaise sauce will provide you with plenty of fuel for recreation. **Known for:** locally sourced and foraged ingredients; smoked-salmon Benedict; funky, rustic vibe. [$] *Average main: $21* ✉ *107 Doe Bay Rd.* ☎ *360/376–8059* 🌐 *www.doebay.com* ⏲ *Closed Tues. and Wed. Limited hours Oct.–May; call ahead.*

$$ PIZZA Fodor's Choice ★ 🍴 **Hogstone's Wood Oven.** An intimate, minimalist space with large windows and just a handful of tables, this hip locavore-minded pizza joint serves wood-fired pies with creative toppings—consider the one with new potatoes, crispy pork fat, chickweed, cultured cream, and uncured garlic. The bounteous, farmers'-market-sourced salads are another strength, and the wine list, with varietals from the Northwest and Europe, is exceptional. **Known for:** wildly inventive pizzas with

unusual toppings; extensive wine list; long wait on the weekend. [$] *Average main: $20* ✉ *460 Main St.* ☎ *360/376–4647* 🌐 *www.hogstone.com* 🕒 *Closed Tues. and Wed. (and some additional days in winter; call first). No lunch.*

$$$ PACIFIC NORTHWEST 🍴 **Inn at Ship Bay.** This restaurant at this stylish, contemporary inn just a mile from Eastsound offers among the most memorable dining experiences on the island. Tucked into a renovated 1869 farmhouse, the dining room and bar serve food that emphasizes local, seasonal ingredients. **Known for:** outstanding wine list; house-made sourdough bread made from a century-old starter yeast. [$] *Average main: $26* ✉ *326 Olga Rd.* ☎ *360/376–5886* 🌐 *www.innatshipbay.com* 🕒 *Closed Sun. and Mon. and mid-Dec.–mid-Mar. No lunch.*

$ ASIAN 🍴 **The Kitchen.** Seating at this casual, affordable Asian restaurant adjacent to the distinctive boutiques of Prune Alley is in a compact dining room or, when the weather is nice, at open-air picnic tables in a tree-shaded yard. The pan-Asian food here is filling and simple, using local seafood and produce, with plenty of vegetarian options. **Known for:** hearty ramen and Thai noodle soups; chocolate-ginger cookies for dessert; nice selection of craft brews on tap. [$] *Average main: $8* ✉ *249 Prune Alley* ☎ *360/376–6958* 🌐 *www.thekitchenorcas.com* 🕒 *Closed Sun.*

$$$$ PACIFIC NORTHWEST 🍴 **Mansion Restaurant.** For a special-occasion dinner (or lunch on weekends), it's worth the drive to this grandly romantic dining room inside the historic main inn at Rosario Resort, where you'll be treated to polished service, sweeping bay views, and exquisitely plated seasonal Northwest cuisine. You might start with the house-made rabbit pâté with dried apples and candied pecans, followed by either the signature bouillabaisse in a Pernod-tomato broth or pan-roasted filet mignon rossini (topped with duck-liver mousse). **Known for:** lovely views of Cascade Bay; bouillabaisse teeming with local seafood; flourless chocolate decadence cake. [$] *Average main: $31* ✉ *1400 Rosario Rd.* ☎ *360/376–2222* 🌐 *www.rosarioresort.com* 🕒 *No lunch Mon.–Thurs.*

$$ MEXICAN FAMILY 🍴 **Mijitas.** A bustling family-friendly Mexican restaurant with a cozy dining room and a sprawling shaded garden patio is helmed by Raul Rios, who learned to cook during his years growing up outside Mexico City. The flavorful food here isn't entirely authentic—expect of mix of Mexican and Mexican-American dishes, many featuring local ingredients. **Known for:** sweet, tangy margaritas; expansive garden patio; braised short ribs with blackberry-mole sauce. [$] *Average main: $19* ✉ *310 A St.* ☎ *360/376–6722* 🕒 *No lunch.*

$$ MODERN AMERICAN 🍴 **Roses Bakery & Cafe.** Set inside a cheerfully renovated former Eastsound fire station, this bustling café known for its house-baked breads and an impressive selection of artisanal gourmet groceries (from cheeses to fine wines) is also a fine spot for breakfast or lunch. The fare is French-Italian influenced but using local ingredients: try the croque monsieur or house-cured gravlax in the morning. **Known for:** rhubarb galette with fennel ice cream; outstanding assortment of cheese, sweets, and wines to go; thin-crust pizzas with interesting toppings. [$] *Average main: $19* ✉ *382 Prune Alley* ☎ 🌐 *www.rosesbakerycafe.com* 🕒 *No dinner.*

8

WHERE TO STAY

$$
B&B/INN
All Dream Cottages and Kingfish Inn. Spacious units in this atmospheric 1902 house are equipped with a king or queen bed, private bath, and all the serenity a guest could ever want, while four lovely cottages come with plenty of privacy and beautiful views. **Pros:** decor is tasteful and contemporary; good café; water views. **Cons:** somewhat small bathrooms in some rooms; although on the lesser-visited shore of West Sound, the rooms do get some noise from road and busy marina; two-night minimum. $ *Rooms from: $198* ⊠ *Crow Valley Rd., at Deer Harbor Rd.* ☎ *360/376–2500* ⊕ *www.kingfishinn.com* ☉ *Closed early Jan.–mid-Feb.* ☞ *3 rooms, 1 suite, 4 cottages* ⦿ *Breakfast.*

$$
B&B/INN
Inn on Orcas Island. Innkeepers Jeremy Trumble and John Gibbs welcome guests to their handsome, contemporary, adults-only inn, with spacious, plush rooms in the main house and two in separate outbuildings. **Pros:** among the most opulent accommodations on the island; serene setting; delicious breakfasts (and fresh-baked chocolate-chip cookies); overlooking the northern tip of Deer Harbor and within walking distance of the community's bustling marina. **Cons:** 20-minute drive from Eastsound shopping and dining. $ *Rooms from: $225* ⊠ *114 Channel Rd.* ☎ *360/376–5227* ⊕ *www.theinnonorcasisland.com* ☞ *1 room, 3 suites, 2 cottages* ⦿ *Breakfast.*

$
HOTEL
Fodor's Choice
★
Outlook Inn. This nice range of accommodations in the center of Eastsound includes small budget-oriented rooms with twin beds and shared bathrooms, rooms with queen or double beds, and rambling bay-view suites with gas fireplaces, kitchenettes, and two-person Jacuzzi tubs. **Pros:** steps from Eastsound dining and shops (and great restaurant on-site); superfriendly and helpful staff; broad mix of rates. **Cons:** in-town location can be a little noisy; only some rooms have water view; least expensive rooms have shared bath. $ *Rooms from: $99* ⊠ *171 Main St.* ☎ *360/376–2200, 888/688–5665* ⊕ *www.outlookinn.com* ☞ *24 rooms, 14 with shared bath, 16 suites* ⦿ *No meals.*

$$
RESORT
FAMILY
Fodor's Choice
★
Rosario Resort and Spa. Shipbuilding magnate Robert Moran built this Arts and Crafts–style waterfront mansion in 1909, and it is now the centerpiece of a 40-acre resort that comprises several different buildings with sweeping views of Cascade Bay and Rosario Point—accommodations range from moderately priced standard guest rooms to deluxe one- and two-bedroom suites with fireplaces, decks, and full kitchens. **Pros:** gorgeous, peaceful location; management continues to make improvements and upgrade the rooms; first-rate spa and several dining options. **Cons:** often busy with weddings and special events. $ *Rooms from: $164* ⊠ *1400 Rosario Rd.* ☎ *360/376–2222, 800/562–8820* ⊕ *www.rosarioresort.com* ☞ *16 rooms, 51 suites* ⦿ *No meals.*

$$
B&B/INN
Turtleback Farm Inn. Eighty acres of meadow, forest, and farmland in the shadow of Turtleback Mountain surround these pleasant and homey rooms in the carefully restored late-19th-century green-clapboard farmhouse and the newer cedar Orchard House. **Pros:** lovely grounds to stroll through; peaceful location; smartly furnished rooms. **Cons:** not near the water; two-night minimum in high season; some rooms are quite cozy. $ *Rooms from: $165* ⊠ *1981 Crow Valley Rd.* ☎ *360/376–3914, 800/376–4914* ⊕ *www.turtlebackinn.com* ☞ *11 rooms* ⦿ *Breakfast.*

$$ 🏠 **West Beach Resort.** This old-school cottage compound with a dazzling
RESORT beachfront location on the island's northwest shore, just a 10-min-
FAMILY ute drive from Eastsound, is a good value for families and groups
of friends—most of these compact, rustic cottages sleep four to six
guests, and all have kitchens. **Pros:** many cabins are right on the beach;
great for families and groups; good value, especially considering these
water views. **Cons:** furnishings in some cottages are a bit dated and
basic; no restaurants within walking distance. $ *Rooms from: $169*
✉ *190 Waterfront Way* ☎ *360/376–2240, 877/937–8224* ⊕ *www.west-
beachresort.com* 🛏 *21 cottages* ❖ *No meals.*

NIGHTLIFE

Fodor'sChoice **The Barnacle.** This quirky hole-in-the-wall bar with an insider-y, speak-
★ easy vibe is across the lawn from the Kitchen restaurant, and has
developed a cult following for its sophisticated, well-made craft cock-
tails—many infused with house-made bitters and local herbs and ber-
ries—and interesting wines. On this quiet, early-to-bed island, it's a
nice late-night option. Light tapas are served, too. ✉ *249 Prune Alley*
☎ *206/679–5683.*

Island Hoppin' Brewery. Set in an otherwise inauspicious industrial area
near the airport, this craft brewery and taproom (open nightly till 9 pm)
has quickly earned a reputation throughout the archipelago—and even
on the mainland as far away as Seattle—for well-made beers, includ-
ing the faintly citrusy Elwha Rock IPA and the silky Old Salts Brown
Ale. Smoked salmon, cheese and crackers, and a few other snacks are
sold in the homey taproom. ✉ *33 Hope La.* ☎ *360/376–6079* ⊕ *www.
islandhoppinbrewery.com.*

SPORTS AND THE OUTDOORS

BICYCLES AND MOPEDS

Mountain bikes rent for about $30 per day or $100 per week. Tandem,
recumbent, and electric bikes rent for about $50 per day.

Wildlife Cycles. This trusty shop rents bikes and can recommend great
routes all over the island. ✉ *350 N. Beach Rd.* ☎ *360/376–4708*
⊕ *www.wildlifecycles.com.*

BOATING AND SAILING

Kruger Escapes. Three-hour day adventures and sunset cruises around the
islands are offered on two handsome sailboats that were both designed
and formerly used for racing. The boats are also available for multiday
charters. ✉ *Orcas Island* ☎ *360/201–0586* ⊕ *www.krugerescapes.com.*

Orcas Boat Rentals. You can rent a variety of sailboats, outboards, and
skiffs for full- and half-day trips, as well as book custom charter cruises,
with this company. ✉ *5164 Deer Harbor Rd.* ☎ *360/376–7616* ⊕ *www.
orcasboatrentals.com.*

West Beach Resort Marina. This is a good option for renting motorized
boats, kayaks and canoes, and fishing gear on the island's northwest
shore. The resort is also a popular spot for divers, who can fill their
tanks here. ✉ *190 Waterfront Way* ☎ *360/376–2240, 877/937–8224*
⊕ *www.westbeachresort.com.*

8

SEA KAYAKING

All equipment is usually included in a rental package or tour. Three-hour trips cost around $80; and day tours, $110 to $135.

Orcas Outdoors Sea Kayak Tours. This outfitter offers one-, two-, and three-hour journeys, as well as day trips, overnight tours, and rentals. ⊠ *Orcas Ferry Landing* ☎ *360/376–4611* ⊕ *www.orcasoutdoors.com.*

Shearwater Kayak Tours. This established company holds kayaking classes and runs three-hour, day, and overnight tours from Rosario, Deer Harbor, West Beach, and Doe Bay resorts. ⊠ *138 N. Beach Rd.* ☎ *360/376–4699* ⊕ *www.shearwaterkayaks.com.*

WHALE-WATCHING

Cruises, which run about four hours, are scheduled daily in summer and once or twice weekly at other times. The cost is around $90 to $110 per person, and boats hold 20 to 40 people. Wear warm clothing and bring a snack.

Deer Harbor Charters. This eco-friendly tour company (the first in the San Juans to use biodiesel) offers whale-watching cruises around the island straits, with departures from both Deer Harbor Marina and Rosario Resort. Outboards and skiffs are also available, as is fishing gear. ⊠ *Deer Harbor Rd.* ☎ *360/376–5989, 800/544–5758* ⊕ *www. deerharborcharters.com.*

Eclipse Charters. In addition to tours that search around Orcas Island for whale pods and other sea life, this charter company offers lighthouse tours. ⊠ *Orcas Island Ferry Landing* ☎ *360/376–6566* ⊕ *www. orcasislandwhales.com.*

SHOPPING

Crow Valley Gallery. This colorful gallery in Eastsound's village exhibits beautiful and distinctive ceramics, metalworks, blown glass, and sculptures. ⊠ *296 Main St.* ☎ *360/376–4260* ⊕ *www.crowvalley.com.*

Darvill's Bookstore. This island favorite, with a coffee bar and a couple of cozy seats with panoramic views of the water, specializes in literary fiction and nautical literature. ⊠ *296 Main St.* ☎ *360/376–2135* ⊕ *www. darvillsbookstore.com.*

Kathryn Taylor Chocolates. This sweet sweetshop in Eastsound village sells the creative bonbons (pistachio-fig, black raspberry) of Kathryn Taylor. It's also a good stop for ice cream and Stumptown coffee drinks. ⊠ *68 N. Beach Rd.* ☎ *360/376–1030* ⊕ *www.kathryntaylorchocolates.com.*

Fodor'sChoice ★ **Orcas Island Artworks.** Stop by this cooperative gallery to see the impressive displays pottery, sculpture, jewelry, art glass, paintings, and quilts by resident artists. Following a devastating fire in 2013, the gallery has reopened in its original beautifully restored 1937 barn in the village of Olga. A café serves tasty breakfast and lunch fare. ⊠ *11 Point Lawrence Rd.* ☎ *360/376–4408* ⊕ *www.orcasartworks.com.*

Fodor'sChoice ★ **Orcas Island Pottery.** A stroll through the historic house, outbuildings, and gardens of this enchanting arts complex on a bluff overlooking President Channel and Waldron Island is more than just a chance to browse beautiful pottery—it's a great spot simply to relax and soak up the views. More than a dozen regular and guest potters exhibit and sell their wares here, everything from functional dinnerware and mugs to fanciful vases and wall hangings. ⊠ *338 Old Pottery Rd.* ☎ *360/376–2813* ⊕ *www.orcasislandpottery.com.*

SAN JUAN ISLAND

45 mins by ferry from Orcas Island, 75–90 mins by ferry from Anacortes or Sidney, BC (near Victoria).

San Juan is the cultural and commercial hub of the archipelago that shares its name. Friday Harbor, the county seat, is larger and both more vibrant and crowded than any of the towns on Orcas or Lopez, yet San Juan still has miles of rural roads, uncrowded beaches, and rolling woodlands. It's easy to get here, too, making San Juan the preferred destination for travelers who have time to visit only one island.

Several different Coast Salish tribes first settled on San Juan, establishing encampments along the north end of the island. North-end beaches were especially busy during the annual salmon migration, when hundreds of tribal members would gather along the shoreline to fish, cook, and exchange news. Many of the indigenous early inhabitants were killed by smallpox and other imported diseases in the 18th and 19th centuries. Smallpox Bay was where tribal members plunged into the icy water to cool the fevers that came with the disease.

The 18th century brought explorers from England and Spain, but the island remained sparsely populated until the mid-1800s. From the 1880s Roche Harbor and its newspaper were controlled by lime-company owner and Republican bigwig John S. McMillin, who virtually ran this part of the island as a personal fiefdom from 1886 until his death in 1936. Friday Harbor ultimately emerged as the island's largest community. The town's main street, rising from the harbor and ferry landing up the slopes of a modest hill, hasn't changed much in the past few decades, though the cafés, inns, and shops have become increasingly urbane.

GETTING HERE AND AROUND

With ferry connections from both Anacortes and Sidney, BC (on Vancouver Island, near Victoria), San Juan is the most convenient of the islands to reach, and the island is easily explored by car; public transportation and bicycles also work, but require a bit more effort. However, if you're staying in Friday Harbor, you can get from the ferry terminal to your hotel as well as area shops and restaurants easily on foot.

AIR TRAVEL   One-hour flights from Seattle to San Juan Airport, Friday Harbor, or Roche Harbor cost about $130 to $170 each way.

BUS TRAVEL   San Juan Transit & Tours operates shuttle buses daily from mid-May to mid-September. Hop on at Friday Harbor, the main town, to get to all the island's significant points and parks, including the San Juan Vineyards, Krystal Acres Alpaca Farm, Lime Kiln Point State Park, and Snug Harbor and Roche Harbor resorts. Different buses call on different stops, so be sure to check the schedule before you plan your day. Tickets are $5 one way, or $15 for a day pass. From mid-June through mid-September, the Friday Harbor Jolly Trolley offers trips around the island—also stopping at all of they key attractions—in an old-fashioned trolley-style bus; tickets cost $20 and are good for the entire day.

Contact Friday Harbor Jolly Trolley. ☎ *360/298–8873* ⊕ *www.fridayharbor-jollytrolley.com.* **San Juan Transit & Tours.** ✉ *Cannery Landing, Friday Harbor* ☎ *360/378–8887* ⊕ *sanjuantransit.com.*

BOAT AND FERRY TRAVEL The Washington State Ferries crossings from Anacortes to Friday Harbor takes about 75 to 90 minutes; round-trip fares in high season are about $14 per person, $65 for a car and driver. It's about the same distance from Sidney, BC, on Vancouver Island—this service is available twice daily in summer and once daily spring and fall (there's no BC service in winter). Round-trip fares are about $25 per person, $85 for car and driver. Clipper Navigation operates the passenger-only *San Juan Clipper* jet catamaran service between Pier 69 in Seattle and Friday Harbor. Boats leave Seattle daily mid-June–early September, Thursday–Monday mid-May–mid-June, and weekends early September–early October at 8:15 am and return from Friday Harbor at 5 pm; reservations are strongly recommended. The journey costs $80 to $100 round-trip, depending on the day and whether you purchase in advance (which is cheaper). Clipper also offers optional whale-watching excursions, which can be combined ferry passage.

Contacts Clipper Navigation. ☎ *206/448–5000, 800/888–2535* ⊕ *www.clippervacations.com.*

ESSENTIALS

The San Juan Island Chamber of Commerce has a visitor center (open daily 10 to 4) in Friday Harbor where you can grab brochures and ask for advice.

Visitor Information San Juan Island Chamber of Commerce. ✉ *165 1st St., Friday Harbor* ☎ *360/378–5240* ⊕ *www.sanjuanisland.org.*

EXPLORING

TOP ATTRACTIONS

FAMILY

Fodor's Choice

★

Lime Kiln Point State Park. To watch whales cavorting in Haro Strait, head to these 36 acres on San Juan's western side just 9 miles from Friday Harbor. A rocky coastal trail leads to lookout points and a little, white, 1919 lighthouse. The best period for sighting whales is from the end of April through September, but resident pods of orcas regularly cruises past the point. This park is also a beautiful spot to soak in a summer sunset, with expansive views of Vancouver Island and beyond. ✉ *1567 Westside Rd.* ☎ *360/378–2044* ⊕ *www.parks.wa.gov/parks* ⊠ *$10* ⊙ *Interpretive center closed mid-Sept.–late May.*

FAMILY

Pelindaba Lavender Farm. Wander a spectacular 20-acre valley smothered with endless rows of fragrant purple-and-gold lavender blossoms. The oils are distilled for use in therapeutic, botanical, and household products, all created on-site. The farm hosts the very popular San Juan Island Lavender Festival in mid- to late July. If you can't make it to the farm, stop at the outlet in the Friday Harbor Center at 150 1st Street, where you can buy their products and sample delicious lavender-infused baked goods, ice cream, and beverages. ✉ *33 Hawthorne La., Friday Harbor* ☎ *360/378–4248, 866/819–1911* ⊕ *www.pelindabalavender. com* ✉ *Free* ⊙ *Closed Nov.–Apr.*

FAMILY
Fodor's Choice
★

Roche Harbor. It's hard to believe that fashionable Roche Harbor at the northern end of San Juan Island was once the most important producer of builder's lime on the West Coast. In 1882 John S. McMillin gained control of the lime company and expanded production. But even in its heyday as a limestone quarrying village, Roche Harbor was known for abundant flowers and welcoming accommodations. McMillin transformed a bunkhouse into private lodgings for his invited guests, who included such notables as Teddy Roosevelt. The guesthouse is now the Hotel de Haro, which displays period photographs and artifacts in its lobby. The staff now has maps of the old quarry, kilns, and the Mausoleum, an eerie Greek-inspired memorial to McMillin.

McMillin's heirs operated the quarries and plant until 1956, when they sold the company to the Tarte family, who developed it into an upscale resort (but no longer own it)—the old lime kilns still stand below the bluff. Locals say it took two years for the limestone dust to wash off the trees around the harbor. McMillin's former home is now a restaurant, and workers' cottages have been transformed into comfortable visitors' lodgings. With its rose gardens, cobblestone waterfront, and well-manicured lawns, Roche Harbor retains the flavor of its days as a hangout for McMillin's powerful friends—especially since the sheltered harbor is very popular with well-to-do pleasure boaters. ✉ *End of Roche Harbor Rd.* ⊕ *www.rocheharbor.com.*

FAMILY
Fodor's Choice
★

San Juan Island National Historic Park. Fortifications and other 19th-century military installments commemorate the Pig War, in which the United States and Great Britain nearly went into battle over their respective claims on the San Juan Islands. The dispute began in 1859 when an American settler killed a British settler's pig, and escalated until roughly 500 American soldiers and 2,200 British soldiers with five warships were poised for battle. Fortunately, no blood was spilled, and the disagreement was finally settled in 1872 in the Americans' favor, with Kaiser Wilhelm I of Germany as arbitrator.

The park comprises two separate areas on opposite sides of the island. English Camp, in a sheltered cove of Garrison Bay on the northern end, includes a blockhouse, a commissary, and barracks. A popular (though steep) hike is to the top of Young Hill, from which you can get a great view of northwest side of the island. American Camp, on the southern end, has a visitor center and the remains of fortifications; it stretches along driftwood-strewn beaches. Many of the American Camp's walking trails are through prairie; in the evening, dozens of rabbits emerge from their warrens to nibble in the fields. Great views greet you from the top of the Mt. Finlayson Trail—if you're lucky, you might be able to see Mt. Baker and Mt. Rainier along with the Olympics. From June to August you can take guided hikes and see reenactments of 1860s-era military life. ✉ *Park headquarters, 125 Spring St., American Camp, 6 miles southeast of Friday Harbor; English Camp, 9 miles northwest of*

8

Friday Harbor, Friday Harbor ☎ *360/378–2240* ⊕ *www.nps.gov/sajh* ✉ *Free* ⊙ *American Camp visitor center closed mid-Dec.–Feb. English Camp visitor center closed early Sept.–late May.*

San Juan Islands Museum of Art. Previously known as the Visual Arts Museum, this facility now generally referred to as the SJIMA presents rotating art shows and exhibits with an emphasis on island and Northwest artists, including the highly touted Artists' Registry Show in winter, which features works by nearly 100 San Juan Islands artists. The museum has been in its sleek, angular, contemporary permanent building since 2014. ⊠ *540 Spring St., Friday Harbor* ☎ *360/370–5050* ⊕ *www.sjima.org* ✉ *$10* ⊙ *Closed Tues.–Thurs.*

FAMILY **San Juan Islands Sculpture Park.** At this serene 20-acre park near Roche Harbor, you can stroll along five winding trails to view more than 150 colorful, in many cases large-scale sculptures spread amid freshwater and saltwater wetlands, open woods, blossoming fields, and rugged terrain. The park is also a haven for birds; more than 120 species nest and breed here. It's a great spot for picnicking, and dogs are welcome. ⊠ *Roche Harbor Rd., just before entrance to Roche Harbor Resort, Roche Harbor* ⊕ *www.sjisculpturepark.com* ✉ *$5.*

WORTH NOTING

FAMILY **Krystal Acres Alpaca Farm.** Kids and adults love admiring the more than 70 alpacas from South America at this sprawling 80-acre ranch on the west side of the island. The shop in the big barn displays beautiful, high-quality clothing and crafts, all handmade from alpaca hair. ⊠ *152 Blazing Tree Rd., Friday Harbor* ☎ *360/378–6125* ⊕ *www.krystalacres.com* ✉ *Free.*

FAMILY **Whale Museum.** A dramatic exterior mural depicting several types of whales welcomes you into a world filled with models of whales and whale skeletons, recordings of whale sounds, and videos of whales. Head around to the back of the first-floor shop to view maps of the latest orca pod trackings in the area. ⊠ *62 1st St. N, Friday Harbor* ☎ *360/378–4710* ⊕ *www.whalemuseum.org* ✉ *$6.*

WHERE TO EAT

$$ ✕ **Backdoor Kitchen.** This local favorite has become well-known beyond
ECLECTIC the San Juans, thanks to the stellar service and inventive, globally
Fodor's Choice inspired cuisine and craft cocktails. As the name might indicate, it's
★ a bit hard to find, tucked in an elegant courtyard a few blocks uphill from the water. **Known for:** "noodle Bowl Monday" lunch specials; some of the best pan-Asian dishes on the island; relaxing and scenic outdoor dining in a landscaped courtyard. $ *Average main: $23* ⊠ *400b A St., Friday Harbor* ☎ *360/378–9540* ⊕ *www.backdoorkitchen.com* ⊙ *Closed Mon., Tues., and additional days in winter; call off-season. No lunch Tues.–Sun.*

$$ ✕ **Cask and Schooner.** This convivial pub decked out with nautical trap-
AMERICAN pings and steps from the ferry terminal serves reliably filling, tasty, English-inspired pub fare with contemporary twists. Among the popular dishes are spicy braised short ribs with mashed potatoes and horseradish crème and a lamb burger with tomato chutney, watercress, and feta. **Known for:** convivial ambience; excellent brunch; strong selection

of craft beers. $ *Average main: $21* ✉ *1 Front St., Friday Harbor* ☎ *360/378–2922* ⊕ *www.caskandschooner.com* ⊘ *Closed Tues.*

$$
PACIFIC
NORTHWEST

✕ **Downriggers.** This snazzy, contemporary, seafood-driven restaurant overlooking the harbor is helmed by one of the most celebrated chefs in the islands, Aaron Rock. The light-filled dining room is a terrific spot to watch boats and ferries come and go while sampling such tempting fare as Penn Cove mussels and pan-seared sockeye salmon with sweet-corn grits, and caramel-chicken and ginger-spiced waffles drizzled with warm honey. **Known for:** pub fare with creative twists; extensive list of craft cocktails; Asian-inspired chicken and waffles. $ *Average main: $21* ✉ *10 Front St., Friday Harbor* ☎ *360/378–2700* ⊕ *www.downriggerssanjuan.com.*

$
ECLECTIC

✕ **Ernie's Cafe.** Ask a local for the best lunch recommendation in town, and you may be surprised by the answer—plenty of folks will send you to this casual diner at the airport, fun as much for watching planes take off and land as for the laid-back, friendly vibe and delicious, casual fare. You'll find a few Asian-fusion dishes on the menu, including Korean-style *bulgogi* (grilled marinated beef), and hearty noodle bowls, plus diner classics like hefty cheeseburgers, breakfast sandwiches, and flaky popovers. **Known for:** popovers at breakfast; several Korean-inspired dishes; watching airplanes. $ *Average main: $10* ✉ *744 Airport Circle Dr., Friday Harbor* ☎ *360/378–6605* ⊘ *Closed weekends. No dinner.*

$
CAFÉ

✕ **The Market Chef.** Only 50 yards from the ferry holding area, this café makes fantastic sandwiches (try the roast-beef-and-rocket version, which is served on a house-baked roll with spicy chili aioli). The soups and deli items—including a decadent macaroni and cheese—are also top-notch. **Known for:** mac and cheese; picnic and to-go lunches. $ *Average main: $9* ✉ *225 A St., Friday Harbor* ☎ *360/378–4546* ⊘ *Closed weekends. No dinner.*

$$$
PACIFIC
NORTHWEST
Fodor's Choice
★

✕ **Restaurant at Friday Harbor House.** Creativity and dedication to local ingredients are hallmarks of this stylish, contemporary restaurant that serves daily brunch and dinner most evenings. The brunch burger, topped with a fried egg and green-tomato-and-bacon jam, and breakfast poutine with duck confit and cheese curds make for decadent starts to your day. **Known for:** brunch served every day; excellent wine and cocktail lists; panoramic views of Friday Harbor. $ *Average main: $26* ✉ *Friday Harbor House, 130 West St., Friday Harbor* ☎ *360/378–8455* ⊕ *www.fridayharborhouse.com* ⊘ *No dinner Tues. and Wed.*

WHERE TO STAY

$$
HOTEL

🛏 **Birdrock Hotel.** The range of spiffy lodging options ranges from affordably priced if compact rooms that have private baths down the hall to downright cushy two-bedroom suites with gas fireplaces, spacious sitting rooms, pitched ceilings, and terrific harbor views. **Pros:** handy downtown Friday Harbor location; tasteful, unfussy furnishings; great value. **Cons:** central location means some street noise and crowds. $ *Rooms from: $188* ✉ *35 1st St., Friday Harbor* ☎ *360/378–5848, 800/352–2632* ⊕ *www.birdrockhotel.com* ⇲ *10 rooms, 5 suites* ⦿| *Breakfast.*

$$$$ **Friday Harbor House.** At this bluff-top getaway with floor-to-ceiling
HOTEL   windows, sleek, modern wood furnishings and fabrics in beige hues
Fodor's Choice   fill the rooms, all of which have gas fireplaces, deep jetted tubs, and at
★   least partial views of the marina, ferry landing, and San Juan Channel
below (be sure to request a marina-view room at booking). **Pros:** great
views; excellent restaurant; steps from downtown shopping and dining.
Cons: limited views from some rooms; among the priciest hotels in the
San Juan Islands. $ *Rooms from: $309* ✉ *130 West St., Friday Harbor*
☎ *360/378–8455, 866/722–7356* ⊕ *www.fridayharborhouse.com* ⤳ *23
rooms* |○| *Breakfast.*

$$ **Island Inn at 123 West.** There's a pretty striking mix of accommoda-
HOTEL   tion styles at this cosmopolitan complex that tumbles down a hillside
Fodor's Choice   overlooking Friday Harbor, from intimate Euro-style rooms that lack
★   exterior windows to expansive suites with water views to ginormous
bi-level penthouses with two bedrooms, private decks, gorgeous full
kitchens, and astounding views. **Pros:** penthouse suites are great for
luxurious family getaways; Euro-style standard rooms are a good deal;
handy in-town location. **Cons:** suites are quite spendy; standard rooms
have no outlooks. $ *Rooms from: $209* ✉ *123 West St., Friday Harbor*
☎ *360/378–4400, 877/512–9262* ⊕ *www.123west.com* ⤳ *5 rooms, 11
suites* |○| *No meals.*

$$$ **Kirk House Bed and Breakfast.** Rooms are all differently decorated in
B&B/INN   this 1907 Craftsman bungalow, the summer home of steel magnate
Peter Kirk: the Garden Room has a botanical motif, the sunny Trellis
Room is done in soft shades of yellow and green, and the Arbor Room
has French doors leading out to the garden. **Pros:** gorgeous house full of
stained glass and other lovely details; within walking distance of town.
Cons: occasional noise from nearby airport; a couple of the rooms
are on the small side. $ *Rooms from: $245* ✉ *595 Park St., Friday
Harbor* ☎ *360/378–3757, 800/639–2762* ⊕ *www.kirkhouse.net* ⤳ *4
rooms* |○| *Breakfast.*

$$$ **Roche Harbor Resort.** This sprawling resort, with several types of accom-
RESORT   modations ranging from historic hotel rooms to luxurious contemporary
waterfront suites, occupies the site of the lime works that made John
S. McMillin his fortune in the late 19th century. **Pros:** lots of different
options for families and groups; very convenient for boaters; beautiful
grounds; gorgeous full-service spa. **Cons:** condos have less character and
are away from the waterfront; a bit isolated from the rest of the island
if you don't have a car; standard rooms in Hotel de Haro have private
baths down the hall. $ *Rooms from: $239* ✉ *248 Reuben Memorial Dr.,
Roche Harbor* ☎ *360/378–2155, 800/451–8910* ⊕ *www.rocheharbor.
com* ⤳ *16 rooms, 18 suites, 9 cottages, 20 condos* |○| *No meals.*

$$$ **Snug Harbor Resort.** At this popular cottage resort and marina on the
RESORT   northwest side of the island, all of the units were completely rebuilt
FAMILY   in 2014 with tall windows overlooking the water, high ceilings, well-
equipped kitchens, knotty-pine wood paneling, gas fireplaces, and private
decks. **Pros:** beautiful, contemporary decor; quiet location; nice views of
the harbor. **Cons:** no pets; 20-minute drive from Friday Harbor; expensive. $ *Rooms from: $299* ✉ *1997 Mitchell Bay Rd., Friday Harbor*
☎ *360/378–4762* ⊕ *www.snugresort.com* ⤳ *17 cottages* |○| *No meals.*

SPORTS AND THE OUTDOORS

BEACHES

San Juan County Park. You'll find a wide gravel beachfront at this park 10 miles west of Friday Harbor, overlooking waters where orcas often frolic in summer, plus grassy lawns with picnic tables and a small campground. **Amenities:** parking (free); toilets. **Best for:** walking. ⊠ *380 Westside Rd., Friday Harbor* ☎ *360/378–8420* ⊕ *www. co.san-juan.wa.us.*

South Beach at American Camp. This 2-mile public beach on the southern end of the island is part of San Juan Island National Historical Park. **Amenities:** parking (free); toilets. **Best for:** solitude; walking. ⊠ *Off Cattle Point Road* ⊕ *www.nps.gov/sajh.*

BICYCLES

You can rent standard, mountain, and BMX bikes for $40 to $50 per day or about $200 to $240 per week. Tandem, recumbent, and electric-assist bikes rent for about $55 to $80 per day.

Discovery Adventure Tours. The noted Friday Harbor outfitter (aka Discovery Sea Kayaks) also rents conventional road bikes and electric-assist bikes. ⊠ *260 Spring St., Friday Harbor* ☎ *360/378–2559, 866/461–2559* ⊕ *www.discoveryadventuretours.com.*

Island Bicycles. This full-service shop rents bikes. ⊠ *380 Argyle Ave., Friday Harbor* ☎ *360/378–4941* ⊕ *www.islandbicycles.com.*

BOATING AND SAILING

At public docks, high-season moorage rates are $1 to $2 per foot (of vessel) per night.

Port of Friday Harbor. The marina at the island's main port offers guest moorage, vessel assistance and repair, bareboat and skippered charters, overnight accommodations, and wildlife- and whale-watching cruises. ⊠ *204 Front St., Friday Harbor* ☎ *360/378–2688* ⊕ *www. portfridayharbor.org.*

Roche Harbor Marina. The marina at Roche Harbor Resort has a fuel dock, pool, grocery, and other guest services. ⊠ *248 Reuben Memorial Dr., Roche Harbor* ☎ *360/378–2155* ⊕ *www.rocheharbor.com.*

Snug Harbor Resort Marina. This well-located marina adjoins a popular, upscale small resort. It provides van service to and from Friday Harbor and rents small powerboats. ⊠ *1997 Mitchell Bay Rd., Friday Harbor* ☎ *360/378–4762* ⊕ *www.snugresort.com.*

SEA KAYAKING

You'll find many places to rent kayaks in Friday Harbor, as well as outfitters providing classes and tours. Be sure to make reservations in summer. Three-hour tours run about $75 to $100, day tours cost around $110 to $125, and overnight tours start around $175 per day. Equipment is always included in the cost.

Crystal Seas Kayaking. Sunset trips and multisport tours that might include biking, kayaking, yoga, and camping are among the options with this respected guide company. ⊠ *40 Spring St., Friday Harbor* ☎ *360/378–4223, 877/732–7877* ⊕ *www.crystalseas.com.*

Discovery Sea Kayaks. This outfitter offers both sea-kayaking adventures, including sunset trips and multiday excursions, and whale-watching paddles. ⊠ *260 Spring St., Friday Harbor* ☎ *360/378–2559, 866/461–2559* ⊕ *www.discoveryseakayak.com.*

San Juan Kayak Expeditions. This reputable company has been running kayaking and camping tours in two-person kayaks since 1980. ⊠ *85 Front St., Friday Harbor* ☎ *360/378–4436* ⊕ *www.sanjuankayak.com.*

Sea Quest Expeditions. Kayak eco-tours with guides who are trained naturalists, biologists, and environmental scientists are available through this popular outfitter. ⊠ *Friday Harbor* ☎ *360/378–5767, 888/589–4253* ⊕ *www.sea-quest-kayak.com.*

WHALE-WATCHING

Whale-watching expeditions typically run three to four hours and cost around $100–$120 per person. Note that tours departing from San Juan Island typically get you to the best whale-watching waters faster than those departing from the mainland. ■ **TIP→ For the best experience, look for tour companies with small boats that carry under 30 people. Bring warm clothing even if it's a warm day.**

Fodor's Choice **Maya's Legacy Whale Watching.** These informative tours on small, ★ modern, and speedy boats ensure great views for every passengers; departures are from Friday Harbor and Snug Harbor Marina. ⊠ *14 Cannery Landing, Friday Harbor* ☎ *360/378–7996* ⊕ *www.sanjuan-islandwhalewatch.com.*

San Juan Excursions. Whale-watching cruises are offered aboard a converted 1941 U.S. Navy research vessel. ⊠ *40 Spring St., Friday Harbor* ☎ *360/378–6636, 800/809–4253* ⊕ *www.watchwhales.com.*

San Juan Island Whale & Wildlife Tours. Tours from Friday Harbor leave daily at noon and are led by highly knowledgeable marine experts. ⊠ *1 Front St., Friday Harbor* ☎ ⊕ *www.sanjuanislandwhales.com.*

Western Prince Whale & Wildlife Tours. Narrated whale-watching tours last three to four hours. ⊠ *1 Spring St., Friday Harbor* ☎ *360/378–5315, 800/757–6722* ⊕ *www.orcawhalewatch.com.*

SHOPPING

Friday Harbor is the main shopping area, with dozens of shops selling a variety of art, crafts, and clothing created by residents, as well as a bounty of island-grown produce.

Arctic Raven Gallery. The specialty here is Northwest native art, including scrimshaw and wood carvings. ⊠ *130 S. 1st St., Friday Harbor* ☎ *360/378–3433* ⊕ *www.arcticravengalleryfridayharbor.com.*

San Juan Island Farmers Market. From April through October, this open-air market with more than 30 vendors selling local produce and crafts takes place at Friday Harbor Brickworks on Saturdays from 10 to 1. The market is also open once or twice a month on Saturdays in winter; check the website for the schedule. ⊠ *150 Nichols St., Friday Harbor* ⊕ *www.sjifarmersmarket.com.*

San Juan Vineyards. This winery 3 miles north of Friday Harbor has a tasting room and gift shop, and organizes such special events as a harvest festival in October and November barrel tastings. Noteworthy varietals here include Chardonnay, Riesling, Merlot, and Cabernet Franc. ✉ *3136 Roche Harbor Rd., Friday Harbor* ☎ *360/378–9463* ⊕ *www.sanjuanvineyards.com.*

Waterworks Gallery. This respected gallery represents about 30 eclectic, contemporary artists, from painters to jewelers. ✉ *315 Argyle Ave., Friday Harbor* ☎ *360/378–3060* ⊕ *www.waterworksgallery.com.*

MOUNT RAINIER NATIONAL PARK

Updated by
Shelley Arenas

Like a mysterious, white-clad chanteuse, veiled in clouds even when the surrounding forests and fields are bathed in sunlight, Mt. Rainier is the centerpiece of its namesake park. The impressive volcanic peak stands at an elevation of 14,411 feet, making it the fifth-highest peak in the lower 48 states. Nearly 2 million visitors a year enjoy spectacular views of the mountain and return home with a lifelong memory of its image.

The mountain holds the largest glacial system in the contiguous United States, with more than two dozen major glaciers. On the lower slopes you find silent forests made up of cathedral-like groves of Douglas fir, western hemlock, and western red cedar, some more than 1,000 years old. Water and lush greenery are everywhere in the park, and dozens of thundering waterfalls, accessible from the road or by a short hike, fill the air with mist.

MOUNT RAINIER PLANNER

8

WHEN TO GO

Rainier is the Puget Sound's weather vane: if you can see it, skies will be clear. Visitors are most likely to see the summit July through September. Crowds are heaviest in summer, too, meaning the parking lots at Paradise and Sunrise often fill before noon, campsites are reserved months in advance, and other lodgings are reserved as much as a year ahead.

True to its name, Paradise is often sunny during periods when the lowlands are under a cloud layer. The rest of the year, Rainier's summit gathers flying-saucer-like lenticular clouds whenever a Pacific storm approaches; once the peak vanishes from view, it's time to haul out rain gear. The rare periods of clear winter weather bring residents up to Paradise for cross-country skiing.

PLANNING YOUR TIME

MOUNT RAINIER IN ONE DAY

The best way to get a complete overview of Mount Rainier in a day is to enter via Nisqually and begin your tour by browsing in **Longmire Museum.** When you're done, get to know the environment in and around Longmire Meadow and the overgrown ruins of Longmire Springs Hotel on the ½-mile **Trail of the Shadows** nature loop.

From Longmire, Highway 706 East climbs northeast into the mountains toward Paradise. Take a moment to explore two-tiered **Christine Falls,** just north of the road 1½ miles past Cougar Rock Campground, and the cascading **Narada Falls,** 3 miles farther on; both are spanned by graceful stone footbridges. Fantastic mountain views, alpine meadows crosshatched with nature trails, a welcoming lodge and restaurant, and the excellent **Jackson Memorial Visitor Center** combine to make lofty Paradise the primary goal of most park visitors. One outstanding (but challenging) way to explore the high country is to hike the 5-mile roundtrip **Skyline Trail** to Panorama Point, which rewards you with stunning 360-degree views.

Continue eastward on Highway 706 East for 21 miles and leave your car to explore the incomparable, 1,000-year-old **Grove of the Patriarchs.** Afterward, turn your car north toward White River and **Sunrise Visitor Center,** where you can watch the alpenglow fade from Mt. Rainier's domed summit.

GETTING HERE AND AROUND
AIR TRAVEL
Seattle–Tacoma International Airport, 15 miles south of downtown Seattle, is the nearest airport to the national park.

CAR TRAVEL
The Nisqually entrance is on Highway 706, 14 miles east of Route 7; the Ohanapecosh entrance is on Route 123, 5 miles north of U.S. 12; and the White River entrance is on Route 410, 3 miles north of the Chinook and Cayuse passes. These highways become mountain roads as they reach Rainier, winding up and down many steep slopes, so cautious driving is essential: use a lower gear, especially on downhill sections, and take care not to overheat brakes by constant use. These roads are subject to storms any time of year and are repaired in the summer from winter damage and washouts.

Side roads into the park's western slope are narrower, unpaved, and subject to flooding and washouts. All are closed by snow in winter except Highway 706 to Paradise and Carbon River Road, though the latter tends to flood near the park boundary. (Route 410 is open to the Crystal Mountain access road entrance.)

Park roads have a maximum speed of 35 mph in most places, and you have to watch for pedestrians, cyclists, and wildlife. Parking can be difficult during peak summer season, especially at Paradise, Sunrise, Grove of the Patriarchs, and at the trailheads between Longmire and Paradise; arrive early if you plan to visit these sites. All off-road-vehicle use—4X4 vehicles, ATVs, motorcycles, snowmobiles—is prohibited in Mount Rainier National Park.

PARK ESSENTIALS
PARK FEES AND PERMITS
The entrance fee of $25 per vehicle and $10 for those on foot, motorcycle, or bicycle is good for seven days. Annual passes are $50. Climbing permits are $46 per person per climb or glacier trek. Wilderness camping permits must be obtained for all backcountry trips, and advance reservations are highly recommended.

PARK HOURS

Mount Rainier National Park is open 24/7 year-round, but with limited access in winter. Gates at Nisqually (Longmire) are staffed year-round during the day; facilities at Paradise are open daily from late May to mid-October; and Sunrise is open daily July to early September. During off-hours you can buy passes at the gates from machines that accept credit and debit cards. Winter access to the park is limited to the Nisqually entrance, and the Jackson Memorial Visitor Center at Paradise is open on weekends and holidays in winter. The Paradise snow-play area is open when there is sufficient snow.

CELL-PHONE RECEPTION

Cell-phone reception is unreliable throughout much of the park, although access is clear at Paradise, Sunrise, and Crystal Mountain. Public telephones are at all park visitor centers, at the National Park Inn at Longmire, and at Paradise Inn at Paradise.

EDUCATIONAL OFFERINGS

RANGER PROGRAMS

FAMILY **Junior Ranger Program.** Youngsters ages 6 to 11 can pick up an activity booklet at a visitor center and fill it out as they explore the park. When they complete it, they can show it to a ranger and receive a Mount Rainier Junior Ranger badge. ⊠ *Visitor centers, Mt. Rainier National Park* ☎ *360/569–2211* ⊕ *www.nps.gov/mora/learn/kidsyouth/index. htm* ⬚ *Free with park admission.*

FAMILY **Ranger Programs.** Park ranger-led activities include **guided snowshoe walks** in the winter (most suitable for those older than eight) as well as **evening programs** during the summer at Longmire/Cougar Rock, Ohanapecosh, and White River campgrounds, and at the Paradise Inn. Evening talks may cover subjects such as park history, its flora and fauna, or interesting facts on climbing Mt. Rainier. There are also daily guided programs that start at the Jackson Visitor Center, including meadow and vista walks, tours of the Paradise Inn, a morning ranger chat, and evening astronomy program. ⊠ *Visitor centers, Mt. Rainier National Park* ☎ *360/569–2211* ⊕ *www.nps.gov/mora/planyourvisit/ rangerprograms.htm* ⬚ *Free with park admission.*

RESTAURANTS

A limited number of restaurants are inside the park, and a few worth checking out lie beyond its borders. Mount Rainier's picnic areas are justly famous, especially in summer, when wildflowers fill the meadows. Resist the urge to feed the yellow pine chipmunks darting about.

HOTELS

The Mount Rainier area is remarkably bereft of quality lodging. Rainier's two national park lodges, at Longmire and Paradise, are attractive and well maintained. They exude considerable history and charm, especially Paradise Inn, but unless you've made summer reservations a year in advance, getting a room can be a challenge. Dozens of motels, cabin complexes, and private vacation-home rentals are near the park entrances; while they can be pricey, the latter are convenient for longer stays. *Hotel reviews have been shortened. For full information, visit Fodors.com.*

8

VISITOR INFORMATION

Park Contact Information Mount Rainier National Park. ⊠ *55210 238th Ave. East, Ashford* ☏ *360/569–2211, 360/569–6575* ⊕ *www.nps.gov/mora.*

VISITOR CENTERS

Jackson Memorial Visitor Center. High on the mountain's southern flank, this center houses exhibits on geology, mountaineering, glaciology, and alpine ecology. Multimedia programs are staged in the theater; there's also a snack bar and gift shop. This is the park's most popular visitor destination, and it can be quite crowded in summer. ⊠ *Hwy. 706 E, 19 miles east of Nisqually park entrance, Mt. Rainier National Park* ☏ *360/569–6571* ⊕ *www.nps.gov/mora/planyourvisit/paradise.htm* ⊘ *Weekdays mid-Oct.–April.*

Longmire Museum and Visitor Center. Glass cases inside this museum preserve the park's plants and animals, including a stuffed cougar. Historical photographs and geographical displays provide a worthwhile overview of the park's history. The adjacent visitor center has some perfunctory exhibits on the surrounding forest and its inhabitants, as well as pamphlets and information about park activities. ⊠ *Hwy. 706, 10 miles east of Ashford, Longmire* ☏ *360/569–6575* ⊕ *www.nps.gov/ mora/planyourvisit/longmire.htm.*

Sunrise Visitor Center. Exhibits at this center explain the region's sparser alpine and subalpine ecology. A network of nearby loop trails leads you through alpine meadows and forest to overlooks that have broad views of the Cascades and Rainier. The visitor center has a snack bar and gift shop. ⊠ *Sunrise Rd., 15 miles from the White River park entrance, Mt. Rainier National Park* ☏ *360/663–2425* ⊕ *www.nps.gov/mora/plany-ourvisit/sunrise.htm* ⊘ *Mid-Sept.–June.*

EXPLORING

SCENIC DRIVES

Chinook Pass Road. Route 410, the highway to Yakima, follows the eastern edge of the park to Chinook Pass, where it climbs the steep, 5,432-foot pass via a series of switchbacks. At its top, take in broad views of Rainier and the east slope of the Cascades. The pass usually closes for the winter in November. ⊠ *Mt. Rainier National Park* ⊕ *www.wsdot. wa.gov/traffic/passes/chinook-cayuse.*

Mowich Lake Road. In the northwest corner of the park, this 24-mile mountain road begins in Wilkeson and heads up the Rainier foothills to Mowich Lake, traversing beautiful mountain meadows along the way. Mowich Lake is a pleasant spot for a picnic. The road is open mid-July to mid-October. ⊠ *Mt. Rainier National Park* ⊕ *www. nps.gov/mora/planyourvisit/carbon-and-mowich.htm* ⊘ *Closed Mid-Oct.-mid-July.*

Paradise Road. This 9-mile stretch of Highway 706 winds its way up the mountain's southwest flank from Longmire to Paradise, taking you from lowland forest to the ever-expanding vistas of the mountain above. Visit early on a weekday if possible, especially in peak summer months, when the road is packed with cars. The route is open year-round though there may be some weekday closures in winter. From November through April, all vehicles must carry chains. ⊠ *Mt. Rainier National Park* ⊕ *www.nps.gov/mora/planyourvisit/paradise.htm.*

Sunrise Road. This popular (and often crowded) scenic road to the highest drivable point at Mount Rainier carves its way 11 miles up Sunrise Ridge from the White River Valley on the northeast side of the park. As you top the ridge there are sweeping views of the surrounding lowlands. The road is open late June to early October. ⊠ *Mt. Rainier National Park* ⊕ *www.nps.gov/mora/planyourvisit/sunrise.htm* ⊗ *Usually closed Oct.–June.*

HISTORIC SITES

National Park Inn. Even if you don't plan to stay overnight, you can stop by year-round to view the architecture of this inn, built in 1917 and on the National Register of Historic Places. While you're here, relax in front of the fireplace in the lounge, stop at the gift shop, or dine at the restaurant. ⊠ *Longmire Visitor Complex, Hwy. 706, 10 miles east of Nisqually entrance, Longmire* ☎ *360/569–2411* ⊕ *www.mtrainierguestservices.com/accommodations/national-park-inn.*

SCENIC STOPS

Christine Falls. These two-tiered falls were named in honor of Christine Louise Van Trump, who climbed to the 10,000-foot level on Mt. Rainier in 1889 at the age of nine, despite having a crippling nervous-system disorder. ⊠ *Next to Hwy. 706, about 2½ miles east of Cougar Rock Campground, Mt. Rainier National Park.*

Fodor's Choice ★ **Grove of the Patriarchs.** Protected from the periodic fires that swept through the surrounding areas, this small island of 1,000-year-old trees is one of Mount Rainier National Park's most memorable features. A 1½-mile loop trail heads through the old-growth forest of Douglas fir, cedar, and hemlock. ⊠ *Rte. 123, west of the Stevens Canyon entrance, Mt. Rainier National Park* ⊕ *www.nps.gov/mora/planyourvisit/ohanapecosh.htm.*

Narada Falls. A steep but short trail leads to the viewing area for these spectacular 168-foot falls, which expand to a width of 75 feet during peak flow times. In winter the frozen falls are popular with ice climbers. ⊠ *Along Hwy. 706, 1 mile west of the turnoff for Paradise, 6 miles east of Cougar Rock Campground, Mt. Rainier National Park* ⊕ *www.nps.gov/mora/planyourvisit/longmire.htm.*

FAMILY   **Tipsoo Lake.** The short, pleasant trail that circles the lake—ideal for families—provides breathtaking views. Enjoy the subalpine wildflower meadows during the summer months; in early fall there is an abundant supply of huckleberries. ⊠ *Off Cayuse Pass east on Hwy. 410, Mt. Rainier National Park* ⊕ *www.nps.gov/mora/planyourvisit/sunrise.htm.*

SPORTS AND THE OUTDOORS

MULTISPORT OUTFITTERS

RMI Expeditions. Reserve a private hiking guide through this highly regarded outfitter, or take part in its one-day mountaineering classes (mid-May through late September), where participants are evaluated on their fitness for the climb and must be able to withstand a 16-mile round-trip hike with a 9,000-foot gain in elevation. The company also arranges private cross-country skiing and snowshoeing guides. ⊠ *30027 Hwy. 706 E, Ashford* ☎ *888/892–5462, 360/569–2227* ⊕ *www.rmiguides.com* ▣ *From $1,087 for 4-day package.*

Whittaker Mountaineering. You can rent hiking and climbing gear, skis, snowshoes, snowboards, and other outdoor equipment at this all-purpose Rainier Base Camp outfitter, which also arranges for private cross-country skiing and hiking guides. ⊠ *30027 SR 706E, Ashford* ☎ *800/238–5756, 360/569–2982* ⊕ *www.whittakermountaineering.com.*

BIRD-WATCHING

Be alert for kestrels, red-tailed hawks, and, occasionally, golden eagles on snags in the lowland forests. Also present at Rainier, but rarely seen, are great horned owls, spotted owls, and screech owls. Iridescent rufous hummingbirds flit from blossom to blossom in the drowsy summer lowlands, and sprightly water ouzels flutter in the many forest creeks. Raucous Steller's jays and gray jays scold passersby from trees, often darting boldly down to steal morsels from unguarded picnic tables. At higher elevations, look for the pure white plumage of the white-tailed ptarmigan as it hunts for seeds and insects in winter. Waxwings, vireos, nuthatches, sapsuckers, warblers, flycatchers, larks, thrushes, siskins, tanagers, and finches are common throughout the park.

HIKING

Although the mountain can seem remarkably benign on calm summer days, hiking Rainier is not a city-park stroll. Dozens of hikers and trekkers annually lose their way and must be rescued—and lives are lost on the mountain each year. Weather that approaches cyclonic levels can appear quite suddenly, any month of the year. All visitors venturing far from vehicle access points, with the possible exception of the short loop hikes listed here, should carry day packs with warm clothing, food, and other emergency supplies.

EASY

Nisqually Vista Trail. Equally popular in summer and winter, this trail is a 1¼-mile round-trip through subalpine meadows to an overlook point for Nisqually Glacier. The gradually sloping path is a favorite venue for cross-country skiers in winter; in summer, listen for the shrill alarm calls of the area's marmots. *Easy.* ⊠ *Mt. Rainier National Park* ✛ *Trailhead: at Jackson Memorial Visitor Center, Rte. 123, 1 mile north of Ohanapecosh, at the high point of Hwy. 706* ⊕ *www.nps. gov/mora/planyourvisit/day-hiking-at-mount-rainier.htm.*

Sunrise Nature Trail. The 1½-mile-long loop of this self-guided trail takes you through the delicate subalpine meadows near the Sunrise Visitor Center. A gradual climb to the ridgetop yields magnificent views of Mt. Rainier and the more distant volcanic cones of Mt. Baker, Mt. Adams, and Glacier Peak. *Easy.* ⊠ *Mt. Rainier National Park* ✛ *Trailhead: at Sunrise Visitor Center, Sunrise Rd., 15 miles from the White River park entrance* ⊕ *www.nps.gov/mora/planyourvisit/sunrise.htm.*

Trail of the Shadows. This ¾-mile loop is notable for its glimpses of meadowland ecology, its colorful soda springs (don't drink the water), James Longmire's old homestead cabin, and the foundation of the old Longmire Springs Hotel, which was destroyed by fire around 1900. *Easy.* ⊠ *Mt. Rainier National Park* ✛ *Trailhead: at Hwy. 706, 10 miles east of Nisqually entrance* ⊕ *www.nps.gov/mora/planyourvisit/day-hiking-at-mount-rainier.htm.*

MODERATE

Fodor's Choice
★

Skyline Trail. This 5-mile loop, one of the highest trails in the park, beckons day-trippers with a vista of alpine ridges and, in summer, meadows filled with brilliant flowers and birds. At 6,800 feet, Panorama Point, the spine of the Cascade Range, spreads away to the east, and Nisqually Glacier tumbles downslope. *Moderate.* ⊠ *Mt. Rainier National Park* ✛ *Trailhead: Jackson Memorial Visitor Center, Rte. 123, 1 mile north of Ohanapecosh at the high point of Hwy. 706* ⊕ *www.nps.gov/mora/planyourvisit/skyline-trail.htm.*

Van Trump Park Trail. You gain an exhilarating 2,200 feet on this route while hiking through a vast expanse of meadow with views of the southern Puget Sound. The 5¾-mile track provides good footing, and the average hiker can make it up and back in five hours. *Moderate.* ⊠ *Mt. Rainier National Park* ✛ *Trailhead: Hwy. 706 at Christine Falls, 4½ miles east of Longmire* ⊕ *www.nps.gov/mora/planyourvisit/van-trump-trail.htm.*

DIFFICULT

Fodor's Choice
★

Wonderland Trail. All other Mount Rainier hikes pale in comparison to this stunning 93-mile trek, which completely encircles the mountain. The trail passes through all the major life zones of the park, from the old-growth forests of the lowlands to the alpine meadows and goat-haunted glaciers of the highlands—pick up a mountain-goat sighting card from a ranger station or visitor center if you want to help in the park's effort to learn more about these elusive animals. Wonderland is a rugged trail; elevation gains and losses totaling 3,500 feet are common in a day's hike, which averages 8 miles. Most hikers start out from Longmire or Sunrise and take 10–14 days to cover the 93-mile route. Snow lingers on the high passes well into June (sometimes July); count on rain any time of the year. Campsites are wilderness areas with pit toilets and water that must be purified before drinking. Only hardy, well-equipped, and experienced wilderness trekkers should attempt this

Mount Rainier,
Looking North

MOUNT RAINIER

Columbia Crest
14,411 ft

Liberty Cap
14,122 ft

Point Success
14,153 ft

Little Tahoma Peak
11,138 ft

Disappointment
Cleaver

Ingraham Glacier

CATHEDRAL ROCKS

Anvil Rock
9,584 ft

Paradise Glaciers

McClure Rock
7,385 ft

Unicorn Peak
6,917 ft

Camp Muir
10,188 ft

Muir
Snowfield

Gibraltar Rock
12,660 ft

Nisqually Glacier

Panorama Point
6,800 ft

Louise
Lake

Paradise

The Castle

Reflection
Lakes

Wilson Glacier

Skyline Trail

Alta
Vista

Pinnacle
Peak
6,562 ft

SUNSET
AMPHITHEATER

Henry M. Jackson
Memorial Visitor Center

St. Andrews Rock
10,992 ft

Van Trump Glaciers

SUCCESS CLEAVER

Kautz Glacier

Success Glacier

WAPOWETY CLEAVER

CUSHMAN CREST

Lane Peak
6,012 ft

Plummer Peak
6,370 ft

TATOOSH RANGE

VAN TRUMP
PARK

Success Glaciers

Pyramid Glaciers

South Tahoma
GLACIER ISLAND

Tahoma Glacier

Wahpenoyo Peak
6,231 ft

Mildred Point

Chutla Peak

PUYALLUP CLEAVER

Tahoma Glacier

SUCCESS DIVIDE

Eagle Peak
5,958 ft

Tokaloo Rock
7,684 ft

Pyramid Peak
6,937 ft

PYRAMID
PARK

Creek

Trail Ridge

Cougar Rock

EMERALD RIDGE

Iron Mountain
6,283 ft

Pyramid

Rampart Ridge Trail

RAMPART

THE RAMPARTS

Longmire

KEY

——— Paved Roads
– – – Hiking Trails
·········· Climbing Routes

trip, but those who do will be amply rewarded. Wilderness permits are required, and reservations are strongly recommended. *Difficult.* ⊠ *Mt. Rainier National Park* ⊹ *Trailheads: Longmire Visitor Center, Hwy. 706, 17 miles east of Ashford; Sunrise Visitor Center, Sunrise Rd., 15 miles west of the White River park entrance* ⊕ *www.nps.gov/mora/ planyourvisit/the-wonderland-trail.htm.*

MOUNTAIN CLIMBING

Climbing Mt. Rainier is not for amateurs; each year, adventurers die on the mountain, and many become lost and must be rescued. Near-catastrophic weather can appear quite suddenly, any month of the year. If you're experienced in technical, high-elevation snow, rock, and ice-field adventuring, Mt. Rainier can be a memorable adventure. Climbers can fill out a climbing card at the Paradise, White River, or Carbon River ranger stations and lead their own groups of two or more. Climbers must register with a ranger before leaving and check out on return. A $46 annual climbing fee applies to anyone heading above 10,000 feet or onto one of Rainier's glaciers. During peak season it is recommended that climbers make their camping reservations ($20 per site) in advance; reservations are taken by fax and mail beginning in mid-March on a first-come, first-served basis (find the reservation form at ⊕ *www.nps. gov/mora/planyourvisit/climbing.htm*).

SKIING AND SNOWSHOEING

Mount Rainier is a major Nordic ski center for cross-country and telemark skiing. Although trails are not groomed, those around Paradise are extremely popular. If you want to ski with fewer people, try the trails in and around the Ohanapecosh–Stevens Canyon area, which are just as beautiful and, because of their more easterly exposure, slightly less subject to the rains that can douse the Longmire side, even in the dead of winter. Never ski on plowed main roads, especially around Paradise—the snowplow operator can't see you. Rentals aren't available on the eastern side of the park.

Deep snows make Mount Rainier a snowshoeing pleasure. The Paradise area, with its network of trails, is the best choice. The park's east-side roads, Routes 123 and 410, are unplowed and provide other good snowshoeing venues, although you must share the main routes with snowmobilers.

Paradise Snowplay Area and Nordic Ski Route. Sledding on flexible sleds (no toboggans or runners), inner tubes, and plastic saucers is allowed only in the Paradise snow-play area adjacent to the Jackson Visitor Center. The area is open when there is sufficient snow, usually from late December through mid-March. The easy, 3½-mile Paradise Valley Road Nordic ski route begins at the Paradise parking lot and follows Paradise Valley/Stevens Canyon Road to Reflection Lakes. Equipment rentals are available at Whittaker Mountaineering in Ashford or at the National Park Inn's General Store in Longmire. ⊠ *Adjacent to the Jackson Visitor Center at Paradise, Mt. Rainier National Park* ☎ *360/569–2211* ⊕ *www.nps.gov/mora/planyourvisit/winter-recreation.htm.*

DID YOU KNOW?

Named after British admiral Peter Rainier in the late 18th century, Mt. Rainier had an earlier name. Tahoma (also Takhoma), its American Indian name, means "the mountain that was God." Various unsuccessful attempts have been made to restore the aboriginal name to the peak. Of course, to most Puget Sound residents, Rainier is simply "the mountain."

TOURS AND OUTFITTERS

General Store at the National Park Inn. The store at the National Park Inn in Longmire rents cross-country ski equipment and snowshoes. It's open daily in winter, depending on snow conditions. ⊠ *National Park Inn, Longmire* ☎ *360/569–2411* ⊕ *www.mtrainierguestservices.com/ activities-and-events/winter-activities/cross-country-skiing.*

WHAT'S NEARBY

NEARBY TOWNS

Ashford sits astride an ancient trail across the Cascades used by the Yakama Indians to trade with the coastal tribes of western Washington. The town began as a logging railway terminal; today it's the main gateway to Mount Rainier—and the only year-round access point to the park—with lodges, restaurants, grocery stores, and gift shops. Surrounded by Cascade peaks, **Packwood** is a pretty mountain village on U.S. 12, below White Pass. Between Mount Rainier and Mount St. Helens, it's a perfect jumping-off point for exploring local wilderness areas.

Visitor Information Destination Packwood Association. ⊠ *13011B U.S. Hwy. 12, Packwood* ☎ *360/494–2223* ⊕ *www.destinationpackwood.com.*

NEARBY ATTRACTIONS

Goat Rocks Wilderness. The crags in Gifford Pinchot National Forest, south of Mt. Rainier, are aptly named. You often see mountain goats here, especially when you hike into the backcountry. Goat Lake is a particularly good spot for viewing these elusive creatures. See the goats without backpacking by taking Forest Road 21 to Forest Road 2140, south from U.S. 12. The goats will be on Stonewall Ridge looming up ahead of you. ⊠ *NF-21 and NF-2140, Randle* ☎ *360/891–5000* ⊕ *www.fs.usda.gov/giffordpinchot.*

Johnston Ridge Observatory. With the most spectacular views of the crater and lava dome of Mt. St. Helens, this observatory also has exhibits that interpret the geology of the mountain and explain how scientists monitor an active volcano. ⊠ *Rte. 504, 53 miles east of I–5, 24000 Spirit Lake Hwy., Castle Rock* ☎ *360/274–2140* ⊕ *www. fs.usda.gov/recarea/mountsthelens/recarea/?recid=31562* ⊠ *$8* ☉ *Nov.–mid-May.*

Mount St. Helens Science and Learning Center. The Mt. St. Helens Institute operates this center, which offers family camps, field trips, and learning experiences throughout the year. It's open to the public on weekends in the off-season when the Johnston Ridge Observatory is closed. Exhibits document the great 1980 blast of Mt. St. Helens and its effects on the surrounding 150,000 acres. A ¼-mile trail leads from the visitor center to Coldwater Lake. ⊠ *Rte. 504, 43 miles east of I–5, 19000 Spirit Lake Hwy., Toutle* ☎ *360/274–2131* ⊕ *www.mshslc.org* ☉ *Closed May–Oct. and weekdays except special events.*

Mount St. Helens Visitor Center. This facility, one of three visitor centers along Route 504 on the west side of the mountain, has exhibits documenting the eruption, plus a walk-through volcano. ⊠ *Rte. 504, 5* *miles east of I–5, 3029 Spirit Lake Hwy., Silver Lake* ☎ *360/274–0962* 🌐 *parks.state.wa.us/245/Mount-St-Helens* 🎟 *$5* 🕒 *Closed Nov.–Feb., Tues. and Wed.*

FAMILY **Mt. Rainier Scenic Railroad and Museum.** This trip takes you through lush forests and across scenic bridges, covering 14 miles of incomparable beauty. Trains depart from Elbe, 11 miles west of Ashford, then bring passengers to a lovely picnic area near Mineral Lake before returning. Seasonal theme trips, such as the Fall Leaves excursion and the Snowball Express, are also available. At Mineral Lake, guests can tour the museum containing old train memorabilia and artifacts, as well as exhibits on the area's old railroad camps, which served as the hub of logging operations by rail. ✉ *54124 Mountain Hwy. E, Elbe* ☎ *360/569–7959, 888/783–2611* 🌐 *www.mtrainier-railroad.com* 🎟 *Rides $39–$49* 🕒 *Closed Nov.–Apr. (except for holiday excursions).*

FAMILY **Northwest Trek Wildlife Park.** This spectacular, 435-acre wildlife park 35 miles south of Puyallup is devoted to native creatures of the Pacific Northwest. Walking paths wind through natural surroundings—so natural that a cougar once entered the park and started snacking on the deer (it was finally trapped and relocated to the North Cascades). See beavers, otters, and wolverines; get close to wolves, foxes, coyotes; and observe several species of big cats and bears in wild environments. Admission includes a 50-minute tram ride through fields of wandering moose, bighorn sheep, elk, bison, and mountain goats. The most adventurous way to see the park is via one of five ziplines, which traverse the park canopy—rides are available early May through late September. ✉ *11610 Trek Dr. E, Eatonville* ☎ *360/832–6117* 🌐 *www.nwtrek.org* 🎟 *$22.25* 🕒 *Closed Mon.–Thurs. in Oct.–mid-Mar. (except holidays).*

AREA ACTIVITIES

SPORTS AND THE OUTDOORS

Crystal Mountain Ski Area. Washington State's biggest and best-known ski area has 9 lifts (plus a children's lift and a gondola) and 57 runs. In summer, it's open for hiking, rides on the Mt. Rainier Gondola, and meals at the Summit House, all providing sensational views of Rainier and the Cascades. **Facilities:** 57 trails; 2,600 acres; 3,100-foot vertical drop; 11 lifts. ✉ *Crystal Mountain Blvd., off Rte. 410, Crystal Mountain* ☎ *360/663–2265* 🌐 *www.crystalmountainresort.com* 🎟 *Lift ticket: $74 including gondola, $39 beginner chair only; $22 gondola only.*

WHERE TO EAT

IN THE PARK

$$$ ECLECTIC 🍴 **National Park Inn Dining Room.** Photos of Mt. Rainier taken by top photographers adorn the walls of this inn's large dining room, a bonus on the many days the mountain refuses to show itself. Meals are simple but tasty: pot roast with mashed potatoes, seared halibut, cedar-plank trout, and blackberry cobbler à la mode. [$] *Average main: $22* ✉ *Hwy. 706, Longmire* ☎ *360/569–2411* 🌐 *www.mtrainierguestservices.com.*

$ ✕ **Paradise Camp Deli.** Grilled meats, sandwiches, salads, and soft drinks
AMERICAN   are served daily from May through early October and on weekends
FAMILY   and holidays during the rest of the year. Ⓢ *Average main: $9* ⊠ *Jack-son Visitor Center, Paradise Rd. E, Paradise* ☎ *360/569–6571* ⊕ *www.mtrainierguestservices.com* ⊙ *Closed weekdays early Oct.–Apr.*

$$$ ✕ **Paradise Inn.** Where else can you enjoy Sunday brunch in a historic,
AMERICAN   heavy-timbered lodge halfway up a mountain? Tall windows provide
terrific views of Rainier, and the warm glow of native wood permeates the large dining room, where hearty Pacific Northwest fare is served. Ⓢ *Average main: $24* ⊠ *E. Paradise Rd., near Jackson Visitor Center, Paradise* ☎ *360/569–2275* ⊕ *www.mtrainierguestservices.com* ⊙ *Closed Oct.–late May.*

$ ✕ **Sunrise Day Lodge Food Service.** A cafeteria and grill serve inexpensive
AMERICAN   hamburgers, chili, and hot dogs from July through September. Ⓢ *Av-erage main: $9* ⊠ *Sunrise Rd., 15 miles from the White River park entrance, Mt. Rainier National Park* ☎ *360/663–2425* ⊕ *www.mtrainierguestservices.com* ⊙ *Closed Oct.–June.*

PICNIC AREAS

Park picnic areas are usually open only from late May through September.

Sunrise Picnic Area. Set in an alpine meadow that's filled with wildflowers in July and August, this picnic area provides expansive views of the mountain and surrounding ranges in good weather. ⊠ *Sunrise Rd., 11 miles west of the White River entrance, Mt. Rainier National Park* ⊕ *www.nps.gov/mora/planyourvisit/sunrise.htm* ⊙ *Road to Sunrise usually closed Oct.–June.*

WHERE TO STAY

IN THE PARK

$$$ 🏨 **National Park Inn.** A large stone fireplace warms the common room
B&B/INN   of this country inn, the only one of the park's two inns that's open year-round. **Pros:** classic ambience; open all year. **Cons:** jam-packed in summer; must book far in advance; some rooms have shared bath. Ⓢ *Rooms from: $177* ⊠ *Longmire Visitor Complex, Hwy. 706, 6 miles east of Nisqually entrance, Longmire* ☎ *360/569–2275, 855/755–2275* ⊕ *www.mtrainierguestservices.com* ⊸ *25 rooms, 18 with bath* 🍽 *No meals.*

$$$ 🏨 **Paradise Inn.** With its hand-carved Alaskan cedar logs, burnished par-
HOTEL   quet floors, stone fireplaces, Indian rugs, and glorious mountain views,
Fodor'sChoice   this 1917 inn is a classic example of a National Park lodge. **Pros:** central
★   to trails; pristine vistas; nature-inspired details. **Cons:** rooms are small and basic; many rooms have shared bathrooms; no elevators, a/c, cell service, or Wi-Fi. Ⓢ *Rooms from: $182* ⊠ *E. Paradise Rd., near Jackson Visitor Center, Paradise* ☎ *360/569–2275, 855/755–2275* ⊕ *www.mtrainierguestservices.com* ⊙ *Closed mid-Oct.–mid-May* ⊸ *121 rooms* 🍽 *No meals.*

Best Campgrounds in Mount Rainier

Three drive-in campgrounds are in the park—Cougar Rock, Ohanapecosh, and White River—with almost 500 sites for tents and RVs. None has hot water or RV hookups. The nightly fee is $20. The more primitive Mowich Lake Campground has 10 walk-in sites for tents only; no fee is charged. For backcountry camping, get a free wilderness permit at a visitor center on a first-come, first-served basis. Primitive sites are spaced at 7- to 8-mile intervals along the Wonderland Trail.

Cougar Rock Campground. A secluded, heavily wooded campground with an amphitheater, Cougar Rock is one of the first to fill up. Reservations are accepted for summer only. ⊠ *2½ miles north of Longmire* ☎ *877/444–6777.*

Mowich Lake Campground. This is Rainier's only lakeside campground and has just 10 primitive campsites. At 4,959 feet, it's also peaceful and secluded. ⊠ *Mowich Lake Rd., 6 miles east of park boundary* ☎ *360/569–2211.*

Ohanapecosh Campground. This lush, green campground in the park's southeast corner has an amphitheater and self-guided trail. It's one of the first campgrounds to open for the season. ⊠ *Rte. 123, 1½ miles north of park boundary* ☎ *877/444–6777.*

White River Campground. At an elevation of 4,400 feet, White River is one of the park's highest and least wooded campgrounds. Here you can enjoy campfire programs, self-guided trails, and partial views of Mt. Rainier's summit. ⊠ *5 miles west of White River entrance* ☎ *360/569–2211.*

8

OLYMPIC NATIONAL PARK

Updated by
Shelley Arenas

A spellbinding setting is tucked into the country's far northwestern corner, within the heart-shape Olympic Peninsula. Edged on all sides by water, the forested landscape is remote and pristine, and works its way around the sharpened ridges of the snowcapped Olympic Mountains. Big lakes cut pockets of blue in the rugged blanket of pine forests, and hot springs gurgle up from the foothills. Along the coast the sights are even more enchanting: wave-sculpted boulders, tidal pools teeming with sea life, and tree-topped sea stacks.

OLYMPIC PLANNER

WHEN TO GO

Summer, with its long stretches of sun-filled days, is prime touring time for Olympic National Park. June through September are the peak months; Hurricane Ridge, the Hoh Rain Forest, Lake Crescent, and Ruby Beach are bustling by 10 am.

Late spring and early autumn are also good bets for clear weather; anytime between April and October, you'll have a good chance of fair skies. Between Thanksgiving and Easter, it's a toss-up as to which days will turn out fair; prepare for heavy clouds, rain showers, and chilly temperatures, then hope for the best.

Winter is a great time to visit if you enjoy isolation. Locals are usually the only hardy souls during this time, except for weekend skiers heading to the snowfields around Hurricane Ridge. Many visitor facilities have limited hours or are closed from October to April.

FESTIVALS AND EVENTS

FAMILY **Chocolate on the Beach Festival.** Venues in the North Beach towns of Seabrook, Moclips, and Pacific Beach host this annual celebration of chocolate the last weekend of February. Activities include classes, contests, demonstrations, and dining and sampling events. ⊠ *Pacific Beach* ⊕ *www.chocolateonthebeachfestival.com.*

Irrigation Festival. For more than a century, the people of Sequim have been celebrating the irrigation ditches that brought life-giving water here. Highlights of the 10-day festival include a beauty pageant, logging demonstrations, arts and crafts, a classic car show, a strongman competition, parades, and a picnic. ⊠ *Sequim* ☎ *360/461–6511* ⊕ *www. irrigationfestival.com.*

Centrum Summer Arts Festival. This summerlong lineup of concerts and workshops is held at Fort Worden State Park, a 19th-century Army base near Port Townsend. ⊠ *Port Townsend* ☎ *360/385–3102* ⊕ *www. centrum.org.*

Olympic Music Festival. A variety of classical concerts are performed in a renovated barn on weekends from July through early September; picnic on the farm while you listen. ☎ *360/385–9699 office,* ⊕ *www. olympicmusicfestival.org.*

Forks Old-Fashioned Fourth of July. A salmon bake, parade, demolition derby, arts-and-crafts exhibits, kids' activities, and plenty of fireworks mark Forks's weekend-long celebration. ⊠ *Forks* ☎ *360/374–2531, 800/443–6757* ⊕ *www.forkswa.com.*

Sequim Lavender Festival. The third weekend in July, a street fair and free self-guided farm tours celebrate Sequim's many fragrant lavender fields. ⊠ *Sequim* ☎ *360/681–3035* ⊕ *www.lavenderfestival.com.*

Wooden Boat Festival. Hundreds of antique boats sail into Port Townsend for the weekend; there's also live music, education programs, and demonstrations. ⊠ *Port Townsend* ☎ *360/385–3628* ⊕ *www.woodenboat.org.*

PLANNING YOUR TIME

OLYMPIC IN ONE DAY

Start at the **Lake Quinault Lodge**, in the park's southwest corner. From here, drive a half hour into the Quinault Valley via **South Shore Road**. Tackle the forested **Graves Creek Trail**, then head up **North Shore Road** to the Quinault Rain Forest Interpretive Trail. Next, head back to U.S. 101 and drive to **Ruby Beach**, where a shoreline walk presents a breathtaking scene of sea stacks and sparkling, pink-hued sands.

Forks, and its **Timber Museum**, are your next stop; have lunch here, then drive 20 minutes to the beach at **La Push**. Next, head to **Lake Crescent**, around the corner to the northeast, where you can rent a boat, take a swim, or enjoy a picnic next to the sparkling teal waters. Drive through **Port Angeles** to **Hurricane Ridge**; count on an hour's drive from

GOOD READS

■ Robert L. Wood's *Olympic Mountains Trail Guide* is a great resource for both day hikers and those planning longer excursions.

■ Craig Romano's *Day Hiking Olympic Peninsula: National Park/ Coastal Beaches/Southwest Washington* is a detailed guide to day hikes in and around the national park.

■ Stephen Whitney's *A Field Guide to the Cascades and Olympics* is an

excellent trailside reference, covering more than 500 plant and animal species found in the park.

■ The park's newspaper, the *Olympic Bugler,* is a seasonal guide for activities and opportunities in the park. You can pick it up at the visitor centers.

■ A handy online catalog of books, maps, and passes for northwest parks is available from Discover Your Northwest (⊕ *www.discovernw.org*).

bottom to top if there aren't too many visitors. At the ridge, explore the visitor center or hike the 3-mile loop to **Hurricane Hill,** where you can see over the entire park north to Vancouver Island and south past Mt. Olympus.

GETTING HERE AND AROUND

You can enter the park at a number of points, but since the park is 95% wilderness, access roads do not penetrate far. The best way to get around and to see many of the park's top sites is on foot.

AIR TRAVEL

Seattle–Tacoma International Airport is the nearest airport to Olympic National Park. It's roughly a two-hour drive from the park.

BOAT TRAVEL

Ferries provide another unique (though indirect) link to the Olympic area from Seattle; contact **Washington State Ferries** (☎ *800/843–3779, 206/464–6400* ⊕ *www.wsdot.wa.gov/ferries*) for information.

BUS TRAVEL

Grays Harbor Transit runs buses Monday through Saturday from Aberdeen and Hoquiam to Amanda Park, on the west end of Lake Quinault. Jefferson Transit operates a Forks–Amanda Park route Monday through Saturday.

Bus Contacts Grays Harbor Transit. ☎ *360/532–2770, 800/562–9730* ⊕ *www.ghtransit.com.* **Jefferson Transit.** ☎ *800/371–0497, 360/385–4777* ⊕ *www.jeffersontransit.com.*

CAR TRAVEL

U.S. 101 essentially encircles the main section of Olympic National Park, and a number of roads lead from the highway into the park's mountains and toward its beaches. You can reach U.S. 101 via Interstate 5 at Olympia, via Route 12 at Aberdeen, or via Route 104 from the Washington state ferry terminals at Bainbridge or Kingston.

PARK ESSENTIALS

ADMISSION FEES AND PERMITS

Seven-day vehicle admission is $25; an annual pass is $50. Individuals arriving on foot, bike, or motorcycle pay $10. An overnight wilderness permit, available at visitor centers and ranger stations, is $7 per person per night. An annual wilderness camping permit costs $45. Fishing in freshwater streams and lakes within Olympic National Park does not require a Washington state fishing license; however, anglers must acquire a salmon-steelhead catch record card when fishing for those species. Ocean fishing and harvesting shellfish require licenses, which are available at sporting-goods and outdoor-supply stores.

ADMISSION HOURS

Six park entrances are open 24/7; gate kiosk hours (for buying passes) vary according to season and location, but most are staffed during daylight hours. Olympic National Park is in the Pacific time zone.

CELL-PHONE RECEPTION

Note that cell reception is sketchy in wilderness areas. There are public telephones at the Olympic National Park Visitor Center, Hoh River Rain Forest Visitor Center, and lodging properties within the park— Lake Crescent, Kalaloch, and Sol Duc Hot Springs. Fairholme General Store also has a phone.

EDUCATIONAL OFFERINGS

CLASSES AND SEMINARS

FAMILY **NatureBridge.** This rustic educational facility offers talks and excursions focusing on park ecology and history. Trips range from canoe trips to camping excursions, with a strong emphasis on family programs. ⊠ *111 Barnes Point Rd., Port Angeles* ☎ *360/928–3720* ⊕ *www.naturebridge. org/olympic.*

RANGER PROGRAMS

FAMILY **Junior Ranger Program.** Anyone can pick up the booklet at visitor centers and ranger stations and follow this fun program, which includes assignments to discover park flora and fauna, ocean life, and Native American lore. Kids get a badge when they turn in the finished work. ⊠ *Olympic National Park* ☎ *360/565–3130* ⊕ *www.nps.gov/olym/ forkids/beajuniorranger.htm.*

RESTAURANTS

The major resorts are your best bets for eating out in the park. Each has a main restaurant, café, and/or kiosk, as well as casually upscale dinner service, with regional seafood, meat, and produce complemented by a range of microbrews and good Washington and international wines. Reservations are either recommended or required.

Outside the park, small, easygoing cafés and bistros line the main thoroughfares in Sequim, Port Angeles, and Port Townsend, offering cuisine that ranges from hearty American-style fare to more eclectic local flavor.

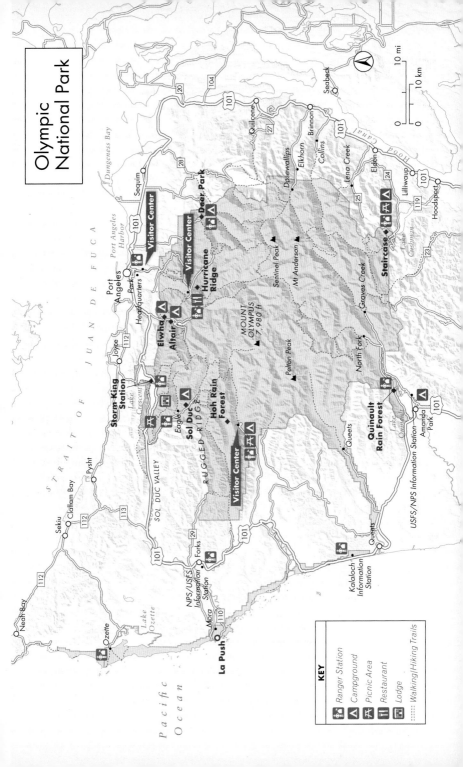

Olympic National Park

HOTELS

Major park resorts run from good to terrific, with generally comfortable rooms, excellent facilities, and easy access to trails, beaches, and activity centers. Midsize accommodations, like Sol Duc Hot Springs Resort, are often shockingly rustic—but remember, you're here for the park, not for the rooms.

The towns around the park have motels, hotels, and resorts for every budget. For a full beach-town vacation experience, base yourself in a home or cottage in the coastal community of Seabrook (near Pacific Beach). Sequim and Port Angeles have many attractive, friendly B&Bs, plus lots of inexpensive chain hotels and motels. Forks is basically a motel town, with a few guesthouses around its fringes.

Hotel reviews have been shortened. For full information, visit Fodors.com.

VISITOR INFORMATION

Park Contact Information Olympic National Park. ⊠ *Olympic National Park Visitor Center, 3002 Mount Angeles Rd., Port Angeles* ☎ *360/565–3130* ⊕ *www. nps.gov/olym.*

VISITOR CENTERS

Hoh Rain Forest Visitor Center. Pick up park maps and pamphlets, permits, and activities lists in this busy, woodsy chalet; there's also a shop and exhibits on natural history. Several short interpretive trails and longer wilderness treks start from here. ⊠ *Hoh Valley Rd., Forks* ✛ *31 miles south of Forks* ☎ *360/374–6925* ⊕ *www.nps.gov/olym/planyourvisit/ visitorcenters.htm* ☉ *Closed Jan., Feb., and weekdays off-season.*

Hurricane Ridge Visitor Center. The upper level of this visitor center has exhibits and nice views; the lower level has a gift shop and snack bar. Guided walks and programs start in late June. In winter, find details on the surrounding ski and sledding slopes and take guided snowshoe walks. ⊠ *Hurricane Ridge Rd., Olympic National Park* ☎ *360/565– 3131 for road conditions* ⊕ *www.nps.gov/olym/planyourvisit/visitor- centers.htm* ☉ *Operating hours/days vary off-season.*

Olympic National Park Visitor Center. This modern, well-organized facility, staffed by park rangers, provides everything: maps, trail brochures, campground advice, weather forecasts, listings of wildlife sightings, educational programs and exhibits, information on road and trail closures, and a gift shop. ⊠ *3002 Mount Angeles Rd., Port Angeles* ☎ *360/565– 3130* ⊕ *www.nps.gov/olym/planyourvisit/visitorcenters.htm.*

South Shore Quinault Ranger Station. The National Forest Service's ranger station near the Lake Quinault Lodge has maps, campground information, and program listings. ⊠ *353 S. Shore Rd., Quinault* ☎ *360/288–2525* ⊕ *www.fs.usda.gov/main/olympic/home* ☉ *Weekends early Sept.–late May.*

Wilderness Information Center (WIC). Located behind Olympic National Park Visitor Center, this facility provides all the information you'll need for a trip in the park, including trail conditions, safety tips, and weather bulletins. The office also issues camping permits, takes campground reservations, and rents bear-proof food canisters. ⊠ *3002 Mount Angeles Rd., Port Angeles* ☎ *360/565–3100* ⊕ *www.nps.gov/olym/planyour- visit/wic.htm* ☉ *Mon.–Thurs. off-season.*

EXPLORING

Most of the park's attractions are found either off U.S. 101 or down trails that require hikes of 15 minutes or longer. The west-coast beaches are linked to the highway by downhill tracks; the number of cars parked alongside the road at the start of the paths indicates how crowded the beach will be.

SCENIC DRIVES

Fodor's Choice ★ **Port Angeles Visitor Center to Hurricane Ridge.** The premier scenic drive in Olympic National Park is a steep ribbon of curves, which climbs from thickly forested foothills and subalpine meadows into the upper stretches of pine-swathed peaks. At the top, the visitor center at Hurricane Ridge has some spectacular views over the heart of the peninsula and across the Strait of Juan de Fuca. A mile past the visitor center, there are picnic tables in open meadows with photo-worthy views of the mountains to the east. Hurricane Ridge also has an uncommonly fine display of wildflowers in spring and summer. In winter, vehicles must carry chains and the road is usually open Friday–Sunday only (call first to check conditions). ⊠ *Olympic National Park* ⊕ *www. nps.gov/olym.*

HISTORIC SITES

La Push. At the mouth of Quileute River, La Push is the tribal center of the Quileute Indians. In fact, the town's name is a variation on the French *la bouche,* which means "the mouth." Offshore rock spires known as sea stacks dot the coast here, and you may catch a glimpse of bald eagles nesting in the nearby cliffs. ⊠ *Rte. 110, 14 miles west of Forks, La Push* ⊕ *www.nps.gov/olym/planyourvisit/ upload/mora.pdf.*

Lake Ozette. The third-largest glacial impoundment in Washington anchors the coastal strip of Olympic National Park at its north end. The small town of Ozette, home to a coastal tribe, is the trailhead for two of the park's better one-day hikes. Both 3-mile trails lead over boardwalks through swampy wetland and coastal old-growth forest to the ocean shore and uncrowded beaches. ⊠ *Ozette* ✣ *At the end of Hoko-Ozette Rd., 26 miles southwest of Hwy. 112 near Sekiu* ☎ *360/565–3130 Ozette Ranger Station* ⊕ *www.nps.gov/olym/planyourvisit/visiting-ozette.htm.*

SCENIC STOPS

Fodor's Choice ★ **Hoh River Rain Forest.** South of Forks, an 18-mile spur road links Highway 101 with this unique temperate rain forest, where spruce and hemlock trees soar to heights of more than 200 feet. Alders and big-leaf maples are so densely covered with mosses they look more like shaggy prehistoric animals than trees, and elk browse in shaded glens. Be prepared for precipitation: the region receives 140 inches or more each year. ⊠ *Olympic National Park* ✣ *From Hwy. 101, at about 20 miles north of Kalaloch, turn onto Upper Hoh Rd. 18 miles east to Hoh Rain Forest Visitor Center* ☎ *360/374–6925* ⊕ *www.nps.gov/olym/planyourvisit/visiting-the-hoh.htm.*

8

Fodor's Choice **Hurricane Ridge.** The panoramic view from this 5,200-foot-high ridge
★ encompasses the Olympic range, the Strait of Juan de Fuca, and Vancouver Island. Guided tours are given in summer along the many
paved and unpaved trails, where wildflowers and wildlife such as
deer and marmots flourish. ⊠ *Hurricane Ridge Rd., 17 miles south of
Port Angeles, Olympic National Park* ☎ *360/565–3130 visitor center* ⊕ *www.nps.gov/olym/planyourvisit/visiting-hurricane-ridge.htm*
⊘ *Closed when road is closed.*

Kalaloch. With a lodge and restaurant, a huge campground, miles of
coastline, and easy access from the highway, this is a popular spot.
Keen-eyed beachcombers may spot sea otters just offshore; they were
reintroduced here in 1970. ⊠ *Hwy. 101, 32 miles northwest of Lake
Quinault, Kalaloch* ☎ *360/565–3130 visitor center* ⊕ *www.nps.gov/
olym/planyourvisit/visiting-kalaloch-and-ruby-beach.htm.*

Lake Crescent. Visitors see Lake Crescent as Highway 101 winds along
its southern shore, giving way to gorgeous views of teal waters rippling in a basin formed by Tuscan-like hills. In the evening, low
bands of clouds caught between the surrounding mountains often
linger over its reflective surface. ⊠ *Hwy. 101, 16 miles west of Port
Angeles and 28 miles northeast of Forks, Olympic National Park
☎ 360/565–3130 visitor center* ⊕ *www.nps.gov/olym/planyourvisit/
visiting-lake-crescent.htm.*

Lake Quinault. This glimmering lake, 4½ miles long and 300 feet deep,
is the first landmark you'll reach when driving the west-side loop of
U.S. 101. The rain forest is thickest here, with moss-draped maples
and alders, and towering spruce, fir, and hemlock. Enchanted Valley,
high up near the Quinault River's source, is a deeply glaciated valley
that's closer to the Hood Canal than to the Pacific Ocean. A scenic
loop drive circles the lake and travels around a section of the Quinault
River. ⊠ *Hwy. 101, 38 miles north of Hoquiam, Olympic National Park
☎ 360/288–2525 Quinault Rain Forest ranger station* ⊕ *www.nps.gov/
olym/planyourvisit/visiting-quinault.htm.*

Second and Third Beaches. During low tide these flat, driftwood-strewn
expanses are perfect for long afternoon strolls. Second Beach, accessed
via an easy forest trail through Quileute lands, opens to a vista of Pacific
Ocean and sea stacks. Third Beach offers a 1.3-mile forest hike for a
warm-up before reaching the sands. ⊠ *Hwy. 101, 32 miles north of
Lake Quinault, Olympic National Park* ☎ *360/565–3130 visitor center*
⊕ *www.nps.gov/olym.*

Sol Duc. Sol Duc Valley is one of those magical places where all the
Northwest's virtues seem at hand: lush lowland forests, sparkling river
scenes, salmon runs, and serene hiking trails. Here, the popular Sol
Duc Hot Springs area includes three attractive sulfuric pools ranging
in temperature from 98°F to 104°F. ⊠ *Sol Duc Rd., Olympic National
Park* ✛ *South of U.S. 101, 12 miles past the west end of Lake Crescent*
☎ *360/565–3130 visitor center* ⊕ *www.nps.gov/olym/planyourvisit/
visiting-the-sol-duc-valley.htm.*

Staircase. Unlike the forests of the park's south and west sides, Douglas
fir is the dominant tree on the east slope of the Olympic Mountains. Fire

CLOSE UP

Plants and Wildlife in Olympic

Along the high mountain slopes hardy cedar, fir, and hemlock trees stand tough on the rugged land; the lower montane forests are filled with thickets of silver firs; and valleys stream with Douglas firs and western hemlock. The park's famous temperate rain forests are on the peninsula's western side, marked by broad western red cedars, towering red spruces, and ferns festooned with strands of mosses and patchwork lichens. This lower landscape is also home to some of the Northwest's largest trees: massive cedar and Sitka spruce near Lake Quinault can measure more than 700 inches around, and Douglas firs near the Queets and Hoh rivers are nearly as wide.

These landscapes are home to a variety of wildlife, including many large mammals and 15 creatures found nowhere else in the world. Hikers often come across Roosevelt's elk, black-tailed deer, mountain goats, beavers, raccoons, skunks, opossums, and foxes; Douglas squirrels and flying squirrels populate the heights of the forest. Less common are black bears (most prevalent from May through August); wolves, bobcats, and cougar are rarely seen. Birdlife includes bald eagles, red-tailed hawks, osprey, and great horned owls. Rivers and lakes are filled with freshwater fish, while beaches hold crabs, sea stars, anemones, and other shelled creatures. Get out in a boat on the Pacific to spot seals, sea lions, and sea otters—and perhaps a pod of porpoises, orcas, or gray whales.

Beware of jellyfish around the shores—beached jellyfish can still sting. In the woods, check for ticks after every hike and after each shower. Biting nasties include black flies, horseflies, sand fleas, and the ever-present mosquitoes. Yellowjacket nests populate tree hollows along many trails; signs throughout the Hoh Rain Forest warn hikers to move quickly through these sections. If one or two chase you, remain calm and keep walking; these are just "guards" making sure you're keeping away from the hive. Poison oak is common, so familiarize yourself with its appearance. Bug repellent, sunscreen, and long pants and sleeves will go a long way toward making your experience more comfortable.

has played an important role in creating the majestic forest here, as the Staircase Ranger Station explains in interpretive exhibits. ⊠ *Olympic National Park* ✛ *At end of Rte. 119, 15 miles from U.S. 101 at Hoodsport* ☎ *360/565–3130 visitor center* ⊕ *www.nps.gov/olym/planyourvisit/visiting-staircase.htm.*

SPORTS AND THE OUTDOORS

BICYCLING

The rough gravel car tracks to some of the park's remote sites were meant for four-wheel-drive vehicles, but can double as mountain-bike routes. The Quinault Valley, Queets River, Hoh River, and Sol Duc River roads have bike paths through old-growth forest. Graves Creek Road, in the southwest, is a mountain-bike path; Lake Crescent's north

8

side is also edged by the bike-friendly Spruce Railroad Trail. More bike tracks run through the adjacent Olympic National Forest. Note that U.S. 101 has heavy traffic and isn't recommended for cycling, although the western side has broad roads with beautiful scenery and can be biked off-season. Bikes are not permitted on foot trails.

TOURS AND OUTFITTERS

All Around Bikes. This bike, gear, and repair shop is a great resource for advice on routes around the Olympic Peninsula. Bike rentals cost $30 per half day, $50 all day, and $60 for 24 hours. ✉ *150 W. Sequim Bay Rd., Sequim* ☎ *360/681–3868* ⊕ *www.allaroundbikes.com.*

Sound Bike & Kayak. This sports outfitter rents and sells bikes, kayaks, and related equipment. Kayak rentals run $15 per hour and $50 per day. Bikes rent for $10 per hour and $45 per day. ✉ *120 E. Front St., Port Angeles* ☎ *360/457–1240* ⊕ *www.soundbikeskayaks.com.*

CLIMBING

At 7,980 feet, Mt. Olympus is the highest peak in the park and the most popular climb in the region. To attempt the summit, climbers must register at the Glacier Meadows Ranger Station. Mt. Constance, the third-highest Olympic peak at 7,743 feet, has a well-traversed climbing route that requires technical experience; reservations are recommended for the Lake Constance stop, which is limited to 20 campers. Mt. Deception is another possibility, though tricky snows have caused fatalities and injuries in the last decade.

Climbing season runs from late June through September. Note that crevasse skills and self-rescue experience are highly recommended. Climbers must register with park officials and purchase wilderness permits before setting out. The best resource for climbing advice is the Wilderness Information Center in Port Angeles.

TOURS AND OUTFITTERS

Mountain Madness. Adventure through the rain forest to the glaciated summit of Mt. Olympus on a five-day trip, offered several times per year by Mountain Madness. ☎ *800/328–5925, 206/937–8389* ⊕ *www. mountainmadness.com* ✍ *From $1,350 for 5-day climb.*

FISHING

There are numerous fishing possibilities throughout the park. Lake Crescent is home to cutthroat and rainbow trout, as well as petite kokanee salmon; Lake Cushman, Lake Quinault, and Ozette Lake have trout, salmon, and steelhead. As for rivers, the Bogachiel and Queets have steelhead salmon in season. The glacier-fed Hoh River is home to chinook salmon April to November, and coho salmon from August through November; the Sol Duc River offers all five species of salmon. Rainbow trout are found in the Dosewallips, Elwha, and Skykomish rivers. Other places to go after salmon and trout include the Duckabush, Quillayute, Quinault, and Salmon rivers. A Washington state punch card is required during salmon-spawning months; fishing regulations vary throughout the park. Licenses are available from sporting-goods and outdoor-supply stores.

TOURS AND OUTFITTERS

Bob's Piscatorial Pursuits. This company, based in Forks, offers salmon and steelhead fishing trips around the Olympic Peninsula from mid-September through May. ⊠ *Forks* ☎ *866/347–4232* ⊕ *www.piscatorialpursuits.com* ✉ *From $225 per person for 2 people; $340 for 1 person.*

HIKING

Know your tides, or you might be trapped by high water. Tide tables are available at all visitor centers and ranger stations. Remember that a wilderness permit is required for all overnight backcountry visits.

EASY

FAMILY
Fodor'sChoice
★
Hoh River Trail. From the Hoh Visitor Center, this rain-forest jaunt takes you into the Hoh Valley, wending its way for 17½ miles alongside the river, through moss-draped maple and alder trees and past open meadows where elk roam in winter. *Easy.* ⊠ *Olympic National Park* ✛ *Trailhead: Hoh Visitor Center, 18 miles east of U.S. 101* ⊕ *www.nps.gov/olym/planyourvisit/hoh-river-trail.htm.*

Hurricane Ridge Meadow Trail. A ¼-mile alpine loop, most of it wheelchair accessible, leads through wildflower meadows overlooking numerous vistas of the interior Olympic peaks to the south and a panorama of the Strait of Juan de Fuca to the north. *Easy.* ⊠ *Olympic National Park* ✛ *Trailhead: Hurricane Ridge Rd., 17 miles south of Port Angeles* ⊕ *www.nps.gov/olym/planyourvisit/visiting-hurricane-ridge.htm.*

MODERATE

FAMILY
Cape Alava Trail. Beginning at Ozette, this 3-mile boardwalk trail leads from the forest to wave-tossed headlands. *Moderate.* ⊠ *Ozette* ✛ *Trailhead: end of the Hoko-Ozette Rd., 26 miles south of Hwy. 112, west of Sekiu* ⊕ *www.nps.gov/olym/planyourvisit/visiting-ozette.htm.*

Graves Creek Trail. This 6-mile-long moderately strenuous trail climbs from lowland rain forest to alpine territory at Sundown Pass. Due to spring floods, a fjord halfway up is often impassable in May and June. *Moderate.* ⊠ *Olympic National Park* ✛ *Trailhead: end of S. Shore Rd., 23 miles east of U.S. 101* ⊕ *www.nps.gov/olym.*

FAMILY
Fodor'sChoice
★
Sol Duc River Trail. The 1½-mile gravel path off Sol Duc Road winds through thick Douglas fir forests toward the thundering, three-chute Sol Duc Falls. Just 0.1 mile from the road, below a wooden platform over the Sol Duc River, you'll come across the 70-foot Salmon Cascades. In late summer and autumn, thousands of salmon negotiate 50 miles or more of treacherous waters to reach the cascades and the tamer pools near Sol Duc Hot Springs. The popular 6-mile **Lovers Lane Loop Trail** links the Sol Duc falls with the hot springs. You can continue up from the falls 5 miles to the **Appleton Pass Trail**, at 3,100 feet. From there you can hike on to the 8½-mile mark, where views at the High Divide are from 5,050 feet. *Moderate.* ⊠ *Olympic National Park* ✛ *Trailhead: Sol Duc Rd., 12 miles south of U.S. 101* ⊕ *www.nps.gov/olym/planyourvisit/sol-duc-river-trail.htm.*

8

Sol Duc Trail

DIFFICULT

High Divide Trail. A 9-mile hike in the park's high country defines this trail, which includes some strenuous climbing on its last 4 miles before topping out at a small alpine lake. A return loop along High Divide wends its way an extra mile through alpine territory, with sensational views of Olympic peaks. This trail is only for dedicated, properly equipped hikers who are in good shape. *Difficult.* ⊠ *Olympic National Park* ✢ *Trailhead: end of Sol Duc River Rd., 13 miles south of U.S. 101* ⊕ *www.nps.gov/olym/planyourvisit/high-divide-loop.htm.*

KAYAKING AND CANOEING

Lake Crescent, a serene expanse of teal-color waters surrounded by deep-green pine forests, is one of the park's best boating areas. Note that the west end is for swimming only; no speedboats are allowed here.

Lake Quinault has boating access from a gravel ramp on the north shore. From U.S. 101, take a right on North Shore Road, another right on Hemlock Way, and a left on Lakeview Drive. There are plank ramps at Falls Creek and Willoughby campgrounds on South Shore Drive, 0.1 mile and 0.2 mile past the Quinault Ranger Station, respectively.

Lake Ozette, with just one access road, is a good place for overnight trips. Only experienced canoe and kayak handlers should travel far from the put-in, since fierce storms occasionally strike—even in summer.

TOURS AND OUTFITTERS

Fairholme General Store. Kayaks and canoes on Lake Crescent are available to rent from $20 per hour to $55 for eight hours. The store is at the lake's west end, 27 miles west of Port Angeles. ✉ *221121 U.S. 101, Port Angeles* ☎ *360/928–3020* ⊘ *Closed after Labor Day–Apr. and Mon.–Thurs. in May.*

Lake Crescent Lodge. You can rent canoes and kayaks here for $20 per hour and $55 per half day. Two-hour guided kayak tours are offered and include instructions; they cost $55 in a single kayak and $75 in a double kayak. ✉ *416 Lake Crescent Rd., Olympic National Park* ☎ *360/928– 3211* ⊕ *www.olympicnationalparks.com* ⊘ *Closed Jan.–Apr.*

Log Cabin Resort. This resort, 17 miles west of Port Angeles, has paddle-boat, kayak, canoe, and paddleboard rentals for $20 per hour and $55 per day. The dock provides easy access to Lake Crescent's northeast section. ✉ *3183 E. Beach Rd., Port Angeles* ☎ *360/928–3325* ⊕ *www. olympicnationalparks.com* ⊘ *Closed Oct.–mid-May.*

Rainforest Paddlers. This company takes kayakers down the Lizard Rock and Oxbow sections of the Hoh River and rafters on both the Hoh and Sol Duc rivers. They also offer river rafting and kayak rentals. ✉ *4883 Upper Hoh Rd., Forks* ☎ *360/374–5254, 866/457–8398* ⊕ *www.rain-forestpaddlers.com* ▣ *Tours from $44; kayak rentals from $11/hr.*

RAFTING

Olympic has excellent rafting rivers, with Class II to Class V rapids. The Elwha River is a popular place to paddle, with some exciting turns. The Hoh is better for those who like a smooth, easy float.

TOURS AND OUTFITTERS

Olympic Raft and Kayak. Based in Port Angeles, this rafting outfit offers trips on the Sol Duc and Hoh rivers, and on the restored Elwha River when conditions allow. It also offers half-day kayaking trips on the Salish Sea, launching from a county park in Port Angeles. ✉ *123 Lake Aldwell Rd., Port Angeles* ☎ *888/452–1443* ⊕ *www.raftandkayak.com* ▣ *From $65.*

WINTER SPORTS

Hurricane Ridge is the central spot for winter sports. Miles of downhill and Nordic ski tracks are open late December through March, and a ski lift, towropes, and ski school are open 10 to 4 weekends and holidays. A snow-play area for children ages eight and younger is near the Hurricane Ridge Visitors Center. Hurricane Ridge Road is open Friday through Sunday in the winter season; all vehicles are required to carry chains.

TOURS AND OUTFITTERS

Hurricane Ridge Visitor Center. Rent snowshoes and ski equipment here December through March. ✉ *Hurricane Ridge Rd., Port Angeles* ☎ *360/565–3131 road condition information* ⊕ *www.nps.gov/olym/ planyourvisit/hurricane-ridge-in-winter.htm* ⊘ *Closed Mon.–Thurs.*

8

WHAT'S NEARBY

NEARBY TOWNS

Although most Olympic Peninsula towns have evolved from their exclusive reliance on timber, **Forks**, outside the national park's northwest tip, remains one of the region's logging capitals. Washington state's wettest town (100 inches or more of rain a year), it's a small, friendly place with just 3,500 residents and a modicum of visitor facilities. **Port Angeles**, a city of 19,000, focuses on its status as the main gateway to Olympic National Park and Victoria, British Columbia. Set below the Strait of Juan de Fuca and looking north to Vancouver Island, it's an enviably scenic settlement filled with attractive, Craftsman-style homes.

The Pacific Northwest has its very own "Banana Belt" in the waterfront community of **Sequim**, 15 miles east of Port Angeles along U.S. 101. The town of 6,600 is in the rain shadow of the Olympics and receives only 16 inches of rain per year (compared with the 140 inches that drench the Hoh Rain Forest just 40 miles away). The beach community of **Seabrook**, near Pacific Beach, is 25 miles from the southeast corner of the national park via the Moclips Highway. Many of its several hundred high-end vacation homes are available for short-term rentals; the community has parks, swimming pools, bike trails, special events, and a growing retail district.

Visitor Information Forks Chamber of Commerce Visitor Center. ⊠ *1411 S. Forks Ave. (U.S. 101), Forks* ☎ *800/443–6757, 360/374–2531* ⊕ *www.forkswa. com.* **Port Angeles Chamber of Commerce Visitor Center.** ⊠ *121 E. Railroad Ave., Port Angeles* ☎ *360/452–2363* ⊕ *www.portangeles.org.* **Sequim-Dungeness Valley Chamber of Commerce.** ⊠ *1192 E. Washington St., Sequim* ☎ *360/683–6197, 800/737–8462* ⊕ *www.sequimchamber.com.*

NEARBY ATTRACTIONS

FAMILY

Fodor's Choice

★

Dungeness Spit. Curving 5½ miles into the Strait of Juan de Fuca, the longest natural sand spit in the United States is a wild, beautiful section of shoreline. More than 30,000 migratory waterfowl stop here each spring and fall, but you'll see plenty of birdlife any time of year. The entire spit is part of the **Dungeness National Wildlife Refuge.** Access is through the **Dungeness Recreation Area,** which serves as a portal to the shoreline. ⊠ *554 Voice of America Rd., Sequim* ✛ *Entrance 3 miles north from U.S. 101, 4 miles west of Sequim* ☎ *360/457–8451 wildlife refuge* ⊕ *www.clallam.net/parks/dungeness.html* ⊠ *$3 per family.*

New Dungeness Lighthouse. At the end of the Dungeness Spit is the towering white 1857 New Dungeness Lighthouse; tours are available, though access is limited to those who can hike or kayak out 5 miles to the end of the spit. Guests also have the opportunity to serve as lighthouse keepers for a week at a time. An adjacent, 66-site camping area, on the bluff above the Strait of Juan de Fuca, is open year-round. ⊠ *Sequim* ✛ *Entrance 3 miles north of Hwy. 101 via Kitchen Dick Rd.* ☎ *360/683–6638* ⊕ *www.newdungenesslighthouse.com.*

Port Angeles Fine Arts Center. This small, sophisticated museum is inside the former home of late artist and publisher Esther Barrows Webster, one of Port Angeles's most energetic and cultured citizens; displays are modern, funky, and intriguing. Outside, Webster's Woods Art Park is dotted with oversize sculptures set before a vista of the city and harbor. Exhibitions emphasize the works of emerging and well-established Pacific Northwest artists. ✉ *1203 E. Lauridsen Blvd., Port Angeles* ☎ *360/457–3532* 🌐 *www.pafac.org* 🎟 *Free* 🕓 *Closed Oct.–Mar.*

Timber Museum. The museum highlights Forks's logging history since the 1870s; a garden and fire tower are also on the grounds. ✉ *1421 S. Forks Ave., Forks* ☎ *360/374–9663* 🌐 *www.forkstimbermuseum.org* 🎟 *$3.*

WHERE TO EAT

IN THE PARK

$$$ AMERICAN

🍴 **Creekside Restaurant.** A tranquil country setting and ocean views at Kalaloch Lodge's restaurant create the perfect backdrop for savoring Pacific Northwest dinner specialties like grilled salmon, fresh shellfish, and vegan lasagne. Tempting seasonal desserts include local berry tart in summer and organic winter squash bread pudding in winter; warm vegan chocolate brownies are enjoyed year-round. [$] *Average main: $24* ✉ *157151 Hwy. 101, Forks* ☎ *866/662–9928, 360/962–2271* 🌐 *www.thekalalochlodge.com/dine.aspx.*

$$$ AMERICAN

🍴 **Lake Crescent Lodge.** Part of the original 1916 lodge, the fir-paneled dining room overlooks the lake; you won't find a better spot for sunset views. Dinner entrées include wild salmon, thyme roasted halibut, grilled steak, pork shank, and roasted chicken breast; the lunch menu features elk cheeseburgers, inventive salads, and a variety of sandwiches. [$] *Average main: $29* ✉ *416 Lake Crescent Rd., Port Angeles* ☎ *360/928–3211* 🌐 *www.olympicnationalparks.com/stay/dining/lake-crescent-lodge.aspx* 🕓 *Closed Jan.–Apr.*

$$$ AMERICAN

🍴 **The Springs Restaurant.** The main Sol Duc Hot Springs Resort restaurant is a rustic, fir-and-cedar-paneled dining room surrounded by trees. In summer big breakfasts are turned out daily 7:30 to 10; dinner is served between 5 and 9, and features comfort foods like pan-roasted salmon, chicken with garlic mashed potatoes, short ribs, burgers, fish-and-chips, mac and cheese, and sandwiches. [$] *Average main: $21* ✉ *12076 Sol Duc Rd., at U.S. 101, Port Angeles* ☎ *360/327–3583* 🌐 *www.olympicnationalparks.com/stay/dining/sol-duc-hot-springs-resort-.aspx* 🕓 *Closed Nov.–late Mar.*

PICNIC AREAS

All Olympic National Park campgrounds have adjacent picnic areas with tables, some shelters, and restrooms, but no cooking facilities. The same is true for major visitor centers, such as Hoh Rain Forest. Drinking water is available at ranger stations, interpretive centers, and inside campgrounds.

East Beach Picnic Area. Set on a grassy meadow overlooking Lake Crescent, this popular swimming spot has six picnic tables and vault toilets. ✉ *East Beach Rd., Port Angeles* ✥ *At far east end of Lake Crescent, off Hwy. 101, 17 miles west of Port Angeles.*

8

Best Campgrounds in Olympic

Note that only a few places take reservations; if you can't book in advance, you'll have to arrive early to get a place. Each site usually has a picnic table and grill or fire pit, and most campgrounds have water, toilets, and garbage containers; for hookups, showers, and laundry facilities, you'll have to head into the towns. Firewood is available from camp concessions, but if there's no store you can collect dead wood within 1 mile of your campsite. Dogs are allowed in campgrounds, but not on most trails or in the backcountry. Trailers should be 21 feet long or less (15 feet or less at Queets Campground) though a few campgrounds can accommodate up to 35 feet. There's a camping limit of two weeks. Nightly rates run $15–$22 per site.

If you have a backcountry pass, you can camp virtually anywhere throughout the park's forests and shores. Overnight wilderness permits are $7 per person per night and are available at visitor centers and ranger stations. Note that when you camp in the backcountry, you must choose a site at least ½ mile inside the park boundary.

Kalaloch Campground. Kalaloch is the biggest and most popular Olympic campground, and it's open all year. Its vantage of the Pacific is unmatched on the park's coastal stretch. ⊠ *U.S. 101, ½ mile north of Kalaloch Information Station, Olympic National Park* ☎ *877/444–6777 for reservations.*

Lake Quinault Rain Forest Resort Village Campground. Stretching along the south shore of Lake Quinault, this RV campground has many recreation facilities, including beaches, canoes, ball fields, and horseshoe pits. The 31 RV sites, which rent for $35 per night, are open year-round but bathrooms are closed in winter. ⊠ *3½ miles east of U.S. 101, South Shore Rd., Lake Quinault* ☎ *360/288–2535, 800/255–6936* ⊕ *www.rainforestresort.com.*

Mora Campground. Along the Quillayute estuary, this campground doubles as a popular staging point for hikes northward along the coast's wilderness stretch. ⊠ *Rte. 110, 13 miles west of Forks* ☎ *No phone.*

Ozette Campground. Hikers heading to Cape Alava, a scenic promontory that is the westernmost point in the lower 48 states, use this lakeshore campground as a jumping-off point. ⊠ *Hoko-Ozette Rd., 26 miles south of Hwy. 112* ☎ *No phone.*

Sol Duc Campground. Sol Duc resembles virtually all Olympic campgrounds save one distinguishing feature—the famed hot springs are a short walk away. ⊠ *Sol Duc Rd., 11 miles south of U.S. 101* ☎ *877/444–6777 for reservations.*

Staircase Campground. In deep woods away from the river, this campground is a popular jumping-off point for hikes into the Skokomish River Valley and the Olympic high country. ⊠ *Rte. 119, 16 miles northwest of U.S. 101* ☎ *No phone.*

CLOSE UP

La Poel Picnic Area. Tall firs lean over a tiny gravel beach at this small picnic area, which has several picnic tables and a splendid view of Pyramid Mountain across Lake Crescent. It's closed October to April. ✉ *Olympic National Park* ✣ *Off Hwy. 101, 22 miles west of Port Angeles* ⏲ *Closed mid-Oct.–mid-May.*

Rialto Beach Picnic Area. Relatively secluded at the end of the road from Forks, this is one of the premier day-use areas in the park's Pacific coast segment. This site has 12 picnic tables, fire grills, and vault toilets. ✉ *Rte. 110, 14 miles west of Forks, Forks.*

WHERE TO STAY

IN THE PARK

$$$ HOTEL FAMILY Fodor's Choice ★ 🏨 **Kalaloch Lodge.** Overlooking the Pacific, Kalaloch has cozy lodge rooms with sea views and separate cabins along the bluff. **Pros:** ranger tours; clam digging; supreme storm-watching in winter. **Cons:** no Internet and most units don't have TVs; some rooms are two blocks from main lodge; limited cell-phone service. [$] *Rooms from: $189* ✉ *157151 U.S. 101, Forks* ☎ *360/962–2271, 866/662–9928* 🌐 *www.thekalalochlodge.com* 🛏 *20 rooms, 46 cabins* 🍴 *No meals.*

$$$ HOTEL 🏨 **Lake Crescent Lodge.** Deep in the forest at the foot of Mt. Storm King, this 1916 lodge has a variety of comfortable accommodations, from basic rooms with shared baths to spacious two-bedroom fireplace cottages. **Pros:** gorgeous setting; free wireless access in the lobby. **Cons:** no laundry; Roosevelt Cottages often are booked a year in advance for summer stays. [$] *Rooms from: $195* ✉ *416 Lake Crescent Rd., Port Angeles* ☎ *360/928–3211, 888/896–3818* 🌐 *www.olympicnationalparks.com* ⏲ *Closed Jan.–Apr., except Roosevelt fireplace cabins open weekends* 🛏 *30 motel rooms, 17 cabins, 5 lodge rooms with shared bath* 🍴 *No meals.*

$$$$ HOTEL 🏨 **Lake Quinault Lodge.** On a lovely glacial lake in Olympic National Forest, this beautiful early-20th-century lodge complex is within walking distance of the lakeshore and hiking trails in the spectacular old-growth forest. **Pros:** hosts summer campfires with s'mores; family-friendly ambience; year-round pool and sauna. **Cons:** no TV in some rooms; some units are noisy and not very private. [$] *Rooms from: $229* ✉ *345 South Shore Rd., Quinault* ☎ *360/288–2900, 888/896–3818* 🌐 *www.olympicnationalparks.com* 🛏 *92 rooms* 🍴 *No meals.*

$$ HOTEL FAMILY 🏨 **Log Cabin Resort.** This rustic resort has an idyllic setting at the northeast end of Lake Crescent with lodging choices that include A-frame chalet units, standard cabins, small camper cabins, motel units, and RV sites with full hookups. **Pros:** boat rentals available on-site; convenient general store; pets allowed in some cabins. **Cons:** cabins are extremely rustic; no plumbing in the camper cabins; no TVs. [$] *Rooms from: $111* ✉ *3183 E. Beach Rd., Port Angeles* ☎ *888/896–3818, 360/928–3325* 🌐 *www.olympicnationalparks.com* ⏲ *Closed Oct.–late May* 🛏 *4 rooms, 23 cabins, 22 RV sites, 4 tent sites* 🍴 *No meals.*

8

$$$$ HOTEL [hotel icon] **Sol Duc Hot Springs Resort.** Deep in the brooding forest along the Sol Duc River and surrounded by 5,000-foot-tall mountains, the main draw of this remote 1910 resort is the pool area, with soothing mineral baths and a freshwater swimming pool. **Pros:** nearby trails; peaceful setting; some units are pet-friendly. **Cons:** units are dated; no air-conditioning, TV, or Internet access; pools get crowded. [$] *Rooms from: $207* ✉ *12076 Sol Duc Hot Springs Rd., Olympic National Park* ☎ *888/896–3818* 🌐 *www.olympicnationalparks.com* 🕒 *Closed Nov.–late Mar.* 🛏 *32 cabins, 1 suite, 17 RV sites* 🍴 *No meals.*

TRAVEL SMART SEATTLE

GETTING HERE AND AROUND

Hemmed in by mountains, hills, and multiple bodies of water, Seattle is anything but a linear, grid-lined city. Twisty, turny, and very long, the city can be baffling to navigate, especially if you delve into its residential neighborhoods—and you should. A good map or phone app can help you confidently explore, and you can use the transportation advice in this section to plan your wanderings around the city's sometimes confusing layout. One thing to keep in mind: Seattle's boomtown status shows in the construction sites that seem to dot every block, which can mean closed-off streets and extra traffic snarls. The Washington State Department of Transportation (WSDOT) features helpful real-time updates and camera footage of local traffic (⊕ *www. wsdot.com/traffic*).

▌ AIR TRAVEL

Nonstop flying time from New York to Seattle is approximately 5 hours; flights from Chicago are about 4–4½ hours; flights between Los Angeles and Seattle take 2½ hours; flights between London and Seattle are about 9½ hours; flights from Hong Kong are 13 hours.

Seattle is a hub for regional air service, as well as air service to Alaska, Hawaii, Canada, and Iceland. It's also a convenient North American gateway for flights originating in Australia, New Zealand, and the South Pacific. Nonstop flights between Seattle and Europe are available, though most transatlantic service involves a connection in Atlanta; Boston; Chicago; New York; or Washington, D.C. Several nonstop flights to Asia are offered.

Airlines and Airports AirlineandAirport-Links.com. ⊕ *www.airlineandairportlinks.com.*

Airline Security Issues Transportation Security Administration. ☎ *866/289–9673* ⊕ *www.tsa.gov.*

AIRPORTS

The major gateway is Seattle–Tacoma International Airport (SEA), known locally as Sea-Tac. The airport is south of the city and reasonably close to it—non-rush-hour trips to Downtown sometimes take less than a half hour. Sea-Tac is a midsize, modern airport that is usually pleasant to navigate. Our only complaint: inexplicably long waits for some airlines at the baggage claim, especially at night when they seem to send all flights to one or two carousels. Over the next 20 years, the number of passengers traveling through Sea-Tac is expected to almost double to 66 million annually. The airport has a major $600 million expansion planned, though it's unclear how long it will take.

While the present Sea-Tac doesn't offer a particularly impressive array of shops and restaurants, there are enough sit-down cafés, fast-food joints, and quirky shops to keep you entertained between flights. Comfort-food lovers should proceed directly to Beecher's for their world-famous mac and cheese. Sub Pop, the iconic Seattle music label that helped launch Nirvana, has a shop stocked with albums from bands on its roster. And for longer layovers, stop into Butter London for a manicure or the Massage Bar for a quick, no-appointment-necessary back or foot massage. Charter flights and small carriers, such as Kenmore Air, that operate shuttle flights between the cities of the Pacific Northwest land at Boeing Field, which is between Sea-Tac and Seattle.

Airport Information Boeing Field. ☎ *206/296–7380* ⊕ *www.kingcounty.gov/ transportation/kcdot/Airport.aspx.* **Seattle–Tacoma International Airport.** ☎ *206/787–5388* ⊕ *www.portseattle.org/seatac.*

NAVIGATING SEATTLE

■ Downtown and adjacent Belltown are the easiest neighborhoods to explore and are the parts of the city where you're least likely to need—or want—a car. Also, keep these tips in mind as you navigate the city:

■ Water makes the best landmark. Both Elliott Bay and Lake Union are pretty hard to miss. When you are trying to get your bearings Downtown, Elliott Bay is a much more reliable landmark than the Space Needle.

■ Remember that I-5 literally bisects the city (north–south), and there are limited places at which to cross it (this goes for pedestrians and drivers). From Downtown to Capitol Hill, cross using Pike, Pine, Madison, James, or Yesler; from Lake Union or Seattle Center to Capitol Hill, use Denny; above the Lake Washington Ship Canal (the "canal"), 45th, 50th, and 80th are the major streets running all the way east–west. East–west travel is usually more laborious than north–south trips, so plan accordingly, particularly during rush hour.

■ The major north–south routes connecting the southern part of the city to the northern part are I-5, Aurora Avenue/Highway 99, 15th Avenue NW (Ballard Bridge), and Westlake (Fremont Bridge) and Eastlake Avenues. With the exception of some difficult on-ramps, I-5 is easy to navigate. Note that Aurora has a limited number of signed exits north of the canal (mostly you just turn directly onto side streets) and a limited number of exits in general Downtown (after the Denny exit if you're heading north to south). Some of the Downtown exits are on the left-hand side, making this road a bit more confusing if you don't know where you're going.

■ Public buses provide a sufficient (if sometimes frustrating) system that's best used to move between Downtown and Capitol Hill, the University District, or Queen Anne. To get from Downtown to Seattle Center, use the monorail. To get from Downtown to Pioneer Square, walk down 1st Avenue or jump on a southbound bus on 1st Avenue. (Note that walking is often the fastest way to get around Downtown and Belltown.) Using the bus system to get from Downtown to the neighborhoods above the canal can sometimes be a slow process during nonpeak travel times, but trips directly to downtown Ballard, Fremont, and Phinney Ridge/Greenwood are fairly straightforward and efficient.

■ Streets in the Seattle area generally travel east to west, whereas avenues travel north to south. Downtown roads are straightforward: avenues are numbered west to east (starting with 1st Avenue by Elliott Bay and ending with 39th Avenue by Lake Washington), streets are named, and a rough grid pattern can be discerned. Above the Lake Washington Ship Canal, east to west streets are mostly numbered, starting with North 34th Street in Fremont and going up into the 100s as you head into the northern suburbs. Here, the system for avenues makes much less sense; they're mostly named, but a few are numbered. West of I-5, 1st Avenue NW starts in Fremont, and numbers increase as you go west toward Shilshole Bay, ending with 36th Avenue NW. East of I-5, 1st Avenue NE starts in Wallingford, and the numbers increase as you go toward Lake Washington, ending at 50th Avenue NE.

■ Directionals are often attached to street names. N (north) is for Queen Anne, Seattle Center, and Fremont, Wallingford, and Green Lake. NE (northeast) is for the University District, and NW (northwest) designates Ballard. S (south) marks Downtown streets around Pioneer Square and the International District. SW (southwest) means West Seattle. E (east) designates Capitol Hill and Madison Park, and W (west) means Queen Anne and Magnolia.

GROUND TRANSPORTATION

Sea-Tac is about 15 miles south of Downtown on I–5 (from the airport, follow the signs to I–5 North, then take the Seneca Street Exit for Downtown). Although it can take as little as 30 minutes to ride between Downtown and the airport, if you're traveling during rush hour, it's best to allow at least an hour for the trip in case of heavy traffic; it tends to bottleneck as the freeway narrows through Downtown.

Metered cabs cost around $45 (not including tip) between the airport and Downtown, though some taxi companies offer a $40 flat rate to Sea-Tac from select Downtown hotels. Expect to pay $50–$65 to Capitol Hill, Queen Anne, or the neighborhoods directly north of the canal. Seattle has a small cab fleet, so expect long waits if a lot of flights arrive at the same time, especially late at night. Another option is using Uber (www.uber.com) or Lyft (www.lyft.com). In 2016, both app-based services got the official green light to operate at Sea-Tac as part of a pilot program through the Port of Seattle.

Shuttle Express is the go-to company for scheduled, hourly runs between the airport and Seattle hotels. It's also the only 24-hour door-to-door shared van service. Fares to and from partner hotels start at $19 one way, with additional adults costing $8 per person. Children under 17 are free with a paying adult. Rates to other locations and during nonscheduled times vary depending on destination, number of people in your party, and how many bags you have, but a one-way trip to the Downtown hotel area for one adult with two bags is around $33. You can make arrangements at the Shuttle Express counter upon arrival or make advance reservations online or by phone. For trips to the airport, reservations are required and should be made at least 24 hours in advance. A number of companies offer town car, SUV, and limo service to and from the airport. Use any of the traveler-information boards in the baggage-claim level of the airport to arrange for pickup. ■ TIP➜ Your least expensive transportation option is also probably the best: Sound Transit's Link light-rail, connected to the fourth floor of the airport parking garage, will take you right to Downtown in 36 minutes for just $3 (children under six are free, youth fare up to 18 years old is $1.50; the $1 fare for seniors/disabled requires a permit). You can't purchase tickets on the train, so be sure and buy your ticket at one of the ticket kiosks on the train platform before you board—the machines accept cash, VISA, or MasterCard. Trains depart every 6 or 15 minutes, depending on the time of day, and run from 5 am to 1 am Monday through Saturday and 6 am to midnight on Sunday. If you don't have a lot of luggage, this is a fantastic option for reaching Downtown cheaply. Take the covered walkway from the airport to the garage, then head up one floor to the fourth floor to find the Link light-rail station—be aware that this walk is a bit of a hike. If you have limited mobility, you might want to use another mode of transport. Once you arrive in Downtown Seattle, and if you're feeling adventurous, you can catch a bus from Westlake Center to other areas of the city, or hop back on the Link light-rail and continue on to Capitol Hill or the University of Washington. Metro Transit's website has a great trip planner that provides door-to-door itineraries, explaining any connections you may have to make if you're not staying Downtown; representatives can also help you plan your trip over the phone. Various other shuttle services exist to take passengers directly to surrounding towns and even out to places like the islands or Mt. Rainier. Check out Sea-Tac's website for a list of special shuttles and buses.

Contacts Metro Transit. ☎ *206/553–3000* ⊕ *metro.kingcounty.gov.* **Shuttle Express.** ☎ *425/981–7000* ⊕ *www.shuttleexpress.com.* **Sound Transit.** ☎ *888/889–6368, 206/398–5000* ⊕ *www.soundtransit.org.*

FLIGHTS

American, Delta, and United are among the many major domestic airlines that fly to Seattle from multiple locations. Alaska Airlines and its affiliate Horizon Air provide service from many states, including Alaska and Hawaii.

USAirways has flights from Philadelphia, Charlotte, and Phoenix and connecting routes from most major U.S. cities. Frontier Airlines has direct flights from Denver to Seattle. JetBlue has nonstop service to Seattle from New York, Los Angeles, and Boston. Hawaiian Airlines flies daily from points in Hawaii. Southwest Airlines has direct flights from many cities around the United States, including Las Vegas, St. Louis, Oakland, and Baltimore. Air Canada flies between Seattle and Vancouver, Calgary, and Toronto. Kenmore Air has scheduled and chartered floatplane flights from Seattle's Lake Union and Lake Washington to the San Juan Islands, Victoria, and the Gulf Islands of British Columbia. Delta Airlines, which has major expansion plans for its Sea-Tac hub, offers nonstop flights to Asia and Europe.

▌ BUS TRAVEL

ARRIVING AND DEPARTING

Greyhound Lines and Northwest Trailways have regular service to points throughout the Pacific Northwest, the United States, and Canada. Only a few years old, the regional Greyhound/Trailways bus terminal, located in SoDo ("South of Downtown") just east of the Downtown stadiums at 503 South Royal Brougham Way, is convenient to all Downtown destinations.

GETTING AROUND SEATTLE

The King County Metro Transit's transportation network is inexpensive, fairly comprehensive, and easy to navigate. So why do so many Seattleites own cars? The most definitive reason is because they can—even though traffic is bad and parking can be tight in many areas of Seattle, the city has yet to meet the level of congestion found in cities like New York and Chicago that really necessitates hanging up the driver's license for a bus pass. The city is also fairly spread out and not overly dense in many parts, allowing a good percentage of the residents to park right outside their homes (or at least the same block) for free. Residents will tell you that buses take longer to make most trips, especially if transfers are involved or traffic is particularly bad; and there are long gaps in off-peak schedules. That said, you'll probably find that traveling around Downtown and to and from the commercial centers of Queen Anne, Capitol Hill, Fremont, the University District, Phinney Ridge/Greenwood, and Ballard by bus from Downtown is relatively easy—from Downtown it takes 10 to 15 minutes to get to Fremont center and 25–35 minutes to get to N.W. Market Street and Ballard Avenue in Ballard or the Woodland Park Zoo in Phinney Ridge. On a bus, it takes 15 to 30 minutes to get from Westlake Center to the University District. A better option is the recently expanded Link light-rail service, which takes a mere six minutes and runs every 6 or 15 minutes.

The city's RapidRide is part of an effort to speed up commute times on heavily used corridors. The high-capacity red-and-yellow hybrids come by every 10 to 15 minutes and don't have steps, which allows passengers to quickly hop on and off. These buses are part of the Metro system, and have the same fares—they're just more efficient.

Most buses, which are wheelchair accessible, run until around midnight or 1 am; some run all night, though in many cases taking a cab late at night is a much better solution than dealing with sporadic bus service. The visitor center at the Washington State Convention and Trade Center has maps and schedules, or you can call Metro Transit directly. Better yet, check online at ⊕ *tripplanner.kingcounty.gov*: type in your starting point, how far you're willing to walk, and your destination, and it will tell you where and when to catch your bus. If you have a smartphone, you can trip plan on the go with Metro's transit app. Several other downloadable apps allow you to see if your bus is running on time or late: check out One Bus Away (⊕ *www.onebusaway.org*), Next Bus (⊕ *www.nextbus.com*), or Transit App (⊕ *www.transitapp.com*). Most bus stops have simple schedules posted telling you when buses arrive; bus stops Downtown often have route maps and more information. Drivers are supposed to announce all major intersections (but feel free to ask them to specifically announce your stop), and you won't have to worry about signaling for a stop at hubs or during peak hours (someone else will probably do it or there will be people waiting at each stop, so the bus will have to pull over). At less-traveled stops in residential neighborhoods and during off-peak hours, you may have to signal for the driver to pull into your stop.

Throughout King County, both one-zone fares and two-zone fares at off-peak times are $2.50 for adults; during peak hours (6 am–9 am and 3 pm–6 pm), one-zone fares are $2.75 and two-zone fares $3.25. Unless you travel outside the city limits, you'll pay one-zone fares. Kids ages 6 to 18 are $1.50 at all times and up to four children under the age of 5 ride free with a paying adult. Riders with disabilities are $1 at all times. Onboard fare-collection boxes have prices posted on them. Transfers between metro buses are free for 2½ hours; if you think you'll need one, make sure you ask the driver for a transfer slip when you get on the bus.

If you plan to take advantage of public transit during your visit, invest in a $5 ORCA card (www.orcacard.com), which can be purchased, loaded up, and mailed to you in advance. ORCA cards provide the convenience of not having to fumble for cash and they're easy to use; a quick tap on an electronic reader deducts the proper fare. ORCA cards can be used for trips on King County Metro (Seattle and the Eastside's buses), Community Transit,

Everett Transit, Kitsap Transit, Pierce Transit, Sound Transit (Link light-rail), and the Washington State Ferry system. If your itinerary involves multiple trips around town on public transit, consider a one-day $8 regional pass. It's good for unlimited rides on Metro buses, trains, streetcars, and water taxis for fares up to $3.50. ORCA cards can be purchased online or at King Street Station, Westlake Center, or other Metro offices—a complete list is available online. Cash, debit cards, MasterCard, and Visa are accepted at all offices.

Fares for city buses are collected in cash or ORCA cards *as you board* the front of the bus. There's usually a sign posted on the fare-collection box that tells you when you pay. Fare boxes accept both coins and bills, but drivers won't make change, so don't board the bus with a $5 bill and a hapless grin.

One thing you should prepare yourself for when taking the bus is the overwhelming possibility that there will be at least one crazy or drunk person loudly disturbing the peace. Though Seattleites have countless stories about eventful bus rides, very few of those stories involve actual threats or crimes, so you don't have to worry too much about safety. Just know that commuters rarely want to chat with strangers, so if you respond to that person who's trying a little too hard to get your attention, you're probably in for a 20-minute screed about how the government is spying on them or a way-too-detailed description of a health problem.

Other than that, riding the buses is unpleasant only during rush hours when they're packed with annoyed residents and helmed by frazzled drivers trying to stay on schedule despite the traffic.

City Bus Information Metro Transit.
☎ *206/553–3000 for customer service, schedules, and information, 206/263–3582 for bus-pass and ticket sales* ⊕ *metro.kingcounty. gov.* **OneBusAway.** ⊕ *www.onebusaway.org.* **ORCA Card.** ☎ *888/988–6722* ⊕ *www.orcacard.com.*

▌ CAR TRAVEL

Access to a car is *almost* a necessity if you want to explore the residential neighborhoods beyond their commercial centers. If side trips to the Eastside (besides downtown Bellevue, which is easily reached by bus), neighborhoods north of the Lake Washington Ship Canal, Mt. Rainier, the San Juan Islands, or pretty much any sight or city outside the Seattle limits (with the exception of Portland, Oregon, which is easily reached by train) are on your agenda, you will definitely need a car. Before you book a car for city-only driving, keep in mind that many high-end hotels offer complimentary town-car service around Downtown and the immediate areas.

The best advice about driving in Seattle is to avoid driving during rush hour whenever possible. In 2016, Seattle was ranked the fourth-worst American city for traffic, which is as frustrating as it sounds. The worst tangles are on I–5 and I–90, and any street Downtown that has a major on- or off-ramp to I–5. The Fremont Bridge and the 15th Avenue Bridge also get tied up. Aurora Avenue/SR 99 gets very busy but often moves quickly enough in most stretches. The Alaskan Way Viaduct portion of SR 99, a raised highway that runs along the waterfront and is considered an earthquake risk, is frequently closed; it's slated to be replaced by a much safer deep-bore underground tunnel, a massive project currently in the works. The Mercer East section that accesses South Lake Union, near where much of Seattle's construction boom is happening, can be so backed up that the bottleneck is nicknamed the Mercer Mess. While city driving can be stressful, it's not as bad as other major cities. And though you'll come across the occasional road-rager or oblivious driver who assumes driving an SUV makes one invincible, drivers in Seattle are generally courteous and safety-conscious—though you'll want to pay extra attention in the student-heavy areas of Capitol Hill and the U-District. Also be on the lookout for bicyclists; though most obey the rules of the road and are easy to spot, sometimes they seem to come out of nowhere. Designated bike lanes are clearly marked throughout the city.

PARKING

Parking is a headache and a half in many parts of Seattle, but not anywhere as bad as most major cities. Street parking is only guaranteed in the least dense residential areas—even leafy parts of Capitol Hill are crammed full of cars all hours of the day. The north end typically has enough parking, but the central core of Ballard and Fremont can get a little hairy come evenings and weekends. The city has a good share of pay lots and garages in the central core of the city, but even the pay lots can fill up on weekend nights, particularly in Belltown and Capitol Hill. Metered street parking exists in Downtown Seattle and the commercial stretches of Capitol Hill, but consider yourself lucky if you manage to snag a spot. Meter rates and restrictions vary by neighborhood, and cost between $1 and $4 per hour. Downtown only offers short-term parking, but many areas of the city allow long-term parking up to 10 hours in some neighborhoods. Just about all meters are electronic, as are the easy-to-spot pay stations on every block that take either coins or debit and credit cards (all major cards except Discover). You get a printed sticker noting the time your parking is up, which you affix to the curbside passenger window unless otherwise indicated. Parking is free on Sunday, some holidays, and after 6 pm or 8 pm (depending on the area) weekdays and Saturday. The maximum meter time is two hours in some areas, and four hours in others, even within the same general neighborhood, so check signs carefully. If you plan to be somewhere for a while and won't be nearby to refill the meter, find a parking lot or garage. Make sure you check the signs around your pay station for any additional restrictions.

■TIP→ Out-of-towners are often con-fused by the Pay-to-park stations. The process is simple: first, insert your credit card and quickly remove it (the pay sta-tions also accept coins); next, press the button that says "Add time" until you've reached your desired time; then press "Print receipt" and follow the directions on the back. Some areas Downtown don't allow street parking during the rush hours of 6 to 9 am and 3 to 6 pm. You could park and pay and come back to find your car towed.

Street-level pay lots are the next price tier up, though those Downtown are often just as expensive as (or more expensive than) garages. Rates vary greatly, but expect to pay at least $5 to $7 before tax for a few hours in Capitol Hill, Down-town, or Belltown, with a cap of around $25 for 24 hours. If a rate looks lower, it might not include tax, so read the fine print if you're on a strict budget. Some pay lots have electronic pay stations similar to metered parking—use bills or a debit or credit card to pay at the sta-tion and place the printed ticket on the driver's-side dashboard—but some lots still use old-fashioned pay boxes where you shove folded-up bills into a tiny slot with the same number as the space in which you parked. So make sure you have some cash on you if you're trolling for pay-lot parking. Very few pay lots have attendants, and most lots don't have in-and-out privileges. Some street-level pay lots do double duty as parking for a neighboring store or restaurant, so make sure you're not in a spot designated for customers or you could be towed—which could be a $500 mistake. When in doubt, skip the street lots and opt for a garage or metered parking.

Most Downtown malls and high-rises have garages. Lot and garage rates begin at $5 an hour and cap off at $25 to $30 for the day. Park before 9 am in most lots (as early as 8 am in some and up to 10 am in others) to take advantage of early-bird specials, which typically run $11 to $15 for up to 10 hours of parking. One of the best garages is the one at Pacific Place: rates are reasonable, spaces are plentiful, a valet parking service costs only a few dollars more, and many merchants in the mall, as well as other local businesses, offer parking validation. Most garages take credit and debit cards.

Evening and weekend parking rates are usually cheaper than those on weekdays, around $10 for parking between 6 (or as early as 4 pm at some lots) and mid-night and $5–$12 for parking all day on weekends. Be aware that these lowered rates can go out the window if there are popular events happening near the lots—for example, any lots near Seattle Center will be dramatically higher during a big concert or happening, like Bumbershoot. After 5 pm, it's just $6 to park at Pacific Place for up to four hours. Late-night revelers should head to The Public Mar-ket Parking Garage at Pike Place, where parking is just $5 if you enter after 5 pm and leave by 2 am. Some of the Market's restaurants, including Le Pichet, offer free parking after 5 pm for patrons.

Important: No matter where you park, always lock your car and never leave valuables in your vehicle. The city has plenty of problems with break-ins. Don't be fooled by the laid-back suburban feel of some of the residential areas—they all experience waves of car theft and vandalism.

Last, you may be tempted to park in large private lots like those belonging to supermarkets. You're really rolling the dice: you may get away with it at small businesses and banks after business hours when no one's around to enforce the rules, but large businesses like grocery stores tend to have someone patrolling the lot. If you end up getting a ticket, you'll pay $35, far more money than you'll pay at a garage or pay lot.

RENTAL CARS

Rates in Seattle vary wildly, beginning at $13 a day (if you snag your deal from an Internet discounter like Hotwire.com or Priceline.com) and up to $150 a day. This does not include the car-rental tax of 17.2%. Hunt around for deals online for the best prices—sometimes you'll get to pick up your car at the airport, or you might have to snag your vehicle from a city lot. Try to avoid renting a car from the airport, where rental fees, surcharges, and taxes are higher. Most major rental agencies have offices Downtown or along the waterfront, within easy reach of the main hotel area. Of the major agencies at the airport, Thrifty often has the lowest rates because it does not have a counter in the terminals.

Booking in advance usually ensures the best rates—and is a must on holiday weekends when Seattleites flee the city. Another option that offers flexibility is car sharing. If you're a member of Zipcar in your own city, you can borrow any Zipcar in Seattle for quick trips around town and not have to worry about the hassles of car rentals or parking. At $70 to $80 a day, this isn't the best option for multiday use, but for a couple of hours here or there, it could end up being a bargain.

Car-sharing service Car2Go (⊕ *www. car2go.com*) is an excellent option for shorter one-way trips around town. Using the simple app, you can locate the nearest available Car2Go and reserve it up to 30 minutes in advance. Car2Go's $5 registration fee includes a $10 account credit; car usage is billed at $0.41 per minute or $14.99 an hour. As an added perk, you can park for free at all public parking spots, including meters, within the designated service area, which covers most of the city. For those seeking a touch of luxury in their temporary ride, BMW now offers an app-based car-sharing service in Seattle called ReachNow (⊕ *www. reachnow.com*; currently available only in Portland and Seattle). Drivers can choose from a variety of BMW models and MINI

Coopers and easily locate the nearest available options. The rate is $0.41 per minute of driving and $0.30 a minute to reserve while parked. Public parking is free within the designated service area. ■TIP→ **If you're staying at a Downtown hotel, car sharing can save you a lot of cash. Hotel valet parking runs upwards of $50 per night.**

Almost no popular hiking trips require special vehicles—the road to Mt. Rainier, for example, is paved the whole way—but if driving 20 miles down a bumpy Forest Service dirt road to reach a remote trailhead sounds like something you want to try, you might want to make sure the vehicle you rent can handle it.

Unless you're hauling around kayaks, rent the smallest car possible, especially if you plan to do a lot of city driving. The smaller the car, the easier it'll be to find a parking space.

In Washington State you must be 21 and hold a major credit card (many agencies accept debit cards with the MasterCard or Visa logo) to rent a car. Rates may be higher if you're under 25. You'll pay about $9 to $12 per day per child seat for children under age four or 40 pounds, or per booster seat for children ages four to six or under 60 pounds, both of which are compulsory in Washington State.

When you reserve a car, ask about cancellation penalties, taxes, drop-off charges (if you're planning to pick up the car in one city and leave it in another), and surcharges (for being under or over a certain age, for additional drivers, or for driving across state or country borders or beyond a specific distance from your point of rental). All these things can add substantially to your costs. Request car seats and extras such as GPS when you book.

■TIP→ **Make sure that a confirmed reservation guarantees you a car. Agencies sometimes overbook, particularly for busy weekends and holiday periods.**

ROAD CONDITIONS

Seattle's roads are generally pretty good, though they can get somewhat flooded during heavy rainstorms. Note that many side streets in residential areas are extremely narrow due to people parking on both sides of the street—what should technically be a one-way street is actually a two-way. The basic rule of thumb when you're faced with oncoming traffic on a very narrow stretch is that whoever has space on their side pulls over to let the other driver pass.

Drive slowly around the Pike Place Market area and Pioneer Square—there are stretches of slippery cobblestones, as well as unmarked dips in the road as you crest the hills from west to east that can really bottom out a car.

Residential areas have many blind intersections, some without any stop signs or traffic circles. Sometimes cars are parked so close to the intersection that you have to pull way out into it in order to see what's coming—just another reason to rent a compact car with a short front end.

If there are a lot of construction and road projects going on when you visit, don't panic—detours are usually well signed and reasonably logical.

Note that some Forest Service roads are paved, but many are dirt or gravel and can become treacherous during or after extreme weather conditions—severe rainstorms in the winter of 2006 even washed out a major road into Mount Rainier National Park. Before heading out to a remote trailhead, always check road conditions. The same goes for any trip heading east over the mountain passes (and be aware that even in the summer, the temperatures in the mountains can be quite chilly—bring a warm jacket if you're going up).

Winter snowfalls in the city are not common (generally only once or twice a year), but when snow does fall, traffic grinds to a halt, schools and businesses close, and the roadways become treacherous—many Seattleites don't know how to drive on snow or ice and the city owns only a handful of snowplows—until the snow melts.

Tire chains, studs, or snow tires are essential equipment for winter travel in mountain areas such as Mt. Rainier. If you're planning to drive to high elevations, be sure to check the weather forecast beforehand. Even the main highway mountain passes can be forced to close because of snow conditions. In winter months, state and provincial highway departments operate snow-advisory telephone lines that give pass conditions.

Road-Condition Reports **Washington State Road Condition Reports.** ☎ 888/766–4636 *for mountain pass information* ⊕ *wsdot. wa.gov/traffic.*

▌ FERRY TRAVEL

Ferries are a major part of Seattle's transportation network, and they're the only way to reach such points as Vashon Island and the San Juans. Thousands of commuters hop a boat from Bainbridge Island, Bremerton, and other outer towns to their jobs in the city each day—which makes for a gorgeous and unusual commute. For visitors, ferries are one of the best ways to get a feel for the region and its ties to the sea (plus, they're just plain fun). You'll also get outstanding views of the skyline and the elusive Mt. Rainier from the ferry to Bainbridge.

Passenger-only King County Water Taxis depart from Seattle's Pier 50 weekdays during rush hours on runs to Vashon Island and West Seattle. The Vashon Water Taxi is $6.25 each way in cash (discounts for ORCA card users, seniors, and youth). The West Seattle Water Taxi makes a quick journey from Pier 50 Seacrest Park in West Seattle for $5.25 each way. Pier 50 is served directly by several Metro bus routes—even if you've rented a car, it's a major hassle to park on the waterfront so busing is the way to go. ■ TIP➔ Two free Metro DART shuttles take passengers directly from the West Seattle dock to the West Seattle Junction and Admiral neighborhoods. For a great, inexpensive outing, hop on the Water Taxi to West Seattle, take the free shuttle, and spend the afternoon enjoying the great shopping and restaurants in West Seattle.

Clipper Navigation operates the passenger-only *Victoria Clipper* jet catamaran service between Seattle and Victoria year-round (except Christmas through mid-January) and between Seattle and the San Juan Islands, May through September. These longer journeys are a little pricier: $117–$175 round-trip to Victoria, $99–$112 round-trip to the San Juans. Note that *Victoria Clipper* fares are less expensive if booked at least one day in advance, children under 12 are free with select trips (be sure to ask about any promotions or deals), and there are also some great package deals available online. In general, package deals are your best bet for Clipper trips. You'll get greatly reduced transportation rates for staying even one night in Victoria.

The Washington State Ferry system serves the Puget Sound and San Juan Islands area and is the largest ferry network in the country and the third largest in the world. Peak-season fares are charged May 1 through September 30. However, ferry schedules change quarterly, with the summer schedule running mid-June through mid-September. Ferries around Seattle are especially crowded during the city's weekday rush hours and holiday events, while San Juan Islands ferries can be jammed on weekends, holidays, and all of May through September. Be at the ferry, or have your car in line, at least 20 minutes before departure—and prepare to wait several hours during heavily traveled times (on nice days, the ferry lines can take on something of a party feel, and impromptu, multicar Frisbee games are not unheard of). Walk-on space is always available; if possible, leave your car behind.

You can pick up sailing schedules and tickets on board the ferries or at the terminals, and schedules are usually posted in local businesses around the docks. The Washington State Ferry (WSF) automated hotline also provides travel details, including weekly departure and arrival times, wait times, cancellations, and seasonal fare changes. To ask questions or make international reservations for journeys to Sidney, British Columbia, call the regular WSF hotline. Note that schedules often differ from weekdays to weekends and holidays, and departure times may be altered due to ferry or dock maintenance, severe weather or tides, and high traffic volume.

Regular walk-on fares from Seattle are $8.20 to Bainbridge and Bremerton, and from Edmonds to Kingston; $5.30 from Fauntleroy in West Seattle, Point Defiance in Tacoma, or Southworth to Vashon Island; $4.90 from Mukilteo to Clinton, on Whidbey Island; $3.30 each way between Port Townsend and Coupeville; and $6.25 round-trip between Fauntleroy and Southworth. Round-trip rates from Anacortes to any point in the San Juan Islands run $13.25. If you'd rather head to Sidney, British Columbia, from Anacortes, it will cost you $19 one way; or you can travel to Sidney from the San Juans for $24.05 round-trip. You'll need reservations to visit Sidney. Senior citizens (age 65 and over) and those with disabilities pay half fare; children 5–18 get a smaller discount, and those under age six ride free.

Peak-season vehicle fares (including one adult driver) are $18.10 from Seattle to Bainbridge and Bremerton, and from Edmonds to Kingston; $23.20 from Fauntleroy, Point Defiance, or Southworth to Vashon; $14.05 from Port Townsend to Coupeville, and from Fauntleroy to Southworth; and $10.80 from Mukilteo to Clinton. From Anacortes, peak-season vehicle and driver round-trip fares through the San Juans are $44.80 to Lopez Island, $53.70 to

Orcas and Shaw islands, $63.75 to Friday Harbor, and $82.95 (one way) to Sidney, British Columbia. Shoulder-season rates are lower. The following routes accept reservations in advance (highly recommended) during summer and fall through the Save a Spot program (visit the ferries section of ⊕ *www.wsdot.wa.gov* for more information): Port Townsend/Coupeville, Anacortes/San Juans, and Anacortes/Victoria, BC. For all fares, you can pay with cash, ORCA card, major credit cards, and debit cards with MasterCard or Visa logos.

Information Clipper Vacations. ☎ *206/448–5000 in Seattle, 250/382–8100 in Victoria, 800/888–2535* ⊕ *www.clippervacations.com.* **King County Water Taxi.** ☎ *206/477–3979* ⊕ *kingcounty.gov/transportation/kcdot/ WaterTaxi.* **Washington State Ferries.** ☎ *800/843–3779 automated line in WA and BC, 888/808–7977 WA and BC reservations, 206/464–6400* ⊕ *www.wsdot.wa.gov/ferries.*

▌ LIGHT-RAIL TRAVEL

The popular Central line runs between the airport and Downtown, and continues on to brand-new stations in Capitol Hill and at the University of Washington. An Angle Lake station south of the airport debuted in late 2016. If the funding comes through, plans also are afoot to extend the system north to Northgate, south to Lynnwood and Federal Way, and east to Mercer Island, Bellevue, and Microsoft's main campus in Redmond over the next couple of decades. So, eventually travelers should have a reliable rail route to get them around instead of the hodgepodge of transit options currently offered. For now, definitely take advantage of the easy and inexpensive route from Sea-Tac airport to Downtown, Capitol Hill, and the University District. Simply head to the Link light-rail station on the fourth floor of the airport parking garage and arrive in Downtown in 36 minutes for just $3 (youth fare is $1.50 and senior/disabled fare is $1). Trains

depart every 6 or 15 minutes, depending on the time of day and run from 5 am to 1 am Monday through Saturday and 6 am to midnight on Sunday.

Information Sound Transit. ☎ *888/889–6368, 206/398–5000* ⊕ *www.soundtransit.org.*

▌ MONORAIL TRAVEL

Built for the 1962 World's Fair, the country's first full-scale commercial monorail is a quick, convenient link for tourists, though it travels an extremely short route between the Seattle Center and Downtown's Westlake Mall, located at 4th Avenue and Pike Street. Most travelers could walk the 1-mile route without much of a struggle, but the Monorail is nostalgic, retro fun. Making the journey in just two minutes, the Monorail departs both points every 10 minutes. Monday through Friday the Monorail runs 7:30 am to 11 pm; Saturday and Sunday it runs 8:30 am to 11 pm; it's closed Thanksgiving and Christmas day. The round-trip fare is $4.50; youth and senior citizens receive a discount and children age four and under ride free.

Information Seattle Center Monorail. ☎ *206/905–2620* ⊕ *www.seattlemonorail.com.*

▌ STREETCAR TRAVEL

The city's cute-as-a-button Seattle Streetcar trolleys are a fun way to explore the Downtown core. The South Lake Union Streetcar (SLUS) links South Lake Union and Downtown, with seven stops along the 1½-mile line and connections to light-rail and the Monorail. The 10-stop First Hill line connects Capitol Hill, First Hill, Yesler Terrace, Central Area, Chinatown-International District, and Pioneer Square. Streetcar frequencies vary; the South Lake Union line runs at 15-minute intervals from 9 am to 4 pm, while the First Hill line runs every 12 minutes. Both run more frequently during rush hour and less often in the late evening (the South Lake Union line stops service at 11 pm; First Hill runs until 1 am). A single fare costs $2.50 (senior/disabled $0.75, youth $1.25, children under five are free). Tickets can be purchased from a ticket vending machine (coins and credit cards are accepted) or deducted from an ORCA card. Streetcar-only unlimited day passes cost $4.50 ($2 senior/disabled, $3 youth).

Information Seattle Streetcar.
☎ *866/205–5001, 206/553–3000*
⊕ *www.seattlestreetcar.org.*

▌ TAXI TRAVEL

Seattle has a smaller taxi fleet than most major cities do, and it's not the most reliable. Taking a cab is not a major form of transportation in the city, and the number of taxis is highly controlled by the city; accordingly, you'll find that rates run higher here. Most people take cabs only to and from the airport and when they go out partying on weekends. You'll often be able to hail cabs on the street in Downtown, but anywhere else, you'll have to call. Expect long waits on Friday and Saturday night.

Rides generally run about $2.70 per mile. The meter drop alone is $2.60, and you'll pay 50¢ per minute stuck in traffic. Unless you're going a very short distance, the average cost of a cab ride in the city is $10–$25 before tip. The nice thing about Seattle metered cabs is that they almost always accept credit cards, and an automated system calls you on your cell phone to let you know that your cab has arrived. All cab companies listed here charge the same rates. Visit ⊕ *www.taxifarefinder.com* before your trip to see roughly how much the fare will be, and the best route to tell your driver to take. Techies might opt to hail cabs with the app GoCurb (iTunes or ⊕ *www.gocurb.com*), but be aware they're not linked to all the local cab companies, and reviews have been hit and miss.

In 2016, Sea-Tac chose Eastside for Hire as the exclusive taxi service to Sea-Tac.

Taxis are required to be available to customers within five minutes at the airport.

Metered cabs are not the best way to visit the Eastside or any destination far outside the city—if you get stuck in traffic, you'll pay dearly for it. Take the bus when possible, and ask your hotel for car-service quotes concerning short side trips outside city limits.

Many locals avoid cabs entirely and take advantage of app-based ride services like Uber or Lyft, both of which boast large fleets of drivers in Seattle. The rides tend to be cheaper than cabs and have less of a wait time. You'll need to download the apps in advance and register with a credit card; fares will be automatically deducted at the end of your ride. Before you book, be sure to check the current rates, which fluctuate with demand; during major events, even a short ride can cost a small fortune thanks to surge pricing.

Taxi Companies Eastside For Hire.
☎ *206/242–6200.* **Graytop Cab.** ☎ *206/282–8222.* **Green Cab.** ☎ *206/575–4040.*
Orange Cab. ☎ *206/522–8800 Seattle, 425/453–0919 Eastside* ⊕ *www.orangecab.net.*
Yellow Cab. ☎ *206/622–6500*
⊕ *www.seattleyellowcab.com.*

▌ TRAIN TRAVEL

Amtrak, the U.S. passenger-rail system, has daily service to Seattle from the Midwest and California. The *Empire Builder* takes a northern route from Chicago to Seattle, with a stop in St. Paul. The *Coast Starlight* begins in Southern California, makes stops throughout western Oregon and Washington, including Portland, and terminates its route in Seattle. The *Cascades* travels from Eugene, Oregon, up to Vancouver, British Columbia, with several stops in between. If you want to spend a day or two in Portland, taking the train down instead of driving is a great way to do so. It's fast and comfortable, and the Amtrak station in Portland is centrally located. Sit on the left side of the train on the way down for stunning views of Mt. Rainier. All Amtrak trains to and from Seattle pull into King Street Station off South Jackson Street in the International District.

Trains to and from Seattle have regular and business-class compartments. Cars with private bedrooms are available for multiday trips (such as to Chicago), while business-class cars provide more legroom, quieter cars, and complimentary newspapers. Reservations are necessary (you can book up to 11 months in advance), and major credit cards are accepted.

Sounder Trains, run by Sound Transit, run between Seattle and Everett and Seattle and Lakewood and travel only during peak hours on weekdays. Trains leave Lakewood about every half hour between 4:41 am and 8 am, and then twice in the evening rush hour, with stops in Tacoma, Puyallup, Sumner, Auburn, Kent, and Tukwila prior to Seattle. Southbound trains leave Seattle twice during early-morning rush hour and then every half hour between 3:15 and 6:15 pm. Sounder Trains from Everett have four morning departure times between 5:45 and 7:15 am, stopping in Mukilteo and Edmonds, and offers four return trips from Seattle between 4:05 and 5:35 pm. (Note that there is daily Amtrak service from most of these cities, offering more departure times.)

Fares are based on distance traveled, starting at $3.25 and running up to $5.75 for the Seattle-to-Tacoma trip; youth, senior citizens, and the disabled receive a discounted fare, and kids under six ride free. Tickets can be purchased at machines inside the stations before you board, or you can use your ORCA card.

Information Amtrak. ☎ *800/872-7245, 206/382-4125* ⊕ *www.amtrak.com.* **Sound Transit.** ☎ *888/889-6368, 206/398-5000* ⊕ *www.soundtransit.org.*

ESSENTIALS

▌ ACCOMMODATIONS

There's a something for everyone, accommodation-wise, in this city, from high-end luxury hotels to clever boutique hotels and environmentally friendly options to historic properties and brand-new digs. Seattle also has a number of bed-and-breakfasts, though rooms at them tend to go quickly since they represent the best deals in the city during high season. Many of the favorite B&Bs are in Capitol Hill (although you'll find teeny-tiny ones we don't even list just about anywhere in the city), whereas almost all hotels are Downtown. Though the city does have its share of standard budget chain hotels and motels, most of them are terribly overpriced in high season and in awkward spots in the city. The best rule of thumb to get the room that you want is to book as far in advance as possible.

For more information about lodging options and for prices, see Where to Stay.

Most hotels and other lodgings require you to give your credit-card details before they will confirm your reservation. If you don't feel comfortable booking your hotel online, call the property to give them this information over the phone or ask if you can fax it. However you book, get confirmation in writing and have a copy of it handy when you check in.

Be sure you understand the hotel's cancellation policy. Some places allow you to cancel without any kind of penalty—even if you prepaid to secure a discounted rate—if you cancel at least 24 hours in advance. Others require you to cancel a week in advance or penalize you the cost of one night. Small inns and B&Bs are most likely to require you to cancel far in advance. Most hotels allow children under a certain age to stay in their parents' room at no extra charge, but others charge for them as extra adults; find out the cutoff age for discounts.

▌TIP→ Assume that hotels don't include breakfast in the cost of your room unless we specify that breakfast is included.

Another option for visitors that continues to grow in popularity is Airbnb (⊕ *www.airbnb.com*). Using Airbnb's website, you can browse and book apartments and houses all over the city, from budget-friendly spare bedrooms to truly beautiful and spacious digs. Airbnb is a unique way to experience Seattle like a local and its vast offerings feature a broad range of amenities and prices. VRBO (Vacation Rental By Owner; ⊕ *www.vrbo.com*) offers a similar service.

▌ CRUISES

Seattle's expanding cruise industry now welcomes some of the world's largest ships to docks on Elliott Bay. The city's strategic location along the West Coast means that it's just a day's journey by water to Canada or California, and you can reach Alaska or Mexico in less than a week. In addition to the six major cruise lines that operate weekly service out of Seattle, you can also sail around Elliott Bay, Lake Union, Lake Washington, or along a combination of local waterways in smaller sightseeing boats like Argosy Cruises *(see Day Tours).*

Norwegian Cruise Line, Carnival Cruise Line, Celebrity Cruises, Holland America Line, Princess Cruises, Disney Cruise Line, and Royal Caribbean all offer seven-day summer cruises from Seattle to Alaska. Princess Cruises and Holland America Line also offer 14-day Alaska excursions, if you have more time to explore The Last Frontier. Holland America Line, Princess Cruises, Celebrity Cruises, Carnival Cruise Line, and Royal Caribbean leave from the Smith Cove Cruise Terminal on Pier 91; Norwegian Cruise Line and Oceania Cruises depart from the Bell Street Pier Cruise Terminal at Pier 66.

Cruise Lines Carnival Cruise Line.
☎ 888/227–6482 ⊕ www.carnival.com.
Celebrity Cruises. ☎ 800/647–2251
⊕ www.celebritycruises.com. **Holland
America Line.** ☎ 877/932–4259 ⊕ www.
hollandamerica.com. **Norwegian Cruise Line.**
☎ 866/234–7350 ⊕ www.ncl.com. **Princess
Cruises.** ☎ 800/774–6237 ⊕ www.princess.
com. **Royal Caribbean.** ☎ 866/562–7625
⊕ www.royalcaribbean.com.

▌DAY TOURS AND GUIDES

AIR TOURS

Leaving from Lake Union, Seattle Seaplanes' 20-minute scenic flight for $97.50
per person takes in views of Woodland
Park Zoo, Downtown Seattle, the Cascades and Olympics, the Ballard Locks,
and Lake Washington. The company also
schedules flying lessons, charter trips to
places like Mt. Rainier, and dinner flights
to the San Juans and area islands. Kenmore Air makes scenic flights over the
metro area, as well as to the San Juan
Islands, the Skagit Valley Tulip Festival,
Port Angeles (*Twilight* fans take note),
Victoria, British Columbia, and its surrounding areas.

BOAT TOURS

Argosy Cruises offers sightseeing
cruises, dining cruises, and event
cruises around the Puget Sound region.
Brunch, lunch, and dinner cruises are
available, but of the dining cruises, the
Tillicum Village excursion is a favorite
with tourists—the four-hour trip takes
you to Blake Island, where you'll enjoy
steamed clams and alder-plank-fired
salmon before a performance of dance,
song, and storytelling in the tradition
of Pacific Northwest Coast Indians ($84
for adults, $32 for youth ages 4–12, free
for children under 3). If you just want
to see more of the Sound but don't want
to shell out the bucks, take a quick narrated sightseeing tour around Elliott
Bay with Argosy Cruises (1 hour, from
Pier 55, $22.75–$25 for adults), the
Ballard Locks (2½ hours, from Pier 56,

$35.75–$40.75 for adults), which also
offers a cruise between Lake Union and
Lake Washington (2 hours, from AGC
Marina in South Lake Union, $27–$34).
Let's Go Sailing permits passengers to
take the helm, trim the sails, or simply
enjoy the ride aboard the *Obsession* or
the SC70 *Neptune's Car*, both 70-foot
ocean racers. May through early October, three 1½-hour excursions ($35 for
adults; $22 kids under 12; kids under
5 are free) depart daily from Pier 54. A
2½-hour sunset sail ($51 for adults; kids
5–12 are $33) is also available. Passen-
gers can bring their own food on board,
and catering is available for groups. The
Center for Wooden Boats offers free
boat rides on a first-come, first-served
basis, Sunday at 10 am. Experienced
sailors can also rent boats from them
after completing a check-out process.

BUS TOURS

Several companies offer guided bus tours
of Seattle and nearby attractions ranging
from the Boeing Factory to Mt. Rainier.

Tour Companies Argosy Cruises.
☎ 888/623–1445, 206/622–8687 ⊕ www.
argosycruises.com. **Citypass.** ☎ 888/330–5008
⊕ www.citypass.com/seattle. **Kenmore Air.**
☎ 866/435–9524, 425/486–1257 ⊕ www.
kenmoreair.com. **Let's Go Sailing.** ☎ 206/624–
3931 ⊕ www.sailingseattle.com. **Seattle
Seaplanes.** ☎ 800/637–5553, 206/329–9638
⊕ www.seattleseaplanes.com. **Tours Northwest.** ☎ 888/293–1404, 206/768–1234
⊕ www.toursnorthwest.com.

▌MONEY

Almost all businesses and attractions
accept debit and credit cards, though
small surcharges may apply for charges
under $5. The only exceptions are some
smaller restaurants and shops.

Many metered cabs also accept credit
cards or debit cards with the MasterCard
or Visa logo.

Prices *throughout this guide* are given
for adults. Substantially reduced fees are

almost always available for children, students, and senior citizens.

The hotels and restaurants in this guide typically accept credit cards. If not, we'll say so.

▌ONLINE TRAVEL TOOLS

The tourist boards' sites will no doubt be your first stops. The home page for the Seattle Convention and Visitor's Bureau is ⊕ *www.visitseattle.org.* For insight on the entire state, head to Washington State Tourism's ⊕ *www.experiencewa. com.* Information straight from the city's leaders is at ⊕ *www.seattle.gov/visiting/ default.htm.* Forget driving. Take public transportation—including the bus, streetcar, and water taxi. This site tells you how: ⊕ *metro.kingcounty.gov.* OK. So you have to drive. The site ⊕ *www. wsdot.com/traffic* will help you navigate Seattle's traffic.

Almost every neighborhood in Seattle has its own website, and many have their own blogs, but some are more useful than others. The Downtown Seattle Association offers the very professional-looking ⊕ *www.downtownseattle.com,* with a great calendar page and a helpful "Getting Around" page with good maps (check out their "Find a Happy Hour" tab if you're ready for a cocktail). You can learn more about Pioneer Square at ⊕ *www.pioneersquare.org.* The site has excellent maps of the area along with detailed info on parking and on the popular monthly art walks. Ballard's ⊕ *www.inballard.com* has up-to-date listings and reviews of the neighborhood's major businesses and sights, complete with pictures of each. Fremont's ⊕ *www.fremont.com* provides visitors with the back stories for the neighborhood's iconic art, along with an event calendar, restaurant listings, and a walking guide that can be downloaded. Find out what's going on in the neighborhood around the University of Washington by logging on to ⊕ *www.udistrictdaily.com.*

Stop by ⊕ *phinneywood.com* for the scoop on the Phinney Ridge and Greenwood neighborhoods and information on their excellent monthly art walk (the second Friday of each month). Columbia City's ⊕ *www.columbiacityseattle.com* has a great event calendar, directory, and lowdown on the history of the neighborhood. Travelers with children will appreciate the kid-friendly restaurant listings on ⊕ *www.wallyhood.org,* Wallingford's one-stop shop for event listings, restaurants, and resources in the area. Capitol Hill's very popular blog gone wild, ⊕ *www.capitolhillseattle.com,* provides a wealth of information on the neighborhood. Ignore the crime-report-type info on the site (it will scare you unnecessarily, and the neighborhood really is quite safe) and head directly to the blog's maps, calendar, and business listings. For travelers looking to get off the beaten path, check out Georgetown, at ⊕ *www. georgetownneighborhood.com.* To learn more about Bellevue, a rapidly growing minicity in the Eastside suburbs, look to ⊕ *www.downtownbellevue.com.*

NWSource (⊕ *www.nwsource.com*), which is affiliated with the *Seattle Times,* is an easy-to-search database with information on all neighborhoods (and their businesses) in Seattle and the Eastside. It's like a local version of Citysearch—packed with information, at least half of which is up-to-date. The *Seattle Post-Intelligencer* website (⊕ *www.seattlepi.com*) is full of breaking local and national news. The *Seattle Times* is one of the country's largest independently owned daily newspapers. Its website (⊕ *www.seattletimes. com*) has frequently updated local news and entertainment information. The *Stranger's* site, run by the irreverent free weekly newspaper *The Stranger* (⊕ *www. thestranger.com*), has the best event listings for movie times, literary events, art, theater, and other fun things to do—especially at night. The *Seattle Weekly* (⊕ *www.seattleweekly.com*) focuses on local political coverage and entertainment and is a great resource for event listings and eating out. Use the site's search tool to narrow your culinary options by type of food, neighborhood, price, and feature (such as outdoor dining).

▌SAFETY

Seattle is generally safe. For many visitors the most menacing presence are the panhandlers who tend to frequent Pioneer Square, Belltown, Capitol Hill, the U-District, and some area parks. Even visitors and transplants who come from other major cities with large homeless populations are surprised by how aggressive (and at times, verbally abusive) Seattle's panhandlers can be. You may pass your entire vacation without incident, but don't be surprised if someone curses you out after you refuse to give them money. In certain pockets of downtown, a handful of drug dealers hardly bother hiding their illegal activities from view, particularly at the otherwise picturesque Victor Steinbrueck Park by Pike Place Market.

It also can be jarring to see the large and colorful encampments of tents, tarps, and piles of refuse beneath freeway overpasses along I-5 and in several other parts of the city. In 2015, Seattle declared a state of emergency over the city's escalating homeless crisis, which can be partially attributed to the rapidly increasing cost of living. As one of the most progressive places in the country, Seattle is determined to make homelessness a thing of the past. Some recent initiatives include the city-sanctioned Tent City program, designed for safety, as well as a strong push for more affordable housing. Most of Seattle's homeless steer clear of the public and are harmless, even when they're camped out on sidewalks and in building nooks at night.

The airport, ground transit links, ferries, and popular sights are well monitored by guards and cameras, and the city's knowledgeable travel personnel are on hand to help set visitors in the right direction. Tight rules apply as to what you can bring into stadiums, arenas, and performance venues; expect bag searches, X-ray machines, and/or metal detectors.

Use common sense and you'll avoid trouble. Always lock your car (there are plenty of break-ins, especially in residential areas), don't leave valuables in your vehicle, and park in lighted areas after dark; be careful when walking alone Downtown during late hours; don't flash cash or valuables in heavily visited areas where petty theft might occur. Keep your laptop in the hotel safe when you're not using it.

▌TAXES

There is a 15.6% hotel tax in Seattle for hotels with more than 60 rooms, 9.5% for properties with fewer than 60 rooms (another benefit for staying in bed-and-breakfasts and small boutique properties); in Bellevue the rates are 12% and 9.5%, respectively. Renting a car in Seattle will set you back 17.2% in tax, and there are additional taxes for renting cars at the airport.

The sales tax in Seattle is 9.5% and is applied to all purchases except groceries and prescription drugs.

▌TIME

Washington State is in the Pacific Standard Time zone, which is 2 hours earlier than Chicago, 3 hours earlier than New York, 8 hours earlier than London, and 18 hours earlier than Sydney.

▌TIPPING

Tips and service charges are usually not automatically added to a bill in the United States (except when your party is over six people). If service is satisfactory, customers generally give waitstaff, taxi drivers, barbers, hairdressers, and so forth, a tip of from 15% to 20% of the total bill. (Be aware that tipping waitstaff less than 15% is considered a sign that service was bad.) Bellhops, doormen, and porters at airports and railway stations are generally tipped $1 for each item of luggage. In Seattle there is no recognized system for tipping concierges. A gratuity of $2–$5 is suggested if you have the concierge arrange for a service such as restaurant reservations, theater tickets, or car service, and $10–$20 if the service is more extensive or unusual, such as having a large bouquet of roses delivered on a Sunday. ■TIP➔ In 2015, the Seattle City Council unanimously voted to increase Seattle's minimum wage to $15—the highest in the country—gradually over the next few years. Some area restaurants are already experimenting with alternative tipping models, including getting rid of it altogether in favor of slightly higher food prices. Menus generally make a note of any untraditional policies.

▌ VACATION PACKAGES

Packages *are not* guided excursions. Packages combine airfare, accommodations, and perhaps a rental car or other extras (theater tickets, guided excursions, boat trips, reserved entry to popular museums, transit passes), but you are allowed to do your own thing. During busy periods packages may be your only option, as flights and rooms may be sold out otherwise.

Packages will definitely save you time. They can also save you money, particularly in peak seasons, but—and this is a really big "but"—you should price each part of the package separately to be sure. And be aware that prices advertised on websites and in newspapers rarely include service charges or taxes, which can up your costs by hundreds of dollars.

■TIP➔ Some packages and cruises are sold only through travel agents. Don't always assume that you can get the best deal by booking everything yourself.

Each year consumers are stranded or lose their money when packagers—even large ones with excellent reputations—go out of business. How can you protect yourself?

First, always pay with a credit card; if you have a problem, your credit-card company may help you resolve it. Second, buy trip insurance that covers default. Third, choose a company that belongs to the United States Tour Operators Association, whose members must set aside funds to cover defaults. Finally, choose a company that also participates in the Tour Operator Program of the American Society of Travel Agents (ASTA), which will act as mediator in any disputes.

You can also check on the tour operator's reputation among travelers by posting an inquiry on one of the Fodors.com forums.

Organizations American Society of Travel Agents (*ASTA*). ☎ 703/739–2782 ⊕ *www.travelsense.org.* **United States Tour Operators Association** (*USTOA*). ☎ 212/599–6599 ⊕ *www.ustoa.com.*

■TIP➔ Local tourism boards can provide information about lesser-known and small-niche operators that sell packages to only a few destinations.

▌ VISITOR INFORMATION

The Seattle Convention and Visitors Bureau is really pulling out all the stops these days. Between its incredibly useful and comprehensive website and the eager-to-assist on-site representatives, it's practically like having a personal concierge. The main office in the Washington State Trade and Convention Center on Pike Street (between 7th and 8th Avenues), can help you plan all aspects of your trip from securing events tickets to making accommodations and restaurant reservations to arranging ground transportation and other services. The staff is set up to accept drop-ins (open weekdays 9 to 5 year-round and daily in the summer), and you can also contact the office before your trip with questions and requests. A second information location is at 1st and Pike, open daily from 10 to 6. This office isn't as full-service as the 7th and Pike center, but the staff will be able to answer many questions, offer suggestions, and load you up with maps and brochures.

If you're planning a side trip out of the city, call Washington State Tourism; you can request brochures or speak with a travel planner weekdays from 8 to 5 PST (closed on major holidays).

Contacts Seattle Convention and Visitors Bureau. ☎ *866/732–2695 visitor information,* *206/461–5840 main office* ⊕ *www.visitse-* *attle.org.* **Washington Tourism Alliance.** ☎ *800/544–1800* ⊕ *www.experiencewa.com.*

INDEX

PHOTO CREDITS

Front cover: Joe Daniel Price/Getty Images [Description: Space Needle and EMP Museum, Seattle, Washington]. 1, Jackbluee ǀ Dreamstime.com. 2-3, Irina88w ǀ Dreamstime.com. 5, Mark B. Bauschke/Shutterstock. **Chapter 1: Experience Seattle:** 8-9, Crackerclips ǀ Dreamstime.com. 18, Victrola Coffee/Kent Colony. 19, YinYang/iStockphoto. 22 (left), Lara Swimmer Photography. 22 (top right), HeyRocker/Flickr. 22 (bottom right), Kathmanduphotog/Shutterstock. 23 (top left), Tim Thompson. 23 (bottom left), KingWu/iStockphoto. 23 (top right), Vladimir Menkov/wikipedia.org. 23 (bottom right), Arbotetum Foundation/Joy Spurr. 32, CrackerClips/iStockphoto. 33 (left), Kevin Cruff. 33 (top right), mikeledray/Shutterstock. 33 (bottom), Charles Finkel. 34 (all), Victrola Coffee/Kent Colony. 35 (left), LWY/Flickr. 35 (top), mtcarlson/Flickr. 35 (bottom), Victrola Coffee/Kent Colony. 36 (top), Vaclav Mach/Shutterstock. 36 (bottom), Elysian Brewing Company. 37 (top), David Blaine/Flickr. 37 (bottom), Charles Finkel. 37 (right), Patrick Wright Photography. 38 (left), Greg Vaughn. 38 (right), Chateau Ste. Michelle. 39 (left), Kevin Cruff. 39 (right), Chateau Ste. Michelle. 40, Greg Vaughn. **Chapter 2: Seattle Neighborhoods:** 41, Blvdone ǀ Dreamstime.com. 43, Lara Swimmer Photography. 45, jeffwilcox/Flickr. 47, Andreykr ǀ Dreamstime.com. 48, RonGreer.Com/Shutterstock. 49, Mariusz S. Jurgielewicz/Shutterstock. 52, Jerryway ǀ Dreamstime.com. 55, Singersiddur ǀ Dreamstime.com. 56, Jackbluee ǀ Dreamstime.com. 59, EmeraldUmbrellaStudio ǀ Dreamstime.com. 61, gregobagel/iStockphoto. 63, Deymos ǀ Dreamstime.com. 64, courtesy of Foster/White Gallery. 67, Larjon ǀ Dreamstime.com. 69, Yaoyu Chen ǀ Dreamstime.com. 71, faungg's photos/Flickr, [CC BY-ND 2.0]. 73, F11photo ǀ Dreamstime.com. 74, Wing Luke Museum. 75, rutlo/Flickr. 77, Sue Elias/Flickr. 78, Jill Hardy. 81, neelsky/Shutterstock. 83, wikipedia.org. 84, Paul Gordon / Alamy. 87, dherrera_96/Flickr. 89, Harry Hu/Shutterstock. 92, L.L.Masseth/Shutterstock. 95, Danita Delimont / Alamy. 96, David6135 ǀ Dreamstime.com. 98, RonGreer.Com/Shutterstock. 101, dk / Alamy. 102, Wonderlane/Flickr. 103 and 105, Andrew Waits/Burke Museum. 107, DVD R W/wikipedia.org. 108, L.L.Masseth/Shutterstock. 111, Us40637 ǀ Dreamstime.com. 112, Us40637 ǀ Dreamstime.com. 113, Tammy Wolfe/iStockphoto. 114, Kevin Cruff. 117, Joseph Calev/Shutterstock. **Chapter 3: Where to Eat:** 121, Suzi Pratt/Heartwood Provisions. 122 and 123 (bottom), Redstone Pictures, Inc. 123 (top), Flickr. 124, Geoffrey Smith. **Chapter 4: Where to Stay:** 161, Courtesy of Pan Pacific. 162, Kimpton Hotel Monaco Seattle. **Chapter 5: Nightlife and the Arts:** 179, HeyRocker/Flickr. 180, Mathayward ǀ Dreamstime.com. **Chapter 6: Shopping:** 207, Czuber ǀ Dreamstime.com. 208, MACSURAK/Flickr. 209 (left), SheriW/Flickr. 209 (right), thebittenword.com/Flickr. 210, Vérité Ventures. 211 (left), ChrisDag/Flickr. 211 (right), Hunters Capital. 212, Sam Fu/LIKELIHOOD. 228, Mark B. Bauschke/Shutterstock. 228 (bottom), Charles Amundson/Shutterstock. 230 (left), piroshky bakery. 230 (top), The Tasting Room. 230 (right), Beecherís Handmade Cheese. 231 (left), Phillie Casablanca/Flickr. 231 (top), Nick Jurich of flashpd.com. 231 (right), eng1ne/Flickr. 232 (top left), Liem Bahneman/Shutterstock. 232 (bottom), Pike Place Market PDA. 232 (right), World Pictures/Phot/age fotostock. 233 (left), Stephen Power/Alamy. 233 (right), Rootology/wikipedia.org. **Chapter 7: Sports and Activities:** 245, Danita Delimont / Alamy. 246, Steve Froebe/iStockphoto. 249, rob casey/Alamy. 250, Joe Mabel/wikipedia.org. 251 (left), Nathan Fabro/iStockphoto. 251 (right), Wolfgang Kaehler/Alamy. 252-253, nesneJkraM/iStockphoto. 252 (bottom), wikipedia.org. 253, Chris Howes/Wild Places Photography/Alamy. 255 (left), Danita Delimont/Alamy. 255 (center), jeffwilcox/Flickr. 255 (right), Chad Davis. 256, 400tmax/iStockphoto. **Chapter 8: Side Trips from Seattle:** 265, YinYang/iStockphoto. 266, Tusharkoley ǀ Dreamstime.com. 267 (bottom), Bjulien03 ǀ Dreamstime.com. 267 (top), Bpperry ǀ Dreamstime.com. 268, Aiisha ǀ Dreamstime.com. 272, LegalAdmin/Flickr. 277, Richard Cummins/age fotostock. 281, Joe Becker/age fotostock. 285, Jdanne ǀ Dreamstime.com. 312-313, YinYang/iStockphoto. 324-325, antony spencer/iStockphoto. **Back cover, from left to right:** Crackerclips ǀ Dreamstime.com; Tashka ǀ Dreamstime.com; Jerryway ǀ Dreamstime.com. **Spine:** fotoguy22/iStockphoto.

NOTES

NOTES

NOTES